Clean Air Act

SECOND EDITION

Roy S. Belden

PRACTICE
SERIES

AMERICAN BAR ASSOCIATION

Section of Environment,
Energy, and Resources

Library of Congress Cataloging-in-Publication Data

The Clean Air Act / Roy S. Belden.—2nd ed.
    p. cm.—(Basic practice series)
  Rev. ed. of: The Clean Air Act / by Roy S. Belden.
  Includes bibliographical references and index.
  ISBN 978-1-61438-096-2 (alk. paper)
    1. Air—Pollution—Law and legislation—United States. I. Belden, Roy S., 1963– II. Belden, Roy S., 1963– Clean Air Act.

  KF3812.B45 2011
  344.7304'6342—dc23

                                                                                    2011030792

Contents

Preface

The Clean Air Act is one of the more challenging environmental statutes and has generated a multitude of regulatory requirements. Practicing in the Clean Air Act area often requires an added vigilance due to its complexity and the fact that many of the applicable statutory and regulatory provisions typically are subject to numerous U.S. Environmental Protection Agency (EPA), state, and local regulatory guidance interpretations, which may or may not be readily available. In recent years, EPA and many state and local air agencies have made an effort to make these numerous guidance documents available through agency web pages, and the appendices to this book includes references to some of the key websites.

The goal of this Clean Air Act basic practice guide is to provide legal practitioners, consultants, and other interested individuals with an overview of the Clean Air Act and its implementing regulations. It is not intended to be an exhaustive treatment of the Act; rather, it should be used as a starting point for answering basic Clean Air Act inquiries. In addition to the overview of the Act and the applicable EPA regulations, this book includes many useful reference materials in the appendices that are intended to assist the reader in navigating through the multiple requirements of the Clean Air Act.

Since the first edition of this basic practice guide was published in 2001, there have been many important regulatory developments and numerous case law decisions that have helped to clarify certain aspects of the Clean Air Act, including a Supreme Court case that held that greenhouse gas emissions fall within the broad definition of "air pollutants" under the Act. The second edition of this book includes a new chapter on the emerging regulation of greenhouse gas emissions under the Clean Air Act. While EPA is still very much in the formative stages of regulating greenhouse gas emissions, the chapter on greenhouse gas emissions provides an overview of the regulatory roadmap that the agency has embarked upon.

Acknowledgments

The author would like to thank the ABA Section of Environment, Energy, and Resources Book Publishing Board and staff for their dedication and leadership in helping make this book possible. Most important, the author thanks his family for their patience and indulgence in writing this book. The author also thanks Phillip R. Bower of Whyte Hirschboeck Dudek, S.C. for his assistance with appendix D.

About the Author

Roy Belden is a Senior Vice President, Environmental Support for GE Energy Financial Services in Stamford, Connecticut. Mr. Belden provides Clean Air Act permitting and environmental compliance support to several power plants and other energy assets owned or being developed by GE Energy Financial Services.

Mr. Belden was previously with Chadbourne & Parke LLP, where he counseled corporate clients on environmental issues including Clean Air Act permitting, compliance, and enforcement actions. He has written and lectured extensively on the Clean Air Act and other environmental issues, and currently serves as a Vice-Chair of the ABA Section of Environment, Energy, and Resources Air Quality Committee.

Mr. Belden also previously served as a congressional legislative aide working on environmental and agricultural issues.

Abbreviations

ALJ	administrative law judge
APA	Administrative Procedures Act
AQCR	air quality control region
AQRV	air-quality-related values
BACT	best available control technology
BART	best available retrofit technology
BDT	best demonstrated technology
Btu	British thermal unit
CAA	Clean Air Act
CAIR	Clean Air Interstate Rule
CAM	compliance assurance monitoring
CAMD	Clean Air Markets Division
CAMR	Clean Air Mercury Rule
CASAC	Clean Air Scientific Advisory Committee
CBI	confidential business information
CEMS	continuous emissions monitoring system
CFCs	chlorofluorocarbons
CFR	Code of Federal Regulations
CH$_4$	methane
CO	carbon monoxide
CO$_2$	carbon dioxide
CO$_2$e	carbon dioxide equivalent
CSAPR	Cross-State Air Pollution Rule
DOJ	U.S. Department of Justice
DOT	U.S. Department of Transportation
E10	gasoline and 10 percent ethanol by volume mixture
E15	gasoline and 15 percent ethanol by volume mixture
EAB	Environmental Appeals Board
e-GGRT	electronic GHG reporting tool
EISA	Energy Independence and Security Act of 2007
EPA	U.S. Environmental Protection Agency
ETBE	ethyl tertiary butyl ether
ERP	Equipment Replacement Provision

Fed. Reg.	Federal Register
FIP	federal implementation plan
FLAG	Federal Land Manager's AQRV Work Group
FLM	federal land manager
GACT	generally available control technology
g/bhp-hr	grams per braked-horsepower-hour
gpm	grams per vehicle mile
GCVTC	Grand Canyon Visibility Transport Commission
GHG	greenhouse gas
GWP	global warming potential
HAP	hazardous air pollutant
HBFC	hydrobromofluorocarbons
HCFC	hydrochlorofluorocarbons
HFC	hydrofluorocarbons
HEW	U.S. Department of Health, Education and Welfare
HON	hazardous organic NESHAP
I/M	inspection and maintenance
IPP	independent power produc[er/tion]
LAER	lowest achievable emission rate
lbs/MMBtu	pounds per million Btu
LEV	low-emission vehicle
MACT	maximum achievable control technology
mg/m^3	milligrams per cubic meter
MOU	memorandum of understanding
MTBE	methyl tertiary butyl ether
MVAC	motor vehicle air conditioner
MW	megawatt
NAAQS	National Ambient Air Quality Standards
NESHAP	National Emission Standards for Hazardous Air Pollutants
NLEV	national low emission vehicle
NMHC	nonmethane hydrocarbons
NO	nitric oxide
NO$_2$	nitrogen dioxide
N$_2$O	nitrous oxide
NO$_x$	nitrogen oxides
NOV	notice of violation
NSPS	New Source Performance Standard
NSR	New Source Review
O$_3$	ozone
ODS	ozone-depleting substance

OTAG	Ozone Transport Assessment Group
OTC	Ozone Transport Commission
OTR	ozone transport region
Pb	lead
PFC	perfluorocarbons
PM	particulate matter
$PM_{2.5}$	particulate matter with a diameter of 2.5 microns or less
PM_{10}	particulate matter with a diameter of 10 microns or less
ppb	parts per billion
ppm	parts per million
PSD	Prevention of Significant Deterioration
PTE	potential to emit
QF	qualifying facility
RACM	reasonably available control measure
RACT	reasonably available control technology
RFG	reformulated gasoline
RFP	reasonable further progress
RFS	renewable fuel standard
RGGI	Regional Greenhouse Gas Initiative
RMP	Risk Management Plan
SF_6	sulfur hexafluoride
SIC	Standard Industrial Classification
SIP	state implementation plan
SNAP	Significant New Alternatives Policy
SO_2	sulfur dioxide
SUV	sport utility vehicle
TCM	transportation control measure
TIP	tribal implementation plan
tpy	tons per year
VOC	volatile organic compound
WEPCO	Wisconsin Electric Power Company
$\mu g/m^3$	micrograms per cubic meter

1 Executive Summary

The Clean Air Act (CAA) sets forth both a complex and intricate mechanism for regulating sources of air pollution, and the Act has spawned over 13,500 pages of regulations in the Code of Federal Regulations. Moreover, even though the last major amendments to the Act were enacted in 1990, new regulations are continuing to be developed to implement the broad ranging requirements of the Act. During the Bush administration from 2001 to 2008 and during the Obama administration, the Environmental Protection Agency (EPA) has taken a more activist role in adopting new regulations to further reduce air emissions in the absence of a consensus in Congress on new amendments to the Act. President Bush first announced the Clear Skies Initiative in 2002 to regulate nitrogen oxide, sulfur dioxide, and mercury emissions from electric generating facilities. The legislation to codify the initiative faltered, and EPA moved to implement emission caps and allowance trading programs that would achieve substantially the same reduction target. Those regulations were largely struck down in the courts.

In 2010, we celebrated the fortieth anniversary of what is known as the modern day Clean Air Act, which was enacted into law in 1970. EPA Administrator Lisa Jackson commemorated the event by stating that "since 1970 we have seen a trajectory of less pollution in our communities and greater economic opportunity throughout our nation. We will continue those trends as we face the clean air challenges of the next 40 years, including working to cut greenhouse gas emissions and grow the American clean energy economy." Starting in 2009, EPA embarked on a program to regulate greenhouse gases using many of the tools provided in the CAA. This course of action was in large part a response to the lack of new legislation that would set the parameters for greenhouse gas emission reductions in the United States.

This book is designed to provide a rudimentary overview of the key concepts and provisions of the CAA. It also includes a basic discussion of some of the fundamental regulations implementing the CAA, as well as highlights of the critical precedential cases interpreting the requirements of the CAA.

Chapter 2 begins with a brief discussion of the history of the CAA, and reviews several of the major legislative and regulatory developments that shaped the current CAA, including the 1970, 1977, and 1990 amendments. An overview of the central regulatory programs of the CAA follows in a series of 12 chapters, starting in chapter 3 with the process for establishing National Ambient Air Quality Standards (NAAQS). The NAAQS serve as the key building blocks for the regulatory infrastructure of implementing enforceable emissions limits and standards. Chapter 4 discusses the mechanism for developing state implementation plans, which provide the backdrop of EPA-approved state statutes, strategies, and rules to implement CAA requirements.

Chapters 5 and 6 focus on the standards and review process that applies to new, modified, and reconstructed stationary sources. Chapter 5 addresses the Prevention of Significant Deterioration/New Source Review (PSD/NSR) program that is applicable to sources siting in parts of the country in NAAQS attainment or nonattainment, (respectively) areas. Chapter 6 reviews the unit-specific requirements of the New Source Performance Standards (NSPS) program. An overview of the air toxics program requirements, which are technology-based like the NSPS program, appears in chapter 7. New standards are still being developed and revised for certain industrial categories under the air toxics program, and many facilities are now in the process of installing pollution control technologies to meet hazardous air pollutant standards that have been enacted over the past several years. Chapter 8 deals with the special requirements of the visibility protection program, which applies in areas near national parks and other federally preserved areas.

Chapter 9 addresses the acid rain control program and discusses the Phase I and Phase II requirements that apply to fossil-fuel-fired utility units. The Phase II requirements—which mandate reductions in sulfur dioxide (SO_2) and nitrogen oxide (NO_x) emissions for many fossil-fuel-fired utility units—took effect on January 1, 2000. The Cross-State Air Pollution Rule, which is scheduled to take effect in 2012, is expected to drive further reductions in NO_x and SO_2 emissions from fossil-fuel-fired power plants, and may substantially eclipse the effectiveness of the acid rain control program in the eastern portion of the United States. Chapter 10 discusses the Title V operating permit program that was enacted by the Clean Air Act Amendments of 1990. Congress intended Title V permits to contain all federally applicable CAA requirements for each affected source primarily to facilitate monitoring and compliance.

Chapter 11 is a new chapter that discusses EPA's efforts to regulate greenhouse gas emissions from multiple sources in the wake of the Supreme Court's 2007 decision in *Massachusetts v. EPA*, which included the key holding that carbon dioxide and other greenhouse gas emissions fall within the Act's definition of an "air pollutant."

Chapter 12 surveys the mobile source air pollution control requirements and the program to regulate fuels and fuel additives. These two programs predominantly focus on reducing emissions from motor vehicle engines and fuel combustion. Chapter 13 discusses the requirements for controlling chlorofluorocarbons and other substances that deplete the stratospheric ozone layer. Chapter 14 reviews the enforcement authority provided under the CAA as well as the mechanism for requesting judicial review of new regulations or other final agency actions of the U.S. Environmental Protection Agency under the CAA.

This guide finishes with a number of sections intended to aid the reader who has further questions or needs additional resources. Appendix A is a series of 50 frequently asked questions (FAQs) and answers. The Q&A list is designed to provide a quick reference for some of the basic CAA questions. Appendix B summarizes most of the key CAA cases that have been decided since the early 1970s. Appendices C and D provide an index to the CAA and the Code of Federal Regulation citations for the various air regulations. Appendix E provides a list of the 28 source categories with a 100-ton-per-year "major source" threshold under the PSD program. Following the appendices is a glossary of terms used in this guide.

Finally, there is a resources section that highlights various CAA treatises and books as well as law review articles on CAA topics. Other resources include web page links and a reference to the web page of the Air Quality Committee of the ABA Section of Environment, Energy, and Resources at http://apps.americanbar.org/environ/committees/airquality/, which provides a convenient starting point to access a wide range of Internet resources such as the various EPA web-sites (e.g., headquarters and regional offices) and the web pages for the air permitting agencies for each of the 50 states and other U.S. jurisdictions.

The materials in the appendices and resources section are not intended to be exhaustive, but rather are designed to guide the reader to additional research sources that may apply to a particular CAA matter.

2 History of the Clean Air Act

The genesis of the modern Clean Air Act actually dates back to the 1950s, and the CAA has evolved considerably since then, to the point where it is now one of the most complicated and prescriptive environmental statutes on the books. In July 1955, President Eisenhower signed the Air Pollution Control Act of 1955 into law.[1] This first version of the federal air pollution law only provided federal research monies and set up a mechanism authorizing the U.S. Surgeon General to provide technical and research assistance to the states to implement controls. The provisions of this early statute were extended several times. However, publicity surrounding several hundred deaths attributed to "killer smog" in London and New York fueled a mounting concern over air pollution in the 1960s. In 1963, a new Clean Air Act was passed, which added additional research and grant programs and directed the Department of Health, Education, and Welfare (HEW) to take actions to abate interstate air pollution.[2] A few years later, President Johnson signed the Air Quality Act of 1967, which amended the 1963 Act. The 1967 Air Quality Act was the federal government's initial foray into regulation of sources of air pollution.[3]

---

1. Pub. L. No. 84-159, 69 Stat. 322.
2. Pub. L. No. 88-206, 77 Stat. 392.
3. Pub. L. No. 90-148, 81 Stat. 485.

2.1   Air Quality Act of 1967

The Air Quality Act of 1967 had four main goals:

1. To protect the nation's resources to promote public health and welfare;
2. To stimulate research programs on prevention and control of air pollution;
3. To provide states with assistance in the development and implementation of their air pollution control and prevention programs; and
4. To develop regional air pollution control programs.

Under the Air Quality Act of 1967, HEW was charged with setting national air quality criteria. The states in turn were required to establish ambient air quality standards based on the federal criteria for air quality control regions designated by HEW. States were also required to submit implementation plans to HEW; these plans were intended to create the mechanism for enforcing those standards. The Air Quality Act of 1967 had several shortcomings, including a lack of effective enforcement provisions; nevertheless, it established the initial framework for the current federal-state partnership that is a fundamental tenet of the modern Clean Air Act.

2.2   Clean Air Act Amendments of 1970

Congress enacted a comprehensive set of amendments to the Clean Air Act in 1970, which largely put in place many current requirements of the Act. The 1970 amendments charged the newly created U.S. Environmental Protection Agency (EPA) with the authority to establish National Ambient Air Quality Standards (NAAQS), which define levels of air quality that must be achieved to protect public health and welfare.[4] In addition, Congress directed EPA to develop regulatory guidance for states to use in developing state implementation plans (SIPs) to achieve the health-and-welfare-based NAAQS. If a SIP was not approved

---

4. Pub. L. No. 91-604, 84 Stat. 1676. Under the Clean Air Act Amendments of 1970, HEW's responsibilities for implementing and enforcing the CAA were transferred to EPA.

by EPA, the agency was given the authority to impose a federal implementation plan (FIP) containing source-specific standards. The development of the NAAQS is more fully explained in chapter 3. The 1970 amendments also created the New Source Performance Standards (NSPS) program (codified in CAA section 111), which authorizes EPA to set stringent control technology requirements for new, modified, and reconstructed sources. The 1970 amendments set forth the first program to regulate hazardous air pollutants or air toxics (CAA section 112); they also created the first program to establish technology-based emission standards for motor vehicles and other mobile sources of air pollution. The 1970 amendments generated a fair amount of controversy and resulted in several legal challenges to EPA's implementation of the NAAQS and NSPS. (See appendix B.) These legal challenges spawned several of the precedent-setting decisions that solidified many of the basic principles of the Clean Air Act.

2.3   Clean Air Act Amendments of 1977

The 1977 amendments to the Clean Air Act codified several major changes to the law, but largely preserved its core federal-state partnership.[5] The 1977 amendments were precipitated by a lack of overall progress in achieving the ambitious goals of the 1970 amendments. At the time, many areas of the country were not meeting the applicable NAAQS (i.e., they were nonattainment areas) and were making little progress toward meeting those standards. Moreover, many individual facilities had failed to achieve full compliance with the CAA requirements. As a result, the 1977 amendments were intended to refocus on meeting the goals of the 1970 amendments. In particular, the time for attaining compliance with the NAAQS for certain areas was extended and new emission control requirements for nonattainment areas were added. The amendments also codified EPA's Prevention of Significant Deterioration (PSD) program, which requires a detailed preconstruction review for new and modified major stationary sources located in areas in attainment with the NAAQS in order to prevent degradation of air quality in those areas. The PSD and nonattainment area New Source Review programs are discussed in chapter 5.

---

5. Pub. L. No. 95-95, 91 Stat. 685.

2.4   Clean Air Act Amendments of 1990

In 1990, Congress passed a significant revision to the Clean Air Act that overhauled certain key components of the Act (hazardous air pollutants), added new programs (acid rain title, Title V operating permit program, and the stratospheric ozone program), and continued to build upon the existing structure that was put in place by the 1970 and 1977 amendments (e.g., nonattainment area requirements). The following are the most significant of the 1990 changes to the CAA:

- Title I of the 1990 amendments contains new requirements for areas that do not meet the ozone, carbon monoxide, and particulate matter NAAQS. These amendments fostered an incremental approach to attainment by ranking areas according to the severity of their nonattainment and by creating more stringent controls for areas with more serious nonattainment issues.
- Title II of the 1990 amendments creates more stringent mobile source emission standards. The 1990 amendments required automobile manufacturers to reduce tailpipe emissions of hydrocarbons and nitrogen oxides by 35 percent and 60 percent, respectively, beginning with 40 percent of vehicles sold in 1994 and increasing to 100 percent of vehicles sold in 1996. The amendments also create two new fuels-related programs, the reformulated fuels program and the clean fuel vehicles program.
- Title III shifts the regulation of hazardous air pollutants from a pollutant-by-pollutant health-based approach to the regulation of categories of sources using technology-based standards.
- Title IV creates a new program to deal with acid rain by employing a new market-based emission allowance and trading system.
- Title V imposes an operating permit program for major stationary sources of regulated pollutants. Operating permits must include all Clean Air Act requirements applicable to a source, and EPA has the authority to veto any permits not complying with the CAA requirements.
- Title VI creates a new stratospheric ozone program that is similar to the provisions in the Montreal Protocol on

Substances That Deplete the Ozone Layer, but with more stringent interim reductions.

- Title VII upgrades criminal violations from misdemeanors to felonies. It also allows EPA to issue administrative penalty orders and field citations for minor violations without having to take every violation to court for enforcement.

EPA has now implemented the major new programs promulgated in the 1990 amendments, but with some difficulty in a few areas. Most notably, EPA's program to promulgate maximum achievable control technology (MACT) standards for certain types of sources emitting hazardous air pollutants has been subject to legal challenges, and as discussed in chapter 7, MACT limits for a few source categories are still not finalized.

The agency continues to use its authority under the CAA to advance major new initiatives, including the regulation of greenhouse gases. In the wake of the *Massachusetts v. EPA* Supreme Court decision in 2007—in which the court concluded that carbon dioxide and other greenhouse gases fall within the broad definition of "air pollutant" under the CAA—EPA has embarked on developing a regulatory program to reduce greenhouse gas emissions, which now consists of several final rules that are reviewed in chapter 11.

3 National Ambient Air Quality Standards

As noted in chapter 2, the framework of the present regulatory structure for addressing air pollution was largely put in place by the 1970 amendments to the Clean Air Act (CAA), and has remained the same since that time. The health-and-welfare-based National Ambient Air Quality Standards (NAAQS) are nationwide air quality goals that serve as one of the key building blocks of the scheme for addressing air pollution. The NAAQS are ambient air standards, and *ambient air* is generally defined to mean all outdoor air that is external to buildings. Congress authorized the Environmental Protection Agency (EPA) to develop primary and secondary NAAQS with the understanding that the primary standards are to be set at a level designed to protect public health; the secondary standards are intended to focus on impacts to the environment, including potential damage to plants and trees.[1] Although the standards themselves are not directly enforceable, certain state implementation plan (SIP) regulations are directly linked to achieving compliance with the NAAQS. The SIP regulations are intended to set standards to "attain" or "maintain" the NAAQS. Moreover, the permitting requirements applicable to the construction of new major sources and major modifications of existing major sources of regulated pollutants are also tied to whether a particular region is in attainment or nonattainment with a NAAQS. The following discussion of the NAAQS reviews the ways in which they are established, implemented, and enforced.

---

1. CAA § 109; 42 U.S.C. § 7409.

3.1   Current NAAQS

Under the CAA, EPA was delegated the authority to develop NAAQS based on a careful and thorough review of the science. EPA has currently identified six common air pollutants (called *criteria pollutants*) that have scientifically demonstrated effects on health and the environment at certain levels. These pollutants are sulfur dioxide (SO_2), particulate matter (PM), carbon monoxide (CO), ozone (O_3), nitrogen dioxide (NO_2), and lead (Pb). The primary and secondary standards for these criteria pollutants, which are set out in 40 C.F.R. part 50, establish a ceiling of emission levels that applies throughout the nation. The NAAQS are generally expressed as a maximum acceptable mass of pollutant (micrograms) per standard volume of air (cubic meters) or as a concentration (parts per million (ppm) or parts per billions (ppb)) measured for a specific period of time (e.g., 1 hour, 8 hours, or 24 hours), NO_2, for example, has a one-hour standard and an annual arithmetic mean NAAQS. An exceedance of a NAAQS is typically measured based on exceeding the standard within a certain period of time. The one-hour NO_2 NAAQS is exceeded if the three-year average of the 98th percentile of the daily maximum one-hour average at monitors within an area is above 100 ppb.[2] Conversely, the 24-hour and annual arithmetic average SO_2 NAAQS are exceeded if there is more than one measurement above the standard at area monitors in a year. The six criteria pollutants are summarized as follows:

Sulfur dioxide is primarily emitted from burning sulfur-containing fossil fuels (oil and coal) as well as during the processing of sulfur-containing fuels and ores. Exposure to high levels of SO_2 may impair lung function and aggravate existing respiratory and cardiovascular disease. SO_2 is the major precursor of acid rain, which has demonstrated deleterious effects on water bodies, trees, and plants.

Particulate matter consists of particles (either liquid droplets or solids) that are emitted from a variety of combustion processes, motor vehicles, and material handling processes. There are generally two types of particulate classifications, based on size: PM_{10} (coarse particulates with an aerodynamic diameter of less than 10 micrometers) and $PM_{2.5}$ (fine particulates with a diameter of less than 2.5 micrometers). Both PM_{10} and $PM_{2.5}$ present potential health concerns from inhalation, which may result in physical ailments (lung irritation) or chemical exposures (allowing lead or

---

2. The 98th percentile corresponds approximately to the seventh or eighth highest one-hour daily average in a year (i.e., 1 percent of 365 days equals 3.65 days). *See* 75 Fed. Reg. 6474, 6491 (Feb. 9, 2010).

other metal particles to enter the body). Fine particulate matter is a mixture of extremely small particles and liquid droplets that can reach the deepest region of the lungs. EPA has established separate PM_{10} and $PM_{2.5}$ NAAQS. Recent developments in setting two separate PM NAAQS are discussed below in section 3.3.

Carbon monoxide is a colorless, odorless gas primarily emitted from combustion sources such as motor vehicles and power plants. Relatively low levels of CO exposure have been demonstrated to aggravate cardiovascular disease and to affect the central nervous system. High levels of CO are toxic to humans and other mammals.

Ozone forms in the lower atmosphere or troposphere, and results from chemical reactions of volatile organic compounds (VOCs), nitrogen oxides (NO_x), and oxygen in the presence of sunlight. Tropospheric ozone is the primary component of smog. High concentrations of O_3 can damage lung tissue and reduce lung function. Ozone precursors—VOCs and NO_x—are emitted by a variety of sources, including most combustion sources (such as boilers, furnaces, power plants, and motor vehicles), the storage of petroleum, and the application of paints and solvents.

Nitrogen dioxide, at high concentrations, can affect respiratory functions. NO_2 is formed when nitric oxide (NO) is oxidized in the atmosphere. NO and NO_2 are often referred to as nitrogen oxides (NO_x). NO_x is generated by high-temperature combustion from boilers, furnaces, and power plants as well as from motor vehicle engines. NO_x is a precursor to smog formation and acid rain.

Lead is emitted by motor vehicles burning leaded fuel and from certain types of manufacturing processes involving combustion (for example, incinerators, refineries, and lead smelters). Lead particles may be inhaled or ingested. Extensive exposure to lead may result in neurological impairments, and it can affect the kidneys, liver, and the blood system since it tends to accumulate in the body rather than being excreted. Lead levels in the ambient air have been reduced substantially since leaded gasoline was phased out.

The first NAAQS were promulgated in 1971 for photochemical oxidants (or O_3), CO, SO_2, NO_2, PM, and hydrocarbons. The lead standard was added in 1978. Hydrocarbons were delisted as a criteria pollutant in 1983 because EPA concluded that hydrocarbons have no direct adverse health effect.[3] Nevertheless, reactive hydrocarbons are a subset of VOCs, which are regulated as precursors of O_3 formation.

---

3. 48 Fed. Reg. 628 (Jan. 5, 1983).

The current primary and secondary NAAQS are set out in the table below.

National Ambient Air Quality Standards

Pollutant	Averaging Time	National Primary Standards[a]	National Secondary Standards[a]
Sulfur dioxide[b]	Max. 24-hour concentration[c]	0.14 ppm (365 µg/m³)	None
	Annual arithmetic mean	0.03 ppm (80 µg/m³)	None
	1-hour avg. concentration[d]	75 ppb	None
	3-hour avg. concentration	None	0.5 ppm (1300 µg/m³)
Particulate matter (PM$_{10}$)[e]	24-hour avg. concentration	150 µg/m³	150 µg/m³
(PM$_{2.5}$)[f]	24-hour avg. concentration	35 µg/m³	35 µg/m³
	Annual arithmetic mean	15 µg/m³	15 µg/m³
Carbon monoxide[g]	8-hour avg. concentration	9.0 ppm (10 mg/m³)	None

Note: The primary and secondary standards are set forth as follows: SO$_2$ (40 C.F.R. §§ 50.4 and 50.5), PM$_{10}$ (40 C.F.R. § 50.6), PM$_{2.5}$ (40 C.F.R. § 50.7), CO (40 C.F.R. § 50.8), O$_3$ (40 C.F.R. § 50.9), NO$_2$ (40 C.F.R. § 50.10), and Pb (40 C.F.R. § 50.11).

a. Parenthetical value is an estimated equivalent concentration.

b. The SO$_2$ annual arithmetic mean and the 24-hour concentration standards were revoked in the 2010 rule establishing a new 1-hour SO$_2$ standard. *See* 75 Fed. Reg. 35,520 (June 22, 2010). The SO$_2$ annual and 24-hour standards will remain in effect for one year following the effective date of the initial nonattainment area designations for the new 1-hour SO$_2$ NAAQS, and for any SIP and FIP rules containing the annual and 24-hour SO$_2$ NAAQS until replaced by new SIP or FIP rules addressing the 1-hour SO$_2$ NAAQS. *See* 75 Fed. Reg. at 35,581.

c. The 24-hour standard, annual arithmetic average, and secondary standard are not to be exceeded more than once per year.

d. To meet the 1-hour SO$_2$ standard, the three-year average of the 99th percentile of the daily maximum one-hour average at area monitors must not exceed 75 ppb.

Pollutant	Averaging Time	National Primary Standards[a]	National Secondary Standards[a]
Carbon monoxide (*cont'd*)	1-hour avg. concentration	35 ppm (40 mg/m³)	None
Ozone	1-hour avg. concentration[h]	0.12 ppm (235 µg/m³)	0.12 ppm (235 µg/m³)
	8-hour avg. concentration— 1997 standard[i]	0.08 ppm (157 µg/m³)	0.08 ppm (157 µg/m³)
	8-hour avg. concentration— 2008 standard[j]	0.075 ppm	0.075 ppm
Nitrogen dioxide	Annual arithmetic mean	53 ppb	53 ppb
	1-hour avg. concentration[k]	100 ppb	100 ppb
Lead	Quarterly arithmetic mean	1.5 µg/m³	1.5 µg/m³
	Rolling 3-month average	0.15 µg/m³	0.15 µg/m³

e. Standard is not to be exceeded more than once per year on average over three years.

f. To meet the 24-hour average standard, the three-year average of the 98th percentile of the 24-hour concentrations at area monitors must not exceed 35 µg/m³. To meet the annual arithmetic mean, the three-year average of the weighted annual mean $PM_{2.5}$ concentrations from area monitors must not exceed 15 µg/m³.

g. The 8-hour concentration and 1-hour average concentration are not to be exceeded more than once per year.

h. EPA revoked the 1-hour standard on June 15, 2005, for all areas except the 8-hour ozone nonattainment Early Action Compact Areas (i.e., those that do not yet have an attainment date established for their 8-hour designations). *See* 40 C.F.R. § 50.9(b). The former 1-hour ozone designations and classifications are retained for purposes of the antibacksliding provisions of 40 C.F.R. § 51.905.

i. To meet the 1997 8-hour standard, the three-year average of the fourth-highest daily maximum 8-hour average ozone concentration measured at area monitors over each year must not exceed 0.08 ppm.

j. To meet the 2008 8-hour ozone standard, the three-year average of the fourth-highest maximum 8-hour average ozone concentrations measured at area monitors over each year must not exceed 0.075 ppm. EPA is in the process of reconsidering the 2008 standards, and is expected to announce a revised ozone NAAQS in 2011.

k. To meet this standard, the three-year average of 98th percentile of the daily maximum 1-hour average at monitors within an area must not exceed 100 ppb.

3.2   Procedures to Establish NAAQS

Sections 108 and 109 of the Clean Air Act authorize EPA to establish, review, and revise NAAQS.[4] Section 108(a) requires the agency to first list those air pollutants that "may reasonably be anticipated to endanger public health or welfare" and whose presence "in the ambient air results from numerous or diverse mobile and stationary sources."[5] Courts have recognized that EPA has a mandatory duty to list a substance if the agency determines that (1) the substance is an air pollutant, (2) the pollutant is emitted by numerous or diverse sources, and (3) the pollutant's presence in the atmosphere may reasonably be anticipated to endanger public health or welfare.[6]

As noted in section 3.1, EPA has thus far "listed" or identified six criteria pollutants subject to regulation. For each listed pollutant, EPA must issue *air quality criteria*—scientific support for regulating such pollutants—which are embodied in a Criteria Document. Within 12 months of listing a pollutant pursuant to CAA section 108, EPA must issue a Criteria Document, which is intended to "accurately reflect the latest scientific knowledge useful in indicating the kind and extent of all identifiable effects on public health or welfare, which may be expected from the presence of [a] pollutant in the ambient air."[7] Preparation of the Criteria Document begins with an extensive review of available health and welfare scientific information on the criteria pollutant. EPA will also publish a notice in the *Federal Register*, requesting submissions of relevant scientific studies and reports. The Criteria Document is developed in chapters and peer-reviewed extensively during the process. EPA is required by the Clean Air Act to submit the document to the Clean Air Scientific Advisory Committee (CASAC) of EPA's Science Advisory Board to obtain their recommendations.[8] The CASAC's primary responsibility is to advise the agency of any appropriate revisions to the existing NAAQS or recommend adoption of a new NAAQS.

CAA Section 109 establishes mechanisms for actually proposing and adopting national primary and secondary NAAQS for each pollutant for which air quality criteria have been issued. For

---

4. CAA §§ 108–109; 42 U.S.C. §§ 7408–7409.
5. CAA § 108(a)(1)(A), (B); 42 U.S.C. § 7408(a)(1)(A), (B).
6. Nat. Res. Def. Council v. Train, 411 F. Supp. 864 (S.D.N.Y. 1976), *aff'd*, 545 F.2d 320 (2d Cir. 1976).
7. CAA § 108(a)(2); 42 U.S.C. § 7408(a)(2).
8. CAA §§ 108(b), 109(d); 42 U.S.C. §§ 7408(b), 7409(d).

any air pollutant listed after December 31, 1970, section 109 provides that the agency shall issue proposed primary and secondary NAAQS at the time the air quality criteria are issued, and such proposed NAAQS shall be finalized after EPA considers any public comments.[9] A primary NAAQS shall be set at a level that will protect public health with an "adequate margin of safety."[10] EPA has interpreted this phrase to require setting the NAAQS at levels below those at which adverse health effects have been detected or expected for sensitive groups of people (e.g., children and asthmatics). Secondary standards are created to protect public welfare from known or anticipated adverse effects from exposure to a pollutant in the ambient air.[11] CAA section 302 defines *public welfare* to include effects on the environment in soils, water bodies, vegetation, wildlife, animals, and so forth.[12]

There is some confusion over how much evidence is necessary to demonstrate that a pollutant may cause an "adverse health effect." However, courts have generally deferred to EPA's policy judgment so long as the agency has provided an explanation of why the evidence in the record supports a particular conclusion and that such conclusion is not irrational or contrary to the statute. In *Lead Industries Ass'n v. EPA*,[13] the D.C. Circuit upheld EPA's promulgation of the NAAQS for lead, which was established at a level below what was known to be clearly harmful to health. The court reasoned that Congress had directed EPA to allow an adequate margin of safety to "protect against effects which have not yet been uncovered by research and effects whose medical significance is a matter of disagreement."[14] In *Lead Industries*, the court concluded that as long as there is evidence in the record that substantiates the conclusions about the health effects on which the standards are based, they will be upheld.[15] Conversely, in *American Lung Ass'n v. EPA*, the court concluded that EPA had not explained its decision to not revise the SO_2 NAAQS with precision; thus, it remanded the matter to the agency for further proceedings.[16] In *American Lung Association*, the court stated that

---

9. CAA § 109(a)(1)(B), (a)(2); 42 U.S.C. § 7409(a)(1)(B), (a)(2).
10. CAA § 109(b)(1); 42 U.S.C. § 7409(b)(1).
11. CAA § 109(b)(2); 42 U.S.C. § 7409(b)(2).
12. CAA § 302(h); 42 U.S.C. § 7602(h).
13. Lead Indus. Ass'n v. EPA, 647 F.2d 1130 (D.C. Cir. 1980), *cert. denied*, 449 U.S. 1042 (1980).
14. 647 F.2d at 1154.
15. *Id.* at 1155.
16. Am. Lung Ass'n v. EPA, 134 F.3d 388, 393 (D.C. Cir. 1998).

the "agency has the heaviest obligation to explain and expose every step of its reasoning."[17] In addition to the statutory requirements of CAA sections 108 and 109, EPA has interpreted the CAA to allow other factors to be evaluated in setting a NAAQS at a level that is protective of public health with an adequate margin of safety. In particular, EPA evaluates the nature and severity of the health effects in question, the types of health evidence, the kind and degree of uncertainties involved, and the size and nature of the sensitive populations at risk. Generally, the scientific evidence reveals no bright-line standard in the scientific evidence for setting a NAAQS for a criteria pollutant; however, the courts have granted a fair amount of deference to EPA's scientific judgments in setting NAAQS. In *American Trucking Ass'n v. EPA*, the D.C. Circuit reviewed the 1997 O_3 and $PM_{2.5}$ NAAQS, and held that "EPA has no obligation either to identify an accurate 'safe level' of a pollutant or to quantify precisely the pollutant's risks prior to setting primary NAAQS. Rather, EPA must err on the side of caution . . . setting the NAAQS at whatever level it deems is necessary and sufficient to protect public health with an adequate margin of safety, taking into account both the available evidence and the inevitable scientific uncertainties."[18]

EPA also takes the position that the economic and technological feasibility of controls needed to implement the NAAQS are not to be considered in setting the standards. This position has been supported by several D.C. Circuit decisions.[19] For example, in *Lead Industries*, the court, in reviewing the CAA's legislative history, determined that economic and technological feasibility are not to be considered in setting a NAAQS.[20] In 2001, the U.S. Supreme Court reached the same conclusion in *Whitman v. American Trucking Ass'n*, noting that "[t]he text of [section] 109, interpreted in its statutory and historical context and with appreciation for its importance to the CAA as a whole, unambiguously bars cost considerations from the NAAQS-setting process."[21]

---

17. *Id.* at 392.
18. Am. Trucking Ass'n v. EPA, 283 F.3d 355, 378 (D.C. Cir. 2002).
19. *Lead Indus.*, 647 F.2d at 1161 (D.C. Cir. 1980); Am. Petroleum Inst. v. Costle, 665 F.2d 1176, 1185 (D.C. Cir. 1981); Nat. Res. Def. Council v. EPA, 902 F.2d 962, 969 (D.C. Cir. 1990), *vacated in part on other grounds*, NRDC v. EPA, 921 F.2d 326 (D.C. Cir. 1991); *Am. Lung Ass'n,* 134 F.3d at 389 (D.C. Cir. 1998).
20. *Lead Indus.*, 647 F.2d at 1148–49.
21. Whitman v. Am. Trucking Ass'n, 531 U.S. 457, 471 (2001).

3.3   NAAQS Developments

Under the CAA, EPA is required to review the NAAQS every five years, and if appropriate, revise the standards.[22] There have been a number of developments in the NAAQS since the mid-1990s, and the O_3, SO_2, NO_2, and PM standards have been significantly revised. Further reductions in the O_3 standards are planned by the Obama administration. The following summarizes some of the background on implementing the NAAQS listed in the table in section 3.1.

On July 18, 1997, EPA promulgated a revised O_3 NAAQS that substituted a new 0.08 ppm primary standard measured over eight hours for the previously existing one-hour standard of 0.12 ppm.[23] New fine particulate ($PM_{2.5}$) and coarse particulate (PM_{10}) NAAQS were also promulgated on July 18, 1997.[24] Several industry groups and states challenged EPA's new eight-hour ozone standard and the new PM standards, and in a 2001 U.S. Supreme Court decision, the court largely affirmed EPA's statutory authority to establish and revise NAAQS.[25] In the *Whitman v. American Trucking Ass'n* decision, the Supreme Court upheld the constitutionality of EPA's process for establishing NAAQS, and concluded that the CAA properly delegated legislative authority to EPA to develop the NAAQS. The Supreme Court also reaffirmed that EPA is required to set the standards based on public health considerations, and it is not to consider implementation costs in its standard-setting process.[26]

EPA issued two final rules implementing the eight-hour O_3 NAAQS and named over 450 new eight-hour ozone nonattainment areas. Provisions of EPA's implementation rules were challenged in the U.S. Court of Appeals for the D.C. Circuit, and in December 2006, the D.C. Circuit vacated portions of EPA's implementation rule.[27] Although the court concluded that EPA

---

22. CAA § 109(d)(1); 42 U.S.C. § 7409(d)(1).
23. 62 Fed. Reg. 38,856 (July 18, 1997). The one-hour ozone standard was revoked in June 2005, but it remains in effect for certain eight-hour ozone non-attainment areas that do not yet have an attainment date set for their eight-hour designations.
24. 62 Fed. Reg. 38,652 (July 18, 1997).
25. *See* Whitman v. Am. Trucking Ass'n, 531 U.S. 457 (2001).
26. 531 U.S. at 471.
27. S. Coast Air Quality Mgmt. Dist. v. EPA, 472 F.3d 882 (D.C. Cir. 2006), *decision clarified on denial of reh'g*, 489 F.3d 1245 (D.C. Cir. 2007), *cert. denied sub nom.* Nat'l Petrochemical & Refiners Ass'n v. S. Coast Air Quality Mgmt.

had the authority to revoke the one-hour ozone standard, the decision held that EPA had improperly failed to retain the measures required for one-hour nonattainment areas under the CAA's antibacksliding provisions and impermissibly classified nonattainment areas under subpart 1 of Title I.[28] The implementation rule provisions relating to ozone classifications under subpart 2 of Title I and the timing for emission reductions under the new eight-hour ozone NAAQS largely remained intact. EPA is in the process of implementing further rule revisions to implement the 1997 eight-hour O_3 NAAQS.

On a separate but parallel track, EPA completed its five-year review of the eight-hour ozone NAAQS, and the agency issued a revised eight-hour ozone standard in March 2008.[29] In the final rule, EPA ratcheted down the eight-hour primary ozone standard from 0.08 ppm to 0.075 ppm. (The prior standard was effectively 0.084 ppm due to rounding.) EPA also made the secondary standard identical to the primary eight-hour ozone standard. In September 2009, EPA announced that it would reconsider the 2008 O_3 NAAQS, noting that the 2008 standards were not as protective as recommended by the Clean Air Scientific Advisory Committee. In January 2010, EPA proposed a new O_3 NAAQS ranging from 0.060 to 0.070 ppm, and a final rule is expected to be issued in 2011. During the interim period until a new O_3 NAAQS is finalized, EPA will stay implementation of the 2008 O_3 NAAQS; however, new sources being permitted under the New Source Review program will need to evaluate compliance with both the 1997 and 2008 O_3 NAAQS.

EPA issued a final rule to implement the 1997 $PM_{2.5}$ NAAQS in March 2007. EPA has identified over 200 counties in 39 metropolitan areas that are not in compliance with the fine particulate matter NAAQS, and states were required to meet the $PM_{2.5}$ attainment date by 2010 unless EPA granted an extension. The agency can grant extensions of up to five years, but states must meet the NAAQS no later than 2015.

Dist., 552 U.S. 1140 (2008), and *cert. denied sub nom.* Chamber of Greater Baton Rouge v. S. Coast Air Quality Mgmt. Dist., 552 U.S. 1140 (2008).

28.   Subpart 1 of Title 1 sets out the mechanism for classifying areas as either in attainment, nonattainment, or unclassifiable with respect to the NAAQS. Subpart 2 of Title I sets out specific classifications based on the severity of nonattainment for areas that do not yet meet the O_3 NAAQS. Subpart 2 classifies areas as either extreme, severe, serious, moderate, or marginal.

29.   73 Fed. Reg. 16,436 (Mar. 27, 2008).

In September 2006, EPA announced that it has completed its most recent five-year review of the $PM_{2.5}$ NAAQS. In its final rule, issued on October 17, 2006, the agency maintained the annual $PM_{2.5}$ standard and lowered the daily standard from 65 µg/m^3 to 35 µg/m^3.[30] In October 2009, EPA designated 120 counties (or portions of counties) as $PM_{2.5}$ nonattainment areas under the 2006 rule. State SIP rules to comply with the 2006 $PM_{2.5}$ NAAQS are due to be submitted to EPA within three years after the designations are effective, and attainment is required no later than five years after the date of the nonattainment area designations unless an extension is granted.

In addition, in May 1996, EPA announced that it would not revise the SO_2 NAAQS and this final decision was appealed by several nongovernmental organizations. In 1998, the D.C. Circuit held in *American Lung Association v. EPA*[31] that the agency had not adequately explained its decision and remanded EPA's SO_2 determination to the agency for further proceedings. EPA took action in June 2010 to revise the SO_2 NAAQS by establishing a new one-hour SO_2 NAAQS at 75 ppb.[32] EPA revoked the prior annual standard because the agency concluded that it would not add to the public health protections afforded by the new one-hour standard. EPA also retained the existing secondary SO_2 NAAQS.

In February 2010, EPA established a new one-hour NO_2 NAAQS at 100 ppb.[33] The standard set a maximum concentration limit for anywhere within an area. EPA also retained with no changes the current annual average standard of 53 ppb. The lead NAAQS was revised in November 2008, and the primary NAAQS was reduced from 1.5 µg/m^3 to 0.15 µg/m^3 measured as total suspended particles.[34]

3.4   NAAQS Implementation

The distinction between primary and secondary standards has become less important over the years. Most secondary standards (those for O_3, NO_2, $PM_{2.5}$, PM_{10}, and Pb) are the same as the pri-

---

30.   71 Fed. Reg. 61,144 (Oct. 17, 2006).
31.   134 F.3d 388 (D.C. Cir. 1998).
32.   75 Fed. Reg. 35,520 (June 22, 2010).
33.   75 Fed Reg. 6474 (Feb. 9, 2010).
34.   73 Fed. Reg. 66,964 (Nov. 12, 2008).

mary NAAQS because EPA has found this standard to protect both public health and the environment. Only SO_2 has a different secondary standard, and there is no secondary NAAQS for CO.

Each of the standards is expressed in terms of a maximum acceptable concentration of the regulated pollutant in the ambient air, including either a parts per million (ppm) or parts per billion (ppb) concentration or a mass of pollutant per volume of air averaged over a period of time. For example, the CO one-hour primary NAAQS is an average concentration standard of 35 ppm, which is equivalent to 40 micrograms per cubic meter ($\mu g/mg^3$).

The Clean Air Act requires a periodic review, at five-year intervals, of the latest scientific and technical data on each criteria pollutant. If supported by the scientific and technical assessment, EPA may propose revisions to the existing air quality criteria and ambient air quality standard. Periodic review of the NAAQS is a time-consuming and often controversial process. EPA typically takes longer than five years to review the status of the science on particular criteria pollutants. This delay has often resulted in litigation being filed against the agency to force it to establish a schedule for the revision process. For example, prior to the 1997 promulgation of a revised O_3 NAAQS, EPA last completed a review of the ozone standard in 1993 pursuant to a court-ordered schedule. The 1993 review was started in the early 1980s, and the 1993 decision was based primarily on data in a Criteria Document completed in 1986 and supplemented in 1989. At the end of the agency's periodic review of a NAAQS, the EPA administrator will make a decision on whether a revision to a NAAQS is warranted. As noted in section 3.3, EPA decided to revise the O_3 and PM NAAQS in 1997, and adopted a revised $PM_{2.5}$ NAAQS in 2006 and an updated O_3 standard in 2008. Conversely, in 1996, it declined to revise the SO_2 standards,[35] but more recently adopted a new one-hour SO_2 NAAQS to replace the annual and 24-hour concentration standards.[36]

The NAAQS represent a ceiling of air pollution concentrations that apply throughout the nation. As such, the primary NAAQS form the basis for regulating air emissions for the entire country and provide the foundation for setting specific emission rate limits for most types of large stationary sources, such as

---

35.   61 Fed. Reg. 25,566 (May 22, 1996).
36   75 Fed. Reg. 35,520 (June 22, 2010).

power plants and manufacturing facilities. Although the NAAQS are theoretically not directly enforceable, they do set ambient air levels that should not be exceeded and thus serve as the basis for the development and approval of SIP rules and emission limits in air permits. In situations where an air modeling analysis predicts violations of a NAAQS, a Prevention of Significant Deterioration/New Source Review permit cannot be issued without some mitigation measures (e.g., tighter emission limits, offsetting emission reductions at the source) to address the impact.[37] A permit applicant may, in some situations, be able to demonstrate that the emissions increase from the proposed source will have only a de minimis contribution to the modeled violation, and the permit could still be issued.[38] Such a situation may then put the onus on the permitting authority to impose emission reduction requirements on other sources in the area through either approved SIP revision or through permit modifications.[39]

Section 107 of the CAA requires that EPA, in consultation with appropriate state and local authorities, designate separate air quality control regions (AQCRs) throughout the entire country. Many AQCRs are delineated around major urban population centers and across state lines. For example, portions of northern Virginia, the District of Columbia, and southern Maryland make up the Washington, D.C., metropolitan AQCR. A listing of AQCRs is set forth in 40 C.F.R. part 81.

The AQCRs or portions thereof are classified as being either in attainment with the NAAQS (i.e., where air pollution concentrations are below the NAAQS) for each particular criteria pollutant, or in nonattainment (i.e., above the NAAQS). Because there are six criteria pollutants, an AQCR could be in attainment with five of the NAAQS and in nonattainment for the remaining NAAQS. The attainment/nonattainment designations trigger separate air regulatory requirements. For example, for attainment areas, the goal is to make sure the AQCR stays in attainment with each NAAQS. To help accomplish this goal, the CAA and EPA implementing regulations set out an elaborate procedure for permitting new sources and major modifications of existing sources. For nonattainment

---

37. Memorandum from Stephen D. Page, Dir., Office of Air Quality Planning & Standards, to the EPA Reg'l Air Div. Dirs., Guidance Concerning the Implementation of the 1-hour SO_2 NAAQS for the Prevention of Significant Deterioration Program, at 8 (Aug. 23, 2010).
38. *Id.* at 7.
39. *Id.* at 8.

areas, each state initiates a step-by-step-process to adopt enforce-able SIP emission control regulations designed to achieve attain-ment status. To meet the objective of achieving attainment, the state or local air emission control agency will adopt various emis-sion control standards for specific sources or categories of sources such as reasonably available control technology (RACT) standards that apply to existing sources and heightened permitting reviews and control technology standards for new major sources and major modifications of existing major sources. Each of the emis-sion reduction strategies and standards for attainment and nonat-tainment areas will ultimately be incorporated into the SIP. The development of SIP emission control regulations is discussed in chapter 4.

It is unlikely that EPA will take steps to regulate any new criteria pollutants other than the six that are currently regulated for the simple reason that almost all air pollutants with known or suspected effects on public health or the environment are cur-rently regulated under the CAA. In December 2009, nongovern-mental organizations filed a petition requesting that EPA declare carbon dioxide (CO_2) a criteria pollutant, and establish a NAAQS limit. As of 2011, EPA had not taken action on the petition, and as discussed in chapter 11, EPA has instead taken steps to regulate greenhouse gas emissions under Title I (stationary sources) and Title II (mobile sources) of the CAA. As discussed in this chap-ter, the process of establishing the NAAQS is lengthy and time-consuming, and at present the agency appears to have no plans to seek to regulate greenhouse gases under a new NAAQS.

4 State Implementation Plans

As noted in chapter 3, the country is divided into those areas that are in "attainment" with the National Ambient Air Quality Standards (NAAQS), and those areas that are not meeting the NAAQS, which are said to be in "nonattainment." Each air quality control region (AQCR) is designated as being either in attainment or nonattainment for each pollutant.[1] However, if it cannot be determined whether an area meets a NAAQS, that area is identified as "unclassifiable" for that criteria pollutant and generally is not subject to the more rigorous nonattainment area requirements. To enforce the NAAQS in each AQCR, the Clean Air Act requires the implementation of source-specific emission limitations and other regulatory restrictions and control strategies for criteria pollutant emissions that are established through state implementation plans (SIPs). Although the implementation plan concept was introduced in the Air Quality Act of 1967, the current SIP framework was largely established by the Clean Air Amendments of 1970. This framework was later augmented by the 1990 amendments, which added several new nonattainment SIP provisions.

A SIP is a collection of Environmental Protection Agency-approved control strategies and regulations, which may include state statutes, rules, transportation control measures, emission inventories, and local ordinances (hereinafter referred to as SIP rules) that are designed to prevent air quality deterioration for areas that are in attainment with the NAAQS or to reduce criteria pol-

---

1. AQCRs are either (1) designated by the EPA administrator after consultation with appropriate state and local authorities or (2) previously designated as AQCRs before December 31, 1970, and (3) any portion of a state not designated as a AQCR under (1) or (2) shall be an AQCR. CAA § 107(b)(c); 42 U.S.C. § 7407(b)(c).

lutants emitted in nonattainment areas to levels that will achieve compliance with the NAAQS. Most new and modified sources in attainment areas must demonstrate that their projected emissions will not cause the area to exceed the NAAQS or contribute to any significant deterioration of the air quality. In nonattainment areas, new and modified sources must typically meet more stringent emission reduction requirements, including securing offsetting emission reduction credits from other sources. Generally, existing sources in nonattainment areas (and some attainment areas) must meet specific emission limitations codified in the SIP. Some SIP rules may apply to a class of emission sources, such as power plants or pulp and paper mills, and others may apply to a specific plant.

The various state SIPs have historically been an unwieldy collection of state statutes, rules, and control strategies mixed with a disjointed series of EPA approval and partial approval letters. These various "approvals" are set out in state-specific subparts of 40 C.F.R. part 52 with minimal descriptions. However, pursuant to the 1990 amendments, EPA undertook an effort to "collect" all of the various SIP rules and approvals for each state in the various EPA regions. These individual state SIP collections are available from the respective EPA regional offices, and some regions have put the data on their Internet web pages.[2] EPA headquarters has also assembled a comprehensive SIP status website with some helpful links.[3] A word of caution: Practitioners should conduct their own review of the SIP rules for a particular state to confirm that EPA has accurately listed it as part of the federally approved SIP. For instance, EPA SIP approval letters may have only approved certain portions of a state rule as part of the SIP while rejecting other portions.

Once EPA approves a SIP submittal it becomes enforceable under both state and federal law. Thus, as explained in chapter 14, EPA and citizen groups can prosecute a SIP violation even if the state environmental agency declines to pursue it. Each state will adopt SIP rules for the AQCR areas in that state. Some SIP rules may apply statewide, whereas others will apply only to a particular AQCR. For example, nonattainment areas will often have a host of SIP rules specifically aimed at bringing the AQCR into attainment.

---

2. Availability of Federally-Enforceable State Implementation Plans for All States, 63 Fed. Reg. 63,986 (Nov. 18, 1998).

3. *See* EPA, State Implementation Plan Status and Information, http://www.epa.gov/air/urbanair/sipstatus/.

Conversely, areas that are already in attainment will typically be subject to fewer and less stringent emission requirements.

4.1 Elements of a SIP

Section 110(a) of the CAA requires that a SIP rule to implement a NAAQS or a NAAQS revision be submitted not later than three years after the NAAQS standard is promulgated unless EPA establishes a shorter deadline. EPA also may issue a "SIP call" requiring revisions to a state SIP when the agency determines that the SIP does not contain adequate provisions to implement the CAA or it does not include adequate measures restricting the interstate transport of pollutants that contribute significantly to downwind nonattainment area violations.

State SIPs are required pursuant to section 110(a)(2) of the Act to contain 13 general elements. The required elements of SIPs are as follows:

- setting enforceable emission limitations and other control measures, including scheduling and compliance timetables
- providing for monitoring, compiling, and analyzing data on ambient air quality
- establishing a program for enforcement of emission limitations and control measures, including permit programs implementing the PSD requirements for attainment areas and the nonattainment area New Source Review (NSR) requirements
- prohibiting emission activities that contribute significantly to the nonattainment of or interfere with maintenance of a NAAQS in downwind areas of another state
- ensuring that adequate funding, staff, and legal authority are available to implement the SIP
- providing for the monitoring of emissions and the submittal of periodic reports, which must be available to the public for inspection at reasonable times
- authorizing the implementation of contingency plans to restrict emissions that present imminent and substantial endangerment to public health and welfare
- providing for revisions of the SIP to expedite attainment of a NAAQS
- meeting the requirements applicable to nonattainment areas

- meeting the requirements applicable to attainment areas (i.e., PSD requirements)
- providing for air quality modeling
- requiring payment of permit fees
- allowing for consultation and soliciting participation by local political subdivisions

Needless to say, it has taken the states many years to put EPA-approvable rules in place to satisfy all these requirements. Not surprisingly, the procedure for adopting a SIP rule is often time-consuming and complicated. Typically, EPA will promulgate a rule directing the states to adopt certain emission standards (e.g., emission limitations or work practices) to implement a portion of the CAA or it will issue guidance on what provisions states should adopt to implement a new or revised NAAQS. The states must then enact the rule through a rulemaking procedure that requires a period of public notice and comment. If a state chooses to adopt its own rule, it must submit the rule to EPA for approval. Alternatively, states may adopt EPA rules verbatim or seek EPA delegation of authority to implement a federal rule or program in a particular state (e.g., PSD permit program for stationary sources in attainment areas). Either way, EPA will review the SIP submittal and decide whether it should be approved and thus become part of the SIP. To assist states and the public, EPA has issued guidance on what constitutes an "approvable" SIP submittal.[4]

States have the flexibility to adopt their own specific rules and emission limitations to meet the Act's section 110(a)(2) requirements.[5] Courts have recognized that EPA may not prescribe the specific manner in which states meet the primary and secondary NAAQS. In other words, EPA may not condition approval of a SIP rule on the state's adoption of a specific control measure.[6] Moreover, EPA may not make a state SIP more stringent than a state originally intends by rejecting portions of a particular proposed SIP rule if the rule otherwise meets the requirements of section 110(a)(2).[7] Further, EPA is not allowed to consider economic

---

4. EPA, Office of Air Quality Planning & Standards, http://www.epa.gov/oar/oaqps/.

5. Train v. Nat. Res. Def. Council, 421 U.S. 60, 79 (1975).

6. Virginia v. EPA, 108 F.3d 1397, 1408–10 (D.C. Cir. 1997), *modified on other grounds*, 116 F.3d 499 (D.C. Cir. 1997).

7. Bethlehem Steel Corp. v. Gorsuch, 742 F.2d 1028 (7th Cir. 1984).

costs and technological feasibility when reviewing and approving a state SIP submittal.[8]

Similar to SIPs, EPA has developed regulations and guidance to develop tribal implementation plans (TIPs) to achieve the NAAQS on tribal lands. A TIP is substantially similar to a SIP, and is often one component of a comprehensive set of air emission reduction programs that are implemented on tribal lands. The Clean Air Act Amendments of 1990 authorized EPA "to treat Indian tribes in the same manner as states," and the agency was directed to promulgate regulations identifying components of the CAA that could be implemented by Indian tribal authorities similar to states.[9] In February 1998 EPA promulgated its Tribal Authority Rule, which authorizes tribes to have the same rights and responsibilities as states under the Clean Air Act.[10] EPA's direct implementation requirements under the Clean Air Act require the agency to administer CAA-mandated programs on tribal lands if a tribe does not elect to implement its own programs.[11] If a TIP is not adopted for tribal lands to achieve the NAAQS, EPA has authority to establish one or more federal implementation plans (FIPs).

4.2   Complete and Approvable SIP Submittals

To be approved, a SIP submission must provide for emission reductions through standards that are quantifiable, enforceable, replicable, and accountable.[12] A SIP rule is generally designed to control emissions, so if it is to effectively track and substantiate emission reductions, the SIP rule must be quantified against an emissions "baseline." Most SIP submittals are quantified against a relatively current baseline of the states emissions inventory. The emission reductions must also be "clear, unambiguous, and measureable

8. Union Elec. Co. v. EPA, 427 U.S. 246 (1976), *reh'g denied*, 429 U.S. 873 (1976).

9. EPA Office of Air Quality Planning & Standards, Developing a Tribal Implementation Plan 7 (Oct. 2002); CAA § 301(d)(2); 42 U.S.C. § 7601(d)(2).

10. 63 Fed. Reg. 7254 (Feb. 12, 1998) (codified at 40 C.F.R. pt. 49).

11. Direct implementation programs include the Title V Operating Permit program, New Source Performance Standards, the Prevention of Significant Deterioration program, the CAA section 112 air toxics program, and implementation of FIP rules to achieve the NAAQS.

12. State Implementation Plans: General Preamble for the Implementation of Title I of the Clean Air Act Amendments of 1990, 57 Fed. Reg. 13,498, 13,568 (Apr. 16, 1992).

requirements" that are enforceable through CAA section 113 as well as being "practicably enforceable."[13] The *practicably enforceable* concept generally means that objective limits or specific work practices must be in effect, rather than an ill-defined subjective standard. The replicability and accountability requirements typically mean not only that the reductions must be permanent, but also that the standards should generally achieve the same level of reductions from similarly situated sources.

EPA guidance states that SIP control measures must be surplus in that the reductions are not otherwise already relied on in other SIP-approved emission reduction programs.[14] In other words, emission reductions cannot be assumed for meeting a SIP requirement if they have already been counted toward achieving a certain level of reductions in another rule. EPA guidance also notes that SIP control measures must demonstrate that the anti-backsliding restrictions of CAA sections 110(l) and 193 are met.[15]

Once a SIP provision is submitted, EPA generally has 60 days to determine whether the completeness criteria have been met.[16] In other words, EPA will evaluate whether the basic administrative and technical information is provided. EPA's completeness criteria are set forth in 40 C.F.R. part 51, appendix V.[17] A SIP submission will automatically be viewed as complete if EPA does not make a determination within six months.[18] Once a SIP submission is complete, EPA is generally required to approve or disapprove the submittal within 12 months.[19] Nevertheless, EPA frequently misses this 12-month deadline, and it is not uncommon for a decision on a SIP submittal to drag on for years.

EPA has several options when considering a SIP submittal: it may grant full approval or decide on full disapproval, or it may partially approve or partially disapprove of the submittal.[20] EPA also has authority to grant conditional approval, which is contingent on the state adopting specific corrective measures to "fix" the SIP submittal.

---

13. 57 Fed. Reg. at 13,568.
14. EPA Office of Air & Radiation, Incorporating Emerging and Voluntary Measures in a State Implementation Plan (SIP) 3 (Sept. 2004).
15. *Id.* at 4.
16. CAA § 110(k)(1)(A); 42 U.S.C. § 7410(k)(1)(A).
17. *See also* Memorandum from John Seitz, Dir. of EPA Office of Air Quality Planning & Standards, to EPA Regions, November 1994 Submittal Policy (Aug. 29, 1994) [hereinafter Seitz Memo].
18. CAA § 110(k)(1)(B); 42 U.S.C. § 7410(k)(1)(B).
19. CAA § 110(k)(2); 42 U.S.C. § 7410(k)(2).
20. Memorandum from John Calcagni, Dir. of EPA Air Quality Mgmt. Div., to EPA Regions, Processing of State Implementation Plan (SIP) Submittals (July 9, 1992).

SIP submittals are generally required to be submitted as a final rule with schedules and timetables for compliance. In *Natural Resources Defense Council v. EPA*,[21] the U.S. Court of Appeals for the D.C. Circuit rejected EPA's attempt to approve a "committal SIP," which contained a state's commitment to adopt and implement a SIP rule. The court concluded that a "committal SIP" does not qualify as an implementable rule and could not be used to circumvent the SIP deadlines. EPA has, however, issued guidance indicating that as long as the rule is substantially in implementable form (i.e., 80 percent or more), the submittal may be deemed complete.[22]

If a state fails to make a required SIP submittal, or if EPA determines that a submittal is incomplete, or if EPA disapproves a submittal, the agency then must promulgate a federal implementation plan (FIP) within two years.[23] If the state rectifies the SIP deficiency before EPA promulgates a FIP, a FIP is not required. In addition, 18 months after an EPA finding that a state has failed to submit an approvable SIP submittal or that a state is not implementing an approved part of a SIP, the agency is required to impose one of the two types of sanctions identified in CAA section 179.[24] Sanctions include either a loss of highway funding or a requirement that emission offsets on at least a two-to-one basis be obtained for new or modified sources.[25] If the SIP deficiency has not been corrected within another six months (i.e., two years total), the second sanction must be imposed. EPA has the additional sanction authority to withhold grant funding for air pollution planning and control programs.[26] The sanctions are designed to severely hamper a state's efforts to foster new economic growth. Typically, most states correct any SIP deficiencies within 18 months (i.e., before the first sanction must be imposed) and thus far EPA has used its sanction authority infrequently. To date, EPA has only rarely advanced to the stage of proposing and implementing a FIP. In May 2009, for example, EPA issued *Federal Register* notices of proposed disapproval of ozone attainment demonstrations for five states and two findings of a failure to submit ozone attainment demonstrations with respect to the 1997 eight-hour O_3 NAAQS.[27] The sanctions clock will not start

---

21. 22 F.3d 1125 (D.C. Cir. 1994).
22. *See* Seitz Memo, *supra* note 17.
23. CAA § 110(c)(1); 42 U.S.C. § 7410(c)(1).
24. CAA § 179(a); 42 U.S.C. § 7509(a).
25. CAA § 179(b); 42 U.S.C. § 7509(b).
26. CAA § 179(a)(4); 42 U.S.C. § 7509(a)(4).
27. 74 Fed. Reg. 21,568 (May 8, 2009); 74 Fed. Reg. 21,578 (May 8, 2009); 74 Fed. Reg. 21,588 (May 8, 2009); 74 Fed. Reg. 21,594 (May 8, 2009); 74 Fed.

for the five states until EPA issues a final disapproval action, but the sanctions clock did start upon publication of the notice for the two findings of failure to submit an ozone attainment demonstration.

As noted in section 4.1, EPA also has independent authority to determine that a SIP is "substantially inadequate" to obtain or maintain a NAAQS or comply with other requirements of the CAA, or that a SIP fails to mitigate transport of interstate pollutants affecting a downwind nonattainment area. In these situations, EPA may issue a "SIP call" that identifies the SIP deficiency and establishes a deadline for submission of applicable SIP revisions. For example, in October 1998, EPA made a determination that the SIPs in 22 states east of the Mississippi were inadequate to address the impact of NO_x emissions from upwind sources on downwind ozone nonattainment areas.[28] EPA's "NO_x SIP call" rule set in motion a timeline for submission of SIP revisions and implementation of new NO_x limits on power plants and certain other combustion sources.[29]

4.3   Nonattainment Area Requirements

In addition to the basic required elements of a state SIP (set forth in section 110), CAA section 172 requires states with nonattainment areas to provide additional regulatory provisions designed to achieve and maintain attainment of the relevant NAAQS.[30] Nonattainment area SIPs must provide for the implementation of reasonably available control measures (RACM) as expeditiously as practicable.[31] Moreover, the CAA generally requires that an area designated as nonattainment achieve attainment no later than five years from the nonattainment designation date, although EPA may extend this date for another five years with the possibility of two additional one-year extensions under certain circumstances. As a practical matter, over the years, many nonattainment areas have failed to meet these deadlines, and ultimately either Congress or EPA has stepped in to provide relief. For example, the 1975 deadline for attainment established by the 1970 amendments was generally not met and it has been

---

Reg. 21,599 (May 8, 2009); 74 Fed. Reg. 21,604 (May 8, 2009); 74 Fed. Reg. 21,550 (May 8, 2009).

28. 63 Fed. Reg. 57,356 (Oct. 27, 1998).
29. See section 4.8.3 for further discussion of the NO_x SIP call.
30. CAA § 172; 42 U.S.C. § 7502.
31. CAA § 172(c)(1); 42 U.S.C. § 7502(c)(1).

extended by both the 1977 amendments and the 1990 amendments. As explained in section 4.4, in the 1990 amendments, Congress crafted an entirely new compliance timeline for ozone nonattainment areas as well as certain CO and PM nonattainment areas.

CAA Section 172(c) provides a list of additional nonattainment area SIP requirements designed to help attain the applicable NAAQS. These provisions require

- imposition of reasonably available control measures, including (at a minimum) the requirement that existing sources achieve reasonably available control technology (RACT) standards
- a plan for reasonable further progress toward attaining the NAAQS by the applicable attainment date
- a comprehensive, accurate, and current inventory of actual emissions from all sources
- identification and quantification of emissions that will be allowed from certain new or modified major stationary sources, and a demonstration that they will meet the reasonable further progress requirement
- permits for the construction and operation of new or modified major stationary sources
- enforceable emission limitations and other control measures and techniques, as well as schedules and timetables for compliance, as necessary
- contingency measures that will be implemented if an area fails to meet compliance targets for attaining the NAAQS

EPA may also allow states to use equivalent techniques for modeling, emission inventories, and planning.

The CAA section 172 nonattainment provisions are referred to as the "subpart 1" standards, which generally offer EPA greater discretion in establishing nonattainment area requirements. The 1990 amendments augmented the above requirements by adding several additional requirements for certain O_3, CO, and PM_{10} nonattainment areas. For these nonattainment areas, Congress set new attainment deadlines, and in general imposed more stringent requirements for controlling emissions. In the 1990 amendments, Congress created the "subpart 2" nonattainment classifications and measures that established much more prescriptive requirements for achieving the O_3 NAAQS. A summary of the attainment deadlines set forth in the 1990 amendments for the one-hour O_3,

CO, and PM_{10} nonattainment areas is shown in table 4.1. Table 4.2 sets out the revised O_3 NAAQS design values and attainment dates set out for implementation of the eight-hour standard.

Table 4.1   Attainment Deadlines under the 1990 Amendments

O_3 Nonattainment		
Area	**Design Value (ppm)**	**Attainment Date**
Marginal	0.121 to 0.137	November 15, 1993
Moderate	0.138 to 0.159	November 15, 1996
Serious	0.160 to 0.179	November 15, 1999
Severe I	0.180 to 0.189	November 15, 2005
Severe II	0.190 to 0.279	November 15, 2009
Extreme	0.280 and above	November 15, 2010

CO Nonattainment		
Area	**Design Value (ppm)**	**Attainment Date**
Moderate	9.1 to 16.4	December 31, 1995
Serious	16.5 and above	December 31, 2000

PM_{10} Nonattainment	
Area	**Attainment Date**
Moderate	December 31, 1994 (6 years for future areas)
Serious	December 31, 2001 (10 years for future areas)

Table 4.2   Attainment Deadlines under the 2004 Eight-Hour O_3 NAAQS (40 C.F.R. § 51.903)

O_3 Nonattainment		
Area Classification	**Design Value (ppm)[a]**	**Attainment Date (Max. period after effective designation date)**
Marginal	0.085 to 0.092	3 years (June 2007)
Moderate	0.092 to 0.107	6 years (June 2010)
Serious	0.107 to 0.120	9 years (June 2013)
Severe—15	0.120 to 0.127	15 years (June 2019)
Severe—17	0.127 to 0.187	17 years (June 2021)
Extreme	0.187 and above	20 years (June 2024)

a.   EPA defines the design categories as "from up to, but not including." 40 C.F.R. § 51.903, tbl. 1.

4.4   Ozone Nonattainment Areas

Under the 1990 amendments, Congress enacted subpart 2 to reclassify ozone nonattainment areas into five categories based on the severity of the nonattainment.[32] These categories are marginal, moderate, serious, severe, and extreme. The 1990 amendments provided that each ozone nonattainment area would be subject to the requirements for its own classification as well as the requirements for each lower classification. For ozone nonattainment areas, the threshold for defining a *major source* is also lowered to 50 tons per year (tpy) of VOCs or NO_x for severe areas and 10 tpy of VOCs or NO_x for extreme areas. A more detailed discussion of the revised 1990 nonattainment area provisions applicable to O_3, CO, and PM_{10} nonattainment areas is beyond the scope of this book; however, some of the general requirements include the following:

Marginal Areas
- Inventory of emission sources.
- RACT corrections for existing sources.
- Basic vehicle inspection and maintenance program.
- Additional NSR permit program requirements.
- Preparation of periodic inventories (every three years).
- NO_x and volatile organic compound (VOC) emission statements from sources.
- Emission offset requirements of at least 1.1 to 1 for new and modified sources.

Moderate Areas
- Meet requirements for marginal areas.
- Achieve 15 percent reasonable further progress (RFP) reduction in VOC emissions within six years.
- RACT for all sources covered by EPA Control Technique Guidelines (28 source categories) and all other major VOC sources.
- Gasoline vapor recovery systems required at certain facilities.
- Emission offset requirements of at least 1.15 to 1 for new and modified sources.

---

32.   As explained in chapter 3, ozone forms in the lower atmosphere or troposphere, and results from chemical reactions of VOCs, NO_x, and oxygen in the presence of sunlight. Ozone precursors—VOCs and NO_x—are emitted by numerous sources, including fossil-fuel-fired combustion sources (e.g., boilers, motor vehicles), petroleum storage, and the use of paints and solvents.

Serious Areas
- Meet requirements for moderate areas.
- RFP demonstrations; demonstrations must include an additional 3 percent reduction per year from baseline for each consecutive three-year period after the initial six-year RFP.
- Enhanced vehicle inspection and maintenance program and a clean fuel vehicle program.
- Transportation control measures.
- Enhanced monitoring of ambient concentrations of O_3, NO_x, and VOCs.
- More stringent NSR permitting (*major source* is defined as emitting at least 50 tons per year of VOCs or NO_x).
- Emission offset requirements of at least 1.2 to 1 for new and modified sources.

Severe Areas
- Meet requirements for serious areas.
- More stringent NSR permitting (*major source* is defined as emitting at least 25 tons per year of VOCs or NO_x).
- Transportation control programs to reduce vehicle miles traveled.
- Emission offset requirements of at least 1.3 to 1 unless all existing major sources are required to use best available control technology (BACT), in which case the ratio is 1.2 to 1.

Extreme Areas
- Meet requirements for severe areas.
- Any increase in emissions from a discrete operation of a major stationary source is considered a modification for NSR purposes.
- More stringent NSR permitting (*major source* is defined as emitting at least 10 tons per year of VOCs or NO_x).
- Transportation control measures may be imposed during heavy traffic hours.
- Electric utility and industrial commercial borders that emit more than 25 tons per year of NO_x must use clean fuels or use advanced control technology.
- Emission offset requirements of 1.5 to 1; however, if all existing major sources are required to use BACT, the ratio may be reduced to 1.2 to 1.

The 1990 amendments recognize that NO_x is also a precursor to the formation of ozone, and CAA section 182(f) provides that major sources of NO_x shall be subject to the emission reduction requirements for serious, severe, and extreme O_3 nonattainment areas. However, EPA has the authority to grant a waiver from these requirements where it can be demonstrated that greater air quality benefits would be achieved without NO_x emission reductions or that additional NO_x emission reductions would not contribute to attaining the O_3 NAAQS.[33] Several ozone non-attainment areas (e.g., the Chicago metropolitan AQCR) have received NO_x waivers due to the fact that NO_x emission reductions would not help achieve attainment with the O_3 NAAQS.[34] [34]In addition, the CAA provides that NO_x emission reduction controls may be substituted for required VOC control measures if the NO_x measure will achieve reductions at least equivalent to the required VOC standards.[35] This provision gives states flexibility to develop an appropriate mix of VOC and NO_x control measures and emission reduction strategies for serious and above ozone nonattainment areas.

As noted in chapter 3, on July 18, 1997, EPA promulgated a revised O_3 NAAQS that established a new 0.08 ppm eight-hour standard and revoked the previously existing one-hour standard of 0.12 ppm.[36] In the *South Coast Air Quality Management District v. EPA* decision, the U.S. Court of Appeals for the D.C. Circuit concluded that EPA had the authority to revoke the one-hour O_3 standard provided that adequate antibacksliding provisions were in place. The former one-hour designations and classifications are being retained in 40 C.F.R. part 81 for purposes of the antibacksliding provisions under 40 C.F.R. part 51.905(c) and for the eight-hour O_3 nonattainment Early Action Compact Areas (i.e., those areas that do not yet have an effective date for the eight-hour standard).

The D.C. Circuit in *South Coast Air Quality Management District v. EPA* also ruled that EPA had impermissibly classified certain eight-hour O_3 nonattainment areas under subpart 1 of

---

33. CAA § 182(f)(1); 42 U.S.C. § 7511a(f)(1).

34. *See, e.g.,* 76 Fed. Reg. 9655 (Feb 22, 2011) (NO_x RACT waiver request to exempt sources in the Illinois portions of the Chicago–Gary–Lake County, Illinois–Indiana and St. Louis, Missouri–Illinois O_3 nonattainment areas).

35. CAA § 182(c)(2)(C); 42 U.S.C. § 7511a(c)(2)(C).

36. 62 Fed. Reg. 38,856 (July 18, 1997). Revocation of the one-hour ozone standard was implemented in June 2005, but it remains in effect for certain eight-hour ozone nonattainment areas that do not yet have an attainment date set for their eight-hour designations.

Title I.[37] EPA's rule implementing the eight-hour O_3 NAAQS allowed eight-hour nonattainment areas meeting the old one-hour standard to be subject to more flexible nonattainment provisions of subpart 1. The court disagreed, and held that the more stringent mandatory classification scheme of subpart 2 should apply to eight-hour O_3 nonattainment areas that have air quality that is equivalent to or worse than the level of the old one-hour O_3 NAAQS.[38]

In April 2004, EPA issued nonattainment area designations and classifications to implement the 1997 eight-hour O_3 NAAQS. Table 4.2 sets out the revised eight-hour design values and attainment dates that apply to these areas. As of April 2011, EPA identified 44 AQCRs and 242 counties that were subject to the various eight-hour O_3 nonattainment area requirements; a total of 69 former nonattainment areas and 192 counties have been redesignated to attainment.[39]

4.5   CO and PM Nonattainment Areas

For CO, the 1990 amendments added requirements for moderate and serious nonattainment areas that are similar to some of the O_3 nonattainment area requirements. The *major source* threshold for moderate CO nonattainment areas is 100 tons per year, and the threshold is 50 tons per year for serious CO nonattainment areas. States with moderate CO nonattainment areas must implement enhanced vehicle inspection and maintenance programs as well as submit an initial CO emission inventory, periodic inventories, and attainment demonstrations. Serious CO areas must meet the moderate CO area requirements, adopt transportation control measures, and use oxygenated gasoline to reduce CO. As of September 2010, all CO nonattainment areas have been redes-

37. S. Coast Air Quality Mgmt. Dist. v. EPA, 472 F.3d 882, 899 (D.C. Cir. 2006), *decision clarified on denial of reh'g*, 489 F.3d 1245 (D.C. Cir. 2007), *cert. denied sub nom.* Nat'l Petrochemical & Refiners Ass'n v. S. Coast Air Quality Mgmt. Dist., 552 U.S. 1140 (2008), and *cert. denied sub nom.* Chamber of Greater Baton Rouge v. S. Coast Air Quality Mgmt. Dist., 552 U.S. 1140 (2008).
38. 472 F.3d at 892.
39. EPA Green Book, 8-Hour Ozone Nonattainment Area Summary, http://www.epa.gov/oaqps001/greenbk/gnsum.html (Apr. 21, 2011); EPA Green Book, 8-Hour Ozone Maintenance Area Summary, http://www.epa.gov/oaqps001/greenbk/gmsum.html (Apr. 21, 2011).

ignated to maintenance areas.[40] EPA recently completed a review of the CO NAAQS, and the agency proposed to retain the current standards.[41]

The 1990 amendments also added two classifications for PM_{10} nonattainment areas—moderate and serious. The major source threshold is 100 tons per year for moderate PM_{10} nonattainment areas and 70 tons per year for serious PM_{10} nonattainment areas. States with moderate PM_{10} nonattainment areas were required to submit SIP revisions assuring that reasonably available control measures (RACM) for PM_{10} reductions would be implemented as well as providing an attainment demonstration. In addition to meeting the requirements for moderate areas, serious PM_{10} nonattainment areas are required to apply best available control measures (BACM) for PM_{10} emissions. As of April 2011, there were a total of 8 AQCRs and 11 counties that were classified as serious PM_{10} nonattainment areas, and 37 AQCRs and 39 counties that were categorized as moderate.[42]

In January 2005, EPA issued a final rule setting forth the initial air quality designations and classifications for $PM_{2.5}$ nonattainment areas.[43] The $PM_{2.5}$ nonattainment areas are classified under CAA section 107(d)(1) (subpart 1),[44] and as of April 2011, there are 39 AQCRs and 208 counties in nonattainment with the 1997 $PM_{2.5}$ NAAQS.[45] EPA revised the $PM_{2.5}$ NAAQS 24-hour standard to 35 $\mu g/m^3$ in October 2006, and retained the annual $PM_{2.5}$ NAAQS at 15 $\mu g/m^3$.[46] EPA completed its designation of nonattainment areas with the 2006 $PM_{2.5}$ NAAQS in November 2009.[47] Under the 2006 $PM_{2.5}$ NAAQS, EPA has designated 32 AQCRs and 121 counties in nonattainment as of April 2011.[48]

---

40. EPA Green Book, Carbon Monoxide Information, http://www.epa.gov/oaqps001/greenbk/cindex.html (Apr. 21, 2011).

41. 76 Fed. Reg. 8158 (Feb. 11, 2011).

42. EPA Green Book, Particulate Matter (PM-10) Nonattainment Area Summary, http://www.epa.gov/oaqps001/greenbk/pnsum.html (Apr. 21, 2011).

43. 70 Fed. Reg. 944 (Jan. 5, 2005); 70 Fed. Reg. 19,844 (Apr. 15, 2005) (supplemental amendments).

44. CAA § 107(d)(1); 42 U.S.C. § 7407(d)(1).

45. EPA Green Book, Particulate Matter (PM-2.5) 1997 Standard Nonattainment Area Summary, http://www.epa.gov/oaqps001/greenbk/qnsum.html (Apr. 21, 2011).

46. 71 Fed. Reg. 61,144 (Oct. 17, 2006).

47. 74 Fed. Reg. 58,688 (Nov. 13, 2009).

48. EPA Green Book, Particulate Matter (PM-2.5) 2006 Standard Nonattainment Area Summary, http://www.epa.gov/oaqps001/greenbk/rnsum.html (Apr. 21, 2011).

4.6   Transportation Conformity

CAA section 176(c) prohibits federal funding or federal approval or licensing of highway and transit projects unless the responsible federal entity makes a determination that the projects are consistent with the applicable SIP rules and will not cause or contribute to any new violations of or worsen existing violations or delay timely attainment of the NAAQS.[49] Although CAA conformity requirements have been in effect since the 1977 amendments, the 1990 amendments refocused the requirements and more closely linked the conformity requirement to the state SIPs. For example, the ozone nonattainment area requirements discussed earlier included numerous transportation-related actions such as transportation control programs to reduce vehicle miles traveled.

EPA's regulations apply the conformity requirement to nonattainment areas and areas that are subject to maintenance plans for O_3, CO, $PM_{2.5}$, PM_{10}, or NO_x. Conformity applies to transportation plans, transportation improvement plans, and transportation projects funded or approved by the Federal Highway Administration or the Federal Transit Administration.[50] Conformity determinations typically must be completed before the federal entity approves a transportation-related action, and generally conformity determinations must be updated at least every three years.[51]

The initial Transportation Conformity Rule was issued by EPA in November 1993, and the requirements have been modified several times since then.[52] The conformity rule sets out procedures to ensure interagency consultation, and typical participants include federal, state, and local transportation agencies, EPA, and state and regional air quality agencies.[53] The conformity provisions signal Congress's intent that federal actions to fund or approve transportation projects not interfere with or cause a delay in attaining the NAAQS.

---

49. CAA § 176(c); 42 U.S.C. § 7506(c).
50. Fed. Highway Admin., Transportation Conformity: A Basic Guide for State and Local Officials (Apr. 2005), http://www.fhwa.dot.gov/environment/air_quality/conformity/guide/guide01.cfm.
51. Id.
52. 58 Fed. Reg. 62,188 (Nov. 24, 1993), 40 C.F.R. pt. 51.390, 40 C.F.R. pt. 93 et seq. See also EPA Office of Transp. & Air Quality, EPA-420-B-09-002, Guidance for Implementing the Clean Air Act Section 176(c)(8) Transportation Control Measure Substitution and Addition Provision (Jan. 2009).
53. Fed. Highway Admin., Transportation Conformity Reference Guide, chapter 2 (Mar. 2006), http://www.fhwa.dot.gov/environment/air_quality/conformity/reference/reference_ guide/chap2.cfm.

4.7 Failure to Attain and Redesignation

EPA is required to determine, as expeditiously as practicable after an applicable attainment date for a nonattainment area (but no later than six months after such date) whether the area has attained the applicable NAAQS. The determination is based on the air quality as of the designated attainment date.[54] Upon making such a determination, EPA is required to publish a notice in the *Federal Register*. If an area has failed to reach attainment by the attainment date, then the state must submit a SIP revision to generally include such additional measures as EPA may reasonably prescribe that can be feasibly implemented in light of technological availability, costs, and any non-air-quality- and other air-quality-related health and environmental impacts to achieve attainment with the applicable NAAQS.[55] EPA has the authority under CAA section 172(a)(2) to issue a new attainment date. In addition, states may apply to EPA to extend the attainment date for one more year.[56] However, no more than two one-year extensions may be issued for a single nonattainment area.[57] For ozone nonattainment areas that fail to achieve attainment by the statutorily prescribed dates, the CAA requires the particular ozone nonattainment area be reclassified generally to the next higher classification, that is, "bumped up."[58]

Areas may be redesignated to either attainment, nonattainment, or unclassifiable status by a state or by EPA; however, nonattainment areas may not be redesignated as unclassifiable.[59] EPA has issued guidance explaining the criteria used to determine whether the statutory requirements for redesignation have been met.[60] Any state may request that a nonattainment area be redesignated to attainment or EPA may redesignate a nonattainment area to attainment on its own. The agency may not promulgate a redesignation of a nonattainment area to attainment unless (1) the area has attained the NAAQS, (2) there is a fully approved SIP in

---

54. CAA § 179(c)(1); 42 U.S.C. § 7509(c)(1).
55. CAA § 179(d); 42 U.S.C. § 7509(d).
56. CAA § 172(a)(2)(C); 42 U.S.C. § 7502(a)(2)(C).
57. *Id.*
58. CAA § 181(b)(2), 42 U.S.C. § 7511(b)(2). An area cannot be bumped up to an extreme classification under this section.
59. CAA § 107; 42 U.S.C. § 7407.
60. *See* State Implementation Plans: General Preamble for the Implementation of Title I of the Clean Air Act Amendments of 1990, 57 Fed. Reg. 13,498, 13,561–64 (Apr. 16, 1992).

place, (3) the improvement in air quality is due to permanent and enforceable reductions in emissions, and (4) the agency has fully approved a "maintenance plan" for maintaining compliance with NAAQS for the area.[61]

4.8   Regional Air Quality Planning

In the 1990s, regional air quality planning has become an important mechanism for addressing air pollution. Traditionally, EPA and the states focused on whether individual AQCRs complied with the NAAQS. Despite years of effort, many AQCRs remain in nonattainment for certain pollutants. The Clean Air Act Amendments of 1990 reflect an awareness by Congress that air pollution is not merely a local problem but also a regional concern. The 1990 amendments provided new statutory tools to tackle air pollution on a regional basis, as it is suspected that the atmospheric transport of air contaminants over large distances and other regional effects hinder NAAQS compliance by certain parts of the country. Additionally, voluntary regional efforts have played a key role in regional air quality planning.

Regional air quality planning is now a key element in EPA's approach to address air pollution. This regional focus stems from the realization that air pollution transport must be addressed if certain areas of the country are ever going to reach attainment status with the NAAQS. Interstate and international transport of air pollution has long been suspected of contributing to the nonattainment of certain NAAQS in downwind states. To address this concern, Congress adopted several provisions to address transboundary air pollution. First, CAA section 110 requires each state's SIP to contain adequate provisions to prohibit emissions that "contribute significantly to nonattainment in, or interfere with maintenance" of a NAAQS in a downwind state.[62] Second, CAA section 126 empowers downwind states to petition EPA to initiate action against specific sources of interstate pollution that are determined to contribute significantly to another state's NAAQS violation.[63] Third, the

---

61. CAA § 107(d)(3); 42 U.S.C. § 7407(d)(3).
62. CAA § 110(a)(2)(D); 42 U.S.C. § 7410(a)(2)(D).
63. CAA § 126; 42 U.S.C. § 7426. There was some discrepancy on whether section 126 authorized states to petition EPA for relief only from new sources of air pollution or whether existing sources were also covered. The plain language of

1990 amendments to the Clean Air Act added two new programs to address regional planning for interstate transport of air pollution. In CAA section 176A, the 1990 amendments set up a mechanism for creating interstate transport commissions. In addition, CAA section 184 was added to create the ozone transport region (OTR) to address ozone transport in the eastern United States (i.e., from Maine to northern Virginia). The OTR is governed by an Ozone Transport Commission (OTC) composed of government leaders and environmental officials from the 12 northeastern and mid-Atlantic states, including the District of Columbia. To date, aside from the OTC, no other interstate transport commissions have been created pursuant to the new section 176A mechanism.

4.8.1   Interstate Transport Commission

An interstate transport region may be created by EPA, on its own accord or by acting on a petition from the governor of a state, when EPA has reason to believe that interstate transport of air pollutants is contributing significantly to a NAAQS violation in one or more states.[64] Any state in which NAAQS violations occur may petition EPA to establish a transport region or to add one or more states (or portions of states) to an existing region. An interstate transport region created pursuant to CAA section 176A may include both upwind and downwind states. A petition to set up an interstate transport region must be acted on within 18 months. An interstate transport commission is the governing body of a transport region and is required to consist of the governor of each state or a designee, the EPA administrator or a designee, the EPA regional administrator or a designee, and the air pollution control officer for each included state.[65]

Transport commissions are designed to assess whether and to what extent control measures should be included in the SIPs of the states in the region to satisfy the Clean Air Act requirements. The

section 126, as amended by the 1990 amendments, provides that states may only petition for relief from new sources of air pollution. However, EPA took the position that Congress made a "typographical error" in its changes to section 126 and that it really intended to subject both new and existing sources to potential emission controls where there is a finding that the source significantly contributes to a violation of a NAAQS. *See* 63 Fed. Reg. 56,292, 56,299–301 (Oct. 21, 1998). The U.S. Court of Appeals for the D.C. Circuit upheld EPA's interpretation in *Appalachian Power Co. v. EPA*, 249 F.3d 1032. 1043–44 (D.C. Cir. 2001).

   64.   CAA § 176A(a); 42 U.S.C. § 7506a(a).
   65.   CAA § 176A(b); 42 U.S.C. § 7506a(b).

commission may develop and submit recommendations to EPA on strategies for mitigating pollution transport, and may request that EPA issue a SIP call to states in a transport region directing that such states revise their SIPs to add the recommended control measures or other measures to address pollutant transport.

4.8.2   Ozone Transport Commission

As noted in section 4.8, in the Clean Air Act Amendments of 1990 (CAA sections 176A and 184), Congress created the OTR and the OTC, and directed the OTC to (1) assess the degree of interstate transport of ozone and its precursors in the northeastern and mid-Atlantic transport region, (2) assess strategies for mitigating inter-state pollution, and (3) recommend to the EPA administrator such measures as the commission may determine to be necessary to ensure that states attain and maintain the NAAQS for ozone in the northeastern United States.

The OTC established six committees to address technical and regulatory issues. Based on the work of its committees and other available information, the OTC has adopted several memoranda of understanding (MOUs) that specify joint state actions to control VOCs and NO_x. These and future MOUs are intended to form a policy framework so that SIPs will be modified and developed to achieve the attainment and maintenance of the ambient O_3 standard throughout the northeastern United States. The OTC has issued several MOUs addressing the controlling of emissions from mobile sources and addressing regional strategies for controlling stationary source NO_x emissions.[66]

On September 24, 1997, 11 of the 12 OTC signatory states agreed to implement a regional NO_x emission program (the NO_x Budget Program) that called for significant reductions in NO_x emissions from utility and large industrial combustion facilities within the OTR through an emissions "cap and trade" program. The NO_x reduction requirements under the NO_x Budget Program started on May 1, 1999.[67] The reductions were only required dur-ing the ozone season—May 1 to September 30 of each year—and were implemented by nine OTC states from 1999 to 2002 when

---

66. A listing of the OTC's formal actions is available on its website at http://www.otcair.org/index.asp.

67   As part of the compliance strategy, the OTC developed a model NO_x emission trading rule that served as a template for states in the OTR to adopt their own rules to implement the OTC NOx emission reduction requirements.

the program was replaced by the NO_x Budget Trading Program under the NO_x SIP call rule starting in 2003.

The OTC NO_x budget model rule implemented the MOU emission reduction requirement through a market-based cap-and-trade program that was based on the acid rain SO_2 emission allowance trading program set forth in CAA Title IV. The OTC program capped NO_x emissions at 219,000 tons in 1999. The OTC NO_x Budget Program successfully reduced regional ozone season emissions in 2002 by almost 280,000 tons from the 1990 baseline of approximately 490,000 tons, approximately a 60 percent reduction in emissions from the baseline.[68] Most of the OTC NO_x trading rules were approved as part of the state SIPs, and EPA implemented a tracking system to record NO_x trades in the OTR.

4.8.3 NO_x SIP Call

The Ozone Transport Assessment Group (OTAG) was formed to evaluate and address the transport of ozone and its precursors in the eastern half of the country. It was started in May 1995 in response to a March 2, 1995, memorandum from EPA's assistant administrator for Air and Radiation to EPA's regional administrators. This memorandum called for a collaborative process among the states in the eastern half of the country and EPA to evaluate and address the transport of ozone and its precursors (NO_x and VOCs). The OTAG process was a voluntary consultative process among the 37 member states (basically the eastern, midwestern, and southern states), EPA, and interested parties, including several environmental groups and various industries. The collaborative effort was initiated because many states with urban nonattainment areas (primarily the northeast OTC-member states) were unable to meet the November 1994 deadlines requiring submittal of SIP revisions addressing NO_x and VOC reductions. The OTAG was formed to forge a consensus on emission inventory calculations, analyze ozone transport predictions, measure the effectiveness of existing control strategies, and develop additional NO_x and VOC control strategies on a regional basis. The goal of the OTAG process was to reach an agreement on the additional regional, local, and national emission reductions that would be needed to ensure that the northeast OTC-member states reached attainment with the O_3 NAAQS standard.

---

68. Ozone Transp. Comm'n, NOx Budget Program—1999–2002 Progress Report 6 (Mar. 2003).

EPA's October 1998 NO_x SIP call rule was based on the recommendations and analysis completed by the OTAG.[69] In the NO_x SIP call rule, EPA determined that the SIPs in 22 states (and the District of Columbia) east of the Mississippi were inadequate to address the effects of NO_x emissions on downwind nonattainment areas.[70] In particular, EPA concluded that many ozone nonattainment areas in the east (e.g., OTC member states) could not achieve attainment by implementing control measures in those areas alone. The NO_x SIP call was challenged by several affected states and industry groups. In March 2000, the D.C. Circuit essentially affirmed EPA's NO_x SIP call rule, which requires that most northeast states implement NO_x emission reduction controls by May 31, 2004, to meet mandated NO_x budget targets for each state by 2007.[71] In *Michigan v. EPA*, the Court upheld EPA's determination that 19 of the 22 NO_x SIP call states were contributing significantly to ozone NAAQS compliance problems experienced by downwind states. Thus, those 19 states were required to implement NO_x emission control levels to meet NO_x emission reduction budget targets. These states also had the option of adopting EPA's NO_x emission trading rule, which established a cap-and-trade program that could be used as a method for achieving compliance with the NO_x budget requirements.[72] The court vacated the inclusion of three states—Georgia, Missouri, and Wisconsin—holding that there was a lack of evidence demonstrating that NO_x emissions from these states contributed to ozone nonattainment in downwind states.[73] Key requirements of the final NO_x SIP call that applied

---

69. 63 Fed. Reg. at 57,369.

70. States included in the original NOx SIP call rule included Alabama, Connecticut, Delaware, District of Columbia, Georgia, Illinois, Indiana, Kentucky, Maryland, Massachusetts, Michigan, Missouri, New Jersey, New York, North Carolina, Ohio, Pennsylvania, Rhode Island, South Carolina, Tennessee, Virginia, West Virginia, and Wisconsin.

71. Michigan v. EPA, 213 F.3d 663 (D.C. Cir. 2000). The original target implementation of May 1, 2003, contained in the NO_x SIP call rule was extended to May 31, 2004, by the U.S. Court of Appeals for the D.C. Circuit. Eight northeastern states and the District of Columbia implemented the NO_x SIP call rule starting in May 2003. The remaining 11 states began compliance with the NO_x SIP call rule in May 2004.

72. 40 C.F.R. pt. 96.

73. The inclusion of Georgia and Missouri in the NO_x SIP call was remanded to EPA for further rulemaking, and in April 2004, EPA finalized a supplemental rule that included portions of Georgia and Missouri in the NOx SIP call with a compliance date of May 1, 2007. *See* 69 Fed. Reg. 21,604 (Apr. 21, 2004).

to 19 states (and the District of Columbia) east of the Mississippi River and the District of Columbia included the following:

- *State NO$_x$ budgets.* The rule established a NO$_x$ emissions budget for each state.
- *Non-utility boilers.* Recommendation of 60 percent reduction of emissions from large-sized sources (e.g., more than 250 mmBtu/hr) such as industrial boilers and combustion turbines.
- *Utility sources.* Recommendation of a NO$_x$ emission rate of 0.15 lb/mmBtu on all applicable sources (fossil-fuel-burning electric utility units serving an electricity generator of 25 megawatts or greater) to reduce emissions from about 1.5 million tons to about 500,000 tons for the ozone season.
- *NO$_x$ cap-and-trade program.* The final rule includes an interstate cap-and-trade program to implement a fixed-tonnage NO$_x$ budget.

For each of the SIP call jurisdictions, EPA calculated a NO$_x$ budget that was required to be achieved by 2007, and states were required to implement controls by May 31, 2004.[74] The NO$_x$ budgets were limited to the ozone season months of May through September, and were calculated for each major source sector, including separate components for highway vehicles and non-road engines. Each state retained discretion for determining the size of its trading program and its individual allocation of emission allowances to affected sources so long as its trading budget and emissions from other nonparticipating affected sources did not exceed the NO$_x$ SIP call budget.

The NO$_x$ SIP call was in place from 2004 to 2008, and was replaced in 2009 by the Clean Air Interstate Rule (CAIR). EPA reported that the NO$_x$ SIP call program was successful in reducing ozone season emissions throughout the region, and at the end of the program the NO$_x$ emissions of approximately 481,000 tons were 9 percent below the 2008 cap, and 62 percent lower than NO$_x$ ozone season emissions in 2000.[75]

---

74. 63 Fed. Reg. at 57,492 (40 C.F.R. §§ 51.21(b)(1)(ii), (e)(1)). As indicated in note 71, the original implementation date of May 1, 2003, was extended to May 31, 2004.

75. EPA Clean Air Mkts. Div., NO$_x$ Budget Trading Program 2008 Highlights, http://www.epa.gov/airmarkets/progress/NBP_4.html.

4.8.4   Section 126 Petitions

Another mechanism for addressing interstate transport of pollution is CAA section 126,[76] which authorizes a downwind state to petition EPA to make a finding that any new or existing major stationary source or group of stationary sources upwind of the state emits of or would emit air pollution in violation of CAA section 110(a)(2)(D)(i) such that the emissions contribute significantly to nonattainment of or interfere with maintenance of a NAAQS.[77] If EPA issues a finding that the offending sources in the upwind state are contributing to downwind NAAQS noncompliance, the sources must shut down within three months from the finding unless EPA directly regulates the sources by establishing emission limits and a compliance schedule to eliminate the prohibited impact on the NAAQS compliance status of the downwind state.[78] The compliance schedule may extend no later than three years.[79]

The CAA section 126 authority provides a fairly draconian remedy of potentially shutting a source down if there is an adverse finding, but to date EPA has taken the approach of establishing source-specific emission limitations. The CAA section 126 mechanism differs from EPA's authority to initiate a SIP call, and propose a FIP if states do not take steps to adopt SIP rules to reduce interstate transport of pollution. Section 126 is a source-specific approach, and it may be initiated only by a state or local political subdivision.

Once a CAA section 126 petition is filed, EPA is allowed 60 days under the Act to respond to the petition, but EPA has frequently extended the deadline to respond to section 126 petitions due to the complexity of the issues raised in evaluating alleged NAAQS compliance impacts from sources in upwind states on the downwind states.

EPA has analyzed several section 126 petitions in recent years. In August 1997, eight northeastern states filed petitions seeking a finding that major stationary sources in 12 states and the District of Columbia were affecting air quality in the downwind states. The petitions were handled by EPA on a parallel track with the NO$_x$ SIP call rule. In January 2000, EPA issued its findings concluding that the major sources in the upwind areas were affecting the down-

---

76.   CAA § 126; 42 U.S.C. § 7426.
77.   65 Fed. Reg. 2674, 2675 (Jan. 18, 2000).
78.   *Id.*; CAA § 126(c); 42 U.S.C. 7426(c),
79.   CAA § 126(c); 42 U.S.C. § 7426(c).

wind states compliance with the one-hour O_3 NAAQS.[80] EPA finalized a cap-and-trade rule similar to the NO_x SIP call that applied directly to the covered sources in the upwind states, and EPA ultimately harmonized the compliance deadlines between the NO_x SIP call and the January 2000 section 126 rule.[81] EPA's authority to promulgate the January 2000 section 126 rule was largely upheld in a May 2001 decision in *Appalachian Power Company v. EPA*.[82]

Other section 126 petitions have been issued over the years, including petitions filed by North Carolina in 2004 and New Jersey in 2010 alleging that major sources (primarily power plants) in upwind states are significantly contributing to or interfering with the maintenance of various NAAQS. EPA denied North Carolina's section 126 petition largely on the basis that the reductions in NO_x and SO_2 emissions under the Clean Air Interstate Rule (CAIR) would eliminate the significant contribution of emissions from upwind sources into North Carolina.[83] New Jersey's section 126 petition is focused on one major source in Pennsylvania, and in April 2011, EPA issued a proposed rule to make a finding that the upwind coal-fired power plant was emitting air pollutants in violation of the CAA.[84]

Section 126 authority is a powerful tool to compel action by specific sources in upwind states to curtail their emissions; however, it has been invoked with mixed success. So far, states appear to have primarily used the authority as a mechanism to prod EPA to take action under its more widely used SIP call and FIP authority.

4.8.5   Clean Air Interstate Rule

In 2005, EPA issued CAIR, which was intended to require power plants in 28 states and the District of Columbia to adopt rules to achieve substantial reductions in NO_x and SO_2 emissions. The centerpiece of the rule was a cap-and-trade program that targeted reductions from power plants in two stages starting in 2009 for NO_x and 2010 for SO_2. Various petitioners, including the State of North Carolina and industry petitioners, challenged several provisions of CAIR. On July 11, 2008, the U.S. Court of Appeals for the

---

80. 65 Fed. Reg. 2674, 2675 (Jan. 18, 2000).
81. 67 Fed. Reg. 21,522 (Apr. 30, 2002).
82. 249 F.3d 1032 (D.C. Cir. 2001).
83. 71 Fed. Reg. 25,328 (Apr. 28, 2006).
84. 76 Fed. Reg. 19,662 (Apr. 7, 2011). *See also* State of N.J., Petitions Pursuant to Section 126 of the Clean Air Act, http://www.state.nj.us/dep/baqp/petition/126petition.htm.

D.C. Circuit vacated CAIR, holding that the rule was fundamentally flawed.[85] In December 2008, the court temporarily reinstated CAIR while the agency conducted further rulemaking to address the flaws in the rule. The court concluded that a remand without vacatur was appropriate in order to preserve the environmental benefits covered by CAIR.[86]

In identifying a number of flaws in CAIR, the court noted the following as the most significant:

- CAA section 110 requires an analysis of sources that contribute significantly to downwind nonattainment or interfere with the maintenance of attainment areas, and the cap-and-trade emissions programs were region-wide programs that were not based on individual source contributions.
- In the rule, EPA neglected to analyze the "interfere with maintenance" prong of the section 110 requirements.
- The NO_x and SO_2 emission reduction deadline of 2015 needed to correlate with the Title I deadlines of achieving compliance with the applicable NAAQS. The court noted that the 1997 $PM_{2.5}$ NAAQS required compliance by 2010.
- The allocation of NO_x and SO_2 allowances under CAIR was not based on each upwind state's contribution to downwind nonattainment areas or interference with maintenance of attainment areas.
- The NO_x allowances were weighed toward coal states and EPA's equitable allocation of the state budgets based on fuel type was not a valid criteria under CAA section 110.
- EPA did not have the statutory authority to require the retirement of SO_2 allowances under the acid rain program.

The court's decision highlighted the tension between the "command and control" provisions of the Clean Air Act and EPA's desire to use more flexible market-based solutions to implement significant reductions in NO_x and SO_2 emissions. The court's remand of CAIR has a number of implications for EPA rulemaking and approval of SIPs. For example, a number of states relied on emission reductions to be achieved by CAIR as a basis for coming into compliance with applicable NAAQS.

---

85. North Carolina v. EPA, 531 F.3d 896 (D.C. Cir. 2008) (per curiam), *on reh'g in part*, 550 F.3d 1176 (D.C. Cir. 2008).
86. North Carolina v. EPA, 550 F.3d 1176, 1178 (D.C. Cir. 2008).

As discussed in the next section, EPA is moving forward to implement a replacement rule to CAIR, called the Cross-State Air Pollution Rule.

4.8.6   Cross-State Air Pollution Rule

On July 6, 2011, EPA issued the final Cross-State Air Pollution Rule (CSAPR), which will take effect in January 2012.[87] CSAPR is intended to further limit the interstate transport of NO_x, and SO_2 emissions to downwind nonattainment and maintenance areas.[88] The final rule applies only to power plants (electric generating units) serving generators of more than 25 megawatts, and does not address some of the industrial units that were covered under the NO_x SIP call and CAIR. CSAPR will require 27 states in the eastern United States and the District of Columbia to implement three different programs to reduce NO_x and SO_2 emissions, including an annual NO_x program, an annual SO_2 program, and an ozone season NO_x program.[89] A total of 23 states will be subject to both the annual NO_x and SO_2 programs to help attain the 2006 24-hour $PM_{2.5}$ NAAQS and the 1997 annual $PM_{2.5}$ NAAQS, and 20 states will be required to achieve NO_x emission reductions during the ozone season to help meet the 1997 eight-hour O_3 NAAQS.[90] In the CSAPR, EPA establishes emission budgets for each of the states and allows interstate emission trading among sources within the same program (e.g., NO_x ozone season program) subject to the emissions cap within each state plus a variability limit. To ensure that the rule is timely implemented to reduce pollution affecting downwind states, the CSAPR annual NO_x and SO_2 programs take effect in January 2012, with a second phase of more stringent emission reduction requirements starting January 2014. Starting in 2012, the NO_x ozone season program will run from May 1 through September 30. EPA projects that once implemented, CSAPR will reduce NO_x emissions

---

87   See http://www.epa.gov/airtransport/. As this book was going to print, the final Cross-State Air Pollution Rule had not yet been published in the *Federal Register*.

88   Federal Implementation Plans to Reduce Interstate Transport of Fine Particulate Matter and Ozone, 75 Fed. Reg. 45,210 (Aug. 2, 2010).

89   The final CSAPR contains a supplemental proposal to include six states in the NO_x ozone season program (i.e., Iowa, Kansas, Michigan, Missouri, Oklahoma, and Wisconsin). Oklahoma is the only state that is not already included in the CSAPR annual NO_x program. If Oklahoma is included, a total of 28 states will be subject to the CSAPR program.

90   If the supplemental proposal is finalized as proposed, a total of 26 states will be required to comply with the NO_x ozone season program.

by 1.4 million tons (54 percent) and SO_2 by 6.4 million tons (73 percent) compared to 2005 emissions.[91]

Once in place, the CSAPR program may substantially reduce the effectiveness of the acid rain program. In the 23 states subject to the annual CSAPR limitations, the CSAPR NO_x and SO_2 emission reduction requirements will be more stringent than the current acid rain program restrictions. The SO_2 emission reduction levels under CSAPR also should ensure that there is a continued surplus of acid rain program allowances.

---

91.   U.S. EPA Fact Sheet, The Cross-State Air Pollution Rule: Reducing the Interstate Transport of Fine Particle Pollution and Ozone (July 6, 2011), and U.S. EPA, Office of Air and Radiation, Final Cross-State Air Pollution Rule (July 6, 2011).

5 Prevention of Significant Deterioration and New Source Review

As discussed in chapter 3, the Clean Air Act requires all areas of the country to meet or strive to comply with the requirements of the National Ambient Air Quality Standards (NAAQS). One of the key programs designed to achieve compliance with the NAAQS is the preconstruction review process for new and modified major stationary sources. This preconstruction review process is implemented through the New Source Review (NSR) program, which has two component parts: the Prevention of Significant Deterioration (PSD) program for attainment areas, and the nonattainment area NSR program. Practitioners generally refer to New Source Review for nonattainment areas as NSR even though both components (i.e., PSD and NSR) make up the NSR program. This is somewhat confusing; however, for ease of reference, this chapter refers to the combined program as "PSD/NSR" and the two component parts as PSD and nonattainment NSR.

The PSD/NSR program has a number of policy goals in mind, with the key goal of ensuring that state-of-the-art pollution control technologies are evaluated in setting emission limits and standards when permitting a new major source or a major modification to an existing major source. The PSD requirements are designed to ensure that the air quality in attainment areas or areas that are already "clean" will not degrade. Typically new major sources and major modifications to existing major sources located in attainment areas must install best available control technology (BACT) pollution controls on the emission-emitting equipment to ensure that the ambient air will not degrade. The nonattainment NSR program is designed to ensure that any new industrial growth in a nonattainment area will comply with stringent emission limitations, with the goal of improving air quality overall to meet the NAAQS. The nonattainment NSR program often extracts a heavy price—the most protective pollution controls and obtaining emission offsets– when a new major source is to be built or a major modification to an existing major source occurs in a nonattainment area. In nonattainment areas, new and modified major sources must install emission controls meeting the lowest achievable emissions rate (LAER) technology.

The PSD/NSR program has had a long and fairly controversial history. The PSD program grew out of regulations that the Environmental Protection Agency (EPA) promulgated in December 1974 to prevent the deterioration of air quality in attainment areas. In 1977, Congress codified the PSD program in CAA sections 160 to 169. EPA quickly issued final regulations implementing the 1977 statutory requirements and these were promptly challenged by several industry groups in *Alabama Power Co. v. Costle*.[1] The *Alabama Power* decision rejected certain aspects of the PSD regulations and confirmed EPA's interpretation of several other provisions; the decision still remains as one of the fundamental cases interpreting provisions of the Clean Air Act. After the *Alabama Power* ruling, new PSD regulations were promulgated on August 7, 1980, and most of these provisions remain in place today.[2] As discussed in this chapter, EPA adopted significant reforms to five provisions of the PSD program in 2002. Three of these provisions survived judicial challenge (i.e., emission increase calculations, baseline emission calculations, and plantwide applicability limits), and to varying degrees these reforms have been implemented by many, but not all, states.

EPA's pre-1977 position on permitting new growth in nonattainment areas was essentially designed to prohibit the construction or modification of a facility if that activity would interfere with the attainment or maintenance of a NAAQS. In December 1976, EPA adopted its "offset policy," which allowed growth in nonattainment areas so long as offsetting emission reductions were obtained from existing sources in the area. The offsetting emission reductions, coupled with installation of state-of-the-art pollution controls on facilities subject to nonattainment NSR, are intended to allow air quality in the area to continue to improve.

---

1.   636 F.2d 323 (D.C. Cir. 1979).
2.   45 Fed. Reg. 52,676 (Aug. 7, 1980).

The present nonattainment NSR program also largely originated from the Clean Air Act Amendments of 1977, although it was significantly changed by the 1990 amendments. As discussed in chapter 3, in the 1990 amendments, Congress further classified ozone, CO, and PM_{10} nonattainment areas and added several new requirements to the nonattainment NSR preconstruction permitting program.

5.1 Applicability of the PSD/NSR Requirements

The key question for new sources and existing sources undergoing an expansion or other equipment or operational changes is whether the proposed action is subject to PSD/NSR program review. Determining PSD/NSR program applicability often involves a complicated factual and legal analysis, and in general there is a separate analysis for each pollutant that is a "regulated NSR pollutant." In analyzing whether a particular source or project is subject to the PSD/NSR program, a threshold question is which preconstruction program or programs apply. Both the PSD program and the nonattainment NSR program can apply to an individual source if it is located in a nonattainment area for certain criteria pollutants, and a separate PSD/NSR analysis must be undertaken for each pollutant. For example, a source that is major for NO_x emissions could be subject to the NO_2 PSD program and to the nonattainment NSR program if the facility is located in an ozone nonattainment area.

Some states also apply different PSD rules.[3] In general, EPA could be implementing the PSD program directly pursuant to the federal rules set forth at 40 C.F.R. part 52. A few states also implement the federal PSD rules pursuant to a delegation of authority (i.e., a "delegated" state). Most of the states have adopted their

---

3. 40 C.F.R. §§ 51.166, 52.21. The PSD program has two sets of regulatory rules, which are virtually the same. One set—40 C.F.R. § 51.166—applies if adopted by a state into an EPA-approved SIP. The other set—40 C.F.R. § 52.21—applies if EPA delegates the program to a state or administers the program itself. The majority of states operate EPA-approved PSD programs that are incorporated in a SIP. In a minority of states, the PSD program is implemented either (1) by a state, through a delegation of EPA's rules (40 C.F.R. § 52.21) or a combination of SIP-approved and EPA-delegated authority, or (2) by EPA, which issues the PSD permits directly.

own PSD program rules into state implementation plans (SIPs). These "SIP approved" PSD programs either directly incorporate the federal rules or have adopted certain changes that are at least as stringent as the federal rules.[4]

Practitioners should not only check the PSD program status of the particular state, but should also review which PSD rules are being applied in the state. As discussed more fully below, a few states have not adopted the 2002 reforms, and thus adhere to the pre-2002 PSD program rules.

5.1.1   Major Stationary Sources

The PSD program applies to new major stationary sources and major modifications to existing major sources. A *major stationary source* under the PSD program is any source belonging to a list of 28 source categories that emits or has the potential to emit 100 tons per year (tpy) or more of any pollutant subject to regulation under the CAA (except hazardous air pollutants (HAP) regulated under CAA section 112) or any other source type that emits or has the potential to emit such pollutants in amounts equal to or greater than 250 tpy.[5] Potential emissions are generally calculated as the maximum annual emissions that a unit would generate if it ran at full capacity 8,760 hours a year (365 days × 24 hours) or otherwise in compliance with any federally or practically enforceable limit on hours of operation.[6]

The PSD program broadly defines a *stationary source* as "any building, structure, facility, or installation," which phrase is in turn defined to include all pollutant-emitting activities that belong to the same industrial grouping (i.e., Standard Industrial Classification (SIC) code), that are located on one or more contiguous or adjacent properties, and that are under the control of the same person or persons under common control.[7] Thus, two adjacent

---

4. EPA has compiled a useful summary of the status of PSD permit programs in each state, identifying which PSD rules are SIP-approved, delegated, or implemented by EPA. *See* EPA New Source Review, Where You Live, http://www.epa.gov/nsr/where.html.

5. 40 C.F.R. §§ 51.166(b)(1)(i)(a), 52.21(b)(1)(i)(a). The 28 source categories include, for example, kraft pulp mills, fossil-fuel-fired steam electric plants, iron and steel mills, portland cement plants, and petroleum refineries. A complete listing of the 28 source categories is included in appendix E.

6. Sources may voluntarily take limitations on hours of operation or other emission restrictions that may keep a source below the major source thresholds.

7. 40 C.F.R. §§ 51.166(b)(5), (6); 52.21(b)(5), (6).

Nonattainment Area Major Source Thresholds

Nonattainment Areas	Major Source Threshold
O_3	
Marginal and Moderate	100 tpy (VOC/NO_x)
Ozone Transport Region[a] (Serious or less)	100 tpy (VOC/NO_x)[b]
Serious	50 tpy (VOC/NO_x)
Severe	25 tpy (VOC/NO_x)
Extreme	10 tpy (VOC/NO_x)
CO	
Serious	50 tpy (CO)
All other areas	100 tpy (CO)
PM_{10}	
Serious	70 tpy (PM_{10})
All other areas	100 tpy (PM_{10})

a. In the Northeast Ozone Transport Region (i.e., Connecticut, Delaware, District of Columbia, Maine, Maryland, Massachusetts, New Hampshire, New Jersey, New York, Pennsylvania, Rhode Island, northern Virginia, and Vermont), each state is classified at least as a moderate ozone nonattainment area.

b. Even though no OTR states are currently classified as serious or above for the 8-hour O_3 NAAQS, some OTR states still use lower major source thresholds (e.g., a major VOC source in New York is defined as emitting 50 tpy or more).

plants under the same SIC code and with common ownership or a common operator would be considered one stationary source. Not surprisingly, there has been some dispute over when adjacent facilities owned or operated by the same or related companies should be treated as one source. This issue, which is typically heavily fact-dependent, may be determinative of whether there are two separate minor sources or one major source. In addition, to the extent they are quantifiable, fugitive emissions (e.g., particulates from coal piles or road dust) are also included in the potential to emit calculation for the 28 source categories and certain sources, which, as of August 7, 1980, were regulated by a New Source Performance Standard (NSPS) or a HAP standard.[8] Under the nonattainment NSR program the term *major stationary source* generally takes the same definition as under the PSD program; however, the emissions cutoffs for determining a major source are generally 100 tpy or lower. Unlike the PSD program, the nonattainment NSR program only covers the six criteria pollutants—O_3

8.   40 C.F.R. §§ 51.166(b)(1)(iii), 52.21(b)(1)(iii).

(and its precursors, VOCs and NO_x), CO, NO_2, PM (i.e., $PM_{2.5}$ and PM_{10}), SO_2, and Pb. The table on page 57 highlights the applicable major source cutoffs for O_3, CO, and PM_{10} nonattainment areas.

EPA has interpreted the PSD/NSR program as applying to pollutants that become "subject to regulation" under the Act. For the PSD program, a pollutant becomes subject to regulation on the date that a requirement under the CAA or a new EPA regulation intended to control emissions of that pollutant "takes effect" or otherwise becomes applicable.[9] In the context of determining when greenhouse gas emissions become a regulated NSR pollutant, EPA reaffirmed the mechanism by which a pollutant becomes subject to regulation. In applying the interpretation to the tailpipe emission standards for light-duty vehicles, EPA concluded that the new standards would take effect when the 2012 model year begins, which is no earlier than January 2, 2011.[10] While the light-duty-vehicle rule took effect within 60 days after publication in the *Federal Register* and applied to planning for the 2012 model year vehicles, EPA concluded that the operative requirement was when the emission control requirements in the rule "take effect."[11]

The PSD program applies not only to criteria pollutants but also to other pollutants that are now "subject to regulation" under the CAA. In addition to the six greenhouse gas (GHG) emissions that are subject to regulation under EPA's "GHG Tailoring Rule,"[12] EPA regulates numerous other pollutants that are subject to EPA emission standards. In order to qualify as a regulated NSR pollutant, a pollutant must meet at least one of four standards: (1) a criteria pollutant, (2) a pollutant subject to an NSPS, (3) an ozone-depleting substance, or (4) any "pollutant that is otherwise subject to regulation under the Act."[13] The CAA specifies that the PSD program does not apply to HAPs listed under CAA section 112.[14] For the nonattainment NSR program, only criteria pollutants are covered pollutants.

9. 75 Fed. Reg. 17,004, 17,006–07 (Apr. 2, 2010).
10. 75 Fed. Reg. at 17,007.
11. *Id.*
12. 75 Fed. Reg. 31,514 (June 3, 2010). Under the GHG Tailoring Rule, EPA regulates carbon dioxide, nitrous oxide, methane, hydrofluorocarbons, perfluorocarbons, and sulfur hexafluoride.
13. EPA Office of Air Quality Planning & Standards, PSD and Title V Permitting Guidance for Greenhouse Gases 7 (Mar. 2011); 40 C.F.R. §§ 51.166(b)(50); 52.21(b)(50).
14. CAA § 112(b)(6); 42 U.S.C. § 7412(b)(6).

5.1.2   Major Modifications

A modification is subject to PSD/NSR review only if (1) the existing source that is modified is major, and (2) the net emissions increase is significant.[15] A minor source may also trigger PSD/NSR review if the "modification" itself constitutes a major stationary source. Under the statutory definition of *modification*, any increase in pollution resulting from any "physical change in, or change in the method of operation of, a stationary source" would constitute a modification and would trigger PSD/NSR review.[16] However, by regulation, EPA has limited the application of PSD/NSR review to only those "major" modifications that constitute a physical or operational change and that result in a significant net increase in emissions.[17] The EPA regulations do not define what constitutes a "physical change" or a "change in the method of operation," but rather they list certain categories of activities that are *not* a physical or operational change. For example, some uses of alternative fuels (such as municipal solid waste); routine maintenance, repair, and replacement; a change in ownership; and increases in production rates or operational hours (unless prohibited by a "federally enforceable" permit) are not considered physical or operational changes, and are excluded from PSD/NSR review.[18] Thus, these activities cannot result in a major modification even if they significantly increase emissions.

In general, the steps in analyzing whether a physical change or a change in the method of operation will rise to the level of a major modification are as follows: First, will there be a physical change that affects the emissions unit or a change in the method of operation (e.g., new fuel or raw material)? Second, if there is a physical change or change in the method of operation, does an exclusion apply?[19] Third, if an exclusion does not apply, will the

---

15. The terms "net emissions increase" and "significant" are defined at 40 C.F.R. §§ 51.165(a)(1)(vi) and (x) for the NSR program and at 40 C.F.R. §§ 51.166(b)(3) and (23) and 40 C.F.R. §§ 52.21(b)(3) and (23) for the PSD program.

16. CAA §§ 111(a)(4), 169(2)(C), 171(4); 42 U.S.C. §§ 7411(a)(4), 7479(2)(C), 7501(4).

17. 40 C.F.R. §§ 51.165(a)(1)(v), 51.166(b)(2), 52.21(b)(2).

18. 40 C.F.R. §§ 51.165(a)(1)(v)(C), 51.166(b)(2)(iii), 52.21(b)(2)(iii).

19. *See* EPA Office of Air Quality Planning & Standards, PSD and Title V Permitting Guidance for Greenhouse Gases 6 (Nov. 2010). The exclusions include (1) routine maintenance, repair, and replacement; (2) use of certain alternative fuels; (3) increases in hours of operation or production rates that do not violate a permit limit; (4) a change in ownership; and (5) the use of clean coal technology.

physical change or change in the method of operation result in a significant net emission increase? Fourth, if there will be a significant net emission increase, are there contemporaneous emission reductions elsewhere at the facility that will "net" the emissions to a level below the significance level?

Routine Maintenance, Repair, and Replacement. EPA has tended to view the exclusions from a physical or operational change fairly narrowly. For example, EPA determined in 1988 that a "life-cycle extension program" undertaken by the Wisconsin Electric Power Company (WEPCO) that would rehabilitate aged facilities, including restoring lost generating capacity and extending the plant's retirement date, was subject to PSD review. EPA determined that the replacement of major boiler components that normally last for the life of a facility, together with other upgrades and replacements, was not "routine" maintenance, repair, or replacement. In *Wisconsin Electric Power Co. v. Reilly,*[20] the Seventh Circuit Court of Appeals upheld EPA's interpretation of the physical change definition.

Through guidance, EPA further defined what activities qualify as routine maintenance, repair, and replacement. In a guidance letter issued in 2000 regarding the Detroit Edison "Dense Pack" project, EPA set forth a five-factor test for evaluating whether a project involving a physical change is "routine."[21] These factors are (1) the nature of the change, (2) the extent of the change, (3) the purpose of the change, (4) the frequency of the change, and (5) the cost of the change.[22] EPA noted that these categories are interrelated, and none of the factors standing alone was determinative, but instead the permitting authority should evaluate the totality of the factors in arriving at a conclusion.[23]

In October 2003, EPA promulgated the Equipment Replacement Provision (ERP) rule, which was intended to create a bright-line safe harbor for projects that qualify as routine replacement of equipment.[24] Under the rule, EPA categorized equipment replacement projects as those costing 20 percent or less of an emissions

20. 893 F.2d 901, 909 (7th Cir. 1990).
21. Letter from EPA Reg'l Adm'r Francis X. Lyons to Henry Nickel, Counsel for the Detroit Edison Company (May 23, 2000).
22. *Id.* at 10–11.
23. *Id.* at 11.
24. Equipment Replacement Provision of the Routine Maintenance, Repair and Replacement Exclusion, 68 Fed. Reg. 61,248 (Oct. 27, 2003).

unit so long as the parts were identical or the functional equivalent of the replaced part.[25] Several states challenged EPA's ERP rule, and in 2006 the U.S. Court of Appeals for the D.C. Circuit vacated the rule.[26] In the wake of the vacatur of the ERP rule, the regulated community is left with EPA guidance (e.g., Detroit Edison), the WEPCO case, and other, often conflicting, decisions at the federal district court level. For practitioners, the preamble to the ERP rule provides a useful history of EPA guidance and relevant case law interpreting the routine maintenance, repair and replacement exclusion.

Significant Net Emissions Increase. Once the existence of a physical or operational change in a source is determined, the focus shifts to whether the change would result in a "significant" net emissions increase. Under the PSD program, a significant net increase is 40 tpy, on an annual basis, for NO_x, SO_2, and VOCs; 15 tpy for PM10; 10 tpy for PM2.5; 100 tpy for CO; and 0.6 tpy for lead.[27] The same criteria pollutant significance levels generally apply for the purpose of nonattainment NSR reviews; however; serious CO nonattainment areas have a 50-ton significance threshold.[28] Serious and severe ozone nonattainment areas use a significant emissions threshold of 25 tons for NO_x and VOCs.[29] In addition, for extreme ozone nonattainment areas, any increase in emissions due to a physical or operational change would be viewed as "significant."[30]

The calculation of a "net emissions increase" is one of the more complicated and time-intensive exercises in the air permitting process. The regulations define *net emissions increase* as the sum of any increase in "actual" emissions that would result from the change in question, and any other contemporaneous (i.e., within the previous five years) increases and decreases in actual

25. 68 Fed. Reg. at 61,252.
26. New York v. EPA, 443 F.3d 880 (D.C. Cir. 2006).
27. 40 C.F.R. §§ 51.166(b)(23), 52.21(b)(23). NO_2 is the compound regulated as a criteria pollutant; however, significant emissions are based on the sum of all oxides of nitrogen. Certain other noncriteria pollutants have significant emission rates, including 3 tpy for fluorides (except hydrogen fluoride), 7 tpy for sulfuric acid mist, and 10 tpy for hydrogen sulfide and total reduced sulfur. *See* 45 Fed. Reg. 52,709 (Aug. 7, 1980).
28. CAA § 187(c)(1); 42 U.S.C. § 7512a(c)(1).
29. CAA § 182(c)(6); 42 U.S.C. § 7511a(c)(6). Section 182(f) (42 U.S.C. § 7511a(f)) addresses the NO_x requirements for serious, severe, and extreme ozone nonattainment areas.
30. CAA § 182(e)(2); 42 U.S.C. § 7511a(e)(2).

emissions that are otherwise credible.[31] For existing sources, actual emissions are measured as the annual average emissions over a 24-month period. Calculation of the baseline actual emissions is discussed more fully below. The regulations allow the "netting" of contemporaneous increases and decreases of actual emissions to determine whether a significant net increase in emissions has occurred. This procedure potentially allows a source to net out of a PSD/NSR review by subtracting previous or current emission decreases from emissions increase that may occur from the proposed physical or operational change. In other words, the netting calculation may keep the "net" emission increase below the PSD/NSR significance levels.

The permitting authority may presume that source-specific allowable emissions for an emissions unit are equivalent to actual emissions. However, the permitting authority is not obligated to use allowable emissions as equivalent to actual emissions, and EPA has traditionally required use of actual emissions unless there are compelling reasons to use allowable emissions as actual emissions. Examples of source-specific allowable emissions are NSPS limits, source-specific SIP emission limits, and federally enforceable permit conditions.

Prior to 2003, EPA typically compared a source's past actual emissions to its future "potential" emissions after the modification to determine whether a net emissions increase will occur. This "actual to potential" applicability test is generally regarded as a very conservative method of calculating whether a net emissions increase will take place. In effect, a permitting agency will equate a unit's "potential" emissions with operation on a year-round basis (i.e., 24 hours a day for 365 days) unless there are federally or practically enforceable permit terms that limit the unit's potential to emit.

In response to the *Wisconsin Electric Power Co. v. Reilly* decision, EPA issued its "WEPCO rule" in July 1992; this rule allows existing electric utility steam generating units to compare past actual emissions to future actual emissions where a utility has begun normal operations.[32] The "actual to future actual" emissions applicability test for electric utility steam generating units applies to all physical and operational changes other than the addition of a new unit or the replacement of an existing unit.[33] A projection of

---

31. 40 C.F.R. §§ 51.165(a)(1)(vi), 51.166(b)(3), 52.21(b)(3).
32. 52 Fed. Reg. 32,314 (July 21, 1992).
33. 40 C.F.R. §§ 51.165(a)(1)(xii)(E), 51.166(b)(21)(v), 52.21(b)(21)(v).

future actual emissions generally takes into account how often the unit is expected to operate after the change is made. For example, a combustion turbine may have operated 50 percent of the time prior to the change with actual emissions of 100 tons, and it is now expected to operate at a 60 percent capacity factor with projected emissions of 120 tons. In comparison, the potential to emit at full operation (i.e., 100 percent) might equal 200 tons, which would easily surpass a significance threshold of 40 tons for a major modification.

The following examples summarize situations where PSD/NSR review would be triggered under an "actual to potential" applicability test:

1. Facility subject to the 250 tpy PSD major source threshold
    *   Facility presently has the potential to emit 180 tpy of SO_2 (and is also "minor" for all other pollutants).
    *   A physical change to the facility *increases* its potential to emit SO_2 by 80 tpy (to 260 tpy).
    *   Since the facility is a minor source and the increase is not major in itself, the physical change is not subject to PSD review.
    *   The *next* change at the facility, however, will be subject to PSD review if net emissions of SO_2 increase by more than 40 tpy (i.e., the "significance" level).

2. Facility subject to the 100 tpy PSD major source threshold
    *   Facility presently has the potential to emit 40 tpy of VOCs (and, overall, is a "minor" source).
    *   A physical change to the facility increases its potential to emit VOCs by 110 tpy (to 150 tpy).
    *   Although the existing facility was a minor source, the physical change is subject to PSD review since it resulted in an emissions increase greater than the major source threshold of 100 tpy.

In 2002, after over 10 years of rulemaking deliberations, litigation, over 50 stakeholder meetings and public hearings, and consideration of over 130,000 comments, EPA promulgated important changes to the PSD/NSR program, including the adoption of a new "actual to projected actual" emissions test that generally allows industrial sources to use the WEPCO rule methodology. The new

PSD/NSR applicability rule kept the general structures of the PSD/NSR program in place, and two of the key changes involved a new formula for determining when a "significant net emissions increase" is triggered and how to calculate the "baseline" emissions.[34] EPA's final PSD/NSR reform rule included five key components, but only three survived a challenge in the courts.[35] The two important changes that affect the PSD/NSR applicability analysis include

- *Emissions increase calculations:* The new PSD/NSR rule allows all industrial plants to now use the WEPCO formula for calculating a "significant net emissions increase." Industrial facilities will be able to calculate emission increases by comparing past actual emissions to projected future actual emissions after physical change or change in the method of operation.
- *Baseline emissions:* Industrial units can calculate prechange actual emissions based on a "baseline" period of any consecutive 24-month period in the past ten years. The current policy applicable to power plants (i.e., a baseline period of a consecutive 24-month period in the past five years), was also codified.[36]

The December 31, 2002, changes to the PSD/NSR program took effect on March 3, 2003, and were effective immediately in 11 states and the District of Columbia. These states directly implement federal PSD rules through authority delegated to them by EPA.[37] The remaining 39 states implement the PSD program through EPA-approved SIP rules, and these states had three years to adopt conforming revisions to existing state PSD program rules. Not all states have adopted the 2002 PSD/NSR reform rules, and counsel should determine which rules apply in a particular state. A few states still use the pre-2002 actual to potential emissions test.

---

34. 67 Fed. Reg. 80,186 (Dec. 31, 2002). One other important change involved allowing sources to utilize plantwide applicability limits (PALs). Sources that keep their emissions below a plantwide cap would be able to make operational changes and equipment modifications without undergoing a major source NSR permitting process. A PAL is generally effective for 10 years.

35. New York v. EPA, 413 F.3d 3 (O.C. Cir. 2005).

36. 67 Fed. Reg. at 80,190.

37. In 2003, the 11 states were Hawaii, Illinois, Massachusetts, Michigan, Minnesota, Nevada, New Hampshire, New Jersey, New York, South Dakota, and Washington. The District of Columbia PSD program is partially delegated.

Establishing the baseline emissions for a new or existing unit is an important component of the "actual to projected actual" emissions test. A "new unit" is one that has existed for less than two years, and prior to the initial construction of a new unit, it will have a baseline of zero emissions. Once operational, for the first two years the "new unit" will have baseline emissions that equal the unit's potential to emit. After two years of operation, the unit will be considered an existing unit, and as noted earlier, non-electric generating units may select the emissions from the highest consecutive 24-month period in the past 10 years as a baseline.[38] Electric generating units may use the highest consecutive 24-month period in the past five years.[39] In developing "projected actual emissions," the source must use the "maximum annual rate" in tons per year in any one of the five years (12-month period) following the change.[40] A 10-year period is used if the project involves increasing the emissions unit's design capacity or its potential to emit, and full utilization of the unit would result in a significant net emissions increase.[41] All "relevant information" is required to be considered in preparing the "projected actual emissions" rate, including historical operational data, the company's expected business activities, and the company's highest projected business activity.[42]

When a project involves multiple emission units, the 2002 reform rule requires that only one consecutive 24-month period be used to determine the baseline emissions for a particular regulated NSR pollutant; however, a different consecutive 24-month period may be used for each regulated NSR pollutant.[43]

Reporting and record keeping are required under the 2002 reform rule for a modification where three criteria are met: (1) projected actual emissions are used instead of potential to emit, (2) there is a reasonable possibility that the project will result in a significant emissions increase, and (3) the project will not constitute a major modification.[44] Non-electric generating units and electric generating units are required to maintain the following

38. 67 Fed. Reg. 80,186, 80,194; 40 C.F.R. §§ 51.165(a)(1)(xxxv)(B), 51.166(b)(47)(i), 52.21(b)(48)(i).

39. *Id.*; 40 C.F.R. §§ 51.165(a)(1)(xxxv)(A), 51.166(b)(47)(ii), 52.21(b)(48)(ii).

40. 40 C.F.R. §§ 51.165(a)(1)(xxviii)(A), 51.166(b)(40)(i), 52.21(b)(41)(i).

41. *Id.*

42. 40 C.F.R. §§ 51.165(a)(1)(xxviii)(B), 51.166(b)(40)(ii), 52.21(b)(41)(ii).

43. 40 C.F.R. §§ 51.165(a))(1)(xxxv)(A)(4), (B)(4), 51.166(b)(47)(i)(c), (ii)(d), 52.21(b)(48) (i)(c), (ii)(d).

44. 67 Fed. Reg. 80,186, 80,197; §§ 51.165(a)(6), 51.166(r)(6), 52.21(r)(6).

documentation prior to the start of construction: (1) a description of the project, (2) an identification of the emission units whose emissions could potentially increase due to the project, (3) the baseline actual emissions for each unit, and (4) the projected actual emissions.[45] If a netting calculation is used to stay under the significance levels, then a record of the calculation must be maintained as well.[46] Electric generating units are also required to submit this information to the permitting authority prior to beginning construction, and within 60 days after the end of each year after the change has been made.[47] Industrial units are not required to submit this information to the permitting authority unless after the change, there is an exceedance in baseline actual emissions that is greater than the significance level.[48]

In general, under the 2002 PSD/NSR reform rule, sources must maintain records for at least five years after the physical change or change in the method of operation if such change did not trigger a major modification, there is a reasonable possibility that the project could result in a significant net emissions increase, and the source relied on the "actual to projected actual" emissions test.[49] In certain situations, the record-keeping obligation may be 10 years if there is change in the design capacity or potential to emit.[50]

In December 2007, EPA promulgated a final rule that further defined the "reasonable possibility" record-keeping and reporting standard.[51] Under the final rule, if the subtraction of a source's baseline actual emissions from its projected actual emissions after the equipment change or method of operation change exceeds 50 percent of the PSD/NSR significance levels, then the project is deemed to have a reasonable possibility of triggering a significant net emissions increase.[52] The "reasonable possibility" standard was challenged by the State of New Jersey, and in April 2009, EPA issued a statement

45. *Id.*
46. *Id.*
47. 67 Fed. Reg. 80,186, 80,197; §§ 51.165(a)(6)(ii), (iv), 51.166(r)(6)(ii), (iv), 52.21(r)(6)(ii), (iv).
48. 67 Fed. Reg. 80,186, 80,197; §§ 51.165(a)(6)(v), 51.166(r)(6)(v), 52.21(r)(6)(v).
49. 67 Fed. Reg. 80,186, 80,197.
50. 67 Fed. Reg. 80,186, 80,197; §§ 51.165(a)(6)(iii), 51.166(r)(6)(iii), 52.21(r)(6)(iii).
51. 72 Fed. Reg. 72,607 (Dec. 21, 2007).
52. 40 C.F.R. §§ 51.165(a)(6)(vi), 51.166(r)(6)(vi), 52.21(r)(6)(vi).

stating that the rule is under review, but the agency declined to issue a stay of the rule while the reconsideration is pending.[53]

The following examples summarize situations where PSD/NSR review would be triggered under an "actual to projected actual" emissions test:

1. Facility subject to the 250 tpy PSD major source threshold
   - Facility presently has baseline actual emissions of 180 tpy of NO_x and 220 tpy of SO_2.
   - A physical change to the facility *increases* its projected actual emissions of NO_x by 60 tpy (to 240 tpy) and by 40 tpy of SO_2 (to 260 tpy).
   - Since the facility is a minor source for both NO_x and SO_2 and neither increase is major in itself, the physical change is not subject to PSD review.
   - Similar to the example above, the *next* change at the facility that increases the net emissions of either NO_x or SO_2 by more than 40 tpy will be subject to PSD review.

2. Electric generating facility subject to the 100 tpy PSD major source threshold
   - Facility presently is a major source with baseline emissions of 150 tpy of VOCs.
   - A physical change to the facility increases its projected future actual VOC emissions by 25 tpy (to 175 tpy).
   - The physical change is not subject to PSD review since the increase in projected actual emissions is below the 40 tpy significance level; however, the increase is above the "reasonable possibility" record-keeping and reporting standard (i.e., 50 percent of the significance level). Initial documentation of the physical change must be submitted to the permitting agency before construction begins, and annual reports documenting the facility's emissions after the change must be submitted annually to the permitting authority for at least a five-year period.

---

53. Letter from Elizabeth Craig, Acting Assistant Adm'r for the EPA Office of Air & Radiation, to Anne Milgram, Att'y Gen. for the State of New Jersey (Apr. 24, 2009).

5.1.3   Minor Stationary Sources

Minor stationary sources of pollutants are not subject to PSD/NSR review unless they are subsequently modified and the modification itself triggers the major source PSD/NSR thresholds. Nevertheless, most states have minor source preconstruction permitting programs, and typically require some form of new source review, and possibly the installation of control technology requirements. State minor source NSR programs are often incorporated into SIPs, and the applicable state air permitting regulations should be carefully evaluated for potential minor source preconstruction requirements.

Minor source NSR programs usually set out similar requirements to initiate a control technology review and establish emission limits and standards. Companies often agree to emission limits that will keep sources under the major source thresholds. In order to avoid triggering the federal PSD/NSR review, these "synthetic" minor sources need to incorporate federally or practically enforceable limitations into their state air permits. In general, these provisions will be federally enforceable only if the particular state or local jurisdiction has obtained EPA approval of its minor source NSR program into the SIP.

5.2   PSD Permit Requirements

If the PSD program is triggered, a new major source or a modified existing major source must apply for a PSD permit. A new or modified major source may not be constructed without a permit that meets the PSD requirements. PSD permit applications are fairly complicated undertakings and often require a significant amount of upfront preparation, including collection of air monitoring data and an analysis of whether the project will contribute to a violation of the applicable NAAQS or PSD increment. PSD increments have been established for SO_2, PM_{10}, $PM_{2.5}$, and NO_x at a fraction of the NAAQS level. The statute creates three levels of increments and the most stringent is for Class I areas (national parks and federal wilderness areas).[54] Typically air dispersion modeling is also necessary to demonstrate that the project does not violate a NAAQS or PSD increment.

---

54. *See* discussion of Class I areas in chapter 8.

A project undergoing a PSD review must also employ best available control technology (BACT) on the emission-emitting equipment to reduce emissions of the BACT-triggering pollutant or pollutants.[55] BACT is generally defined as the most effective control technology available for a pollutant emitted by a particular type of source, taking into account energy and economic considerations and other environmental impacts. Technology that is BACT for one type of source, such as a utility boiler, would not necessarily be BACT at another type of source, such as a recovery furnace at a pulp and paper mill. BACT can take many forms: it could be an expensive add-on pollution control device, such as an SO_2 flue gas desulfurization system or "scrubber," or a NO_x selective catalytic reduction system, or a change in the method of operation, such as implementing good combustion practices or using an inherently less polluting raw material or fuel.

The PSD permit application generally must provide a BACT demonstration following EPA's top-down BACT approach, which ranks potentially available technology based on its ability to reduce emissions.[56] EPA takes the position that an applicant is required to use the most effective control technology available or to make a showing why such technology is not "available" for a particular project (including energy, economic, or environmental reasons).

If the "top" technology is not available, then the review continues by evaluating the next most effective technology until an appropriate technology is selected. BACT determinations are reviewed on a case-by-case basis by the applicable permitting agency. A helpful resource for selecting BACT is EPA's RACT/BACT/LAER clearinghouse database, which contains a listing of previous BACT determinations.[57] Moreover, EPA has issued several important guidance documents reviewing PSD/NSR applicability and permitting issues; perhaps the most useful is EPA's draft New Source Review Workshop Manual, released in 1990.[58] EPA Region 7 has put together a searchable database of over 600 EPA-issued PSD/NSR policy and guidance documents that can be accessed at its website.[59]

55. CAA § 165(a)(4); 42 U.S.C. § 7475(a)(5).

56. See EPA Office of Air Quality Planning & Standards, New Source Review Workshop Manual, at B.1–B.55 (Oct. 1990 (draft)).

57. The database can be accessed at http://cfpub1.epa.gov/RBLC.

58. EPA Office of Air Quality Planning & Standards, New Source Review Workshop Manual (Oct. 1990 (draft)).

59. EPA Region 7 Air Program, New Source Review Policy and Guidance Database, http://www.epa.gov/region07/air/nsr/nsr.htm.

Under the PSD program, EPA's "Major for One, Major for All" policy provides that once a source is major for any regulated NSR pollutant, a BACT review is required for each pollutant that is or will be emitted above the respective significant emissions rates.[60] For example, if a new combustion turbine is a 110-ton CO major source, and it has NO_x emissions of 50 tons and $PM_{2.5}$ emissions of 12 tons, the facility would undergo a BACT review not only for CO but also for NO_x and $PM_{2.5}$ because the significance levels were exceeded (i.e., 40 tpy for NO_x and 10 tpy for $PM_{2.5}$). In other words, even if a source is classified as "major" for only one pollutant, it may be subject to PSD review for several more pollutants that are emitted in amounts above the respective significance levels.

An additional source of PSD/NSR guidance is the database of EPA Environmental Appeals Board (EAB) decisions. The EAB has issued over 55 published decisions in PSD permit appeal cases, and the Board has addressed a number of precedent-setting issues. The EAB PSD permit appeal decisions may be accessed at its website.[61]

5.3   NSR Nonattainment Area Permit Requirements

Major sources in nonattainment areas are subject to rigorous permitting requirements. All of the states are required to adopt a major source nonattainment NSR program through the SIP process either directly incorporating the federal program (40 C.F.R. § 51.165) or adopting substantially similar requirements.

New or modified sources in nonattainment areas are required to install technology control systems referred to as the lowest achievable emissions rate (LAER) technology. Similar to a BACT determination, LAER is determined on a case-by-case basis. At a minimum, LAER must be equivalent to the rate achievable with BACT, and in some instances, it may be more stringent. LAER is generally defined as the most stringent emission limitation contained in a SIP rule of any state for the applicable category of

---

60. 75 Fed. Reg. 31,514, 31,520 (June 3, 2010).
61. EPA Environmental Appeals Board, Published Decisions: PSD Permit Appeals (CAA), http://yosemite.epa.gov/oa/EAB_Web_Docket.nsf/PSD+Permit+Appeals+(CAA)?OpenView.

sources or the most stringent emission limitation achieved in practice by a source in the same category as the applicant.[62] Although a LAER analysis involves many similarities to the BACT process, one of the most significant differences is that a LAER analysis generally does not consider economic, energy, or environmental factors.

Emission offset requirements are also imposed for new construction or modification of existing facilities in nonattainment areas. Offset requirements may be imposed at greater than a 1-for-1 ratio depending on the severity of the nonattainment classification. For example, new major sources in serious ozone nonattainment areas must obtain emission offsets of 1.2 tons of VOCs from a nearby source for every ton of VOCs the new source will emit (i.e., an offset ratio of 1.2 to 1). Offsets generally must be obtained before a permitting agency will issue an NSR permit authorizing the construction of a new major source or a major modification to an existing major source in a nonattainment area. Offsets may be bought and sold and can be "banked" for future use. Offsets can be created only from emissions reductions that are real (or creditable), quantifiable, enforceable, permanent, and surplus beyond existing requirements.[63] Typically, offsets are created when nearby sources shut down, add pollution controls, or take enforceable emission limitations. Companies may generate their own offsets or purchase them from a nearby source. Several emissions brokerage firms have sprung up in the wake of the 1990 amendments and sales of emission offsets have become commonplace. The availability of emission offsets largely depends on the particular air quality control region. In certain nonattainment areas, there may be a shortage of certain types of offsets, and the result is a potential limitation on the development of new projects and modifications to existing major sources in the region.

5.4 Consequence for Failing to Obtain a PSD/NSR Permit

The complexity of the NSR program makes it a particularly challenging exercise to determine when a PSD/NSR permit is required,

---

62. 40 C.F.R. § 51.165(a)(2)(xiii).
63. New Source Review Workshop Manual at G.6. EPA has set forth minimum criteria for emission offsets in its Emission Offset Interpretive Ruling, codified as appendix S to 40 C.F.R. pt. 51.

and, not surprisingly, this has been an active area of EPA enforcement. EPA has taken a fairly aggressive approach in requiring the retroactive application of PSD/NSR review to major sources that should have obtained a PSD/NSR permit for major modifications. In November 1998, the EPA Office of Enforcement and Compliance Assurance released a guidance document intended to clarify how the EPA regions should handle cases where a major emissions source failed to obtain a PSD/NSR permit prior to a major modification.[64]

In the 1998 guidance, EPA states that a source violating PSD/NSR permitting requirements should comply fully with all applicable PSD/NSR provisions, including a PSD/NSR permitting review, implementing control technology requirements, generating an air quality impact analysis, and obtaining offsets. The guidance states that as part of an EPA settlement, a consent decree should require a minimum level of emissions control that the agency believes will ensure achievement of BACT/LAER-equivalent emission reductions. The 1998 guidance also reaffirms EPA's long-standing policy that the BACT or LAER determination be made at the time a source goes through PSD/NSR permit review. Thus, if a source violates PSD/NSR in 1985 (e.g., by undertaking a major modification of a major source without a PSD/NSR permit) and finally applies for a permit in 2010, whatever technology is BACT or LAER in 2010 should be required in the PSD/NSR permit.

Starting in the 1990s, EPA significantly stepped up its enforcement of alleged PSD/NSR violations targeting several industry groups. In the early 1990s, EPA focused on the wood products industry and entered into multimillion-dollar settlements with several companies. The settlements typically included a significant penalty component as well as a commitment to install state-of-the-art pollution control technology. In 1999 and 2000, EPA filed civil complaints targeting coal-fired plants owned by several major electric utilities. Several EPA regional offices and some state agencies have also issued notices of violation or initiated investigations of other coal-fired utilities, focusing on the question of whether these plants were modified in the 1970s and 1980s without going through the required permitting reviews. EPA also continued to target PSD/NSR enforcement actions against coal-fired power plants

---

64. *See* Memorandum from Eric Schaeffer, Dir. of EPA Office of Regulatory Enforcement, to EPA Regions, Guidance on the Appropriate Injunctive Relief for Violations of Major New Source Review Requirements (Nov. 17, 1998).

during the 2000s. As of 2011, EPA settled 23 major NSR cases with electric utility owners covering over 70 coal-fired plants. In the settlements, the utility owners agreed to install state-of-the-art control technology on many of the older coal-fired units to control NO_x and SO_2, and/or to repower some units with natural gas. The settling utilities have also agreed to pay multimillion-dollar penalties, implement supplemental environmental projects (e.g., conservation activities), and surrender a substantial number of SO_2 allowances.[65] Petroleum refineries, pulp and paper mills, chemical plants, and steel mini-mills have also recently been subject to similar PSD/NSR investigations by some EPA regional offices.

Several of the agency's PSD/NSR enforcement cases remain pending in the federal courts. One notable PSD/NSR case reached the U.S. Supreme Court, *Environmental Defense v. Duke Energy Corp.*, in which the issue of how a "modification" is determined under the PSD/NSR program was before the Court.[66] EPA's interpretation of the term "modification" has been a source of long-standing disagreement between the agency, the regulated community, and environmental groups, and the issue reached a crescendo in 2005 when two federal appeals courts reached opposite conclusions on how a "modification" is calculated under the PSD/NSR program. The U.S. Court of Appeals for the Fourth Circuit held in *United States v. Duke Energy Corp.* that "modification" had the same meaning for purposes of both the PSD/NSR and NSPS programs (i.e., a modification occurs when there is an increase in the maximum achievable hourly emission rate).[67] However, the D.C. Circuit ruled in *New York v. EPA* that the agency is free to adopt a different interpretation of what constitutes a "modification" for NSR permits.[68] The U.S. Supreme Court upheld EPA's interpretation, and concluded that the agency

---

65. For example, in 2003 the U.S. government settled three major NSR enforcement actions against three major electric utilities. In one of the largest Clean Air Act enforcement settlements with a utility to date, one company agreed to spend as much as $1.2 billion by 2013 to install new pollution controls and upgrade existing pollution controls at eight coal-fired power plants. The company also agreed to pay a $5.3 million civil penalty and to spend at least $13.9 million on environmental mitigation projects. Background on EPA's Coal-Fired Power Plant Enforcement Initiative is available at http://www.epa.gov/compliance/resources/cases/civil/caa/coal/index.html.

66. Envtl. Def. v. Duke Energy Corp., 549 U.S. 561 (2007).

67. United States v. Duke Energy Corp., 411 F.3d 539 (4th Cir. 2005), *rev'd*, Envtl. Def. v. Duke Energy Corp., 549 U.S. 561 (2007).

68. New York v. EPA, 413 F.3d 3 (D.C. Cir. 2005).

was authorized to apply different emissions tests under the two separate programs.

One issue that has emerged from EPA's PSD/NSR enforcement initiatives is that the multitude of EPA guidance letters and memoranda on how particular provisions should be interpreted has not always resulted in clarity on how the extremely complex PSD/NSR rules should be applied. Since the mid-1990s there has been an ongoing effort within EPA to address the regulated community's concerns.[69] During the Bush administration (i.e., 2001 to 2008), EPA adopted the 2002 PSD/NSR reform rule that made some important revisions to the PSD/NSR program. Other proposals by the Bush administration to revise the PSD/NSR program were struck down in the courts or were never finalized.[70]

5.5   GHG Tailoring Rule

As of January 2, 2011, GHG emissions from the largest stationary sources are subject to the PSD program.[71] This step marks a significant expansion of the PSD program, and the agency took a somewhat unique approach that is not without controversy in "tailoring" the major source thresholds for GHGs to stationary sources. In June 2010, EPA issued the GHG Tailoring Rule, which sets major source and significance level thresholds for GHGs to define when the PSD program applies to a new source or a major modification to an existing major source.[72] EPA concluded that the major source emissions thresholds under the CAA (i.e., 100 tons and 250 tons) were based on traditional criteria pollutants, and were not designed to apply to

---

69. 61 Fed. Reg. 38,250 (July 23, 1996). In 1998, EPA also published a notice of availability requesting further comments on certain NSR reform issues. *See* 63 Fed. Reg. 39,857 (July 24, 1998).

70. The Equipment Replacement Provision Rule was vacated by the U.S. Court of Appeals for the D.C. Circuit in 2006. *See* New York v. EPA, 443 F.3d 880 (D.C. Cir. 2006). EPA published a proposed NSR rulemaking on September 14, 2006, designed to clarify and codify the agency's guidance on aggregating emissions from upstream and downstream "debottlenecking" projects. In other words, a change to one piece of equipment may affect the emissions from other units at the source. The proposed rule was controversial, and was withdrawn in January 2009. 74 Fed. Reg. 2460 (Jan. 15, 2009).

71. The six GHGs regulated under the GHG Tailoring Rule are carbon dioxide (CO_2), nitrous oxide (N_2O), methane (CH_4), hydrofluorocarbons (HFCs), perfluorocarbons (PFCs), and sulfur hexafluoride (SF_6).

72. 75 Fed. Reg. 31,514 (June 3, 2011).

GHGs because GHGs are emitted in much higher volumes.[73] For example, a 900 MW natural-gas-fired power plant may emit approximately 400 tons of NO_x annually, but its GHG emissions could be upwards of 2.5 to 3 million tpy. Coal contains more carbon than natural gas, and coal-fired power plants may emit up to twice the level of GHG emissions as a comparable-sized natural-gas-fired power plant.

The GHG Tailoring Rule was phased in starting January 2, 2011, for major sources that have not yet received a PSD permit and that are required to go through PSD permitting "anyway" due to their non-GHG pollutants. The threshold for triggering PSD review of GHGs in the first phase is an increase in GHGs by 75,000 tpy of CO_2 equivalent (CO_2e).[74] The second phase of the rule started on July 1, 2011, and applies to major sources of GHG emissions regardless of whether the facility is subject to the PSD program for other pollutants. The major source threshold is triggered if (1) the source has a potential to emit 100,000 tpy of CO_2e and (2) the source emits GHGs or some other regulated NSR pollutant above the mass-based 100/250 tpy potential to emit threshold.[75] In addition, the significance level for a major modification to an existing major source will be met if the physical change or change in the method of operation results in a significant net GHG emission increase of 75,000 tpy or more and the increase on a mass basis exceeds zero.[76]

As part of the implementation of the GHG Tailoring Rule, EPA has issued PSD and Title V Permitting Guidance for Greenhouse Gases, which provides some analysis on how the agency anticipates that the states and EPA regional offices will apply a PSD review for GHGs to major sources.[77] The guidance document emphasizes that existing EPA guidance on implementation of a PSD permitting review applies equally to GHGs, and states and EPA regional offices should apply existing PSD policy and practices.[78] EPA has also developed a series of technical "white papers" summarizing considerations to be evaluated during the

---

73. 75 Fed. Reg. at 31,516–17.
74. 75 Fed. Reg. at 31,523.
75. *Id.* (The mass-based calculation for GHGs is based on the sum of the six GHG pollutants regulated by the GHG Tailoring Rule.)
76. *Id.*
77. EPA Office of Air Quality Planning & Standards, PSD and Title V Permitting Guidance for Greenhouse Gases (Nov. 2010).
78. *Id.* at 4.

BACT review process.[79] The industrial sectors covered include electric generating units, large industrial/commercial/institutional boilers, pulp and paper mills, cement manufacturing, the iron and steel industry, refineries, and nitric acid plants.[80]

If PSD program review is triggered due solely to GHGs exceeding the major source or major modification thresholds, EPA's GHG Tailoring Rule provides that a PSD BACT analysis would need to be conducted for other pollutants that exceed a significance level.[81] The following are examples of major sources that would trigger PSD program review after July 1, 2011, due to GHG emissions:

1. New facility subject to the 250 tpy (mass-based) and 100,000 CO_2e PSD major source threshold
   - New facility has the potential to emit 1 million tpy (CO_2e) of GHGs, 25 tons of VOCs, 50 tons of NO_x, and 150 tons of CO.
   - Source is major for GHGs, and PSD review is triggered for GHGs as well as NO_x and CO because the significance levels for NO_x and CO are exceeded.
2. Existing major source subject to the 100 tpy (mass-based) and 100,000 CO_2e PSD major source threshold
   - A physical change to the facility increases its projected actual GHG emissions by 90,000 tpy (CO_2e), its projected actual NO_x emissions by 45 tpy, and its projected actual CO emissions by 75 tpy.
   - As an existing major source, a significant net increase in GHGs over 75,000 tpy (CO_2e) triggers a major modification. PSD review is also triggered for NO_x because the significance level for NO_x is exceeded. The CO emissions increase is less than the CO significance level of 100 tpy.

As this book goes to print, EPA is working with the states to ensure that adequate PSD permitting programs are in place for GHG emissions. Aside from states where EPA is the permitting authority for PSD permits, the agency has taken action to imple-

79. *See* EPA New Source Review, Clean Air Act Permitting for Greenhouse Gases, http://www.epa.gov/nsr/ghgpermitting.html.

80. *Id.*

81. 75 Fed. Reg. 31,514, 31,520.

ment a federal implementation plan for eight states that were not able to submit an approvable PSD program for GHG emissions by the January 2, 2011, deadline.[82] In separate rulemakings, EPA has approved a number of the state SIPs implementing the GHG Tailoring Rule provisions.

EPA has also committed to take another look at whether smaller sources of GHG emissions should be subject to PSD permitting. EPA expects to conclude a third phase of the GHG Tailoring Rule by July 1, 2012, and a fourth phase by April 30, 2016.[83] For the third phase, EPA does not expect to regulate sources below 50,000 tpy of CO_2e.[84] As this book was going to print, EPA's GHG Tailoring Rule was being challenged in federal court, and further revisions to the program may result from the litigation.

---

82. 75 Fed. Reg. 82,246 (Dec. 30, 2010), 75 Fed. Reg. 82,430 (Dec. 30, 2010). The states are Arizona, Arkansas, Florida, Idaho, Kansas, Oregon, Texas, and Wyoming.
83. 75 Fed. Reg. 31,514, 31,522.
84. *Id.*

6 New Source Performance Standards

Section 111 of the Clean Air Act requires new, modified, or reconstructed stationary sources to meet New Source Performance Standards (NSPS) for particular industry categories. This section, enacted as part of the Clean Air Act Amendments of 1970, was intended to implement nationwide technology-based standards that would establish a minimum floor of emission limitations or work practice standards applicable to certain categories of industry sources. Section 111 was crafted to apply these standards on new, modified, and reconstructed equipment, regardless of whether the source of emissions was in a National Ambient Air Quality Standards (NAAQS) attainment area or a nonattainment area. In enacting CAA section 111, Congress determined that it would be more cost-effective to impose control technology requirements on new, modified, or reconstructed units than to impose requirements on existing sources. While the primary focus of CAA section 111 is to apply uniform minimum technology and work practice standards to new, modified, or reconstructed sources, CAA section 111(d) also provides authority for the Environmental Protection Agency to regulate existing sources. CAA section 111(d) authorizes EPA to enact standards for pollutants that are not covered by a NAAQS or listed as a hazardous air pollutant (HAP).[1] To date, EPA has exercised its CAA section 111(d) authority sparingly, and so far has only adopted *emission guidelines* for four source categories: municipal waste combustors, municipal solid waste landfills, sulfuric acid production units, and hospital and medical waste incinerators.[2] Once EPA adopts a fed-

---

1. CAA § 111(d)(1)(A); 42 U.S.C. § 7411(d)(1)(A).
2. 40 C.F.R. §§ 60.30b (subpt. Cb), 60.30c (subpt. Cc), 60.30d (subpt. Cd), 60.30e (subpt. Ce).

eral emissions guideline for existing sources pursuant to CAA section 111(d), states have nine months to adopt and submit a plan to EPA for approval.[3]

NSPS under CAA section 111 are intended to reflect "the degree of emission limitation achievable through the application of the best system of emission reduction" that has been "adequately demonstrated" while considering the "costs of achieving such reductions and any nonair quality health and environmental impact and energy requirements."[4] This technology standard is referred to as *best demonstrated technology*, as discussed more fully in section 6.3.

Pursuant to CAA section 111, the EPA administrator is required to develop and update a list of industrial source categories. A source category is listed if the administrator concludes that such a source "causes, or contributes significantly to, air pollution which may reasonably be anticipated to endanger public health or welfare."[5] As of 2011, EPA has promulgated NSPS for over 80 industrial source categories, including most of the major industrial processes (e.g., electric utility steam generating units, kraft pulp mills, and petroleum refineries).[6]

The NSPS were first issued in the early 1970s and the program has evolved considerably since then. In the late 1980s and most of the early 1990s, the technology requirements imposed under the Prevention of Significant Deterioration/New Source Review (PSD/NSR) program eclipsed the NSPS program. In general, emission limitations imposed on new and modified sources under the PSD/NSR program were more stringent than the NSPS emission limits. Moreover, although violations of the NSPS are separate and distinct violations, EPA generally directed its enforcement resources toward PSD/NSR violations, where the anticipated emission reductions were often greater. Now, EPA is once again in the process of adopting additional NSPS in response to statutory requirements imposed by the 1990 amendments to regulate certain source categories that were previously listed, but not regulated under CAA section 111.[7] Since the early 2000s, EPA has adopted over 10 new NSPS, and the

---

3. 40 C.F.R. § 60.23(a).
4. CAA § 111(a)(1); 42 U.S.C. § 7411(a)(1).
5. CAA § 111(b)(1)(A); 42 U.S.C. § 7411(b)(1)(A).
6. See appendix D for current NSPS source categories.
7. CAA § 111(f)(1); 42 U.S.C. § 7411(f)(1).

agency is developing new NSPS for greenhouse gas emissions for two industrial source categories: electric utility steam generating units and petroleum refineries. At the end of 2010, EPA announced that it agreed to propose new NSPS greenhouse gas standards for the two source categories by July 2011, and finalize the rule by May 2012.[8]

The Clean Air Act imposes a duty on the agency to review the individual NSPS at least every eight years, and if necessary, make revisions. In practice, EPA frequently misses this deadline, which potentially leaves the agency open to a citizen suit enforcement action to ensure compliance with this requirement. Congress, of course, can also direct a revision of NSPS, which it did in the 1990 amendments by requiring that the NO_x emission standards for fossil-fuel-fired steam generating units (including both utility and non-utility units) (40 C.F.R. §§ 60.40a and 60.40b) be revised.[9]

The effective date for a specific NSPS is generally the date the NSPS is originally proposed, instead of the date that the final rule is promulgated. After the NSPS effective date for an industrial category, it is unlawful to operate any new, modified, or reconstructed source in violation of that standard.

Each state is required to implement and enforce new source performance standards, and typically each state has been delegated authority from EPA to run the NSPS program. A few states have received partially delegated authority (e.g., for specific source categories), and EPA implements the rest of the NSPS program. States can also adopt their own new source performance standards, but their standards must be at least as stringent as the federal standards.[10] The federal NSPS may be delegated or a separate state NSPS approved as part of the state implementation plan; nevertheless, these standards are enforceable by both EPA and the applicable state.

---

8. EPA, Settlement Agreements to Address Greenhouse Gas Emissions from Electric Generating Units and Refineries—Fact Sheet (Dec. 23, 2010). In June 2011, EPA announced that it was delaying the proposed GHG NSPS for power plants to September 2011.
9. CAA § 407(c); 42 U.S.C. § 7651f(c).
10. 40 C.F.R. § 60.10(a).

6.1   Applicability

Like the PSD/NSR program, the NSPS program applies the same broad definition of a *stationary source*: "any building, structure, facility, or installation" that emits or may emit any air pollutant.[11] The term *new source* means "any stationary source, the construction or modification of which is commenced after the publication of regulations (or, if earlier, proposed regulations) prescribing a standard of performance."[12] Thus, the definition of a new source includes a modified existing source, as well as a reconstructed source, because EPA has interpreted *construction* to include reconstruction activities.[13] The term *construction* is defined to mean "fabrication, erection, or installation of an affected facility."[14] One of the key considerations, for purposes of triggering an applicable NSPS, is when construction actually commences. A source that commences construction prior to the proposal of an NSPS will not be considered a new source. The test for commencing construction is (1) whether a continuous program of construction or modification has been undertaken or (2) whether a contract has been entered to undertake a continuous program of construction or modification.[15]

The EPA regulations implementing the NSPS program apply to the "affected facility" as defined by the various NSPS.[16] This term generally focuses on specific pieces of equipment; for example, each boiler at a power plant would generally be a separate "affected facility." Each NSPS has a different definition of what constitutes an "affected facility." Generally, an existing unit will not become subject to an NSPS standard unless it is modified, reconstructed, or constructed after the trigger date in the relevant NSPS rule. However, as noted at the beginning of this chapter, EPA has established NSPS emission guidelines for existing sources in four source categories pursuant to CAA section 111(d).

---

11. CAA § 111(a)(3); 42 U.S.C. § 7411(a)(3).
12. CAA § 111(a)(2); 42 U.S.C. § 7411(a)(2).
13. 40 C.F.R. § 60.5(a).
14. 40 C.F.R. § 60.2.
15. *Id.*
16. A database of NSPS and National Emissions Standards for Hazardous Air Pollutants (NESHAP) applicability determinations is available at EPA Compliance Monitoring, Applicability Determination Index, http://www.epa.gov/oecaerth/ monitoring/programs/caa/adi.html. The NSPS/NESHAP applicability determination index includes guidance letters and other memoranda issued by EPA headquarters and the EPA regional offices.

6.1.1   Modifications

Similar to the PSD/NSR program, an NSPS *modification* is defined as "any physical change in, or change in the method of operation of, a stationary source which increases the amount of any air pollutant emitted by such source or which results in the emission of any air pollutant not previously emitted."[17] As with the PSD/NSR program, the regulations contain exclusions for routine maintenance, repair, and replacement; for increases in the hours of operation or in the production rate; and for certain types of fuel switches.[18] EPA generally applies the same test as the PSD/NSR program to determine whether a physical change qualifies as an exempt routine maintenance, repair or replacement.

An NSPS modification must involve a physical or operational change to an existing piece of equipment, and also must increase emissions to the atmosphere of any pollutant for which a standard applies.[19] However, the emissions increase step of the NSPS analysis differs significantly from the PSD/NSR rules. Unlike the PSD/NSR program, which considers whether a significant net increase in emissions (based on tons per year) will occur because of a physical or operational change, the NSPS program provides that any increase in emissions to the atmosphere due to the physical or operational change will subject the unit to NSPS, as long as no exclusion applies.[20] Under the NSPS program, emission increases are calculated by comparing the hourly potential "emission rate," at a maximum physical capacity, before and after the physical or operational change.[21] An *hourly emissions rate* is the product of the amount of pollution emitted by a source, after control, per unit of fuel combusted (e.g., lbs. of SO_2 per ton of coal burned) multiplied by the production rate (e.g., tons of coal burned per hour). Emission factors, continuous emission monitor data, material balances, and stack tests may be used to measure or predict the

---

17. 42 U.S.C. § 7411(a)(4).
18. 40 C.F.R. § 60.14(e).
19. 40 C.F.R. §§ 60.2, 60.14.
20. 40 C.F.R. § 60.14(a).
21. 40 C.F.R. § 60.14(b)(2). Unlike the PSD/NSR program, the NSPS emission test does not address annual increases in emissions due to a physical change or change in the method of operation. Under the new 2002 reform rules, the PSD/NSR program generally compares past actual emissions to future projected actual emissions to determine whether there will be a significant net increase in emissions due to the physical or operational change (i.e., a major modification). For states that have not adopted the 2002 PSD/NSR reform rule, the test is a comparison of past actual emissions to potential emissions. *See* 40 C.F.R. §§ 51.165(a)(1)(v)(C), 51.166(b)(2)(iii), 52.21(b)(2)(iii).

emission rate. For purposes of calculating an emissions increase, operational parameters such as fuel quality must be held constant. In addition, any offsetting reductions in the emission rate caused by the addition of pollution controls may reduce the emission rate. In general, an increase in the hourly emissions rate qualifies as a modification, and as noted earlier, the next step in the analysis is to evaluate whether an exemption applies.

As discussed in section 5.4, the U.S. Supreme Court reviewed whether the term "modification" should have the same meaning under both the PSD/NSR program and the NSPS program.[22] In *Environmental Defense v. Duke Energy Corp.*, the Court concluded that EPA could apply different emissions tests under the two programs to determine if a modification will occur due to a physical or operational change.[23]

6.1.2   Reconstruction

The NSPS rules set forth a specific "reconstruction" test, and reconstructed units are basically treated as new units. Under the reconstruction rules, any change that costs at least 50 percent of the total cost of a comparable new facility may subject the facility to NSPS requirements, even if there is no increase in emissions.[24] Once the initial 50 percent replacement cost threshold is reached, EPA will then also consider the following factors in determining whether reconstruction is triggered: (1) the estimated life of the repaired facility vis-à-vis a comparable new facility, (2) the extent the replaced components contribute to the emissions from the facility, and (3) the economic and technological feasibility of meeting the applicable standard.[25]

6.2   Procedures to Establish NSPS

The NSPS requirements applicable to a particular source category are generally composed of two parts: the general NSPS procedural provisions in 40 C.F.R. part 60 *et seq.* and the substantive standards contained in the relevant subpart. The general provisions, for example, include the submission of notifications of the construction date, start-

---

22.   Envtl. Def. v. Duke Energy Corp., 549 U.S. 561 (2007).
23.   549 U.S. at 574–77.
24.   40 C.F.R. § 60.15.
25.   40 C.F.R. § 60.15(f).

up date, and any physical or operational change that may increase the emissions rate.[26] In addition, the general provisions require filing excess emission and monitoring system performance reports, as well as conducting certain performance tests.[27] The substantive NSPS provisions are generally expressed as numerical emission limitations as opposed to a specific type of pollution control technology. However, when the NSPS emission standards are set, they are typically based on the emission reduction levels achievable by a certain type of technology, the "best demonstrated technology" (BDT). Although in theory a source has the latitude to meet the emission limit any way it sees fit, it may, as a practical matter, be limited to only a few types or only one type of technology to meet the standard. If it is not practical to express the standard as a numerical limit, EPA has authority to establish specific work practices or operational limits to reflect the BDT.

As explained in chapter 10, the Title V operating permit program created by the 1990 amendments now mandates that NSPS provisions be incorporated in operating permits; however, air emission sources subject to NSPS that are otherwise minor sources are currently exempted from obtaining a Title V permit. Incorporation of NSPS provisions, including the general record-keeping and reporting requirements, into an operating permit make these standards more easily enforceable by the applicable permitting agency and citizen groups.

As noted earlier, over 80 source categories for different industries have been developed. Courts have recognized that applicable NSPS have to be nationally uniform and nationally achievable standards for a particular industry category. In *National Lime Ass'n v. EPA*,[28] the U.S. Court of Appeals for the D.C. Circuit held that because EPA did not conduct sampling tests that were representative of a particular industry as a whole (i.e., nationwide), the NSPS that was developed was based on inadequate data.[29]

6.3   Best Demonstrated Technology

As noted above, CAA section 111 requires EPA to establish NSPS for new, modified, and reconstructed sources at a level consistent with

26.   40 C.F.R. § 60.7.
27.   40 C.F.R. §§ 60.7(c), 60.8.
28.   627 F.2d 416 (D.C. Cir. 1980).
29.   627 F.2d at 431–33.

the best demonstrated technology that takes into account various factors, including costs, non-air-quality health and environmental inspects, and energy requirements. In setting an NSPS limit, the courts have given the agency the latitude of considering the economic cost to the industry.[30] Courts have also recognized that although EPA is allowed to consider cost in setting a particular NSPS for an industry group, it is under no duty to do a specific cost-benefit analysis.[31]

EPA is also tasked with evaluating the potential energy impacts of setting the BDT at a particular level. In *Portland Cement v. Ruckelshaus*, the D.C. Circuit concluded that Congress intended that the best demonstrated technology should be one that balances the potential impacts and does not do more damage to a particular environmental media than actual benefit to the air quality.[32] EPA must also determine that the BDT "has been adequately demonstrated."[33] Courts have concluded that in order for a technology to be "adequately demonstrated," EPA may rely on application of the technology in other countries or in successful pilot scale operations.[34] Further, in *National Lime Ass'n*, the D.C. Circuit concluded that in order for a technology-based standard to be "achievable," it must be capable of being met by representative sources for all variations of operating conditions.[35]

6.4   Solid Waste Combustion

Congress added a new CAA section 129 in the 1990 amendments to direct EPA to adopt NSPS and emission guidelines for new and existing solid waste incinerators, including municipal waste combustors and hospital and medical waste incinerators. Congress highlighted this category of industrial sources due to public health concerns related to emissions of certain metals (e.g., cadmium, lead, mercury), organics (i.e., dioxin and furans), and acid gases, such as hydrogen chloride.[36] CAA section 129 requires that the performance standards for solid waste incineration units be based on the maximum achievable control technology (MACT) standards developed for air toxics.[37]

---

30. Portland Cement Ass'n v. Ruckelshaus, 486 F.2d 375, 387 (D.C. Cir. 1973), *cert. denied*, 417 U.S. 921 (1974).
31. 486 F.2d at 387; Nat'l Asphalt Pavement Ass'n v. Train, 539 F.2d 775 (D.C. Cir. 1976).
32. 486 F.2d at 387–88.
33. CAA § 111(a)(1); 42 U.S.C. § 7411(a)(1).
34. 486 F.2d at 391.
35. 627 F.2d at 433–34.
36. 60 Fed. Reg. 65,387, 65,390 (1995).
37. CAA § 129(a)(2); 42 U.S.C. § 7429(a)(2).

7 Control of Hazardous Air Pollutants

Section 112 of the Clean Air Act calls for the regulation of hazardous air pollutants (HAPs). In the Clean Air Act Amendments of 1990, Congress completely overhauled the air toxics program, and initiated a new, phased regulatory approach. In doing so, Congress largely scrapped the previous program of listing and setting emission limits for HAPs based solely on a health risk analysis.

When Congress originally enacted CAA section 112 in 1970, it granted EPA broad authority to set stringent emission standards, including a zero emissions level, for HAPs. As explained later, in two decades, the Environmental Protection Agency managed to list only eight HAPs and enacted regulations covering seven of these substances. Given the virtual paralysis of the pre-1990 HAP program, Congress adopted a two-pronged program for regulating HAPs in the 1990 amendments. The first phase is a technology-based program imposed on HAP source categories and subcategories that require the installation of maximum achievable control technology (MACT) on HAP-emitting equipment. After the technology-setting phase is completed, the revised section 112 directs EPA to establish and implement "residual risk" control standards designed to further reduce HAP emissions that still pose an unacceptable health risk after compliance with the initial MACT standards. These residual risk requirements embody several of the underlying concepts from the original section 112 provisions.

7.1   Original Section 112 Requirements

The pre-1990 HAP requirements defined a *hazardous air pollut-ant* as one to which no ambient air quality standard applies and "which in the judgment of the Administrator causes, or contributes to, air pollution which may reasonably be anticipated to result in an increase in mortality or an increase in serious irreversible or incapacitating reversible illness."[1] In implementing the pre-1990 HAP requirements, EPA was directed to develop a list of HAPs that "may reasonably" be expected to cause a serious health risk. Once a HAP was listed, the agency was required to set emission standards within 180 days of the listing. These standards were termed National Emissions Standards for Hazardous Air Pollutants (NESHAPs). In establishing NESHAPs, EPA had to ensure that the limit provided "an ample margin of safety to protect the public health."[2] Setting NESHAPs at such a level proved to be very dif-ficult in practice because EPA felt hard pressed to justify a "safe" standard for carcinogens and other air toxics that caused acute or chronic health effects above a zero emission standard. EPA's hands were further tied because CAA section 112 did not autho-rize the consideration of economic and technological constraints where a zero emissions standard would almost certainly result in industry closures and disruptions.

In setting the vinyl chloride NESHAP in the mid-1970s, EPA outlined an approach that appeared to interject costs and tech-nological feasibility considerations into crafting NESHAPs.[3] EPA's pragmatic approach came under attack by environmental groups, but in *Natural Resources Defense Council v. EPA,*[4] decided in 1987, the U.S. Court of Appeals for the D.C. Circuit rejected a challenge to EPA's decision not to revise its vinyl chloride HAP emission standard, which was based in part on cost consider-ations. Nevertheless, the court set forth a fairly rigid two-step

---

1. CAA § 112 (a)(2); 42 U.S.C. § 7412(a)(1) (1977).
2. CAA § 112(b)(1)(B); 42 U.S.C. § 7412(b)(1)(B) (1977).
3. 41 Fed. Reg. 46,560 (Oct. 21, 1976). In *Natural Resources Defense Coun-cil v. EPA,* the D.C. Circuit explained that EPA's interpretation of CAA section 112 was based on "setting emission standards that require emission reduction to the lowest level achievable by use of the best available control technology . . . , where complete emission prohibition would result in widespread industry closures . . . [and] the cost of such closure would be grossly disproportionate to the benefits of removing the risk that would remain after imposition of the best available control technology." Nat. Res. Def. Council v. EPA, 824 F.2d 1146 (D.C. Cir. 1987) (en banc) (citing 41 Fed. Reg. at 59,534).
4. 824 F.2d 1146 (D.C. Cir. 1987) (en banc).

process for setting NESHAP limits.[5] Under the court's process, economic and technological costs could not be considered in the first step of determining a "safe" exposure level. Such factors could, however, be reviewed in the second step, which addresses whether an "ample margin of safety" is provided. Once again, EPA was in the difficult position of setting NESHAP limits with restrictions on the consideration of economic and technological costs. As a result, the air toxics program continued to languish. In the pre-1990 NESHAP program, EPA listed only eight substances and promulgated standards governing emissions from seven industrial categories emitting these substances.[6]

7.2   1990 Amendments

In the Clean Air Act Amendments of 1990, Congress completely restructured the air toxics program with the goal of developing and implementing new technology-based standards for all listed HAP source categories and subcategories by November 15, 2000, including all major HAP sources and specified nonmajor "area" HAP sources.[7] As noted at the beginning of this chapter, the 1990 amendments contemplate a two-phase NESHAP program. In the first phase, technology-based MACT standards will be promulgated, followed by the development of residual risk standards in the second phase. These two facets of the current NESHAP program are discussed in this chapter.

The Clean Air Act now lists 187 HAPs and specifically defines a *hazardous air pollutant* as "any air pollutant listed pursuant to subsection (b)" of CAA section 112.[8] The CAA directs EPA periodically to review the HAP list; EPA may add or delete substances provided there is adequate scientific data to support

---

5. 824 F.2d at 1164–66.
6. Asbestos, benzene, beryllium, coke oven emissions, inorganic arsenic, mercury, radionuclides, and vinyl chloride. No standards were set for coke oven emissions.
7. CAA § 112(e); 42 U.S.C. § 7412(e).
8. The 1990 amendments originally included 189 HAPs; however, caprolactam was removed in 1996. 61 Fed. Reg. 30,816 (June 18, 1996). In December 2005, EPA issued a final rule removing methyl ethyl ketone (MEK) from the list of HAPS. 70 Fed. Reg. 75,047 (Dec. 19, 2005). EPA has also removed certain compounds form the listed group of glycol ethers, including surfactant alcohol ethoxylates (65 Fed. Reg. 47,342 (Aug. 2, 2000)) and ethylene glycol monobutyl ether (69 Fed. Reg. 69,320 (Nov. 29, 2004)).

such a determination.[9] In addition, any person may petition the EPA administrator to request that a pollutant either be added to or deleted from the list.[10] The agency is currently considering at least two petitions to remove pollutants from the HAP list.[11] To date, only two substances have been completely removed from the HAP list and none have been added.[12]

7.3   Applicability

Section 112 of the Clean Air Act requires categories and sub-categories of "major sources" of listed HAPs to meet maximum achievable control technology (MACT) emission limitations. The CAA generally defines a *major source* as any stationary source or group of stationary sources located within a contiguous area and under common control that emits or has the potential to emit, considering controls, 10 tons per year of any HAP or 25 tons per year of any combination of HAPs.[13] An *area source* is defined as any nonmajor stationary source of HAPs.[14]

The definition of a *major source* under CAA section 112 is different from that used under the Prevention of Significant Deterioration/New Source Review (PSD/NSR) program, but the mechanism for calculating the 10-ton/25-ton triggers is based on the same broad definition of *potential to emit*. EPA has defined *potential to emit* in the general provisions section of the HAP standards as "the maximum capacity of a stationary source to emit a pollutant under physical and operational design" including air pollution controls and other federally enforceable limits on operations.[15] EPA's requirement for "federally enforceable" limits in the CAA section 112 program was rejected in *National Mining Ass'n*

---

9. CAA §§ 112(b)(2), (3); 42 U.S.C. §§ 7412(b)(2), (3).
10. CAA § 112(b)(3); 42 U.S.C. § 7412(b)(3).
11. 69 Fed. Reg. 42,954 (July 19, 2004) (Notice of Petition to Delist Methyl Isobutyl Ketone); 70 Fed. Reg. 30,407 (May 26, 2005) (Notice of Petition to Delist 4,4, Methylene Diphenyl Diisocyanate).
12. Caprolactam was removed in 1996. *See* 61 Fed. Reg. 30,816 (June 18, 1996). MEK was removed in 2005. *See* 70 Fed. Reg. 75,047 (Dec. 19, 2005). EPA has also removed certain compounds form the listed group of glycol ethers. *See* 65 Fed. Reg. 47,342 (Aug. 2, 2000) and 69 Fed. Reg. 69,320 (Nov. 29, 2004).
13. CAA § 112(a)(1); 42 U.S.C. § 7412(a)(1).
14. CAA § 112(a)(2); 42 U.S.C. § 7412(a)(2).
15. CAA § 112(a)(4); 42 U.S.C. § 7412(a)(4); 40 C.F.R. § 63.2.

v. EPA,[16] and remanded to the agency for further rulemaking. In short, the court held that "effective" state and local limits on operation would also serve to restrict a source's potential to emit.[17]

The CAA section 112 requirements apply to both existing sources and new sources. A *new source* is defined as a stationary source where construction is commenced after EPA first proposes regulations establishing an emission standard applicable to the source.[18] CAA section 112(i) states that no person may construct any new major source subject to an emission standard unless EPA determines that the source will comply with the applicable MACT standard. In contrast to new sources, existing sources generally must meet a compliance date specified by EPA for each category of existing sources that shall provide for compliance as expeditiously as practicable, but no later than three years after the standard is promulgated.[19]

EPA headquarters maintains a database of New Source Performance Standard (NSPS) and NESHAP applicability determinations, which includes guidance letters and other memoranda issued by EPA offices.[20]

In regulating HAPs, EPA has adopted "General Provisions" that apply to each regulated source category of new and existing sources. The General Provisions include applicability provisions, common definitions applicable to all categories, performance testing and monitoring provisions, general record-keeping and reporting requirements, and standards for control devices and

---

16. 59 F.3d 1351 (D.C. Cir. 1995).

17. On January 22, 1996, EPA released its Interim Policy on Federal Enforceability of Limitations on Potential to Emit, and the memorandum provided that sources lacking federally enforceable limits may be recognized as minor sources if sources with emissions less than 100 percent of the major source threshold demonstrate that state-enforceable standards are "enforceable as a practical matter." EPA's January 26, 1996, memorandum notes that the part 63 federal enforceability requirements remain in effect because the rule was not vacated, but EPA anticipated conducting further rulemaking. To date, EPA has not initiated further rulemaking, and EPA's policy of recognizing state-enforceable limitations remains in effect as set forth in a memorandum titled Options for Limiting the Potential to Emit (PTE) of Stationary Sources Under Section 112 and Title V of the Clean Air Act (Jan. 25, 1995).

18. CAA § 112(a)(4); 42 U.S.C. § 7412(a)(4).

19. CAA § 112(i)(3); 42 U.S.C. § 7412(i)(3). Existing sources may be granted an additional year for compliance if the extension is necessary to install pollution controls. CAA § 112(i)(4); 42 U.S.C. § 7412(i)(4).

20. The NSPS/NESHAP applicability determination index is available at EPA Compliance Monitoring, Applicability Determination Index, http://www.epa.gov/oecaerth/monitoring/programs/caa/adi.html.

work practice requirements.[21] When evaluating the applicability of CAA section 112 to a particular source, the specific HAP emission standard and the General Provisions should be reviewed.

In regulating HAPs, EPA has taken the position that major sources are required to comply with applicable MACT standards in perpetuity once the first substantive compliance date of an applicable MACT standard becomes effective—the "once in always in" policy.[22] In January 2007, EPA proposed amendments to the General Provisions that would replace the once-in-always-in policy.[23] The proposed amendments would allow a major HAP source to limit its potential to emit HAPs to become an area source (i.e., below the major source thresholds of 10 tpy of any single HAP or 25 tpy of any combination of HAPs) at any time, including after the first substantive compliance date of a MACT standard.[24] As of mid-2011, EPA had not finalized the proposed rule.

7.4   MACT Standard Setting

7.4.1   Source Categories

EPA was required pursuant to CAA section 112(c) to develop categories and subcategories of all major sources by November 15, 1991. EPA is also authorized to list categories of area sources. EPA's initial source category list, promulgated on July 16, 1992, contained 166 major source categories and eight area source categories.[25] EPA may revise the source category list pursuant to the agency's own initiative or based on consideration of a petition filed by any person. EPA has issued several revisions to the industrial and area source category and subcategory listings, and the *Federal Register* notices of the final rules can be accessed online.[26] EPA is required pursuant to CAA section 112(c)(1) to

21.   59 Fed. Reg. 12,430 (Mar. 16, 1994) (codified at 40 C.F.R. §§ 63.1 *et seq.*).
22.   Memorandum from John Seitz, Dir., EPA Office of Air Quality Planning & Standards (OAQPS), to EPA Reg'l Air Div. Dirs., Potential to Emit for MACT Standards—Guidance on Timing Issues (May 16, 1995).
23.   72 Fed. Reg. 69 (Jan. 3, 2007).
24.   72 Fed. Reg. at 69–70.
25.   57 Fed. Reg. 31,591 (July 16, 1992).
26.   *See* EPA Air Toxics Web Site, Source Category List and Promulgation Schedule, http://www.epa.gov/ttn/atw/socatlst/socatpg.html.

update the source and area source categories periodically, but no less than once every eight years.[27] EPA has also delisted a number of source categories.[28]

After the categories and subcategories are listed, the CAA directs EPA to promulgate MACT standards pursuant to section 112(d). The CAA required the agency to promulgate standards for not less than 40 source categories or subcategories by November 1992, another 25 percent by November 1994, an additional 25 percent by November 1997, and the remainder by November 2000.[29] In a December 3, 1993, *Federal Register* notice, EPA committed itself to promulgating at least 50 percent of the MACT standards for the source categories and subcategories (i.e., 87 of 174) by November 15, 1997, with the remaining standards being promulgated by November 15, 2000.[30] In large part, EPA tried to adhere to its regulatory time frames for issuing MACT standards; however, there were delays in meeting the two-year, four-year, and seven-year promulgation targets. EPA did not promulgate all of the MACT standards for the listed source categories and subcategories by the November 15, 2000, statutory deadline, and the CAA section 112(j) "hammer" provision was triggered for over 40 source categories.[31] Under CAA section 112(j), if EPA failed to promulgate all MACT standards by May 15, 2002, then the owner or operator of a major source not currently covered by an applicable MACT standard must file an application for a Title V permit to set a plant-specific case-by-case MACT standard. EPA adopted regulations implementing CAA section 112(j), and the rules required that the owner or operator of a major HAP source affected by a listed source category submit a permit application for a case-by-case standard within 18 months after the missed promulgation deadline.[32]

In 2010, EPA proposed to modify the CAA section 112(j) rules to clarify and streamline the application of case-by-case emission

27. CAA § 112(c)(1); 42 U.S.C. § 6412(c)(1).
28. The list with *Federal Register* citations can be accessed at EPA Air Toxics Web Site, Delisted Source Categories, http://www.epa.gov/ttn/atw/delisted.html.
29. CAA § 112(e)(1); 42 U.S.C. § 6412(e)(1).
30. 58 Fed. Reg. 63,941 (Dec. 3, 1993).
31. *See* 68 Fed. Reg. 32,586, 32,588 (May 30, 2003) (Tables 1 and 2 provide a listing of source categories subject to CAA section 112(j)).
32. 59 Fed. Reg. 26,429 (May 20, 1994), 67 Fed. Reg. 16,582 (Apr. 5, 2002); EPA subsequently modified the 18-month deadline to establish specific permit application due dates. See 68 Fed. Reg. at 32,588, tbl.1. EPA also issued EPA Office of Air Quality Planning & Standards, EPA-453/R-02-001, Guidelines for MACT Determinations Under Section 112(j) Requirements (Feb. 2002).

limits for sources categories where the initial MACT standards for the category were vacated by the U.S. Court of Appeals for the D.C. Circuit.[33] The proposed rule identified four source category rules that have been overturned in the courts, and the proposal sets out deadlines for submitting CAA section 112(j) permit applications.[34] The MACT standard for the oil- and coal-fired electric utility steam generating units source category is scheduled to be promulgated in 2011 pursuant to a consent decree entered between EPA and numerous nongovernmental organizations.[35] As reviewed later in this chapter, EPA initially attempted to regulate air toxics emitted by oil- and coal-fired electric utility steam generating units through the Clean Air Mercury Rule, which was vacated by the D.C. Circuit in 2008.[36]

CAA section 112(l) allows each state to develop and submit a HAP program to EPA for approval.[37] States may seek full or particle delegation of EPA's CAA section 112 authority, but the program "shall not include authority to set standards less stringent than those promulgated by the Administrator."[38] EPA regulations setting out the state HAP program requirements and procedures for seeking the agency's approval are set forth in 40 C.F.R. §§ 63.90–63.99.

7.4.2   Defining MACT

CAA section 112(d) of the Clean Air Act specifies that EPA shall establish HAP emission standards for existing and new sources based on the maximum degree of reduction achievable "taking into consideration the cost of achieving such emission reduction,

---

33.   75 Fed. Reg. 15,655 (Mar. 30, 2010).

34.   75 Fed. Reg. at 15,656. The four categories are (1) polyvinyl chloride and copolymers production, (2) brick and structural clay products, (3) clay ceramics manufacturing, and (4) industrial, commercial, and institutional boilers. The final rule implementing MACT standards for industrial, commercial, and institutional boilers was promulgated in March 2011, and the effective date has been delayed until judicial review is no longer pending or EPA completes its reconsideration of the rules. *See* 76 Fed. Reg. 15,608 (Mar. 21, 2011), 76 Fed. Reg. 15,554 (Mar. 21, 2011), and 76 Fed. Reg. 28,662 (May 18, 2011).

35.   Am. Nurses Ass'n et al. v. Jackson, Civ. No. 1:08-cv-02198 (RMC) (filed Apr. 15, 2010). An up-to-date listing of the status of EPA's promulgation of MACT standards is available at EPA's Air Toxics website, which can be accessed at http://www.epa.gov/ttn/atw/mactfnlalph.html. EPA has also developed several guidance documents to implement various MACT standards that can be found at http://www.epa.gov/ttn/atw/macttools_51805.pdf.

36.   New Jersey v. EPA, 517 F.3d 574 (D.C. Cir. 2008).

37.   CAA § 112(l)(1); 42 U.S.C. § 7412(l)(1).

38.   *Id.*

and any non-air-quality health and environmental impacts and energy requirements."[39] This process for setting technology-based standards is similar to the NSPS program, with a few unique twists as to establishing the minimum level of control. Congress imposed minimum stringency requirements, which EPA calls "MACT floors," that "apply without regard to either costs or the other factors and methods listed in section 7412(d)(2)."[40] These stringency levels are established differently for new and existing sources. For new sources, the minimum level of control shall be set at a level no less stringent than "the emission control that is achieved in practice by the best controlled similar source, as determined by the Administrator."[41] Under this provision, EPA has taken the position that it has little discretion to alter the new source standard. The MACT floor for existing standards is somewhat less stringent and affords the agency more flexibility. CAA section 112(d) provides that the MACT standards shall not be less stringent than "the average emission limitation achieved by the best performing 12 percent of existing sources (for which the Administrator has emissions information) . . . in the category or subcategory for categories and subcategories with 30 or more sources."[42] For categories or subcategories with less than 30 sources, the average limitation shall be based on the five best performing existing sources.[43] EPA has taken the position that the "average emission limitation" of the top 12 percent of best controlled sources should be set at the 94th percentile (i.e., the midpoint of the top 12 percent). Industry, in contrast, has argued that the average limit should be set at the 88th percentile (i.e., the minimum "average" level achieved by all top 12 percent of sources). EPA's use of the "average emission limitation" in its MACT standard setting methodology for existing sources has generally been accepted by the courts.[44] In analyzing how to establish the MACT floor, the U.S. Court of Appeals for the D.C. Circuit held that the floors need to "reflect a reasonable estimate of the emissions 'achieved' in practice by the best-performing sources.[45] The D.C. Circuit also held in *Sierra Club v. EPA* that

---

39. CAA § 112(d)(2); 42 U.S.C. § 7412(d)(2).
40. Nat'l Lime Ass'n v. EPA, 233 F.3d 625, 629 (D.C. Cir. 2000); *see also* NRDC v. EPA, 489 F.3d 1364, 1375–76 (D.C. Cir. 2007).
41. CAA § 112(d)(3); 42 U.S.C. § 7412(d)(3).
42. CAA § 112(d)(3)(A); 42 U.S.C. § 7412(d)(3)(A).
43. CAA § 112(d)(3)(B); 42 U.S.C. § 7412(d)(3)(B).
44. *See, e.g.,* Sierra Club v. EPA, 479 F.3d 875, 880 (D.C. Cir. 2007).
45. Cement Kiln Recycling Coal. v. EPA, 255 F.3d 855, 871–72 (D.C. Cir. 2001); *see also Nat'l Lime Ass'n*, 233 F.3d at 632; *Sierra Club*, 479 F.3d at 880–81.

the agency may not redefine "best performing" to mean that the MACT floors must be actually "achievable by all sources" using a particular technology that is technically feasible.[46] In *Sierra Club v. EPA*, the court vacated the MACT standards for brick and cement kilns, and sent the rule back to EPA to be reworked.[47]

The courts have issued decisions in a number of MACT standard cases, and some key questions regarding implementation of the MACT program have largely been resolved. In *National Lime Ass'n v. EPA*, the D.C. Circuit determined that EPA may use surrogate pollutants, such as PM or opacity, to regulate hazardous pollutants if it is "reasonable" to do so.[48] The D.C. Circuit has also rejected EPA's practice of setting of MACT standards based solely on technology if there are other nontechnology factors (e.g., fuel type) that affect emission levels of the best performing sources.[49] In *Sierra Club v. EPA*,[50] the D.C. Circuit reviewed whether EPA could use available state regulatory data and supplement it with data from its own testing program. The court concluded that the use of regulatory data involving applicable state emissions limits was permissible, but that EPA had not adequately explained the reasonableness of using the agency's supplemental testing data in its calculation of the MACT floor for existing medical waste incinerators. The court remanded the existing source MACT standards for medical waste incinerators to EPA for further explanation of why the combined regulatory/test data provides an accurate picture of the emission performance of the incinerators.[51] The court also held that EPA could set new source MACT standards based on a reasonable estimate of the performance of the "best controlled similar source"; however, these standards were also remanded because EPA did not sufficiently explain its rationale.[52]

The D.C. Circuit has determined that the CAA requires EPA to establish MACT standards for major HAP sources even if there is no control technology currently used by the particular industry to restrict

---

46.   479 F.3d at 883.
47.   479 F.3d at 876.
48.   233 F.3d at 637; *see also* Sierra Club v. EPA, 353 F.3d 976, 984 (D.C. Cir. 2004).
49.   233 F.3d at 640; 255 F.3d at 863–65; 479 F.3d at 882–83.
50.   167 F.3d 658 (D.C. Cir. 1999).
51.   *Id.* at 663–65.
52.   *Id.* at 664–65.

such HAPs.[53] In such situations, the CAA requires EPA to consider "process changes, substitution of materials or other modifications."[54]

Once EPA establishes the minimum level of stringency in setting the MACT floor, the second step in the process is to evaluate whether stricter standards are "achievable."[55] EPA has authority under section 112(d)(2) to go "beyond the floor" for new and existing sources and set standards more stringent than suggested by a MACT floor analysis.[56] In general, EPA must demonstrate that such beyond-the-floor costs of control are reasonable taking into account cost, energy requirements, and certain non-air-quality health and environmental impacts.[57] In *National Lime Ass'n v. EPA*, the D.C. Circuit remanded EPA's MACT standard for portland cement manufacturing facilities back to the agency for further rulemaking, because the agency failed to consider non-air-quality health and environmental impacts in rejecting the need for beyond-the-floor standards for HAP metals.[58] Another important case law development was the D.C. Circuit's decision in *Sierra Club v. EPA* that invalidated EPA's regulation that generally exempted emissions during start-up, shutdown, and malfunction events from compliance with a particular NESHAP.[59] EPA issued guidance in 2009 interpreting the decision as only affecting HAP standards that directly incorporate the two vacated provisions.[60] EPA has since taken steps in some specific source category rules to establish specific emission limits that apply during start-up, shutdown, and malfunction periods.[61]

7.4.3   Compliance Deadlines

For existing sources, MACT standards must be generally achieved within three years of issuance of the final rule.[62] In some instances,

---

53. *Nat'l Lime Ass'n*, 233 F.3d at 633–34; *Sierra Club*, 479 F.3d at 883.
54. *Nat'l Lime Ass'n*, 233 F.3d at 634.
55. CAA § 112(d)(2); 42 U.S.C. § 7412(d)(2).
56. *Nat'l Lime Ass'n*, 233 F.3d at 629.
57. CAA § 112(d)(2); 42 U.S.C. § 7412(d)(2).
58. 233 F.3d at 635.
59. Sierra Club v. EPA, 551 F.3d 1019 (D.C. Cir. 2008). The D.C. Circuit vacated sections 40 C.F.R. §§ 63.6(f)(1) and 63.6(h)(1) of EPA's General Provisions rule.
60. Letter from Adam M. Kushner, Dir. of EPA Office of Enforcement and Compliance Assurance, to Counsel for Industry Intervenors (July 22, 2009).
61. *See, e.g.*, 74 Fed. Reg. 56,008 (Oct. 29, 2009) (specific start-up and shutdown emission limits for nine area source categories); 75 Fed. Reg. 51,570 (Aug. 20, 2010) (requirement to minimize emissions during 30-minute start-up time for reciprocating internal combustion engines).
62. CAA § 112(i)(3)(A); 42 U.S.C. § 7412(i)(3)(A).

a one-year extension of the deadline may be obtained to install the requisite control technology.[63] After the effective date of a MACT standard, new sources generally must comply with the standard from the start of operations.[64] There are some special rules that apply if construction is commenced after the proposal date but before the effective date of the MACT standard.[65] MACT standards and other applicable CAA section 112 requirements will generally be incorporated into a major source's Title V operating permit.

Section 112(i) also provides an early reduction option where an existing source can elect to meet a 90 percent HAP reduction limit (95 percent for HAP particulates) before the applicable MACT standard is proposed.[66] Sources meeting this alternative HAP limit will qualify for a six-year extension of compliance with the final MACT standard for the particular HAP source category or subcategory. In addition, CAA section 112(g)(2) states that after the effective date of a Title V permit program in any state, no person may construct any major source of HAPs unless EPA (or the state permitting agency) determines that MACT for new sources will be met. Such a determination will be made on a case-by-case basis if no applicable MACT emission limitations have been established by EPA.[67] EPA issued a final rule implementing CAA section 112(g) in 1996, and the agency has published guidance outlining steps for state permitting agencies and sources to develop case-by-case MACT standards.[68] Even though most of the CAA section 112 MACT standards have been issued, there remain a few source categories that do not yet have final standards. In 2010, the U.S. Court of Appeals for the Fifth Circuit held that CAA section 112(g)(2)(B) prohibits the act of construction, and not merely the commencement of construction.[69] In *Sierra Club v. Sandy Creek Energy Associates*, construction of a coal-fired power plant started prior to the vacatur of EPA's Clean Air Mercury Rule and Delisting Rule, which exempted the category of fossil-fuel-fired electric utility steam generating units from CAA

---

63. CAA § 112(i)(3)(B); 42 U.S.C. § 7412(i)(3)(B).

64. 40 C.F.R. § 63.6(b)(2).

65. *See* 40 C.F.R. §§ 63.6(b)(1) and (3).

66. CAA § 112(i)(5); 42 U.S.C. § 7412(i)(5).

67. CAA § 112(g)(2); 42 U.S.C. § 7412(g)(2).

68. 61 Fed. Reg. 68,384 (Dec. 27, 1996); EPA, EPA-450/3-92/007b, GUIDELINES FOR MACT DETERMINATIONS UNDER SECTION 112(G) (proposal) (Mar. 1994).

69. Sierra Club v. Sandy Creek Energy Assocs., 627 F.3d 134 (5th Cir. 2010).

section 112.[70] Once the rules were vacated, power plants once again became subject to the CAA section 112 programs.

7.5 GACT Standards

CAA section 112(d)(5) authorizes EPA to set emission standards or work practices for area sources of HAP emissions (i.e., nonmajor HAP emitters). EPA may promulgate NESHAP standards for area sources based on generally available control technologies (GACT), and EPA has broad authority to set GACT standards at levels less stringent than MACT-type standards.[71] GACT does not involve a "floor" technology standard evaluation, and it is generally a less vigorous emission standard than a MACT standard; however, it is not necessarily always less stringent than a MACT standard. For example, in the NESHAP for hazardous waste combustors, EPA determined that the same emissions standards should apply to both major and area HAP sources.[72] EPA concluded that GACT for certain hazardous waste combustors should be the same as MACT because the standards are generally achievable by both types of sources. In setting GACT standards for area sources, EPA can consider costs and technical feasibility.[73] CAA section 112(c)(3) requires EPA to identify and list area sources that represent "90 percent of the area source emissions of the 30 hazardous air pollutants that present the greatest threat to public health in the largest number of urban areas."[74] EPA has identified 70 source categories that represent 90 percent of the emissions of 30 listed HAPs in urban areas. The list was developed as part of EPA's Urban Air Toxic Strategy.[75] To date, EPA has listed GACT standards for most of the source categories.[76]

---

70. Standards of Performance for New and Existing Stationary Sources: Electric Utility Steam Generating Units, 70 Fed. Reg. 28,606 (May 18, 2005); Revision of December 2000 Regulatory Finding, 70 Fed. Reg. 15,994 (Mar. 29, 2005). Both rules were vacated by New Jersey v. EPA, 517 F.3d 574 (D.C. Cir. 2008).
71. CAA § 112(d)(5); 42 U.S.C. § 7412(d)(5).
72. 64 Fed Reg. 52,828, 52,837–38 (Sept. 30, 1999).
73. See 74 Fed. Reg. 30,366, 30,371 (June 25, 2009).
74. CAA § 112(c)(3); 42 U.S.C. § 7412(c)(3).
75. 64 Fed. Reg. 38,706 (July 19, 1999).
76. A listing of the final rules and source categories can be accessed at EPA Air Toxics Web Site, Area Source Standards, http://www.epa.gov/ttn/atw/area/arearules.html#court.

7.6 **Residual Risk Standards**

EPA prepared and submitted its Residual Risk Report to Congress in March 1999, pursuant to CAA section 112(f), which required EPA to report on the methods to be used to assess the residual risks that may remain after MACT standards have been promulgated and applied.[77] EPA's Residual Risk Report includes a discussion of the methodologies the agency will use to analyze potential residual risks as well as providing a framework for addressing the requirements to promulgate standards if necessary. CAA section 112(f)(2) directs EPA to promulgate residual risk standards within eight years after promulgation of applicable MACT standards if such residual risk protections are required "to provide an ample margin of safety to protect public health" or to set more stringent standards, if necessary, "to prevent, taking into consideration costs, energy, safety, and other relevant factors, an adverse environmental effect."[78] In the report, EPA did not identify a need for any additional legislation to address residual risks, but generally concluded that it had the requisite authority to proceed. CAA section 112(d)(6) also requires EPA to review the MACT standards at least every eight years, and revise the standards as necessary to take into account developments in practices, processes, and control technologies.[79]

EPA has developed a "Risk and Technology Review" process to identify, assess, and manage any residual risks remaining following the implementation of the MACT standards for the various source categories and subcategories. On EPA's Risk and Technology Review website, the agency cites its analysis conducted for the petroleum refining and portland cement manufacturing source categories as an example of how EPA conducts its assessments.[80]

EPA is in the process of making residual risk determinations for a number of source categories. EPA completed its residual risk determinations for the first eight categories of HAP sources by

77. EPA Office of Air Quality Planning & Standards, EPA-453/R-99-001, Residual Risk Report to Congress (Mar. 1999).

78. CAA § 112(f)(2); 42 U.S.C. § 7412(f)(2). Standards required to be promulgated by November 15, 1992, are granted a nine-year period before residual risk standards may be implemented. CAA § 112(f)(2)(C); 42 U.S.C. § 7412(f)(2)(C).

79. CAA § 112(d)(6); 42 U.S.C. § 7412(d)(6).

80. EPA, EPA-452/R-09-006, Risk and Technology Review (RTR) Risk Assessment Methodologies: For Review by the EPA's Science Advisory Board with Case Studies—MACT I Petroleum Refining Sources and Portland Cement Manufacturing (June 2009). See http://www.epa.gov/ttn/atw/rrisk/rtrpg.html.

April 2007. These categories are coke ovens, dry cleaning, halogenated solvents, industrial cooling towers, gasoline distribution, ethylene oxidizer sterilizers, magnetic tape, and sources subject to the hazardous organic NESHAP. EPA is now in the process of finalizing the residual risk rules for a number of additional source categories, and a schedule of the standards is listed on EPA's Risk and Technology Review website.[81]

In evaluating each HAP source category or subcategory, EPA makes a determination on whether the existing MACT standards provide for an ample margin of safety or whether the incremental cost for further risk reduction warrants the setting of a residual risk standard.[82] Residual risk standards are generally required to be promulgated if the MACT standards applicable to sources in a particular category or subcategory emitting a known, probable, or possible human carcinogen do not reduce lifetime excess cancer risks to less than one in one million.[83]

In *NRDC v. EPA*,[84] the D.C. Circuit upheld EPA's decision not to impose more stringent residual risk requirements under the hazardous organics NESHAP (HON). The court agreed that CAA section 112(f)(2) requires EPA to promulgate standards whenever the lifetime risk exceeds one in one million, but the provision does not specify what those standards require. The court went on to conclude that EPA's interpretation that 100 in one million provides an ample margin of safety was reasonable.[85] The court found that additional regulation was not required because under the existing HON MACT standard no individual would face an excess lifetime cancer risk of greater than 100 in one million.[86] In *NRDC v. EPA*, the D.C. Circuit also upheld EPA's interpretation that the eight-year review requirement does not impose an obligation to recalculate the MACT floors.[87]

---

81. EPA Air Toxics Web Site, Risk and Technology Review, http://www.epa .gov/ttn/atw/rrisk/rtrpg.html.

82. CAA § 112(f)(2)(C); 42 U.S.C. § 7412(f)(2)(C).

83. CAA § 112(f)(2); 42 U.S.C. § 7412(f)(2).

84. 529 F.3d 1077 (D.C. Cir. 2008).

85. 529 F.3d at 1081–83.

86. *Id.*

87. 529 F.3d at 1084.

7.7   Mercury

One of the more notable HAPs is mercury. Mercury is widely recognized as a highly toxic, persistent pollutant that accumulates in the environment and can transform into methylmercury and build up in the food chain. Humans may consume mercury by eating contaminated fish. In January 2004, EPA proposed two alternative approaches for reducing mercury emissions from coal- and oil-fired electric utility steam generating plants based on different sections of the Clean Air Act. The first alternative involved a CAA section 112 MACT standard. The second alternative was a cap-and-trade approach under CAA section 111 (New Source Performance Standard), which offered a much less prescriptive approach and provided more flexibility in setting mercury standards. As part of its development of a mercury reduction rule, EPA "delisted" the source category of coal- and oil-fired electric utility steam generating plants from the CAA section 112 source category list so that coal- and oil-fired power plants were no longer subject to CAA section 112.[88]

In 2005, EPA finalized the Clean Air Mercury Rule (CAMR), and chose the CAA section 111 alternative by adopting a two-phased "cap and trade" approach with the first phase starting in 2010 and the second phase in 2018. The rule was immediately challenged by several states and numerous nongovernmental organizations. In February 2008, the D.C. Circuit vacated the "delisting rule" and CAMR, concluding that EPA did not follow the proper procedural requirements in making its decision to delist coal- and oil-fired electric utility steam generating plants fom the CAA section 112 source category list.[89]

In May 2011, EPA proposed MACT standards for existing and new coal- and oil-fired electric utility steam generating facilities which would set emission limits for mercury, non-mercury metals, and acid gases (e.g., hydrogen chloride (HCL)).[90] EPA expects to finalize the rule by November 2011.

---

88. 70 Fed. Reg. 15,994 (Mar. 29, 2005).
89. New Jersey v. EPA, 517 F.3d 574 (D.C. Cir. 2008).
90. 76 Fed. Reg. 24,976 (May 3, 2011).

7.8   Accidental Release Program and Risk Management Plans

CAA section 112 also includes a program that is intended to prevent accidental releases of HAPs that may cause catastrophic consequences for the area community. CAA section 112(r) directs the agency to promulgate a list of substances that, if released, "are known to cause death, injury, or serious adverse effects to human health or the environment."[91] EPA promulgated two lists of regulated substances in January 1994—a list of 77 toxic substances and a list of 63 flammable substances—along with the applicable quantity threshold levels.[92] EPA developed its lists of regulated substances based on consideration of three factors: (1) the severity of any acute adverse health effects associated with an accidental release, (2) the likelihood of an accidental release, and (3) the potential magnitude of human exposure to an accidental release.[93]

An owner or operator of a stationary source that has more than a threshold quantity of a regulated HAP substance in a "process" must prepare a Risk Management Plan (RMP) and submit it to EPA by June 21, 1999.[94] A *process* is generally defined as "any activity involving a regulated substance including any use, storage, manufacturing, handling, or on-site movement of such substances, or combination of these activities."[95] EPA's RMP regulations, promulgated in June 1996, set forth the requirements of developing a plan to prevent and respond to an accidental release of a regulated substance.[96] An RMP generally requires three basic components: (1) a hazard assessment, (2) a prevention program, and (3) an emergency response program. An RMP requires a fairly detailed discussion of the regulated substances that are stored at a stationary source and requires development of a worst-case release scenario analysis as part of the hazard assessment. In addition, an RMP generally mandates that a prevention program be put in place, including operating and training procedures and clear instructions on safety precautions. Lastly, a thorough, written emergency response plan must be prepared outlining procedures to address an acci-

---

91.   CAA § 112(r)(3); 42 U.S.C. § 7412(r)(3).
92.   40 C.F.R. § 68.130.
93.   CAA § 112(r)(4); 42 U.S.C. § 7412(r)(4).
94.   40 C.F.R. § 68.10.
95.   40 C.F.R. § 63.3.
96.   64 Fed. Reg. 31,726 (June 20, 1996) (codified at 40 C.F.R. §§ 68.1 et seq.).

dental release. The RMP must be submitted to EPA, the Chemical Safety and Hazard Investigation Board, the applicable state emergency response commission, and any local emergency planning committee.[97] Guidance on preparing an RMP is available at EPA's Risk Management Plan Rule website.[98]

7.9   General Duty Clause

One other key requirement of the CAA section 112(r) accidental release program requirements is the "general duty" clause of this section, which generally applies to all stationary sources using toxic or hazardous substances in plant operations, even if the facility is not subject to EPA's RMP rule. CAA section 112(r)(1) provides in part:

> The owners and operators of stationary sources producing, processing, handling or storing [certain listed and other extremely hazardous] substances have a general duty . . . to identify hazards which may result from [accidental] releases using appropriate hazard assessment techniques, to design and maintain a safe facility taking such steps as are necessary to prevent releases, and to minimize the consequences of accidental releases which do occur.[99]

The statute further specifies that companies have this general duty in the same manner and to the same extent they do under the Occupational Safety and Health Administration's general duty rule requiring employers to maintain a safe workplace. EPA has stated that the general duty clause under CAA section 112(r) applies not only to the regulated substances listed by EPA, but also to any other extremely hazardous substance.[100] The CAA section 112(r) general duty clause does not trigger any requirements under the RMP rule, but it does provide EPA with fairly broad authority to enforce the clause.

---

97.   CAA § 112(r)(7)(B)(iii); 42 U.S.C. § 7412(r)(7)(B)(iii).
98.   EPA Emergency Management, Risk Management Plan (RMP) Rule, http://www.epa.gov/oem/content/rmp/.
99.   CAA § 112(r)(1); 42 U.S.C. § 7412(r)(1).
100.   59 Fed. Reg. 4,478, 4,481 (Jan. 31, 1994).

8 Visibility Protection

Section 169A of the Clean Air Act (CAA), which was added by the Clean Air Act Amendments of 1977, sets forth the national goal of "the prevention of any future, and the remedying of any existing, impairment of visibility" due to man-made air pollution in certain pristine areas of the country. At the heart of the visibility protection program is the protection of scenic vistas in our national parks and other federal lands. The CAA, in section 162(a), lists the areas that are required to be protected under the visibility program as "Class I" areas.[1] Class I areas include (1) international parks, (2) national wilderness areas exceeding 5,000 acres in size, (3) national memorial parks exceeding 5,000 acres in size, and (4) national parks exceeding 6,000 acres in size.[2] The Environmental Protection Agency has codified the list of 156 mandatory Class I areas at 40 C.F.R. §§ 81.400 *et seq.*

Visibility in the Class I areas is monitored by federal land managers (FLMs), who are by definition the secretary of the federal department with responsibility over such lands.[3] For example, the Secretary of Interior is the FLM for National Park Service lands.[4] The secretary of the applicable federal agency may also designate an agency employee to serve as the FLM.[5] As explained later in this chapter, the federal land managers play an integral role in preserving the air quality in Class I areas.

---

1. A map of the 156 Class I areas is available at EPA Visibility, EPA's Regional Haze Program, http://epa.gov/visibility/program.html.
2. CAA § 162(a); 42 U.S.C. § 7472(a).
3. CAA § 302(i); 42 U.S.C. § 7602(i).
4. The FLMs include the Department of Interior/National Park Service (national parks and monuments), the Department of Interior/Fish and Wildlife Service (national wildlife refuges), and the Department of Agriculture/National Forest Service (national wilderness areas).
5. 40 C.F.R. § 51.301.

EPA has monitored visibility at a number of the national parks and wilderness areas since 1988, and submitted a report to Congress in 2001 that summarized visibility trends and analysis based on 1994 to 1998 monitoring data from 46 Class I areas.[6] The report provides a good overview of visibility issues. Visibility impairment or haze is caused when sunlight encounters small particles of dust, soot, and other fine particulate contaminants (e.g., nitrates, sulfates, organic carbon, and elemental carbon), particularly during humid conditions. NO_x and SO_2 are converted in the atmosphere to nitrates and sulfates.

8.1   Protections under the Prevention of Significant Deterioration Program

As explained in chapter 5, the Prevention of Significant Deterioration (PSD) program is designed to preserve the air quality in areas that are in attainment with the National Ambient Air Quality Standards for criteria pollutants. The PSD program requires a preconstruction review and issuance of a permit for new major sources and major modifications of existing major sources. FLMs are authorized to participate in the PSD review process where a new or modified major source is located within 100 kilometers (approximately 62 miles) of a Class I area. Pursuant to CAA section 165, the FLMs are charged with protecting the air-quality-related values (AQRVs), including visibility, of Class I lands and are authorized to consult with the permitting agency on PSD permit applications.[7] Neither the CAA nor EPA regulations currently define what can be considered an AQRV; not surprisingly, this lack of a concrete definition has led to some controversy in the permitting of PSD sources near Class I areas. In 1996, EPA proposed that AQRVs be defined to include "visibility or a scenic, cultural, physical, biological, ecological, or recreational resource which may be affected by a change in air quality."[8] However, this definition has not yet been formally adopted by EPA.

---

6. EPA, EPA 452/R-01-008, Visibility in Mandatory Federal Class I Areas (1994–1998)—A Report to Congress (Nov. 2001).

7. CAA § 165(d)(2)(B); 42 U.S.C. § 7475(d)(2)(B).

8. 61 Fed. Reg. 38,250, 38,332, and 38,339 (July 23, 1996). Portions of the proposed rule to revise the PSD and New Source Review (NSR) programs were

CAA section 165 provides that the permitting authority shall provide notice of a PSD permit application to the applicable FLM overseeing any Class I area that may be affected by emissions from a proposed new or modified major source. The FLM is required to evaluate the proposed project to determine if the anticipated emissions from the project may have a potential adverse impact on the air quality in the Class I area. It is the PSD permit applicant's responsibility to prepare an AQRV analysis to allow the FLM to make an informed decision about potential adverse impacts on AQRVs.[9] In general, the FLM will consider whether a PSD increment will be violated and the overall potential effect of the project's air emissions on the nearby Class I area.[10] The FLM may file comments alleging that the emissions from the proposed new or modified major source may have an adverse affect on an AQRV. The burden is on the FLM to demonstrate to the satisfaction of the permitting authority that the emissions from the proposed project will have an adverse impact on an AQRV.[11] When an increment violation occurs, EPA's regulations place the burden on the applicant to demonstrate that no adverse impact on the Class I area will result.[12] If the permitting authority agrees that the proposed source will have an adverse impact on an AQRV, a PSD permit may not be issued.[13]

The role of the FLM in the PSD program has been somewhat controversial and EPA's efforts to formally codify this role in a federal regulation have thus far been met with strong reservations from the regulated community. In 1996, EPA proposed changes to the Prevention of Significant Deterioration/New Source Review (PSD/NSR) program that would formalize the consultation process between the permitting authority and the FLM.[14] Industry largely opposed the proposed rule, arguing that it would complicate and unnecessarily prolong PSD permitting, as well as impose a largely

adopted in the 2002 NSR Reform rule, but the proposed revisions to the Class I program provisions were not finalized.

9. Fed. Land Managers' Air Quality Related Values Work Group (FLAG), Response to Public Comments on Revised Phase I Report (2010), at 5 (Oct. 2010), http://www.nature.nps.gov/air/pubs/pdf/flag/FLAG_RtC_2010.pdf.

10. As noted in chapter 5, *increments* are the maximum allowable ambient pollutant increases over the baseline for certain criteria pollutants (i.e., SO_2, PM, and NO_2).

11. Fed. Land Managers' Air Quality Related Values Work Group (FLAG), Response to Public Comments on Revised Phase I Report (2010), at 6 (2010), http://www.nature.nps.gov/air/pubs/pdf/flag/FLAG_RtC_2010.pdf.

12. 40 C.F.R. § 52.21(p)(5).

13. CAA § 165(d)(2)(C)(ii); 42 U.S.C. § 7475(d)(2)(C)(ii).

14. 61 Fed. Reg. 38,250 (July 23, 1996).

subjective and unpredictable process on permitting new projects. This proposed rule was never adopted by the agency. When EPA finalized revisions to the PSD/NSR program in 2002, Class I issues were not addressed.

In an effort to provide guidance on the FLM's role in identifying AQRVs, evaluating adverse impacts on AQRVs, and permitting new and modified major sources near Class I areas, the National Park Service, the Fish and Wildlife Service, and the National Forest Service have jointly developed a guidance document titled "Federal Land Managers' Air Quality Related Values Workgroup (FLAG)—Phase I Report."[15] The FLAG Phase I Report is intended to provide coordinated guidance on the procedures each agency will use in reviewing PSD permit applications and evaluating the potential impacts on Class I AQRVs from proposed new and modified major sources. The FLAG Phase I Report was developed by the three agencies to address concerns by the regulated community that each agency used different approaches to identify AQRVs and evaluate PSD permit applications. The FLAG Phase I Report was recently updated in 2010 to incorporate criteria from EPA's 2005 best available retrofit technology (BART) guidelines to implement provisions of the regional haze rule, as well as further clarity on the factors considered for adverse impact determinations.[16]

8.2   1980 Visibility Protection Regulations

CAA section 169A, Visibility Protection for Federal Class I Areas, directs EPA to promulgate regulations to "assure reasonable progress toward meeting the national goal" of preventing future, and remedying existing, visibility impairment in Class I areas.[17] In response to the CAA section 169A mandate, EPA took a phased approach to implementing the required visibility protections. The first phase focused on "reasonably attributable" impairment; in other words, air emissions affecting visibility that are emanating from a single stationary source or a small group of sources.[18]

---

15. Fed. Land Managers' Air Quality Related Values Work Group (FLAG), Phase I Report (Dec. 2000), http://www.fs.fed.us/air/documents/flag.pdf.
16. Fed. Land Managers' Air Quality Related Values Work Group (FLAG), Nat. Res. Rep. NPS/NRPC/NRR 2010/232, Phase I Report Revised (Oct. 2010), http://www.nature.nps.gov/air/pubs/pdf/flag/FLAG_2010.pdf.
17. CAA § 169A(a)(4); 42 U.S.C. § 7491(a)(4).
18. 40 C.F.R. § 51.300.

The second phase focuses on regional haze resulting from a large number of sources and typically covering an expansive area.[19]

In 1980, EPA promulgated the first phase of regulations to address visibility impairment caused by one or a small group of sources.[20] In the 1980 rule, EPA directed the 35 states and 1 territory with Class I areas to revise their state implementation plans (SIPs) to include control strategies and regulations to address sources whose emissions are reasonably anticipated to cause or contribute to visibility impairment in Class I areas.[21] In general, the SIP revision submittals needed to include (1) a long-term strategy, including emission limitations and schedules of compliance; (2) emission limitations representing the BART for stationary sources determined to require such technology; (3) the adoption of measures to assess visibility impacts from new and modified sources; and (4) visibility monitoring in Class I areas. One of the key components of the 1980 visibility regulations was the requirement to implement BART at certain existing stationary sources, namely sources falling within a specific list of 26 categories of sources in existence on August 7, 1977, that were not operated prior to August 7, 1962, and that have a potential to emit at least 250 tons a year of any air pollutant.[22] The 26 source categories include large fossil-fuel-fired steam electric plants, large industrial boilers, and other industrial facilities such as pulp mills, petroleum refineries, iron and steel plants, and portland cement plants.

As defined in the EPA regulations, *BART* means "an emission limitation based on the degree of reduction achievable through the application of the best system of continuous emission reduction for each pollutant which is emitted by an existing stationary facility."[23] The definition further provides that BART limits must be set on a case-by-case basis taking into consideration the technology available, the costs of compliance, the energy and non-air-quality environmental impacts of compliance, any pollution control equipment in use or in existence at the source, the remain-

19. Regional haze is caused primarily by fine particulate emissions (e.g., organic carbon, elemental carbon, and road dust) as well as sulfates and nitrates that are formed from SO_2 and NO_x through chemical reactions in the atmosphere; these compounds potentially obscure the clarity, color, texture, and form of scenic vistas.

20. 45 Fed. Reg. 80,086 (Dec. 2, 1980) (codified at 40 C.F.R. §§ 51.300 et seq.).

21. 40 C.F.R. § 51.302.

22. 40 C.F.R. § 51.301.

23. *Id.*

ing useful life of the source, and the degree of improvement in visibility that could be anticipated from the technology being used.[24]

Most of the states required to submit visibility SIP revisions missed the applicable deadlines and/or failed to make submissions altogether. As a result, EPA ultimately promulgated federal implementation plans (FIPs) to meet the Act's requirements (e.g., visibility monitoring (40 C.F.R. § 52.26), long-term visibility strategies (40 C.F.R. § 52.29)). In many instances, the federal visibility programs have been adopted into state SIPs or states have sought delegated authority to implement the federal regulations. Although each of the state SIPs include the required visibility regulations, these regulations traditionally have not been used as authority to reduce air emission levels. In particular, very few sources have been required to install BART controls. Prior to EPA's adoption of the revised regional haze rule (discussed in section 8.4) in 2005, EPA has exercised its authority to require BART for only one plant, the Navajo Power Plant in Arizona, which was required to install a flue gas desulfurization system to reduce SO_2 emissions that were affecting the Grand Canyon vistas.[25]

8.3   Grand Canyon Visibility Transport Commission and Regional Planning

The Grand Canyon Visibility Transport Commission (GCVTC) was created by section 169B(f) of the 1990 CAA amendments to determine what, if any, steps are needed to preserve and improve visibility in 16 national parks and wilderness areas located on the Colorado plateau.[26] The commission, which started its work in November 1991, developed a comprehensive database on visibility in the Colorado Plateau and conducted extensive modeling of air quality in the Grand Canyon Visibility Transport Region, which includes 9 states and 211 tribal lands. The GCVTC was charged with providing recommendations to EPA on strategies for protecting and improving visual air quality on the Colorado Plateau. This mission was largely completed with the June 1996 sub-

24. *Id.*
25. 40 C.F.R. § 52.145(d).
26. CAA § 169B(f); 42 U.S.C. § 7492(f).

mittal of the GCVTC's recommendations to EPA, which (as noted in section 8.4) played an important role in the development of the regional haze rule. EPA continues to encourage the states and tribes across the United States to address visibility impairment through regional cooperative efforts. EPA has provided funding to five regional planning organizations to support efforts to address regional haze and visibility issues. The organizations included the Western Regional Air Partnership (which is a successor organization to the GCVTC), the Central Regional Air Planning Association, the Western Regional Planning Association, Visibility Improvement State and Tribal Association of the Southeast, and the Mid-Atlantic/Northeast Visibility Union.[27]

8.4   Regional Haze Rule

When EPA enacted its 1980 visibility protection rules, it deferred proposing regulations to address regional haze. Over the years, regional haze impairment has been the focus of several studies, including a 1993 National Academy of Sciences study.[28] In addition, GCVTC's submittal of its June 1996 final report to EPA served as one of the bases for the development of EPA's regional haze rule. Almost 19 years after promulgating the first phase of the visibility protection program, EPA initiated the second phase of the program by issuing a final regional haze rule on July 1, 1999.[29] This rule was intended to reduce the precursors of haze (e.g., sulfate and nitrate particles) that reduce visibility in national parks and wilderness areas. As explained in this section, the regional haze rule was *revised* in 2005 in response to the decision in *American Corn Growers Ass'n v. EPA*.[30]

EPA's regional haze rule was designed to improve visibility in 156 national parks and wilderness areas across the country (i.e., Class I areas). The rule calls for all 50 states to establish long-term strategies for reducing emissions of SO_2, NO_x, and fine particulates

---

27. *See* EPA Visibility, Regional Planning Organizations, http://epa.gov/visibility/regional.html.
28. NAT'L RESEARCH COUNCIL, PROTECTING VISIBILITY IN NATIONAL PARKS AND WILDERNESS AREAS (1993).
29. 64 Fed. Reg. 35,714 (July 1, 1999).
30. 70 Fed. Reg. 39,104 (July 6, 2005); American Corn Growers Ass'n v. EPA, 291 F.3d 1 (D.C. Cir. 2002) (per curiam).

(PM$_{2.5}$), which allegedly contribute to visibility impairment, and to develop SIP provisions addressing regional haze controls.[31] These new regional haze SIP requirements were scheduled to be submitted to EPA as SIP revisions by December 31, 2007. On January 15, 2009, EPA issued a final action finding that 37 states, the District of Columbia, and the U.S. Virgin Islands failed to submit all or part of the SIP rules necessary to implement the regional haze rule.[32] The finding started the two-year clock for promulgation of a FIP by EPA. EPA is not required to issue a FIP if a state submits a SIP rule, and it is approved by EPA within two years of the finding.

The regional haze rule provides that sources that are reasonably anticipated to cause or contribute to Class I visibility impairment must install BART controls. In 2002, in *American Corn Growers Ass'n v. EPA*,[33] the U.S. Court of Appeals for the D.C. Circuit vacated a key provision of EPA's regional haze rule that would have allowed states to impose pollution control requirements on a group of sources instead of on individual sources. The D.C. Circuit noted that states must consider equally the following five factors when deciding what BART controls to place on a source: (1) the costs of compliance, (2) the energy and non-air-quality environmental impacts of compliance, (3) any existing pollution control technology in use at the source, (4) the remaining useful life of the source, and (5) the degree of improvement in visibility that may reasonably be anticipated to result from the use of such technology.[34] In the 1999 rule, EPA required the states to consider the fifth factor (the degree of improvement) on a group basis.[35] The court concluded that before BART controls may be required, the CAA requires a finding that a particular source contributes to visibility impairment at a Class I area.

The goal of the regional haze rule is to attain "natural visibility conditions" within 60 years, that is, by the year 2064.[36] The rule requires each state to conduct an analysis to establish visibility goals for each affected Class I area to improve visibility on the haziest days and to ensure that no degradation occurs

---

31. The regional haze rule applies to all 50 states because EPA concluded that all states contain sources whose emissions are "reasonably anticipated to contribute to regional haze in a Class I area." 64 Fed. Reg. at 35,721.
32. 74 Fed. Reg. 2,392 (Jan. 15, 2009).
33. 291 F.3d 1 (D.C. Cir. 2002) (per curiam).
34. *Id.* at 5.
35. *Id.* at 5–6.
36. 64 Fed. Reg. at 35,731.

on the clearest days. In the *American Corn Growers* decision, the court upheld EPA's adoption of a "natural visibility" goal and the "no degradation" requirement set forth in the regional haze program.[37] In developing long-term strategies to meet the visibility goals, states are directed to address all types of man-made emissions, including those from stationary sources, mobile sources, area sources, and forest fires.

EPA's regional haze rule is intended to ultimately trigger BART pollution control requirements on existing stationary sources as defined under the original 1980 visibility protection regulation; that is, sources in 26 categories that were in existence as of August 7, 1977, and did not operate prior to August 7, 1962, and that have a potential to emit 250 tons or more a year of any air pollutant The regional haze rule requires all 50 states to prepare SIP revisions that identify all "BART-eligible" sources and establish control strategies to provide for reasonable progress in achieving natural visibility conditions for each Class I area located within the state, as well as any Class I areas located outside the state that may be affected by emissions from sources within the SIP-submitting state.[38] These states are then required to establish emission limitations for those BART-eligible sources that are identified as being reasonably anticipated to cause or contribute to regional haze.

On July 6, 2005, EPA published its revised regional haze rule, as well as guidelines for the implementation of BART.[39] The 2005 final rule revised the regional haze rule to require that states conduct a BART analysis with respect to potential visibility impacts from each individual source. The BART guidelines provided further tools for states to evaluate whether a particular source "may reasonably be anticipated to cause or contribute to any impairment of visibility in any mandatory Class I Federal area."[40] In short, the new regional haze rule is intended to spur the states into mandating that BART controls be installed on many pre-1977 plants located near Class I areas.

Under the regional haze rule, states also have the option of developing an emissions trading program applicable to BART sources as long as the trading program achieves greater emission

---

37. 291 F.3d at 9–13.
38. 40 C.F.R. § 51.308(d), (e).
39. 70 Fed. Reg. 39,104 (July 6, 2005).
40. 70 Fed. Reg. at 39,106.

reductions than would be achieved by applying BART to each individual source.[41] The U.S. Court of Appeals for the D.C. Circuit considered EPA's "better than BART" alternative in *Center for Energy & Economic Development v. EPA*, and although the court rejected the Western Regional Air Partnership's use of an optional backup emissions trading program because it was based on a "group BART" approach denied in *American Corn Growers*, the court did not reject the use of an alternative mechanism to comply with the regional haze rule.[42] In 2006, EPA issued a final rule clarifying the processes for making a "better than BART" determination and providing for minimum elements for cap-and-trade programs adopted in lieu of BART.[43]

---

41. 40 C.F.R. § 51.308(e)(2).

42. Ctr. for Energy & Economic Dev. v. EPA, 398 F.3d 653, 659 (D.C. Cir. 2005).

43. 71 Fed. Reg. 60,612 (Oct. 13, 2006).

9 Acid Rain Control

Acid rain results from the amount of sulfuric acid and nitric acids in the atmosphere. Sulfur dioxide (SO_2) and nitrogen oxides (NO_x), which are emitted by many stationary and mobile sources such as power plants and cars, react with water, oxygen, and oxidants to form sulfuric acid and nitric acid. Rainwater, snow, fog, and other precipitation containing these solutions of sulfuric acid and nitric acid fall to earth as acid rain. Rain in the eastern United States has a pH ranging from about 4.0 to 5.0, which is generally more acidic than the national average.[1] Unpolluted rain has a pH of about 5.5. As pH decreases, the acidity increases logarithmically. Thus, a pH of 4.0 has 10 times the acid of a pH of 5.0. Pure water has a pH of 7.0. Acid rain can affect agriculture and forestry yields, and it can accelerate the corrosion of structural materials and cause damage to soils and waterbodies by raising acidity. Acid rain also can aggravate human respiratory and cardiovascular problems.

Sulfate transport is fairly well documented and studies have shown that sulfur can be transported distances that exceed 1,000 miles. Power plants with tall smoke stacks have played a role in sulfur transport. The transport of NO_x is much more complex and the scientific data is not 100 percent conclusive; nevertheless, there is some evidence that NO_x is transported and downwind communities may be affected.

Through most of the 1980s, Congress debated whether acid rain legislation should be adopted. For example, legislation passed the Senate Committee on Environment and Public Works

---

1. See EPA, Introduction to Acid Rain in New England, http://www.epa.gov/ ne/eco/acidrain/intro.html.

in 1982, 1984, and 1987; however, none of that legislation made it much further. In 1989, Clean Air Act legislation advocated by the George H.W. Bush administration was introduced in the House of Representatives and the Senate. It included an acid rain title, which was based on an emissions trading program designed to lessen the costs of compliance. The concept of an emissions trading program was foreign to the overall "command and control" structure of the CAA, but industry generally favored the idea of attempting to use market incentives to address air pollution. The legislation introduced the concept of holding "allowances" to cover SO_2 emissions emitted by fossil-fuel-fired power plants subject to the program. In 1990, the acid rain title (Title IV) was passed as part of that year's CAA amendments.

Title IV was enacted to achieve two goals. First, it aimed to reduce SO_2 emissions by 10 million tons from 1980 levels (which were about 17.3 million tons) and to lower NO_x emissions by 2 million tons from the projected emission levels for 2000 without implementation of Title IV (i.e., approximately 8.1 million tons).[2] Second, Title IV sought to encourage, through various mechanisms, energy conservation, pollution prevention, and the use of renewable and clean alternative technologies.

The Title IV requirements were fairly controversial in that emission reductions from one industry sector—the utility industry—were the primary target.[3] The utilities wanted to avoid being required to install expensive add-on controls—namely, a flue gas desulfurization system, or "scrubber," that typically removes more than 90 percent of the SO_2 from the flue gas stream before it exits the stack. There are generally two types of scrubbers— wet scrubbers and spray dry scrubbers.[4] Scrubbers are extremely large pieces of equipment that may cost over $300 per kW of electricity. For example, installation of a scrubber on an 800 MW

---

2. See http://www.epa.gov/airmarkets/progress/ARP09_html. SO_2 emissions from coal-, gas-, and oil-fired power plants were approximately 5.7 million tons in 2009. NO_x emissions from coal-fired power plants subject to the acid rain program were 2.0 million tons in 2009.

3. Other industries with fossil-fuel-fired boilers and combined cycle combustion turbines generating electricity (e.g., certain nonexempt independent power producers) may be subject to Title IV. Fossil fuels include coal, oil, and natural gas.

4. Wet scrubbers are generally used with larger boilers and typically achieve SO_2 removal rates greater than 95 percent. Spray dry scrubbers usually achieve SO_2 removal rates on the order of 90 percent to 92 percent.

coal-fired utility boiler may cost $240 million or more.[5] Ongoing operation and maintenance of a scrubber can also be costly.

The Title IV acid rain program has been largely successful in reducing SO_2 and NO_x emissions from large coal-fired power plants and in helping improve the health of rivers, streams, lakes, and forests of the northeastern United States. In "Our Nation's Air: Status and Trends through 2008," the Environmental Protection Agency reports that in parts of the Northeast, wet sulfate deposition and wet nitrate deposition decreased more than 30 percent between 1989–1991 and 2006–2008, and SO_2 emissions from fossil-fuel-fired power plants dropped by almost 10 million tons, or about 56 percent, from 1980 levels.[6]

The Title IV acid rain program requirements apply throughout the 48 contiguous states, but the SO_2 program will largely be superfluous in the 23 northeast, mid-Atlantic, and midwestern states subject to the SO_2 program under the Cross-State Air Pollution Rule (CSAPR) that takes effect in 2012. Under CSAPR, SO_2 allowances will be allocated to fossil-fuel-fired power plants, and the affected sources will need to hold sufficient SO_2 allowances to comply with the SO_2 budgets established for each of the states under the CSAPR SO_2 program. The Title IV acid rain program will remain in effect, but because the SO_2 emission reduction levels under the state budget cap are so much more stringent under CSAPR, the cost of complying with the acid rain program will no longer be a driving force for SO_2 emission reductions in the 27 states subject to the CSAPR SO_2 program. Importantly, power plants subject to the Title IV acid rain program will continue to be subject to the SO_2 allowance requirements, NO_x emission limits, and monitoring and record-keeping provisions of the program. Deviations from the acid rain program requirements are subject to enforcement under the CAA.

During 2010 and 2011, the SO_2 Clean Air Interstate Rule (CAIR) program will be in effect until it is replaced by CSAPR. Under the CAIR SO_2 program, acid rain program allowances are used to satisfy the emission reduction requirements. Pre-2010 vintage acid rain program allowances may be used on a one for one basis (i.e., one allowance equates to 1 ton of SO_2 emissions) to

---

5. George W. Sharp, *Update: What's That Scrubber Going to Cost?* POWER MAG., Mar. 1, 2009. There are 1,000 kW in 1 MW.
6. EPA OFFICE OF AIR QUALITY PLANNING & STANDARDS, EPA-454/R-09-002, OUR NATION'S AIR: STATUS AND TRENDS THROUGH 2008, at 35 (Feb. 2010).

meet CAIR SO$_2$ allowance surrender requirements. Acid rain program allowances with a vintage of 2010 and 2011 are retired on a two for one basis (i.e., two allowances equates to 1 ton of SO$_2$ emissions.) The CAIR SO$_2$ and NO$_x$ programs were vacated by the U.S. Court of Appeals for the D.C. Circuit in July 2008, and later temporarily reinstated in order to preserve the environmental benefits of the programs while EPA addressed some of the fundamental flaws in the rule identified in the court's decision.[7]

In July 2011, EPA issued the final CSAPR, and the annual SO$_2$ and NO$_x$ programs under the rule will replace CAIR starting January 1, 2012. Once implemented, CSAPR should spur further reductions in NO$_x$ and SO$_2$ emissions from fossil-fuel-fired power plants, and will be more stringent than the current acid rain program restrictions. As a result, the effectiveness of the acid rain control program in the 23 northeast, mid-Atlantic, and midwestern states subject to the annual CSAPR SO$_2$ and NO$_x$ limitations will likely be superseded by the new rule's emission reduction requirements. Nevertheless, the acid rain program will remain in effect for the CSAPR states, and a failure to comply will carry enforcement risks.

9.1   Applicability

Title IV of the Clean Air Act Amendments of 1990 requires all "affected units"—that is, fossil-fuel-fired electric generating units that produce electricity for sale—to obtain acid rain permits; to hold sufficient allowances to cover their SO$_2$ emissions (which started in 1995 for Phase I units and 2000 for Phase II units); to install a continuous emissions monitoring system (CEMS) meeting the Title IV requirements; and to comply with other monitoring and record-keeping provisions. Title IV specifically lists certain major utility units (Phase I units) that were required to meet the acid rain requirements by January 1, 1995. Phase II units were required to comply with the SO$_2$ requirements by January 1, 2000. An initial list of Phase I and Phase II affected units with corresponding SO$_2$ allowance allocations was provided in EPA's 1993 allowance allocation rules and the 1998 allowance reallocation

---

7. North Carolina v. EPA, 531 F.3d 896 (D.C. Cir. 2008) (per curiam), *on reh'g in part*, 550 F.3d 1176 (D.C. Cir. 2008); *see* discussion in section 4.8.5.

rule.[8] Notably, the Title IV requirements apply only to sources located in the contiguous 48 states and the District of Columbia.

In general, the acid rain program is applicable to existing and new "utility units" serving a generator with a nameplate capacity of greater than 25 megawatts (MW) of electricity.[9] A *utility unit* is a fossil-fueled-fired combustion device, such as a boiler or a combined cycle combustion turbine, serving a generator that produces electricity for sale, whether wholesale or retail. As set forth in 40 C.F.R. § 72.2, a unit may be affected by the acid rain regulations only if it meets the following three conditions:

1. It is a combustion device.
2. It is fossil-fuel-fired (i.e., it combusts any amount of fossil fuel, no matter how small).
3. It supplies electricity for sale or supplies a generator that supplies electricity for sale.

Certain types of utility units, including some industrial boilers, may be exempt or grandfathered from meeting the acid rain requirements. The following paragraphs briefly explain the criteria for qualifying as an exempt or grandfathered unit, and also discuss EPA's position on the continuing requirements that must be met to maintain such status and avoid regulation under the acid rain program.

There are two types of exempt utility units: small new units burning clean fuels, and retired units.[10] A small new unit is exempt if it commenced commercial operation on or after November 15, 1990; it serves a generator(s) with a total nameplate capacity of 25 MW or less; and it combusts "clean" fossil fuels with a sulfur content of 0.05 percent or less.[11] A retired unit may be granted an exemption if it is retired before it needs to obtain a Phase II acid rain permit.[12] To be exempted, a company must submit a written application to EPA requesting an exemption.

---

8. 58 Fed. Reg. 3,687 (Jan. 11, 1993); 58 Fed. Reg. 15,634 (Mar. 23, 1993); 63 Fed. Reg. 51,706 (Sept. 28, 1998) (codified at 40 C.F.R. § 73.10).

9. Utility units subjected to the acid rain program are defined as *affected units,* and an "affected source" may contain one or more affected units. 40 C.F.R. § 72.2.

10. 40 C.F.R. §§ 72.7 and 72.8.

11. 40 C.F.R. § 72.7(a).

12. 40 C.F.R. § 72.8.

Six types of electricity generating units are not affected by the regulations under certain conditions, and qualify as grandfathered units. These include the following:

- existing simple combustion turbines under 40 C.F.R. § 72.6(b)(1)
- existing small units under 40 C.F.R. § 72.6(b)(2)
- cogenerators meeting the requirements of 40 C.F.R. § 72.6(b)(4)
- qualifying facilities (QFs) meeting the requirements of 40 C.F.R. § 72.6(b)(5)
- independent power production (IPP) facilities meeting the requirements of 40 C.F.R. § 72.6(b)(6)
- solid waste incinerators under 40 C.F.R. § 72.6(b)(7)

To be grandfathered, units needed to meet certain threshold requirements as of November 15, 1990. For example, to be a grandfathered QF or IPP, the facility must have had one or more qualifying power purchase agreements to sell at least 15 percent of its total net output as of November 15, 1990.[13] If a unit is grandfathered under more than one provision, it will remain grandfathered until it loses this status for all appropriate categories (e.g., a unit grandfathered as both as an IPP and a QF will remain grandfathered until it loses both its IPP and QF status). EPA does not routinely require a grandfathered unit to submit proof of its status; however, it may be required to submit such documentation if requested.

The issue of retaining grandfathered status is not always simple. For example, almost all of the cogeneration and IPP plants that had contracts in place as of November 15, 1990, have been built and are exempt; however, some contracts are expiring and/or being modified, so a question arises as to whether these units are now subject to Title IV. EPA has interpreted Congress's intent in crafting the grandfathering provisions for IPPs and QFs as providing relief from compliance costs, as these entities had already entered fixed-price, long-term contracts to provide power and those contracts presumably do not provide an opportunity for passing on to the purchaser the cost of acid rain emission controls (or the cost of allowances). As a result, EPA has concluded that if the project has an opportunity to pass through the costs of

---

13. 40 C.F.R. §§ 72.6(b)(5)(i) and 72.6(b)(6)(i).

compliance with the acid rain program, then the unit will lose its grandfathered status. Certain modifications to existing power sales contracts, such as pricing structure changes, may also result in the loss of grandfathered status. Again, once the exempt or grandfathered status is lost, it is incumbent upon the unit to comply with the acid rain program or risk penalties for failure to meet those requirements. As of 2011, EPA had issued over 40 acid rain program applicability determinations.[14]

9.2 SO$_2$ Allowance Trading

Title IV of the 1990 amendments to the CAA creates a mechanism to address the transport and dispersion of acid rain precursors (SO$_2$ and NO$_x$) on a national scale. The program mandates the nationwide reduction of emissions of acid rain precursors from certain fossil-fuel-fired combustion devices producing electricity for sale. The centerpiece of the acid rain program is its market-based emissions trading system, which involves a fixed number of "allowances"; each allowance authorizes the emission of one ton of SO$_2$ during a particular year.

Most utilities that use boilers or combined cycle combustion turbines to operate generators larger than 25 megawatts are allocated allowances based on their past base-year fuel consumption and the Title IV overall emission limits. Newer utilities that began operation after December 31, 1995, were not allocated any allowances, so they must purchase them either from EPA or other sources. An affected source must have allowances that equal or exceed its SO$_2$ emissions. However, use of allowances does not entitle a source to release SO$_2$ in quantities that cause a violation of the National Ambient Air Quality Standards.[15] An allowance can be used by an affected source or it can be sold to others or traded among plants within a particular company. Such transfers require written notice to EPA and a formal recordation. Beginning in the year 2000, total allowances are capped at approximately 8.9 million tons with an additional 50,000 tons of SO$_2$ allow-

---

14. EPA maintains a database of acid rain applicability determinations, available at http://www.epa.gov/airmarkt/progsregs/arp/determination.html.
15. CAA § 403(f); 42 U.S.C. § 7651b(f).

ances (not subject to the cap) being allocated on a pro rata basis among certain Phase I units.[16]

The SO$_2$ requirements of Title IV are divided into two phases. By January 1, 1995, the 110 plants listed in Title IV were required to meet the emission reduction requirements of CAA section 404 or hold allowances sufficient to cover the plant's SO$_2$ emissions. Phase I allowance allocations were based on a formula equivalent to an SO$_2$ emissions rate of 2.5 pounds per million Btu (lbs/MMBtu) multiplied by the applicable unit's baseline fuel consumption, which is the average fuel used in the years 1985 to 1987.[17] Phase I units are large units capable of generating 100 megawatts of electricity or more that have SO$_2$ emission rates over 2.5 lbs/MMBtu. The Phase I requirements had to be met by January 1, 1995, but certain provisions allowed units to extend the compliance date, if scrubbers were installed.[18]

Phase II of the program began on January 1, 2000, and it is generally implemented by states in conjunction with the Title V operating permit program. Under Phase II, SO$_2$ allowance allocations are based on meeting a 1.2 lbs/MMBtu SO$_2$ emission rate multiplied by the plant's baseline fuel use.[19] Cleaner plants generally were provided with 20 percent more allowances during 2000 to 2009 (Phase II bonus allowances) than they would have received based on their baseline consumption.[20] The Phase II affected units are listed in 40 C.F.R. § 73.10.

The 1990 amendments set up EPA reserves of SO$_2$ allowances (approximately 2.8 percent of the total 8.9 million allowances) that are eligible for distribution. The reserves include (1) a reserve for installing qualifying control technology during Phase I; (2) a reserve for emission reduction incentives for renewable energy generation or conservation measures (300,000 annual bonus allowances); and (3) an annual EPA auction reserve of 150,000 allowances during Phase I and 250,000 during Phase II (to assure allowances are available for new entrants).[21] Extra allowances are also available for utilities that replace boilers with new, cleaner, and more efficient technologies. EPA's Clean Air Markets division

---

16. CAA § 403(a) and 405(a); 42 U.S.C. § 7651b(a) and 7651d(a).
17. CAA § 404(e); 42 U.S.C. § 7651c(e). The term "baseline" is defined in CAA § 402(4); 42 U.S.C. § 7651a(4).
18. CAA § 404(d); 42 U.S.C. § 7651c(d).
19. CAA § 405; 42 U.S.C. § 7651d.
20. CAA § 405(a)(2); 42 U.S.C. § 7651d(a)(2).
21. 40 C.F.R. §§ 73.25, 73.26, and 73.27.

tracks the SO_2 allowances of each affected unit.[22] Annual allocations of SO_2 allowances are credited to each unit account, and
companies must notify EPA of any SO_2 allowance transfers so that
their accounts can be credited or debited. At the end of each year,
there is a 60-day grace period during which additional SO_2 allowances may be bought and sold to "true up" the account. Companies may also set up separate "general" accounts for holding SO_2
allowances for trading or company-wide transfers.

All Title IV affected units are required to install a CEMS that
meets specific requirements (and the Title IV CEMS rule generally
imposes more stringent monitoring requirements than the CEMS
provisions for certain New Source Performance Standards).[23]
The CEMS is used to determine the amount of SO_2 emitted by an
affected unit. If a CEMS is not available, the unit is presumed to be
uncontrolled for that period, and there are data substitution provisions for missing data periods.[24] During missing data periods, SO_2
emissions may be artificially inflated, which could trigger an excess
emission penalty. An alternative emission monitoring system may
be installed, but it generally must meet the same precision, reli-
ability, and accessibility requirements for acid rain CEMS.[25]

An affected unit that emits in excess of its allowances or emission limits must pay an "excess emissions penalty" of $2,000 per
ton adjusted each year for inflation ($3,464 in 2010).[26] Excess
emissions must also be offset by an equal tonnage reduction in
the following calendar year.

9.3 Opt-In Program

Title IV also sets up a mechanism for opting into the acid rain program to join the allowance system and become an affected unit.[27]
In Phase I, approximately 180 units opted in to the program. The
opt-in program offers a combustion source a financial incentive to
voluntarily reduce its emissions: namely, it will be allocated allowances that it can sell. All nonaffected fossil-fuel-fired units are eli-

---

22. 40 C.F.R. § 73.30.
23. 40 C.F.R. § 75.11.
24. 40 C.F.R. §§ 75.30–75.39.
25. 40 C.F.R. §§ 75.40–75.48.
26. CAA § 411(a); 42 U.S.C. § 7651j(a); 74 Fed. Reg. 50,962 (Oct. 2, 2009).
27. 40 C.F.R. pt. 74.

gible to opt in. Opt-in units are not subject to the Title IV NO_x requirements discussed in section 9.4, but opt-in units must generally comply with all the other Title IV requirements, including the requirement to install a CEMS and obtain an acid rain permit. The EPA regulations set forth a separate opt-in form and a special opt-in permit.[28] Opt-in sources may withdraw from the acid rain program under certain conditions; as a result, all current-year and subsequent-year SO_2 allowances must be surrendered.

9.4   Title IV NO_x Requirements

The Title IV NO_x requirements apply only to coal-fired utility units. The EPA rules define a *coal-fired utility unit* as one in which coal combustion exceeds 50 percent of its annual heat input.[29] Although the Title IV NO_x requirements establish different emission limits for different types of boilers, they generally restrict EPA to requiring technology no more stringent than "low NO_x burner" technology or other technology that is comparable in cost to low NO_x burner technology.

The NO_x emission limits for boilers are divided into two phases. The Phase I rules set specific annual emission limits, effective January 1, 1996, for tangentially fired boilers and dry bottom wall-fired boilers.[30] These boilers are referred to as *Group 1 boilers*. The Phase I standards ended in 1999 and were replaced with the Phase II rules for Group 1 boilers.[31] On December 19, 1996, EPA promulgated NO_x standards for Phase II coal-fired utility units; these units needed to meet the NO_x standards starting January 1, 2000.[32] In this rule, EPA determined that more effective low NO_x burner technology is available, and thus set more stringent limits for Group 1 boilers (i.e., tangentially fired and dry bottom wall-fired boilers).[33]

In the December 1996 rule, EPA also promulgated emission limits for Group 2 boilers (i.e., wet bottom wall-fired boilers,

---

28.   40 C.F.R. § 74.14.
29.   40 C.F.R. § 76.2.
30.   40 C.F.R. § 76.5.
31.   Group 1 boilers that complied with the Phase I emission limit by January 1, 1997, were exempt from the Phase II NO_x limits until 2008.
32.   61 Fed. Reg. 67,112 (Dec. 19, 1996) (codified at 40 C.F.R. §§ 76 *et seq.*).
33.   40 C.F.R. § 76.7.

cyclone boilers, boilers using cell burner technology, vertically fired boilers, arch-fired boilers, and other non–Group 1 boilers), which also went into effect on January 1, 2000.[34] The limits for these boilers must be based on "the best system of continuous emission reduction" that is comparable in cost to the controls required for Group 1 boilers. Industry challenged the Group 2 boiler standards; however, the U.S. Court of Appeals for the D.C. Circuit upheld these standards in *Appalachian Power Co. v. EPA*.[35] The CAA does allow EPA (or for Phase II, state permitting authorities) to set a less stringent emission limit for an individual unit where there is a showing that the unit cannot meet the emission limits established by EPA.[36] To be eligible for an alternative emission limit, the owner/operator must demonstrate that the appropriate control equipment has been installed and operated for at least three months and that the unit could not have otherwise met the limit.[37] Title IV also allows an owner/operator of two or more units, subject to the NO_x limits, to petition for an alternative NO_x averaging plan.[38] The NO_x averaging plan essentially sets up a "bubble" over two or more units. An averaging plan gives a company flexibility to "overcontrol" certain units to compensate for undercontrolled emissions from other units in a company's fleet. The averaging plan must ensure that the Btu-weighted annual average emission rate for all the units is less than or equal to the annual average rate that the group or units would have had if each unit emitted at its individual applicable rate.[39]

9.5 Acid Rain Permits

In 1993, EPA promulgated a set of "core rules" for the acid rain program that included the requirements for acid rain permits, the allowance trading system, the monitoring and record-keeping requirements, and the enforcement and administrative appeal

---

34. 40 C.F.R. § 76.6.
35. 135 F.3d 791 (D.C. Cir. 1998).
36. CAA § 407(d); 42 U.S.C. § 7651f(d).
37. 40 C.F.R. § 76.10.
38. CAA § 407(e); 42 U.S.C. § 7651f(e).
39. 40 C.F.R. § 76.11.

provisions.[40] These core rules are codified at 40 C.F.R. parts 72, 73, 75, 77, and 78. Title IV sources are required to submit acid rain permit applications and compliance plans. The compliance plans specify the compliance options that the source will use. Unless a source is going to qualify for either a Phase I or Phase II extension plan or designate some other method of compliance with the statute (e.g., NO_x alternative emission limit), generally all that is required is a simple statement that the source will hold enough allowances to cover its SO_2 emissions and will meet any applicable NO_x emission limit.[41]

Title IV permits are good for five years, and Phase I and Phase II permits for existing units should already have been issued.[42] EPA has created a standard, fairly straightforward form to use for both the acid rain permit and compliance plan.[43]

Most states have incorporated the Title IV acid rain permit into the Title V operating permit (discussed in chapter 10). In general, EPA issued the Phase I permits, and many Phase II permits were issued by the applicable state permitting agencies with EPA-approved Title V operating permit programs. Nevertheless, to the extent that a state Title V permit program was not approved prior to July 1, 1996, EPA was required to issue the Phase II permits.[44] According to EPA, all states now have approved or conditionally approved Title V operating permit programs.

---

40. 58 Fed. Reg. 3590–766 (Jan. 11, 1993); General Provisions, *id.* at 3590 (codified at 40 C.F.R. §§ 72.1–72.13); Permits Regulation, *id.* at 3650 (codified at 40 C.F.R. §§ 72.30 *et seq.*); Sulfur Dioxide Allowance System, *id.* at 3687 (codified at 40 C.F.R. pt. 73); Continuous Emission Monitoring, *id.* at 3701 (codified at 40 C.F.R. pt. 75); Excess Emissions, *id.* at 3757 (codified at 40 C.F.R. pt. 77); and Appeal Procedures, *id.* at 3760 (codified at 40 C.F.R. pt. 78).

41. Phase I and II extension plan requirements are set forth at 40 C.F.R. §§ 72.42 and 72.44.

42. Phase II applications for existing units were due by January 1, 1996, with respect to SO_2 requirements and January 1, 1998, with respect to NO_x compliance.

43. The forms are available to download from EPA Clean Air Markets, Forms, http://www.epa.gov/airmarkt/business/forms.html#arp.

44. CAA § 408(d); 42 U.S.C. § 7651g(d).

10 Title V Operating Permits

In one fell swoop, the Clean Air Act Amendments of 1990 brought thousands of facilities into the federal air permitting scheme. Until the 1990 amendments under the CAA, sources were only required to obtain Prevention of Significant Deterioration/New Source Review (PSD/NSR) permits, providing their potential emissions were high enough to trigger this requirement. In 1990, Congress determined that virtually every source that emits pollutants regulated by the CAA should obtain an "operating permit" to continue operations. Prior to 1990, many states had their own individual state operating permit programs and the requirements often varied widely from state to state. Title V directs states to implement minimum operating permit program requirements, which are designed to provide a certain degree of standardization among the states.[1]

Title V of the CAA, added by Title V of the 1990 amendments, charges the Environmental Protection Agency with promulgating regulations to guide the development of individual state operating permit programs that, once approved by the agency, will carry out this mandate. In July 1992, EPA issued its final regulations to implement the Title V operating permit program—the part 70 requirements.[2] There are separate federal operating permit regulations that will be administered by EPA if a state permitting authority is not authorized to implement the part 70 program.[3] The part 71 requirements apply to most major emission sources in

---

1. For purposes of this chapter, the term *state* also generally encompasses territorial and local air permitting authorities. For example, in California there are 35 separate local air permitting authorities and no state-level air permitting agency that issues air permits. In addition, U.S. territories like the U.S. Virgin Islands implement their own Title V operating permit program.
2. 57 Fed. Reg. 32,250 (July 21, 1992) (codified at 40 C.F.R. pt. 70).
3. 61 Fed. Reg. 34,228 (July 1, 1996) (codified at 40 C.F.R. pt. 71).

Indian country and in some U.S. territories, such as Guam and the Northern Marianas.[4]

There were initially several delays in getting the Title V program started, and EPA's final rule was challenged by both industry and environmental groups.[5] One of the major issues in dispute concerned the provisions for revising permits and, particularly, whether public review and comment are required for minor permit revisions. In response to the rule's challenge, EPA negotiated with the interested parties on potential changes to the Title V program, but little consensus was achieved. In 1994 and in 1995, EPA proposed changes to the Title V rule, but it ultimately backed away from these proposals in the wake of strong criticism from the regulated community.[6] Some of the issues raised in *Clean Air Implementation Project v. EPA* were largely resolved in the mid-1990's through the issuance of EPA guidance memoranda.[7]

10.1   Overview of the Title V Program

Congress envisioned that a Title V operating permit would bring together all applicable federally required and/or federally approved air emission limitations, work practice standards, monitoring, record-keeping, and reporting requirements for a facility into one document. As discussed later in this chapter, the Title V operating permit rules (i.e., 40 C.F.R. parts 70 and 71) define these federally enforceable requirements as "applicable requirements." The purpose of the program is not to create new substantive federal requirements but to facilitate source compliance and enforcement by marshaling all of a facility's applicable federal requirements in one document. By including these federal requirements in a single permit, it is now much easier for EPA,

---

4. As of 2007, about 110 sources in Indian country needed Title V permits. *See* EPA Operating Permits, Part 71 Permits, http://www.epa.gov/oaqps001/permits/part71.html. Additional information on EPA's Title V permitting program for Indian country can be found at EPA Operating Permits, Title V Permitting in Indian Country, http://www.epa.gov/oaqps001/permits/indperm.html.

5. Clean Air Implementation Project v. EPA, No. 92-1303 (D.C. Cir. filed July 21, 1992) (Various petitions for review of the final rule were consolidated under No. 92-1303.).

6. 59 Fed. Reg. 44,460 (Aug. 29, 1994); 60 Fed. Reg. 45,530 (Aug. 31, 1995).

7. *See* Lydia N. Wegman, Deputy Dir. of EPA Office of Air Quality Planning & Standards, to EPA Reg'l Air Dirs., White Paper for Streamlined Development of Part 70 Permit Applications (July 10, 1995); EPA Office of Air Quality Planning & Standards, White Paper Number 2 for Improved Implementation of the Part 70 Operating Permits Program (Mar. 5, 1996).

state agencies, and citizen groups to identify all the applicable regulatory limits that apply to a facility; consequently, it also makes enforcement much easier. In addition, Title V authorizes the imposition of permit fees. Permit fees provide an incentive for states to get the operating permit program up and running. The federal regulations require permit fees to be not less than $25 per ton of each regulated pollutant.[8] Congress included the fee requirement largely to make the program self-sustaining.

EPA has reported that is has approved Title V programs for all 113 state, territorial, and local permitting authorities, and as of 2011, virtually all existing plants that meet the Title V applicability requirements have been issued final permits. Many existing major sources are on their first or second renewal applications, but it often takes the permitting agencies a year or more to issue permit renewals. EPA reports that each year approximately 100 new sources are required to obtain a Title V permit, and about 3,000 sources file applications for permit renewals.[9]

As noted earlier, EPA's July 1992 part 70 regulations prescribe the minimum requirements for state operating permit programs. States may go beyond the minimum Title V program requirements and impose additional requirements or incorporate state-specific standards. Thus, in addition to the required federally enforceable requirements, a Title V permit may include state-only enforceable provisions as well. Each state, territory, or local permitting jurisdiction currently has either full approval or interim approval from EPA to implement the Title V program, but there are some jurisdictions where the federal part 71 program currently applies: namely, most Indian lands and certain U.S. territories.[10] In these federal jurisdictions, EPA is the Title V permitting authority and operating permits will be issued pursuant to the 40 C.F.R. part 71 regulations. The part 71 standards generally mirror the requirements of part 70. In 1998, EPA promulgated a rule authorizing Indian tribes to develop and seek approval of their own Title V operating permit programs.[11] A few tribal authorities have sought EPA approval to implement Title V programs covering major air emission sources

---

8. CAA § 502(b)(3)(B); 42 U.S.C. § 7661a(b)(3)(B).
9. *See* EPA Operating Permits, Issuance Status, http://www.epa.gov/oaqps001/permits/issuestatus.html.
10. The federal operating permit program would also potentially apply when a state does not submit an approvable program or EPA withdraws its approval of a state program because it is not adequately administered and enforced.
11. 63 Fed. Reg. 7253 (Feb. 12, 1998).

on Indian lands.[12] For Indian lands where the applicable Indian tribe does not seek to implement its own part 70 program, EPA's part 71 operating permit rule will continue to apply.

Additional background information and EPA guidance on the Title V operating permit program is available at http://www.epa.gov/oar/oaqps/permits/index.html.

10.2   Title V Applicability

The operating permit system is intended to be implemented through individual state programs that meet minimum criteria and are approved by EPA. Section 502(a) of the CAA requires an operating permit for all "major" sources of air contaminants, as well as sources subject to New Source Performance Standard (NSPS) provisions, hazardous air pollutants maximum achievable control technology (HAP MACT) requirements, the Title IV acid rain provisions, the PSD/NSR program, and any other source in a category designated by EPA. In general, "major" sources include sources that emit 100 tons per year of a regulated pollutant, unless a lower threshold exists (e.g., certain ozone nonattainment areas may have thresholds of 50, 25, or 10 tons per year). In addition, sources emitting 10 tons per year of a HAP or 25 tons of any combination of HAPs are "major" sources. EPA's part 70 applicability provisions are extremely expansive and could include many minor stationary sources, that is, sources with emissions below the "major" source trigger, but that are subject to NSPS requirements. Nevertheless, EPA has generally deferred Title V regulation of these nonmajor sources to a later date.

Title V applicability is based on a source's *potential to emit*, considering controls, not on its actual emissions. This is the same definition used under the NSPS, the National Emissions Standards for Hazardous Air Pollutants (NESHAP), and the PSD/NSR programs. In other words, even though a source normally shuts down for two weeks of each year for maintenance, EPA calculates its potential to emit based on operation for every day of the year (i.e., at its maximum capability to emit an air pollutant under its physical and operational design). Sources can take federally enforceable limits to stay below the applicability triggers, and such

---

12. *See, e.g.,* Clean Air Act Proposed Interim Approval of the Title V Operating Permits Program; South Ute Indian Tribe, 76 Fed. Reg. 12,926 (Mar. 9, 2011).

resources are called "synthetic minors." Most states have established "synthetic minor" regulations that offer sources the opportunity to taken an enforceable emissions cap in a state operating permit or other enforceable document, to avoid the need for a Title V permit altogether. EPA has published guidance on the different types of options states may use to make such emission caps federally enforceable.[13] Sources considering this option should carefully evaluate whether "synthetic minor" status will unduly restrict operations or hamper future expansions.

Historically, EPA has only recognized controls that are federally enforceable in order to avoid triggering a CAA requirement. However, the D.C. Circuit, has, in several cases, determined that "effective" state and local controls should also be credited.[14] In response to these decisions, EPA issued a guidance document stating that, for the time being, it will recognize state and local limits on a source's potential to emit that are "legally and practicably enforceable."[15] As of 2011, EPA has not taken any further action to define "effective" state and local controls that can be credited in achieving synthetic minor status.

10.3   Applicable Requirements

As noted earlier, Title V operating permits are required to contain all of a source's "applicable requirements" under the CAA.[16] The term *applicable requirement* is defined in the Title V regulations as any emission limit, standard, control practice, and other operating requirements that apply to the source pursuant to specific provisions

---

13. 54 Fed. Reg. 27,274 (June 28, 1989); *see also* EPA Office of Enforcement & Compliance Monitoring & Office of Air Quality Planning & Standards, Guidance on Limiting Potential to Emit in New Source Permitting (June 13, 1989); EPA Office of Air Quality Planning & Standards, Options for Limiting the Potential to Emit (PTE) of a Stationary Source Under Section 112 and Title V of the Clean Air Act (Jan. 25, 1995).

14. *See* Nat'l Mining Ass'n v. EPA, 59 F.3d 1351 (D.C. Cir. 1995) (D.C. Circuit remanded the federal enforceability requirement of EPA's definition of *potential to emit* in the CAA section 112 air toxics program); Chem. Mfrs. Ass'n v. EPA, 70 F.3d 637 (D.C. Cir. 1995) (D.C. Circuit vacated the federal enforceability requirement of the "potential to emit" definition in the PSD/NSR regulations); Clean Air Implementation Project v. EPA, No. 96-1224, 1996 WL 393118 (D.C. Cir. June 28, 1996) (The D.C. Circuit vacated EPA's "potential to emit" definition used in the Title V operating permit program).

15. EPA Office of Air Quality Planning & Standards, Release of Interim Policy on Federal Enforceability of Limitations on Potential to Emit (Jan. 22, 1996).

16. 40 C.F.R. § 70.3(c).

of the CAA or federally approved requirements of a state implementation plan (SIP).[17] The permits must also incorporate each source's plan for achieving compliance with applicable requirements and must specify its monitoring, reporting, and record-keeping responsibilities. For example, for a pulp and paper mill, the Title V permit would likely contain applicable NSPS provisions, any relevant PSD/NSR permit requirements, and HAP MACT standards as well as other emission limits (e.g., opacity limits) set forth in the applicable SIP.

The CAA was amended in 1990 to include two provisions—sections 504(b) and 114(a)(3)—designed to ensure that sufficient monitoring and reporting requirements are included in Title V permits, to assure compliance with CAA requirements. First, CAA section 504(b) authorizes the EPA administrator to prescribe by rule the "procedures and methods for determining compliance and for monitoring and analysis of pollutants."[18] If an applicable limit or standard does not require monitoring to determine compliance, then the EPA rules require that "periodic monitoring sufficient to yield reliable data" to determine compliance be incorporated in the permit.[19] EPA took this approach to ensure that any "gaps" in monitoring will be addressed, and it issued a guidance document specifying that states should review all applicable standards on a pollutant-by-pollutant basis and upgrade monitoring requirements accordingly. Several industry groups challenged this guidance document on the theory that EPA was imposing new requirements without going through formal notice and comment procedures. The U.S. Court of Appeals for the D.C. Circuit agreed and held that the periodic monitoring guidance was invalid.[20] Further, the court held that EPA's Title V regulations provide that periodic monitoring may be used only as a "gap filler" where the underlying standard contains a one-time compliance test or does not provide for testing or monitoring, or specifies no monitoring frequency. As of 2011, EPA had not yet issued any further guidance to clarify when "gap filler" periodic monitoring may be incorporated into a Title V permit.

Second, CAA section 114(a)(3) allows EPA to require "enhanced monitoring" for major stationary sources. In response, EPA adopted a rule requiring compliance assurance monitoring (CAM) for certain major sources. As a threshold matter, for the

17. 40 C.F.R. § 70.2.
18. CAA § 504(b); 42 U.S.C. § 7661c(b).
19. 40 C.F.R. § 70.6(a)(3).
20. *See* Appalachian Power Co. v. EPA, 208 F.3d 1015 (D.C. Cir. 2000).

CAM rule (40 C.F.R. part 64) to apply, a pollutant-specific emissions unit must meet the following three criteria:

1. The unit must be subject to an emissions limit for the applicable regulated air pollutant (or a surrogate of that pollutant).
2. The unit must use a control device to achieve compliance.
3. The unit must have a precontrol potential to emit that is equal to or greater than the major source cutoff levels.[21]

The preamble to the CAM rule explains that each piece of equipment (e.g., a coal-fired boiler) would be separately classified as a pollutant-specific emissions unit for a host of pollutants.[22] For example, a coal-fired boiler would be viewed as a pollutant-specific emission unit for NO_x, SO_2, VOCs, PM_{10}, and CO. The CAM rule generally requires additional monitoring of indicator parameters, such as pressure drop on a baghouse (i.e., a particulate matter collection device), to help determine whether a piece of equipment is in compliance with the applicable emission standards.

10.4 Permit Applications

The permit application will serve as the foundation of the final Title V permit. Generally, whatever is listed in the application will likely end up in the Title V permit. Thus, if a pollutant is not subject to an applicable requirement, there is no need to provide the information unless the state specifically requests it. Because of the importance of preparing a complete permit application, EPA has issued several different guidance documents to aid the regulated community and the state permitting agencies.[23] The EPA Title V White Paper guidance documents are intended to help streamline

---

21. 40 C.F.R. § 64.2(a).

22. 62 Fed. Reg. 54,900, 54,911 (Oct. 22, 1997).

23. Lydia N. Wegman, Deputy Dir. of EPA Office of Air Quality Planning & Standards to EPA Reg'l Air Dirs., White Paper for Stream-lined Development of Part 70 Permit Applications (July 10, 1995); EPA Office of Air Quality Planning & Standards, White Paper Number 2 for Improved Implementation of the Part 70 Operating Permits Program (Mar. 5, 1996); EPA Office of Air Quality Planning & Standards, Design of Flexible Permits—Operating Permits Program White Paper Number 3 (Draft) (Aug. 7, 2000).

permit applications and offer options for clarifying permit terms when multiple applicable requirements apply to the same piece of equipment. The following briefly summarizes some of the timing concerns and the key components of a complete application.

10.4.1   Timing

A source requiring an operating permit must submit a formal application to the permitting authority no later than 12 months after the source becomes subject to the program or on such earlier date as prescribed by the permitting authority.[24] Generally, states have established specific dates for existing sources to apply for Title V permits. New sources typically must file an application within 12 months of commencing operations. EPA regulations provide that no source may operate after the time it is required to submit an application, except in compliance with an operating permit already issued. In other words, the source will be in violation of the CAA if it continues to operate after missing its permit application deadline.

EPA's regulations provide that a permitting agency has 18 months to process an application, but in practice, it has generally taken states much longer to process applications. EPA estimated that over 20,000 sources were initially required to have Title V operating permits, and the agency projects that approximately 100 new sources a year are required to obtain a Title V permit.[25]

10.4.2   Key Components

The permit application should clearly identify all of the applicable requirements. If an apparently relevant federal requirement does not apply, the application should state this fact so that the statement may be included in the final permit. This is important if the source is to qualify for a permit shield, as explained in section 10.4.3. Applicable federal requirements should be listed in a sep-

---

24.   40 C.F.R. § 70.5(a).
25.   U.S. GEN. ACCOUNTING OFFICE, GAO/RCED-00-72, REPORT TO THE CHAIRMAN, SUBCOMM. ON CLEAN AIR, WETLANDS, PRIVATE PROP., & NUCLEAR SAFETY, COMM. ON ENV'T & PUB. WORKS, U.S. SENATE, STATUS OF IMPLEMENTATION AND ISSUES OF THE CLEAN AIR ACT AMENDMENT THROUGH 1990 (Apr. 2000); *see also* EPA Operating Permits, Issuance Status, http://www.epa.gov/oaqps001/permits/issuestatus.html.

arate "federally enforceable" section. Non-federally enforceable state emission standards, to the extent included in the Title V permit, should be identified as state-only enforceable. The distinction between state enforceable and federally enforceable is significant because citizen suits generally may be filed only to enforce federal requirements, but not state requirements.

EPA guidance also provides that the emissions units and emissions-related information may be identified in broad, general terms if such information is sufficient to identify the applicable requirements, determine compliance, and calculate a permit fee. EPA guidance also provides that "trivial" activities need not be listed in the application; however, all "insignificant" activities (as defined in the applicable states' Title V regulations) should be listed in the application, though they typically will not be subject to any specific emission limitations. Once a piece of equipment qualifies a plant as a major source, then other pieces of equipment emitting minor amounts of air pollutants will have to be included in the permit application, even if only for permit fee determinations.

In preparing an application, companies may propose provisions designed to provide a facility with some operational flexibility. For example, an application may include alternative operating scenarios. *Operating scenarios* are descriptions of alternative ways in which a specific plant might run. Each alternative operating scenario would have a different emissions profile and would need to be included in the final permit. For instance, a paper mill may alternate between producing different grades of paper, which might entail the use of different chemicals in the papermaking process and change the amount of air pollutants emitted from the plant. Title V operating permits generally prohibit operating scenarios that are not described in the permit. In the preceding example, if an alternative scenario is not in the permit, then the paper mill must obtain a permit amendment before it can make the other product. If both scenarios are in the approved permit, the company can generally make the change immediately after notifying the permitting authority.

Most states also allow and encourage the applicant to prepare a draft permit or summary of requested terms and conditions to be included with the application. Some permit terms that might be incorporated include (1) preapproved operational changes (e.g., substitution of raw materials such as switching the types of paints used in a paint spray booth) that may allow the company to make certain future operational changes merely by filing a notice, instead of triggering a permit revision pursuant to Title V; or (2) an emissions cap designed to keep a source below a certain emission level and thus avoid certain requirements (e.g., a limit on HAP emissions below the "major" source designation).

All permit applications must be accompanied by a compliance plan. This requirement will particularly affect sources that are out of compliance, because the source's plan must include a federally enforceable schedule for meeting the applicable requirements. Sources required to have enhanced monitoring must also submit an enhanced monitoring protocol with the application. Perhaps most importantly, the application must be certified as to its truth and accuracy by a responsible official.[26] Submission of inaccurate data or failure to identify emission sources could subject the plant and the responsible official to civil and criminal penalties.

10.4.3   Complete Applications

Timely submission of an application that is deemed "complete" by the permitting authority will allow the permit applicant to continue to operate under an "application shield." In other words, a major source can operate without a Title V permit so long as its application was submitted on time and is complete, and the source submits any supplemental information requested by the state. EPA's rules require states to adopt criteria and procedures for determining when an application is "complete."[27] At a minimum, to be deemed complete, an application must contain (1) information that identifies a source; (2) identification of the requirements that apply to the source (the applicable requirements); (3) a statement of the current compliance status of the source; (4) the source's intended operating regimes and emissions levels; (5) a completed standard application form (or forms); (6) a compliance plan (including a compliance schedule); and (7) a certification of the truth, accuracy, and completeness of the information, sworn to by a responsible official after making a reasonable inquiry.

---

26. 40 C.F.R. § 70.2 defines "responsible official" and identifies those individuals who may sign certification on behalf of corporations, partnerships, and public agencies.

27. 40 C.F.R. §§ 70.5(a)(2) and (c).

The application shield allows a source to operate until the final permit is issued. The state permitting agency has 60 days to determine whether the application is complete; otherwise, the application is automatically deemed complete.

10.5 Permit Terms and Conditions

Each Title V permit is required to include all federally applicable emission limitations and work practice standards, and must specify the legal authority for such limit or standard.[28] Permits also must incorporate monitoring, record-keeping, and reporting requirements specified by the underlying applicable requirements.[29] If more than one monitoring or testing requirement applies, the permitting authority may specify one set of streamlined requirements. In addition, as noted earlier, additional monitoring requirements may be required by the Title V periodic monitoring provision or the CAM rule. Title V permits must also include inspection and entry authorization.[30] Title V permits may be issued for a period not to exceed five years.[31] Any required monitoring and reporting submittals must include a certification of compliance, signed by a responsible official, attesting to the truth, accuracy, and completeness of all information and reports concerning the compliance status of the source.

The 1990 amendments to the Clean air Act allow states to also issue general permits covering certain categories of sources, such as dry cleaners and emergency generators.[32] General permits are used by a number of state permitting agencies to cover categories of small emission sources that are generally homogeneous in terms of operations, processes, and emissions where application of common monitoring, record-keeping and reporting requirements is achievable.[33]

EPA's Title V rules also provide that a permit shield may be included as a term of the permit. A permit shield must be specifically included in the permit, and it generally provides that compliance with the conditions of the permit shall be "deemed compliance with any applicable requirements as of the date of permit issuance," as long as such requirements are specifically

---

28. 40 C.F.R. § 70.6(a)(1).
29. CAA § 504(c); 42 U.S.C. § 7661c(c); 40 C.F.R. § 70.6(a)(3).
30. CAA § 504(c); 42 U.S.C. § 7661c(c).
31. 40 C.F.R. § 70.6(a)(2).
32. CAA § 504(d); 42 U.S.C. § 7661c(d).
33. See 57 Fed. Reg. 32,250, 32,278 (July 21, 1992).

identified in the permit or the permitting agency determines in writing that such requirements do not apply.[34] Thus, if a state permitting agency makes a mistake and incorrectly determines that a standard is not applicable, the permittee will generally be "shielded" from an enforcement action during the term of the permit. There are some exceptions to this general rule, including a prohibition on shielding permittees from complying with an emergency order.[35] In addition, EPA's "credible evidence" rule promulgated in 1997 indicated in the preamble that it is EPA's position that a permit shield does not relieve a source from its obligation to comply with the underlying applicable requirements, even if the required monitoring failed to detect a violation.[36]

10.6   Permit Review and Issuance Process

The applicable permitting agency will prepare a draft permit for review by the applicant, EPA, and the public. In general, public notice of the draft permit is required with at least a 30-day comment period.[37] The public shall also have an opportunity to request a public hearing. A copy of each permit application, each proposed permit, and each final Title V permit are required to be provided to EPA.[38] EPA may also comment on the permit application or draft permit, and it has 45 days after receiving the draft permit to object to its issuance.[39] To the extent its objections are not resolved, EPA may veto the permit issued by the state permitting agency, even over the state's objections. Public citizens and affected states may also petition EPA to object to the issuance of the permit. Any such objection must be based on issues raised during the comment period. A petition requesting review of a permitting authority's decision to issue a Title V permit must be filed with the agency within 60 days after EPA's 45-day review period expires.[40] The petition must be based only on objections that were raised with reasonable specificity during the public comment period unless the petitioner demonstrates that it was impracticable

---

34. 40 C.F.R. § 70.6(f); *see also* CAA § 504(f); 42 U.S.C. § 7661c(f).
35. 42 U.S.C. § 7661c(f).
36. 62 Fed. Reg. 8314, 8320 (Feb. 13, 1997).
37. 40 C.F.R. § 70.7(h).
38. 40 C.F.R. § 70.8(a).
39. CAA § 505(b)(1); 42 U.S.C. § 7661d(b)(1); 40 C.F.R. § 70.8(c).
40. CAA § 505(b)(2); 42 U.S.C. § 7661d(b)(2); 40 C.F.R. § 70.8(d).

to raise the objection.[41] EPA then has 60 days to grant or deny the petition.[42] After a final decision is made on the petition by the EPA administrator, the decision may be appealed to the appropriate federal circuit court of appeals, pursuant to CAA section 307(b). The U.S. Courts of Appeals for the Eighth and Ninth Circuits have determined that a failure to petition EPA for an objection bars any subsequent citizen suit action by a petitioner challenging actions that could have been raised during the permitting process.[43]

There have been several petitions filed with EPA requesting that the agency object to the issuance of certain Title V permits. Under CAA section 505(b)(2), EPA "shall issue an objection . . . if the petitioner demonstrates to the Administrator that the permit is not in compliance with the requirements of" Title V.[44] The case law has focused on what constitutes a sufficient demonstration of noncompliance. The U.S. Courts of Appeals for the Sixth and Eleventh Circuits have held that EPA has the discretion to conclude that the issuance of a notice of violation and civil complaints are insufficient to trigger the EPA administrator's duty to object under CAA section 505(b).[45] In *Sierra Club v. Johnson*, the Eleventh Circuit concluded that a violation notice and the filing of a civil complaint are merely initial steps in an enforcement action, and are not sufficient to demonstrate noncompliance.[46] In contrast, the U.S. Court of Appeals for the Second Circuit reached an opposite conclusion in *New York Public Interest Research Group v. Johnson*, and held that issuance of notices of violation and commencement of civil suits against two power plants by the applicable state permitting agency was a sufficient demonstration of noncompliance to trigger EPA's obligation to object to the plant's Title V permits.[47]

Any renewals or significant modifications of Title V permits are subject to the above public participation and appeal rights under the EPA regulations. When the permit is up for renewal, the permitting agency may also make any necessary changes in the permit provisions.

---

41. *Id.*
42. CAA § 505(b)(2); 42 U.S.C. § 7661d(b)(2).
43. Romoland Sch. Dist. v. Inland Empire Energy Ctr., 548 F.3d 738, 755 (9th Cir. 2008); Sierra Club v. Otter Tail Power Co., 615 F.3d 1008, 1017–18 (8th Cir. 2010).
44. CAA § 504(b)(2); 42 U.S.C. § 7661d(b)(2).
45. Sierra Club v. Johnson, 541 F.3d 1257, 1259 (11th Cir. 2008); Sierra Club v. EPA, 557 F.3d 401, 411–12 (6th Cir. 2009).
46. 541 F.3d at 1259.
47. N.Y. Pub. Interest Research Group v. Johnson, 427 F.3d 172, 180 (2d Cir. 2005).

10.7 **Modifications**

The Title V rules authorize three types of permit modifications: (1) administrative permit amendments, (2) minor permit revisions, and (3) significant permit revisions. In general, it will take a minimum of 45 days and frequently much longer, to obtain a permit revision when significant permit changes are involved. Such changes are subject to the full agency and public participation procedures, and EPA will have an opportunity to veto the proposed revisions before any operational change is implemented.

Administrative permit changes include corrections of typographical errors; changes in names, addresses, and other similar information; incorporation of requirements from preconstruction review permits (i.e., PSD/NSR or state preconstruction permits); and other changes of a ministerial nature. No public notice is required for these changes and such revisions are typically filed with a standard form or notice letter.

Minor permit amendments are those that do not violate any applicable requirement and do not involve significant changes to monitoring, reporting, or record-keeping requirements. Minor amendments may also not involve a case-by-case determination of a change in an emission standard or limitation, nor seek to establish or change a permit term or condition for which there is no underlying applicable requirement, if the source previously accepted such term or condition as an alternative to an applicable requirement.[48] Minor permit amendments require submittal of an application, and are generally subject to limited review requirements and streamlined procedures involving only notice to EPA and the applicable state permitting agency. No formal notification of the public is required.

Significant permit amendments are essentially all permit revisions that do not qualify as either administrative or minor changes. These revisions are subject to the standard procedural requirements applicable to issuance and renewal of a Title V permit.

A permit modification is not required for so-called "off-permit changes," which are changes that are not addressed or prohibited by the permit.[49] States have the discretion to allow off-permit changes without triggering a permit revision. EPA has provided little guidance on what may qualify as an off-permit change, and

---

48. 40 C.F.R. § 70.7(e)(2).
49. 40 C.F.R. § 70.4(b)(14).

generally state permitting agencies are responsible for making such determinations.

10.8 **Reopener Provision**

Title V permits may also be reopened before the permit expires, for a number of reasons—including, in some instances, when additional applicable requirements under the CAA are triggered. Moreover, the permitting authority may seek to reopen a permit for cause; for example, if the permit contains a material mistake or inaccurate statements made in the permit application creates or causes the Title V permit to fail to comply with the requirements of the CAA.[50]

---

50.   40 C.F.R. § 70.7(f).

11 Greenhouse Gas Emissions

In 2007, the U.S. Supreme Court—in a 5–4 decision—concluded in *Massachusetts v. EPA* that greenhouse gas (GHG) emissions fall within the Clean Air Act's broad definition of "air pollutants," and determined that the Environmental Protection Agency has statutory authority to regulate GHG emissions.[1] The Supreme Court's ruling ended the discussion on whether EPA is authorized to regulate GHGs under its current Clean Air Act authority, but it has spurred the debate on how EPA should exercise that authority. Under the Obama administration, EPA has initiated a number of rulemaking activities, and set in motion several programs to regulate GHG emissions from stationary and mobile sources. This chapter will review the current status of EPA's rulemaking activities, and highlight some of the pending legal challenges to the rules.

A discussion of the science of climate change is beyond the scope of this book, but some basic background information is provided. In *Massachusetts v. EPA*, Justice Stevens observed that "a well-documented rise in global temperatures has coincided with a significant increase in the concentration of carbon dioxide (CO_2) in the atmosphere."[2] Justice Stevens went on to note that "respected scientists believe that the two trends are related."[3] CO_2 and other GHGs trap the solar energy of the sun in the atmosphere, much like a greenhouse, and limit the escape of reflected heat.[4] The theory is that increases in atmospheric concentrations of GHGs warm the average temperature of the Earth's surface,

---

1. Massachusetts v. EPA, 549 U.S. 497 (2007).
2. *Id.* at 504–05.
3. *Id.* at 505.
4. *See generally* EPA Climate Change, Basic Information, http://www.epa .gov/climatechange/basicinfo.html.

which changes rainfall and precipitation patterns, glacier coverage, and sea levels.[5]

In general, EPA's GHG rulemaking efforts have focused on six types of greenhouse gas emissions: CO_2, methane (CH_4), nitrous oxide (N_2O), hydrofluorocarbons (HFCs), perfluorocarbons (PFCs), and sulfur hexafluoride (SF_6).[6] EPA evaluates the potential impact of GHGs based on the *global warming potential* (GWP) of the pollutants. Calculating the GWP allows for an exchange rate comparison of the heat-trapping ability of the six primary GHG pollutants.[7] The GWP reflects both the instantaneous heat-trapping intensity of the gas and the time it remains in the atmosphere, and is calculated over a specified time period, which EPA has determined should be 100 years. The GWP would change if a different time period was used.

The GWP of the six individual GHGs are set forth at 40 C.F.R. § 98, subpart A, table A-1. For example, methane has a GWP of 21, which means that over a 100-year time period, a ton of methane will trap 21 times more heat than one ton of CO_2.[8] Nitrous oxide will trap 310 times more heat than CO_2 over a 100-year period.[9] HFCs range from a GWP of 12 to 11,700, and PFCs range from a GWP of 6,500 to 17,340. Sulfur hexafluoride is the most potent of the GHGs, and will trap 23,900 times more heat than an equivalent unit of CO_2 over a 100-year period.[10] The GWP of the non-CO_2 GHGs are often converted to CO_2 equivalent (CO_2e) for purposes of using a functionally equivalent amount of CO_2 as a reference. CO_2e is calculated by multiplying the GHG's GWP by the mass amount of emissions (tons per year) for the particular GHG.

The primary GHG emitted in the United States is CO_2, representing approximately 83 percent of total GHG emissions in 2009 on a CO_2e basis.[11] The largest source of CO_2 is the combustion of fossil fuels, such as coal, gas, or oil, primarily through electricity generation, transportation (such as cars, trucks, airplanes, trains),

---

5. *Id.*
6. *See* 40 C.F.R. § 86.1818-12(a).
7. The GWP of a GHG is defined as the time-integrated radiative forcing from the instantaneous release of 1 kilogram of a trace substance to that of 1 kilogram of the reference gas (CO2). EPA, EPA 430-R-11-005, Inventory of U.S. Greenhouse Gas Emissions and Sinks: 1990–2009, at ES-3 (Apr. 15, 2011) [hereinafter GHG Inventory].
8. 40 C.F.R. § 98, subpt. A, tbl.A-1.
9. *Id.*
10. *Id.*
11. GHG Inventory, *supra* note 7, at ES-6.

and industrial sources.[12] Methane is the next largest source of total GHG emissions, and emissions come from natural gas systems, landfills, and fermentations processes.[13] Nitrous oxide emissions result primarily from agricultural activities and motor vehicles; HFCs are emitted during the manufacturing process, during the product life as a substitute for more powerful ozone-depleting substances, and during disposal; PFCs are primarily emitted during semiconductor manufacturing and aluminum manufacturing; and SF_6 is generally emitted when used as an insulating gas in electrical transmission equipment.[14]

Unlike criteria pollutants such as CO, NO_x, and PM, which can have localized and regional impacts, a ton of GHG emitted in the United States will have the same effect on the atmosphere as a ton of GHG released in Australia. In other words, a ton of GHG emitted anywhere in the world will have the same potential impact as a ton of CO_2 emitted by a passenger car in the United States.[15]

11.1   *Massachusetts v. EPA*

In *Massachusetts v. EPA*, the Supreme Court settled the question of whether CO_2 and other GHGs fall within the broad definition of "air pollutant" under the CAA. In confirming that GHGs qualify as air pollutants, the Court put the question of whether GHGs should be regulated under the CAA squarely before EPA. By way of background, the CAA does not expressly direct EPA to regulate GHGs. The question of whether EPA had implied authority to regulate GHGs was first addressed in a memorandum prepared by EPA's general counsel in 1998.[16] The 1998 EPA memorandum concluded that CO_2 met the definition of an "air pollutant" under

---

12. *Id.* at ES-4, ES-6. The global carbon cycle includes carbon sinks, such as oceans, trees, and land, which remove CO2 from the atmosphere. Changes in forests and land use can also release CO2 through the removal of vegetation and biomass. *Id.* at ES-6 to ES-7.

13. GHG Inventory, *supra* note 7, at ES-5.

14. *Id.* at ES-5 to ES-6.

15. An average passenger car in the United States emits approximately 5.2 metric tons (or 5.75 short tons) of CO_2e per year. *See* EPA, Overview: Pollutants and Programs, Emission Facts: Greenhouse Gas Emissions from a Typical Passenger Vehicle, http://www.epa.gov/oms/climate/420f05004.htm.

16. Memorandum from Jonathan Z. Cannon to EPA Adm'r Carol M. Browner, EPA's Authority to Regulate Pollutants Emitted by Electric Power Generation Sources (Apr. 10, 1998).

the CAA, and noted that there were a number of provisions under Title I that were potentially applicable to regulating CO_2.[17]

In 1999, a group of 19 nongovernmental organizations filed a lawsuit asking EPA to regulate GHG emissions from new motor vehicles under CAA section 202.[18] In August 2003, EPA's general counsel in the Bush administration released a memorandum that reached a different conclusion from the 1998 general counsel memorandum.[19] The 2003 memorandum concluded that the CAA did not authorize EPA to regulate GHGs, and withdrew the 1998 memorandum.[20] In September 2003, EPA formally denied the rulemaking petition requesting that GHGs be regulated under CAA section 202.[21] EPA determined that (1) the CAA does not authorize EPA to issue mandatory regulations to address climate change, and (2) even if EPA had the authority to regulate GHGs, the agency concluded that it would be unwise to do so at that time, in part because it would conflict with separate actions by the Bush administration to address climate change.[22] The nongovernmental organizations and other intevenors filed a petition with the U.S. Court of Appeals for the D.C. Circuit seeking review of the EPA order denying the request for rulemaking under CAA section 202. The D.C. Circuit denied the petition for review.[23]

As noted earlier, the U.S. Supreme Court accepted the *Massachusetts v. EPA* case, and concluded that CO_2 and other GHGs qualify as "air pollutants" under the CAA. The Court also addressed whether the CAA authorizes EPA to regulate GHG emissions from new motor vehicles, and concluded that CAA section 202(a)(1) requires EPA to make a "judgment" on whether an air pollutant "cause[s], or contributes[s] to, air pollution which may reasonably be anticipated to endanger public health or welfare."[24] The Court determined that EPA failed to comply with the statutory mandate of CAA section 202(a)(1), and remanded the petition to EPA for a decision on whether GHGs cause or contribute to climate change in accordance with the statute.[25] The

---

17. *Id.* at 3–4.

18. Massachusetts v. EPA, 549 U.S. 497, 510 (2007).

19. Memorandum from Robert E. Fabricant to EPA Acting Adm'r Marianne L. Horinko, EPA's Authority to Impose Mandatory Controls to Address Global Climate Change Under the Clean Air Act (Aug. 28, 2003).

20. *Id.*

21. 68 Fed. Reg. 52,922 (Sept. 8, 2003).

22. 68 Fed. Reg. at 52,925.

23. Massachusetts v. EPA, 549 U.S. 497, 514 (2007) (citing Massachusetts v. EPA, 415 F.3d 50, 58 (2005)).

24. 549 U.S. at 532–33.

25. 549 U.S. at 534–35.

remand to EPA then set the stage for EPA's "endangerment" and "cause or contribute" findings discussed in the next section.

11.2   Endangerment Finding and Motor Vehicle Rules

In September 2009, EPA issued two findings pursuant to CAA section 202(a)(1) that set in motion the agency's regulation of GHGs under the mobile source program of Title II and the stationary source programs under Title I. In a final rule, the EPA administrator found that six GHGs (CO_2, CH_4, N_2O, HFCs, PFCs, and SF_6), taken in combination endanger the public health and public welfare of current and future generations.[26] The finding was supported by a consideration of both observed and projected effects of GHGs in the atmosphere, the effect on the climate, and the resulting impacts from climate change.[27] In the same final rule, the agency also concluded that the combined emissions of the six GHGs from new motor vehicles and engines contribute to the GHG air pollution that endangers public health and welfare.[28] The EPA administrator determined that the body of scientific evidence compellingly supported the endangerment finding.[29] The EPA administrator compared the concentration of GHGs emitted by mobile sources in the United States to the total global and total U.S. contribution of GHGs, and found that GHG emissions from motor vehicles in the United States clearly contribute to GHG concentrations in the global atmosphere.[30] EPA also noted that in order for the agency to issue emission standards for new motor vehicles under CAA section 202(a)(1), it is a prerequisite that the EPA administrator determine that emissions from classes or categories of new motor vehicles cause or contribute to air pollution

---

26. 74 Fed. Reg. 66,496 (Dec. 15, 2009).
27. 74 Fed. Reg. at 66,497. The preamble to the rule states: "The Administrator is using her judgment, based on existing science, to weigh the threat for each of the identifiable risks, to weigh the potential benefits where relevant, and ultimately to assess whether these risks and effects, when viewed in total, endanger public health or welfare." *Id.*
28. 74 Fed. Reg. at 66,496.
29. 74 Fed. Reg. at 66,497.
30. 74 Fed. Reg. at 66,499.

that may reasonably be anticipated to endanger public health and welfare.[31]

The two findings did not impose any specific regulatory requirements on industry, but the actions were a prerequisite to EPA's issuance of a final rule pursuant to CAA section 202(a)(1) setting GHG emissions standards for passenger cars, light-duty trucks, and medium-duty passenger vehicles, like minivans and SUVs, for the model years 2012 to 2016. As discussed more fully in section 12.3.1, EPA promulgated its first rule to require reductions in GHG emissions from mobile sources in May 2010.[32] EPA also expects to issue GHG emission standards (i) for heavy-duty pickups and vans, combination tractors, including heavy-duty tractor trailer trucks and engines, and vocational vehicles, like buses and refuse or utility trucks,[33] and (ii) the 2017 to 2025 model years for light-duty and medium-duty passenger vehicles and light-duty trucks.[34]

In 2010, several state, nonprofit, and industry groups filed petitions with the U.S. Court of Appeals for the D.C. Circuit seeking judicial review of the "endangerment" and "cause or contribute" findings as well as the motor vehicle rules issued in May 2010. These petitions have been consolidated under the case heading of *Coalition for Responsible Regulation v. EPA*, No. 09-1322.

11.3   Stationary Sources

In the wake of the *Massachusetts v. EPA* case and anticipating that it would need to address the question of what other CAA regulatory programs are triggered once GHGs become "subject to regulation" under the statute, EPA Administrator Johnson issued a guidance memorandum in 2008 that clarified EPA's interpretation of when pollutants become subject to the federal Prevention of Significant Deterioration (PSD) program.[35] The Johnson memorandum stated that the agency would interpret "regulated NSR pollut-

---

31. 74 Fed. Reg. at 66,501.
32. 75 Fed. Reg. 25,324 (May 7, 2010).
33. 75 Fed. Reg. 74,152 (Nov. 30, 2010).
34. The White House, Presidential Memorandum Regarding Fuel Efficiency Standards (May 21, 2010).
35. Memorandum from EPA Adm'r Stephen L. Johnson to EPA Reg'l Adm'rs, EPA's Interpretation of Regulations that Determine Pollutants Covered by Federal Prevention of Significant Deterioration (PSD) Program (Dec. 18, 2009).

ants" to include each pollutant for which EPA regulations require actual control of emissions of that pollutant as opposed to merely monitoring or testing.[36] The EPA interpretation was further refined in a notice establishing that PSD permitting requirements will not apply to a newly regulated pollutant until a regulatory requirement to control emissions of that pollutant "take[s] effect."[37] The agency concluded that the PSD permitting requirements would not apply to major sources and major modifications of major stationary sources until January 2, 2011, when auto manufacturers were expected to start manufacturing vehicles that would meet the GHG emission standards for model year 2012.

As discussed more fully in section 5.5, in June 2010, EPA issued the GHG Tailoring Rule, which establishes major source and significance level emission thresholds for GHGs to define when the PSD program applies to a new source or a major modification.[38] The GHG Tailoring Rule also addresses the applicability of the Title V operating permit program to major sources of GHG emissions.[39] In developing the rule, EPA was faced with the dilemma of potentially applying the CAA major source thresholds of 100 tons or 250 tons per year to GHG emissions, which would greatly increase the number of small sources subject to the CAA requirements, and likely overwhelm permitting authorities. In crafting the rule, EPA sought to tailor the application of the PSD and Title V permitting programs to GHG emissions to avoid "absurd results" in applying the two programs to small sources, such as schools, hospitals, bakeries, and residential sources.[40] The GHG Tailoring Rule has also been challenged by a number of parties, and petitions seeking review of the rule have been consolidated with the *Coalition for Responsible Regulation v. EPA* case.

In December 2010, EPA announced a settlement of challenges to New Source Performance Standards (NSPS) for (1) electric utility steam generating units regulated under 40 C.F.R. part 60, subpart Da, and (2) petroleum refineries regulated under 40 C.F.R. part 60, subparts J and Ja. The challenges were filed by

---

36. *Id.* at 1.
37. 75 Fed. Reg. 17,004 (Apr. 2, 2010).
38. 75 Fed. Reg. 31,514 (June 3, 2011).
39. Title V permitting requirements will apply to new major sources of GHGs starting on July 1, 2011, where (1) potential emissions of GHGs equal or exceed 100,000 tons per year of CO_2e and (2) potential emissions of GHGs equal or exceed 100 tons per year on a mass basis. Major sources that have Title V permits for non-GHG pollutants will need to address GHGs as part of their Title V permit when it is renewed or otherwise revised. 75 Fed. Reg. at 31,523–24.
40. 75 Fed. Reg. at 31,544.

12 states, the City of New York, the District of Columbia, and several nongovernmental organizations, and alleged that EPA was required to include standards for GHG emissions.[41] Under the two settlement agreements, EPA agreed to promulgate GHG emission standards for new sources under CAA section 111(b) and for existing sources under CAA section 111(d) by May 26, 2012, for power plants and November 10, 2012, for petroleum refineries.[42] Promulgation of NSPS for power plants and petroleum refineries will set minimum performance standards for two source categories that account for nearly 40 percent of the GHG emissions in the United States. The new NSPS standards will also serve as the minimum level of control evaluated in top-down best available control technology determinations under the PSD program.

11.4   GHG Mandatory Reporting Rule

In 2007, Congress included a provision in the Consolidated Appropriations Act for fiscal year 2008 authorizing funding for EPA to develop a draft rule requiring the mandatory reporting of GHG emissions "above appropriate thresholds in all sectors of the economy of the United States."[43] In 2009, pursuant to authority under CAA sections 114 and 208, EPA promulgated a Mandatory Reporting of Greenhouse Gases Rule, which requires 41 source categories of industrial facilities to submit GHG emissions data to EPA.[44] The rule is codified at 40 C.F.R. part 98, and requires the collection of GHG data and other information from (1) upstream suppliers or

---

41. The petitioning states include (in order of filing) New York, California, Connecticut, Delaware, Maine, New Hampshire, New Mexico, Oregon, Rhode Island, Vermont, Washington, and Massachusetts. New Hampshire did not join in challenging the final NSPS amendments for power plants. The settlement agreements and related materials can be obtained at EPA Air Quality Planning & Standards, Addressing Greenhouse Gas Emissions, http://www.epa.gov/airquality/ghgsettlement.html.

42. Settlement Agreement between the U.S. EPA and various petitioners resolving a petition for review of "Standards of Performance for Electric Utility Steam Generating Units, Industrial-Commercial-Institutional Generating Units, and Small Industrial-Commercial-Institutional Generating Units," 71 Fed. Reg. 9,866 (Feb. 27, 2006); Settlement Agreement between the U.S. EPA and various petitioners resolving a petition for review of "Standards of Performance for Petroleum Refineries," 73 Fed. Reg. 35,838 (June 24, 2008).

43. Consolidated Appropriations Act, 2008, Pub. L. No. 110-161, 121 Stat. 1844, 2128 (2008).

44. 74 Fed. Reg. 56,260 (Oct. 30, 2009) (codified at 40 C.F.R. § 98).

importers of fossil fuels or industrial gases, and (2) industrial sources directly emitting 25,000 metric tons or more of CO_2e emissions through fuel combustion.[45] Motor vehicle and engine manufacturers are also required to report emissions rate data on their products.[46]

The Mandatory Reporting of Greenhouse Gases Rule requires industrial sources to report their annual GHG emissions in metric tons as opposed to short tons.[47] Unlike other EPA GHG rules, such as the GHG Tailoring Rule, the mandatory reporting rule applies to CO_2, CH_4, N_2O, HFCs, PFCs, and SF_6, as well as other fluorinated gases (such as nitrogen trifluoride and hydrofluorinated ethers). EPA has created an electronic GHG reporting tool (e-GGRT) for the submittal of GHG data, and the regulated community must submit its first GHG reports on or before September 30, 2011, covering 2010 GHG emissions data.[48]

11.5   **Other GHG Programs and GHG Litigation**

Legislation to implement a national cap-and-trade program to regulate GHG emissions from industrial sources was first introduced in 2003 during the 108th Congress, and during the subsequent 109th, 110th and 111th Congresses, but a comprehensive GHG program failed to garner sufficient support to pass. In the absence of a national program, several states stepped forward to regulate GHGs from certain industrial sources. Although a detailed review of the regional GHG programs adopted by 10 northeastern and mid-Atlantic states and the program adopted by California is beyond the scope of this book, the following is a brief summary of these developments.

On December 20, 2005, seven states signed a memorandum of understanding agreeing to implement the Regional Greenhouse Gas Initiative (RGGI) to reduce CO_2 emissions from fossil-fuel-fired power plants by 10 percent by 2018.[49] In 2007 and 2008,

---

45. 74 Fed. Reg. at 56,264.
46. *Id.*
47. A short ton equals 2,000 pounds. The GHG Tailoring Rule, for example, uses short tons as the measurement for determining the major source and significance level thresholds. One short ton equals 0.9072 metric tons.
48. 76 Fed. Reg. 14,812 (Mar. 18, 2011).
49. The original seven states were Connecticut, Delaware, Maine, New Hampshire, New Jersey, New York, and Vermont. *See* Reg'l Greenhouse Gas Initiative, Program Design, http://www.rggi.org/design. In May 2011, Governor Chris

three additional states joined RGGI, and the program was implemented on January 1, 2009.[50] The RGGI states have implemented a cap-and-trade program where each state is allocated a CO_2 emissions budget cap and emission allowances corresponding to the gradual reduction in the cap. The RGGI states have largely agreed to implement a public auction of the allowances as a means of investing the proceeds in consumer benefit programs with the goal of improving energy efficiency and fostering renewable energy technology. The program applies to power plants with units that serve an electricity generator with a nameplate capacity of 25 MWs or greater. More details on the RGGI program are available at http://www.rggi.org/design/overview.

In 2006, the California Legislature passed, and Governor Arnold Schwarzenegger signed into law, Assembly Bill 32, the Global Warming Solutions Act.[51] AB 32 calls for the development of regulations to reduce GHG emissions in California to 1990 levels by 2020. California is in the process of adopting regulations, including a cap-and-trade program, to implement the GHG reduction program. Under AB 32, most of the GHG emission reduction regulations are required to be adopted by 2011, and the program is scheduled to start on January 1, 2012.[52]

In addition to regional efforts by certain states to address climate change, several states and nongovernmental organizations have resorted to the courts to attempt to bring about a change in how industry responds to climate change issues. There have been numerous cases filed against utilities and industry, as well as against EPA and other governmental agencies alleging different common law and statutory-based claims with the goal of reducing GHG emissions. The most notable case is *American Electric Power v. Connecticut*, which was originally filed in 2004 by two groups of plaintiffs: eight state attorneys general and New York City and three public interest land trusts, seeking to abate the

Christie announced that New Jersey would pull out of the RGGI program effective at the end of the first compliance period in December 2011.

50. Massachusetts and Rhode Island joined in 2007, and Maryland joined in 2008.

51. A.B. 32, 2005–06 Leg., Reg. Sess. (Cal. 2006); CAL. HEALTH & SAFETY CODE §§ 38500–38599.

52. Additional detail on California's GHG program may be obtained at Cal. EPA, Air Resources Bd., Assembly Bill 32: Global Warming Solutions Act, http://www.arb.ca.gov/cc/ab32/ab32.htm, and Cal. EPA, Air Resources Bd., Cap-and-Trade, http://www.arb.ca.gov/cc/capandtrade/capandtrade.htm. The AB 32 implementing regulations are expected to become enforceable January 1, 2012; however, covered entities are not expected to have an emissions obligation until 2013.

GHG emission contributions to climate change of six electric utilities.[53] The U.S. Court of Appeals for the Second Circuit reversed
and remanded the lower court decision, holding that the plaintiffs
had stated claims under the common law of public nuisance and
that the CAA had not displaced the public nuisance claim.[54]

The U.S. Supreme Court granted certiorari to hear the appeal
of the Second Circuit's decision, and issued its ruling in June
2011.[55] In an 8–0 decision, the Court reversed the Second Circuit
and held that the Clean Air Act and the EPA actions pursuant to
the CAA to regulate GHG emissions displace the plaintiffs' claims
alleging a federal common law public nuisance. The Court did
not address whether the CAA and EPA's regulatory efforts displace
public nuisance law. As of 2011, a number of other common law
and statutory based climate change cases were pending in the
courts, and to date, several hundred cases have been filed.[56]

53. Am. Elec. Power v. Connecticut, 131 S. Ct. 2527, 2011 WL 2437011
(2011).

54. Connecticut v. Am. Elec. Power, 582 F.3d 309, 392–93 (2d Cir. 2009),
vacated, 131 S. Ct. 2527, 2011 WL 2437011 (2011).

55. Am. Elec. Power v. Connecticut, 131 S. Ct. 2527.

56. A current summary of the pending cases is available at Columbia Law
School, Center for Climate Change Law, http://www.law.columbia.edu/centers/
climatechange.

12 Mobile Sources and the Regulation of Fuels

The Clean Air Act provides the Environmental Protection Agency and states with broad authority to regulate air emissions from mobile sources. The term *mobile sources* does not just encompass cars, trucks, buses, and motorcycles, but also includes aircrafts, ships, locomotives, and other nonroad vehicles and equipment such as tractors, bulldozers, forklifts, lawn mowers, and rototillers. Title II of the CAA prescribes the setting of emission standards for certain types of mobile sources and mandates the regulation of fuels and fuel additives. In addition, Title I of the CAA, which addresses the preparation of state implementation plans (SIPs) and the requirements for nonattainment areas, also includes several transportation-related controls. This chapter reviews some of the key transportation-related requirements of Title I and summarizes the mobile source controls required by Title II, as well as the provisions of the CAA addressing the regulation of fuels and fuel additives.

Mobile source emissions primarily come from four sources: (1) exhaust emissions coming out of the tailpipe, (2) evaporative emissions occurring when the engine is hot or when the temperatures rise during the day heating the fuel tank, (3) refueling emissions when vapors are displaced during filling or spillage occurs, and (4) crankcase or "blow-by" emissions, which are oily aerosols escaping from the piston rings around the engine.

12.1   Control of Mobile Source Emissions

The CAA mobile source provisions focus on reducing CO, non-methane hydrocarbons (NMHC, also known as VOCs), NO_x, and PM. The initial federal standards were set forth in the Motor Vehicle Air Pollution Control Act of 1965, which authorized the U.S. Department of Health, Education, and Welfare (HEW) to establish emission standards, taking into account technological feasibility and economic costs, for any class or classes of new motor vehicles that were determined to cause or contribute to air pollution that endangered the health or welfare of any persons.[1] In 1967, Congress enacted the Air Quality Act, which included the National Emissions Standards Act (in sections 201 to 212).[2] The 1967 Act authorized the regulation of fuels and fuel additives in section 210 and built upon the motor vehicle standards of the 1965 Act. Under section 208 of the 1967 Act, HEW was permitted to preempt the application of national motor vehicle emission standards for any state that had enacted new motor vehicle emission standards before March 30, 1966.[3] As of that date, only California had adopted state emission standards for new motor vehicles. This provision foreshadowed the current dual standard approach, which recognizes both national motor vehicle standards and California standards.

Many of the CAA's current mobile source requirements were enacted as part of the 1970 Clean Air Act, including the requirement to establish emission standards for light-duty vehicles (i.e., cars and small trucks) and the imposition of a mandatory certification process for motor vehicle engines. The 1970 CAA standards required a 90 percent reduction in NMHC and CO emissions from a 1970 baseline to be achieved in light-duty vehicles and engines starting with the 1975 model year.[4] The 1970 CAA also required a 90 percent reduction in NO_x emissions from light-duty vehicles and engines from a 1971 baseline starting with the 1976 model year.[5]

In the 1977 amendments to the CAA, Congress added requirements to set emission standards for heavy-duty vehicles such as

---

1. Pub. L. No. 89-272, 79 Stat. 992 (1965).
2. Pub. L. No. 90-148, 81 Stat. 485 (1967).
3. Pub. L. No. 90-148, § 208.
4. Pub. L. No. 91-604, § 202(b)(1)(A), 84 Stat. 1676, 1690 (1970).
5. Pub. L. No. 91-604, § 202(b)(1)(B), 84 Stat. at 1690.

large trucks and buses, and codified the "California option" as an alternative set of motor vehicle standards for nonattainment areas.[6] Under the California option, states were authorized to adopt the California motor vehicle standards in lieu of the federal standards, as long as what they adopted was identical to the California requirements. In the 1990 CAA amendments, Congress imposed new requirements to regulate nonroad mobile sources, evaporative emissions, and refueling emissions, as well as adopting a clean fuel vehicle program designed to foster development of low-emission vehicles.

12.2   Title I Transportation-Related SIP Controls

The CAA includes several provisions, in Title I, that are intended to reduce air-polluting emissions (primarily CO, NO_x, and VOCs) from motor vehicles. Once such provision, found in CAA section 176, is a general federal "conformity" requirement that prohibits an agency of the federal government from engaging in, supporting, providing financial assistance to (e.g., by federal grants), licensing, issuing permits for, or approving any activity that does not conform to the requirements of the applicable state or federal implementation plan.[7] The onus for assuring such conformity is put on each federal agency. As noted in chapter 4, EPA has promulgated specific transportation conformity rules that apply to projects triggering U.S. Department of Transportation (DOT) involvement.[8] In general, any regional transportation plans or state or local transportation programs requiring DOT funding or approval will trigger application of the conformity standards. The transportation conformity rules require an affirmative determination that the proposed plan, program, or project will not (1) cause or contribute to any new violation of a National Ambient Air Quality Standard (NAAQS), (2) increase the frequency or severity of any existing violation of a NAAQS, or (3) delay the timely attainment of a NAAQS. Several types of projects are exempt from the transportation conformity rules and are listed at 40 C.F.R. §§ 93.126 and 93.127.

---

6. CAA § 177; 42 U.S.C. § 7507.
7. CAA § 176(c); 42 U.S.C. § 7506(c).
8. 40 C.F.R. pt. 93 *et seq.*

As discussed in chapter 4, states with nonattainment areas are required to adopt several transportation-related programs, depending on the severity of the nonattainment status. For example, all states with either ozone or CO nonattainment status are required to implement vehicle inspection and maintenance (I/M) programs. Large metropolitan areas in the northeast ozone transport region, moderate and serious CO nonattainment areas, and serious, severe, and extreme ozone nonattainment areas must have an enhanced I/M program in place. Other ozone and CO nonattainment areas must implement basic I/M requirements. Severe and extreme ozone nonattainment areas must also adopt and implement transportation control measures (TCMs) designed to reduce motor vehicle emissions.[9] These TCMs may include programs to encourage carpooling, greater use of mass transit, or similar measures to reduce work-related vehicle trips.

12.3   Mobile Source Emission Standards

CAA section 202 charges EPA with regulating light-duty vehicles and engines, heavy-duty vehicles and engines, and motorcycles. Nonroad vehicles and engines are addressed in CAA section 213, urban buses in CAA section 219, and aircraft and aircraft engines in CAA section 231. Pursuant to the CAA, EPA has adopted standards for mobile sources that generally set emission limits for the different classes and categories of mobile sources that are based on a mass emissions basis, namely, grams per braked-horsepower-hour (g/bhp-hr) or grams per vehicle mile (gpm). As noted earlier in this chapter, EPA typically has set CO, NMHC, NO_x, and PM limits for most mobile sources.

The emission standards for mobile sources typically focus on technology-driven performance enhancements to the engines that reduce emissions. In setting emission standards for motor vehicles, EPA generally focuses on two types of emissions: tailpipe emissions and evaporative emissions. For tailpipe emissions, EPA will set the standard based on various criteria, including the vehicle weight, the starting model year, the useful life of the vehicle,

---

9.   CAA § 182(d)(1); 42 U.S.C. § 7511a(d)(1).

and the temperature at which the standard is pegged (e.g., cold CO standard for light-duty vehicles and trucks).[10]

12.3.1 Tailpipe Standards

Each manufacturer of a mobile source subject to a tailpipe emission control standard must meet certification requirements. Manufacturers typically must submit test information about a "prototype" engine to EPA and demonstrate that this engine will meet the applicable emission control standards. If the prototype meets the emission standards based on the testing protocols developed by EPA for the particular rules (including longer-term deterioration testing to ensure compliance over the vehicle's or engine's specified "useful life"), then EPA issues a "certificate of conformity" to the manufacturer, and the certificate authorizes the manufacturer to begin production of the mobile source.

To confirm that the mobile source will actually meet the emission standards once full-scale production begins, EPA may order the manufacturer to test samples of the mobile source as part of its selective enforcement audit program. If a substantial number of the production models fail to meet the applicable emission standards, EPA can revoke the certificate of conformity.[11]

Once a motor vehicle or engine is "in use," it must continue to comply with emission standards for the duration of its "useful life." EPA conducts testing of classes and categories of vehicles and engines to determine if a substantial number of the vehicles and engines, even when properly maintained and used, do not conform to the emissions standards.[12] Although *substantial number* is not defined in the CAA, the U.S. Court of Appeals for the D.C. Circuit recognized that the number must be large enough to show that a systematic or pervasive problem in a particular class or category of vehicles or engines exists.[13]

---

10. In the 1990 amendments, Congress raised the "useful life" for light-duty vehicles and trucks from 5 years or 50,000 miles to 10 years or 100,000 miles. CAA § 202(d); 42 U.S.C. § 7521(d).

11. *See, e.g.,* 40 C.F.R. § 86, apps. X and XI (for light-duty vehicles, the "acceptable" quality level is 40 percent).

12. CAA § 207(c)(1); 42 U.S.C. § 7541(c)(1).

13. Chrysler Corp. v. EPA, 631 F.2d 865, 890–91 (D.C. Cir. 1980) (more than 85 percent of the tested vehicles in the recall class exceeded the applicable CO emission standards).

If EPA determines that in-use vehicles or engines are not meeting the applicable standard, then the manufacturer must submit a plan to EPA to remedy the problem, or face a recall order from the agency directing that the manufacturer recall the vehicles.[14] Failure to comply with a recall order can result in stiff penalties. Under statutory warranty requirements, the manufacturer rather than the vehicle owner is responsible for the recall repairs.[15]

Light-Duty Vehicles and Trucks. Light-duty vehicles include all passenger cars; light-duty trucks include pickup trucks, minivans, passenger vans, and sport utility vehicles (SUVs) up to 8,500 pounds gross vehicle weight. In the 1990 CAA amendments, Congress set forth Tier 1 standards that reduced existing tailpipe emission standards for cars and light-duty trucks by 40 and 50 percent, respectively.[16] The Tier 1 standards were phased in over 1994 to 1996, and Congress adopted two sets of standards for light-duty vehicles and trucks up to 6,000 pounds: one for the first 5 years or 50,000 miles and one for 10 years or 100,000 miles.[17] For light-duty trucks over 6,000 pounds, Congress mandated standards for 5 years/50,000 miles and 11 years/120,000 miles starting with model year 1996.[18]

In CAA section 202(i), Congress created a mechanism for EPA to study whether further reductions in light-duty vehicles and trucks was warranted starting with model year 2004. EPA submitted study results to Congress in 1998, which recommended that Tier 2 emission standards be developed in order to help states in meeting required ozone and PM emission reductions needed to help attain and maintain NAAQS.[19]

In February 2000, EPA promulgated a major new rule that starting in 2004 phased in a single set of tailpipe emission standards that applies to all passenger cars and vans, light trucks, and SUVs operated on any fuel.[20] These Tier 2 standards were intended to introduce cleaner vehicle emission control technology. In addition, the rule required refiners to reduce sulfur levels in gasoline nationwide over the 2000 to 2006 time frame. EPA's

14. CAA § 207(c); 42 U.S.C. § 7541(c).
15. *Id.*
16. CAA § 202(g); 42 U.S.C. § 7521(g).
17. CAA § 202(g)(1), (2); 42 U.S.C. § 7521(g)(1), (2).
18. CAA § 202(h); 42 U.S.C. § 7521(h).
19. 65 Fed. Reg. 6698, 6703 (Feb. 10, 2000).
20. 65 Fed. Reg. 6698 (Feb. 10, 2000) (codified at 40 C.F.R. pts. 80, 85, and 86).

Tier 2 program was intended to foster major reductions in NO_x, SO_2, and PM emissions from light-duty vehicles and trucks as well as a new category of medium-duty passenger vehicles, such as minivans and SUVs, between 8,500 and 10,000 pounds.[21]

In 2003, EPA denied a petition for rulemaking filed by 19 nongovernmental organizations seeking to regulate greenhouse gas emissions (GHGs) from motor vehicles under CAA section 202(a).[22] EPA's denial of the petition for rulemaking was upheld by the U.S. Court of Appeals for the D.C. Circuit in 2005,[23] and, as discussed more fully in chapter 11, the U.S. Supreme Court in *Massachusetts v. EPA* ruled in 2007 that GHGs fall within the broad definition of "pollutants" under the CAA, and EPA's decision to deny the rulemaking petition was arbitrary and capricious because the agency did not offer a reasoned explanation for its refusal to determine whether GHGs cause or contribute to climate change.[24]

In the wake of *Massachusetts v. EPA*, in 2009, President Obama called for the reduction in GHG emissions and improved fuel economy in all new light-duty cars and trucks sold in the United States. In May 2010, EPA promulgated national CO_2 emission standards for light-duty vehicles and trucks and medium-duty passenger vehicles.[25] The standards take effect starting with model year 2012 and increase in stringency through model year 2016. The standards will require these vehicles to achieve an average emissions level of 250 grams/mile of CO_2 by model year 2016. According to EPA, mobile sources accounted for about 31 percent of all GHGs (on a CO_2e basis) emitted in the United States in 2007.[26] EPA projects that the 2012–2016 standards will reduce GHG emissions from the U.S. light-duty vehicle fleet by approximately 21 percent by 2030.[27]

On May 21, 2010, President Obama issued a presidential memorandum calling for the development of a coordinated national program under the CAA and the Energy Independence and Security Act of 2007[28] to improve fuel efficiency and to

21. 65 Fed. Reg. at 6702.
22. Massachusetts v. EPA, 549 U.S. 497, 510 (2007).
23. Massachusetts v. EPA, 415 F.3d 50 (D.C. Cir. 2005), *rev'd*, 549 U.S. 497 (2007).
24. 549 U.S. at 534–35 (2007).
25. 75 Fed. Reg. 25,324 (May 7, 2010).
26. 75 Fed. Reg. at 25,326.
27. 75 Fed. Reg. at 25,328.
28. Pub. L. No. 110-140, 121 Stat. 1492 (2007).

reduce GHG emissions from light-duty trucks and vehicles for model years 2017–2025.[29]

Heavy-Duty Engines and Trucks. Under CAA section 202(a)(3) in the 1990 amendments, Congress directed EPA to regulate CO, NOx, NMHC, and PM tailpipe emissions from heavy-duty vehicles (such as trucks and buses) and engines that reflect "the greatest degree of emission reduction achievable through the application of technology" that is "available" while giving "appropriate consideration to cost, energy, and safety factors."[30] The 1990 CAA amendments also directed EPA to reduce NOx emissions from new heavy-duty trucks to 4.0 grams per braked-horsepower-hour by model year 1998.[31] In 1997, EPA promulgated "Phase 1" regulations reducing NOx NMHC and PM emissions from heavy-duty vehicles and gasoline/diesel engines starting with model year 2004.[32] EPA further updated and revised the 1997 Phase 1 heavy-duty vehicle and engine standards in October 2000.[33]

In January 2001, EPA promulgated a new "Phase 2" rule to reduce NO_x, NMHC, and PM emissions from heavy-duty highway engines and vehicles starting with model year 2007.[34] The rule created a comprehensive national program to regulate heavy-duty highway engines and vehicles and fuels used by these vehicles by combining more stringent emission standards for vehicle engines with stricter sulfur content standards for highway diesel fuel. In addition, new diesel fuel standards for use in highway vehicles took effect beginning in 2006, and require a 97 percent reduction in the sulfur content of highway diesel fuel. Starting in June 2006, the prior standard of 500 parts per million was reduced to 15 parts per million.[35] The Phase 2 rule also requires crankcase emissions from heavy-duty diesel engines to be controlled.[36]

In November 2010, EPA issued a proposed rule to create a national program to increase fuel efficiency and reduce GHG

---

29. The White House, Presidential Memorandum Regarding Fuel Efficiency Standards (May 21, 2010) http://www.whitehouse.gov/the-press-office/presidential-memorandum-regarding-fuel-efficiency-standards.
30. CAA § 202(a)(3)(A)(i); 42 U.S.C. § 7521(a)(3)(A)(i).
31. CAA § 202(a)(3)(B)(ii); 42 U.S.C. § 7521(a)(3)(B)(ii).
32. 62 Fed. Reg. 54,694 (Oct. 21, 1997) (codified at 40 C.F.R. pt. 86).
33. 65 Fed. Reg. 59,896 (Oct. 6, 2000) (codified at 40 C.F.R. pt. 86).
34. 66 Fed. Reg. 5001 (Jan. 18, 2001) (codified at 40 C.F.R. pts. 69, 80, and 86).
35. 66 Fed. Reg. at 5006.
36. 66 Fed. Reg. at 5040–41.

emissions from on-road heavy-duty vehicles starting with model year 2014.[37] The program is expected to be fully phased in by 2018. The proposed rule responds to President Barack Obama's May 21, 2010, presidential memorandum calling for a coordinated program to produce cleaner vehicles, and the rule is expected to be finalized in 2011.

12.3.2   Evaporative Standards

EPA has also implemented controls on "evaporative" emissions caused during vehicle refueling, during operation ("running losses"), and during nonoperation when the vehicle is out in the hot sun or high heat. CAA section 182(b)(2) requires states to adopt regulations requiring Stage II gasoline fuel-pump recovery systems for moderate, serious, severe, and extreme ozone nonattainment areas in the country.[38] Stage II systems provide a sheath over the pump nozzle to capture VOC vapors during refueling. CAA section 202(a)(6) also mandates that EPA promulgate regulations requiring onboard refueling vapor recovery for light-duty vehicles and trucks. In 1994, EPA issued regulations that require manufacturers to phase in onboard refueling vapor recovery equipment over three years, starting with the 1998 model year.[39]

12.3.3   Clean Fuel Vehicles

Sections 241–250 of the CAA (added by the 1990 amendments) establish a new clean fuel vehicle program. The program is intended to encourage the development of cars, trucks, and buses that run on "clean alternative fuel," which is defined to include methanol, ethanol or other alcohol fuels, reformulated gasoline, diesel, natural gas, electricity, and other low-emission fuels.[40] The program directly applies to "covered fleets," which means 10 or more motor vehicles owned and operated by a single person in either serious, severe, or extreme ozone nonattainment areas

---

37. 75 Fed. Reg. 74,152 (Nov. 30, 2010).
38. CAA § 182(b)(3); 42 U.S.C. § 7511a(b)(3).
39. 59 Fed. Reg. 16,262 (Apr. 6, 1994).
40. CAA § 241(a); 42 U.S.C. § 7581(2).

or in serious CO nonattainment areas.[41] However, rental cars, motor vehicles held by dealers, vehicles used by law enforcement and other emergency agencies, and nonroad vehicles (e.g., farm equipment) are exempt. Specific standards for various classes and categories of motor vehicles are codified in CAA section 243.[42] In addition, EPA has promulgated regulations implementing the clean fuel vehicles program, requiring states with applicable non-attainment areas to adopt the clean fuel fleet program as part of their SIPs.[43]

A related program is the voluntary National Low Emission Vehicle (NLEV) program, developed by a partnership of EPA, several states, and vehicle manufacturers in the late 1990s. At the time, many northeastern states were facing stringent NO_x and VOC emission reduction requirements to meet target reductions to come into compliance with the NAAQS for ozone, and the Tier 2 emission standards for light-duty vehicles and engines were not scheduled to take effect until the 2004 model year. Starting in 1999, 13 northeastern states agreed to implement the NLEV program. EPA issued a series of composite rules setting out the NLEV standards that were nationally applicable in 2001.[44] Under the NLEV program, light-duty vehicles and engines sold in NLEV program states were required to meet emission standards that were substantially similar to the California low emission vehicle program.

12.3.4   Nonroad Engines, Equipment, and Vehicles

CAA section 213, added by the 1990 amendments, authorized EPA to study whether CO, NO_x, and VOC emissions from nonroad engines and vehicles were significant contributors to ozone and CO in nonattainment areas.[45] If the EPA administrator were to make an affirmative determination, then the agency would be required to identify categories of nonroad engines and vehicles that should be subject to emission standards that achieve "the

---

41.   CAA § 241(5); 42 U.S.C. § 7581(5).
42.   CAA § 243; 42 U.S.C. § 7583.
43.   40 C.F.R. pt. 88 et seq.
44.   62 Fed. Reg. 31,192 (June 6, 1997); 63 Fed. Reg. 925 (Jan. 7, 1998) (codified at 40 C.F.R. pts. 85 and 86).
45.   CAA § 213(a)(1); 42 U.S.C. § 7547(a)(1).

greatest degree of emission reduction achievable through the application of technology" that the EPA administrator determines to be "available," giving appropriate consideration to the cost and to noise, energy, and safety of applying such technology.[46]

EPA's 1991 study concluded that emissions from nonroad engines and vehicles contributed to ozone and CO concentrations in more than one nonattainment area.[47] As a result, EPA moved forward with emission standards for a number of categories of nonroad engines, equipment, and vehicles, including the following general categories:

- aircraft
- marine vessels (including commercial ships, recreational craft, and personal watercraft)
- locomotives
- nonroad diesel engines and equipment (including farm, construction, and mining equipment)
- forklifts, generators, and compressors
- lawn and garden equipment (including lawn mowers, leaf blowers, and chainsaws)
- snowmobiles, dirt bikes, and all-terrain vehicles (ATVs)[48]

In conjunction with the nonroad emission standards program, EPA has developed a National Clean Diesel Program to reduce NO_x and PM emissions from nonroad diesel engines. In 1994, EPA adopted the Tier 1 standards for new nonroad diesel engines greater than 50 horsepower.[49] The Tier 1 standards were phased in during 1996 to 2000. In 1998, EPA adopted more stringent Tier 2 and 3 standards for new nonroad diesel engines, including nonroad engines greater and less than 50 horsepower.[50] The Tier 2 standards were phased in during 2001 to 2006 and the Tier 3 standards were phased in during 2006 to 2008. In 2004, EPA promulgated the Tier 4 standards for nonroad diesel engines, including farm machinery, lawn and garden tractors, industrial trucks, industrial construction machinery, mining equipment, and oil and

---

46.   CAA § 213(a)(3); 42 U.S.C. § 7547(a)(3).
47.   EPA, Office of Air & Radiation, EPA 460/3-91-02, Nonroad Engine and Vehicle Emission Study—Report (Nov. 1991).
48.   Links to the applicable federal regulations for nonroad engines, equipment, and vehicles are available at EPA, Nonroad Engines, Equipment, and Vehicles, http://www.epa.gov/nonroad/#3.
49.   59 Fed. Reg. 31,306 (June 17, 1994) (codified at 40 C.F.R. pt 89).
50.   63 Fed. Reg. 56,968 (Oct. 23, 1998) (codified at 40 C.F.R. pt 89).

gas field machinery.[51] The rule was phased in during 2007 and affects model years 2008 and beyond. The Tier 4 standards are expected to achieve significant reductions in NO_x, PM, and SO_2 emissions by regulating engines from under 25 horsepower to over 750 horsepower.[52]

12.3.5   State Programs

As discussed in section 12.1, under the 1967 Act, Congress pre-empted states from adopting their own emission standards for mobile sources unless a state had enacted motor vehicle standards before March 30, 1966.[53] At the time, only California had adopted state emission standards for mobile sources. CAA section 209(b) codifies the federal waiver of the California motor vehicle regulatory program, and provides that before new state motor vehicle standards may go into effect, EPA is required to approve subsequent waivers.[54] EPA is required to grant a waiver unless it makes one or more of the following findings: (1) the state standards are arbitrary and capricious in the state's finding that the standard is at least as protective of public health and welfare as the applicable federal standards, (2) the standards are not needed to meet compelling and extraordinary conditions, or (3) the proposed standards are not consistent with CAA section 202(a).[55]

In 1990, Congress added CAA section 177 giving states with ozone and/or CO nonattainment areas the option of adopting either the federal standards or the California standards for motor vehicles.[56] Before the 1990 amendments, California was the only state with its own motor vehicle emissions program; however, since then several northeastern states have adopted rules to implement the California low-emission vehicle (LEV) program for light-duty vehicles and light-duty trucks. California has steadily reduced the emission standards applicable to light-duty vehicles and trucks through the initial LEV standards that were in effect

---

51. 69 Fed. Reg. 38,958 (June 29, 2004).
52. 69 Fed. Reg. at 38,960.
53. Pub. L. No. 90-148, § 208.
54. CAA § 209(b)(1); 42 U.S.C. § 7543(b)(1).
55. Id.
56. CAA § 177; 42 U.S.C. § 7507. States adopting the California motor vehicle standards are also referred to as "section 177 states."

from 1994 through 2003, and the LEV II regulations applied starting in 2004.[57]

In 2002, California enacted legislation (Assembly Bill 1493) to set fleet-average motor vehicle standards for GHGs. The standards required automobile manufacturers to achieve a 30 percent reduction in GHG emissions from automobiles through model year 2016.[58] As directed by AB 1493, California adopted regulations in 2004 to control GHG emissions from light-duty vehicles and light-duty trucks and medium-duty passenger vehicles into the LEV program, and the standards are being phased in from 2009 to 2016.[59] In 2005, California applied to EPA for a waiver to implement the GHG regulations. EPA initially denied California's waiver request in March 2008.[60] In May 2009, President Obama announced an agreement among California, EPA, and the automobile industry to develop national fuel economy standards and GHG emission standards covering model years 2012 to 2016.[61] The agreement paved the way for EPA's reconsideration of California's waiver request from federal preemption under the CAA to implement GHG motor vehicle standards. EPA granted the waiver request in June 2009.[62] EPA's decision to grant California's waiver request was challenged, and the U.S. Court of Appeals for the D.C. Circuit dismissed the petition for review in April 2011.[63] To date, 14 states have adopted the California LEV emission standards.[64]

---

57. A link to the LEV standards is available at Cal. Air Res. Bd., Low-Emission Vehicle Program, http://www.arb.ca.gov/msprog/levprog/levprog.htm.

58. *See* Cal. Envt'l Protection Agency, Air Resources Bd., Clean Car Standards—Pavley, Assembly Bill 1493, http://www.arb.ca.gov/cc/ccms/ccms.htm, for a discussion of the bill.

59. A summary of the California GHG emission standards applicable to light-duty vehicles and trucks and medium-duty passenger vehicles is available at DieselNet, California: Cars: Greenhouse Gas Emissions, http://www.dieselnet.com/standards/us/ca_ghg.php.

60. 73 Fed. Reg. 12,156 (Mar. 6, 2008).

61. *See* The White House, Office of the Press Secretary, President Obama Announces National Fuel Efficiency Policy (May 19, 2009).

62. 74 Fed. Reg. 32,744 (July 8, 2009).

63. Chamber of Commerce of U.S. v. EPA, 642 F.3d 192 (D.C. Cir. 2011).

64. The states adopting California's LEV II standards are Arizona, California, Connecticut, Maine, Maryland, Massachusetts, New Jersey, New Mexico, New York, Oregon, Pennsylvania, Rhode Island, Vermont, and Washington. *See* Greencars.org, Guide to Green: Sorting out Standards, http://www.greenercars.org/guide_standards.htm.

12.4   Regulation of Fuels and Fuel Additives

CAA Title II also provides for the regulation of mobile source fuels. In general, CAA section 211 provides EPA with broad authority to regulate fuels, including the ability to prohibit or control fuels and fuel additives, and require the registration, testing, and certification of fuels and fuel additives. Under this authority, EPA has implemented a phaseout of the use of lead and lead additives in motor vehicle fuels.[65] The goal of CAA section 211 is to foster cleaner-burning fuels, with the aim of reducing CO, NMHC (or VOCs), NO_x, PM, and hazardous air pollutants (such as benzene) that are emitted when the fuel is combusted and to preempt damage to emissions control components of vehicles and engines. CAA section 211 authorizes the registration and testing of fuels and fuel additives and provides for the reformulated gasoline program, which sets forth specific standards for the composition of gasoline fuels in certain ozone nonattainment areas. In addition, EPA implemented an oxygenate program for CO nonattainment areas pursuant to CAA section 211(m).

Under the Energy Policy Act of 2005,[66] EPA is required to promulgate regulations to implement a national Renewable Fuel Standard program to ensure that gasoline sold in the United States contains a minimum volume of renewable fuel. As discussed in section 12.8, the Renewable Fuel Standard program was expanded by the Energy Independence and Security Act of 2007.[67]

12.5   Registration of Fuels and the Assessment of Public Health Impacts

One of the key fuel programs administered by EPA is the fuels registration and testing requirements prescribed by CAA section 112(e) and codified at 40 C.F.R. part 79. In general, no manufacturer of any fuel or fuel additives may market a fuel or fuel additive without registering it with EPA. EPA's fuel registration requirements

---

65. EPA initially used its authority under CAA section 112(c) to implement a phaseout of leaded gasoline. CAA section 112(n), added by the 1990 amendments, prohibits the sale of leaded gasoline after December 31, 1995. CAA § 211(n); 42 U.S.C. § 7545(n).

66. Pub. L. No. 109-58, 119 Stat. 594 (2005).

67. Pub. L. No. 110-140, 121 Stat. 1492 (2007).

originally took effect in 1975.[68] In 1994, EPA added mandatory health testing requirements as a prerequisite to fuel/fuel additive registration with three potential levels of testing and review (Tiers 1, 2, and 3).[69] The testing requirement is intended to identify fuels and fuel additives that present a significant risk to public health. Manufacturers of fuels and fuel additives must first perform a Tier 1 review consisting of (1) information on the health and welfare effects of the fuel/fuel additive emissions, (2) a characterization of the emissions generated by evaporation and combustion, and (3) a literature search on the toxicological and other exposure effects of emissions from the fuel/fuel additives.[70] As of May 2011, over 7,150 fuels and fuel additives had been registered.[71]

Tier 2 testing requires in vitro and in vivo biological tests to determine whether the emissions from the fuels and/or fuel additives have carcinogenic, mutagenic, reproductive, pulmonary, or neuro-toxic effects.[72] EPA can also impose additional testing on a case-by-case basis depending on the results from the Tier 1 and Tier 2 review or follow-up studies in a Tier 3 review.[73] Based on the testing and/or study results, EPA will make a decision on whether a particular fuel or fuel additive may be registered and introduced into commerce.

CAA section 211(f)(1)(A) makes it unlawful for fuel manufacturers to introduce into the marketplace or increase the concentration of any fuel or fuel additives for use in light-duty motor vehicles that are not "substantially similar" to fuels or fuel additives used in certifying light-duty vehicle model years 1975 and later.[74] In the 1990 CAA amendments, Congress added CAA section 211(f)(1)(B), which extended the prohibition on the use of certain fuels and fuel additives to all other motor vehicles, including heavy-duty vehicles and trucks.[75] CAA section 211(f)(4) authorizes the EPA administrator to grant waivers to allow the introduction of fuels and fuel additives that are not "substantially similar" to the fuels or additives used to certify a particular model year vehicle.[76] To be eligible for a waiver, the fuel or fuel additive must not cause or contribute to a failure of

68. 40 Fed. Reg. 52,011 (Nov. 7, 1975).
69. 59 Fed. Reg. 33,042 (June 27, 1994).
70. 40 C.F.R. § 79.52.
71. *See* EPA, Fuels and Fuel Additives: Registration and Health Effects Testing, http://www.epa.gov/otaq/additive.htm for a listing of the registered fuels and fuel additives.
72. 40 C.F.R. § 79.53.
73. 40 C.F.R. § 79.54.
74. CAA § 211(f)(1)(A); 42 U.S.C. § 7545(f)(1)(A).
75. CAA § 211(f)(1)(B); 42 U.S.C. § 7545(f)(1)(B).
76. CAA § 211(f)(4); 42 U.S.C. § 7545(f)(4).

an emission control device or system used to achieve compliance with the applicable emission standards.[77] In *Ethyl Corp. v. EPA*, the U.S. Court of Appeals for the D.C. Circuit concluded that CAA section 211(f) requires that the waiver decisions must be based on an analysis of the fuel or fuel additive's effect on emission standards, including an evaluation of how the fuel or fuel additive "causes or contributes" to an emission control device's ability to comply with the requisite emission standards.[78] Over the years, EPA has considered numerous CAA section 211(f) waiver applications. More recently, EPA has granted waivers for fuel and fuel additives containing more than 10 percent volume ethanol (E10) and more than 15 percent volume ethanol (E15). As of 2011, EPA has granted partial waivers to use E10 and E15 in model year 2001 and newer light-duty vehicles, light-duty trucks, and medium-duty passenger cars. The E10 and E15 waivers are subject to certain conditions, including fuel quality and mitigating misfueling in older vehicles.[79]

12.6   Reformulated Gasoline

The reformulated gasoline (RFG) program is mandated by CAA section 211(k)(1); the goal of the program is to foster cleaner-burning gasoline to reduce air emissions, including NO_x, VOCs, and air toxics, like benzene. To achieve this goal, RFG must pass both performance and composition requirements. EPA's final regulations setting forth the standards for reformulated fuels were promulgated in 1994, and are codified at 40 C.F.R. part 80.40 *et seq.*[80] The reformulated fuel requirements took effect on January 1, 1995.[81]

12.6.1   RFG Standards

CAA section 211(k) sets compositional specifications for reformulated gasoline, including (1) a 2.0 weight percent oxygen minimum,

---

77. *Id.*

78. Ethyl Corp. v. EPA, 51 F.3d 1053, 1058–59 (D.C. Cir. 1995). In *Ethyl Corp. v. EPA*, the court determined that EPA was not authorized to consider public health effects in reviewing a CAA section 211(f) waiver application.

79. *See* EPA, Fuels and Fuel Additives: E15, http://www.epa.gov/otaq/regs/fuels/additive/e15/index.htm.

80. 59 Fed. Reg. 7716 (Feb. 16, 1994).

81. In the final rule, EPA required all facilities upstream of retail outlets (i.e., refiners, importers, and oxygenate blenders) to begin selling reformulated fuel on December 1, 1994.

(2) a 1.0 volume percent benzene maximum, (3) a prohibition on heavy metals, (4) a prohibition on increases in NO_x emissions, and (5) achievement of required toxics and VOC reductions (during the high ozone season, June 1 to September 15).[82] These compositional requirements apply to reformulated fuel year round (except for the VOC performance standards) in the worst ozone nonattainment areas, including the following metropolitan areas: Baltimore, Chicago, Dallas–Fort Worth, Houston, Los Angeles, Milwaukee, New York City, Philadelphia, San Diego, and most of Connecticut.[83] Other areas may also apply to opt in to the reformulated fuel program. In addition, 13 states have had certain counties approved to opt in to an RFG program, including the entire states of Massachusetts and Rhode Island. A total of 17 states and the District of Columbia are covered by the RFG program, and approximately 30 percent of the gasoline sold in the United States is reformulated.[84] In the "covered areas" (i.e., worst ozone nonattainment areas and opt-in areas), fuel must be certified as either reformulated or conventional.

Aggregate emissions of VOCs and other air toxics, when using RFG, must be 15 percent lower than emissions from conventional gasoline. Starting in the year 2000, VOCs and other air toxics had to be reduced to 25 percent lower than conventional gasoline emissions.[85] However, EPA can allow a less than 25 percent (but not lower than 20 percent) reduction based on technological feasibility and economic considerations.[86]

Starting January 1, 2000, the RFG composition requirements must be met by meeting the "complex" model requirements of 40 C.F.R. § 80.41. Before January 1, 1998, a "simple" model was also available to certify compliance. The complex model is a statistical model that sets forth various fuel parameters, including Reid Vapor Pressure (a measure of gasoline volatility), fuel oxygen, benzene, and aromatics, which must be met on a per-gallon basis.[87] This

82. In section 211, the Clean Air Act refers to "toxics" reductions, which are the same types of hazardous air pollutants regulated under CAA section 112 (applicable to stationary sources). Also, under the RFG program, the CAA refers to reductions in VOC emissions, in contrast to the motor vehicle standards, which generally address reductions in NMHC. NMHC emissions are also VOCs.

83. Under CAA section 211, the nine cities with the worst smog pollution were defined as "covered areas" that were subject to the RFG program, and areas reclassified to a "severe" ozone nonattainment areas are also required to use RFG fuel. Ozone nonattainment areas classified as "serious," "moderate," or "marginal" may opt in to the RFG program.

84. A listing of the areas subject to the RFG program is available at EPA, Reformulated Gas, Where You Live, http://www.epa.gov/oms/rfg/whereyoulive.htm.

85. CAA § 211(k)(3)(B); 42 U.S.C. § 7545(k)(3)(B).

86. *Id.*

87. 40 C.F.R. § 80.41(i)(3).

model allows a refiner to input the relevant fuel characteristics to determine whether the fuel may automatically be certified as meeting the RFG requirements.

In order to satisfy the 2 percent oxygen by weight requirement, an oxygenate must be added to the fuel. The three most common oxygenates used in the RFG program include methyl tertiary butyl ether (MTBE), ethanol, and ethyl tertiary butyl ether (ETBE). In some instances, MTBE has been found to have contaminated groundwater from leaking underground storage tanks, and states including California, Connecticut, and New York have banned MTBE from the RFG program. A state may seek a waiver from the requirement that an RFG fuel contain 2 percent oxygen, but only by providing clear evidence that the oxygen content requirement will prevent or interfere with the state's ability to meet a NAAQS.[88]

12.6.2   Compliance Requirements

The requirements of the reformulated fuel rule must be met by upstream refiners, importers, and oxygenate blenders. Downstream sellers are not required to submit data to EPA, but are required to ensure that the gasoline meets the reformulated fuel requirements before it is sold. Refiners, importers, and oxygenate blenders were required to register with EPA by November 1, 1994, and keep records on production or importation of gasoline, sampling, testing, and compliance calculations.[89] Quarterly reports must be submitted to EPA to show that the RFG standards have been met, either on a per-gallon basis or on average.[90] In addition, refiners and importers must prepare detailed product transfer documents that specify the type of gasoline and product restrictions. Parties downstream of refiners and importers that transport, store, or dispense gasoline are responsible for ensuring that only reformulated gasoline is sold in the covered areas. In addition, downstream users (i.e., blenders, carriers, distributors, resellers, retailers, and wholesale purchaser-consumers) are responsible for ensuring that reformulated gasoline does not violate the per-gallon minimum and maximum standards.

Typically, either refiners or importers will blend the gasoline to ensure that all the reformulated fuel standards are met. How-

---

88.   CAA § 211(m)(3)AB); 42 U.S.C. § 7545(m)(3)(A).
89.   59 Fed. Reg. at 7757–58.
90.   59 Fed. Reg. at 7757.

ever, oxygenates such as MTBE, ethanol, and ETBE may be added downstream by oxygenate blenders. If gasoline will be blended downstream, the oxygenate blenders must ensure that the oxygenate standards are met, while refiners and importers are required to meet all the other reformulated gasoline standards.[91]

With respect to enforcement liability, downstream sellers can be liable for violations. The regulations provide that when gasoline contained in a storage tank at any facility owned, leased, operated, controlled, or supervised by any refiner, importer, oxygenate blender, carrier, distributor, reseller, retailer, or wholesale purchaser-consumer is found to violate the standards of the rule, most parties involved in the chain of distribution upstream are presumed liable for the violation.[92] (Carriers are only presumed liable only when the product was under their control or custody at the carrier's facility). This is a rebuttable presumption and various affirmative defenses can be raised (for example, the gasoline was tested to show that it was in compliance, or the proper documentation was provided when the party received the gasoline and sufficient quality assurance sampling and testing was conducted).[93]

12.7 Oxygenated Fuels

CAA section 211(m) addresses the oxygenated fuels program for CO nonattainment areas. Since November 1992, gasoline sold in the winter months in areas in nonattainment with the CO NAAQS standard must contain a minimum of 2.7 percent oxygen.[94] In cold temperatures, motor vehicles emit more carbon monoxide. The addition of an oxygenate, like ethanol, MTBE, or ETBE, improves combustion and helps car engines burn cleaner and emit less CO.

12.8 Renewable Fuel Standard Program

As noted in section 12.4, the Renewable Fuel Standard (RFS) program was created by section 1501 of the Energy Policy Act of 2005. Pursuant to the RFS program, EPA promulgated regulations in 2007

---

91. 59 Fed. Reg. at 7769.
92. 59 Fed. Reg. at 7777.
93. 59 Fed. Reg. at 7781–83.
94. CAA § 211(m)(2); 40 U.S.C. § 7545(m)(2).

that are designed to encourage the blending of renewable fuels into gasoline.[95] Renewable fuels include bio-based fuels largely produced from farm crops (e.g., ethanol and biodiesel). Under the RFS program, EPA was required to ensure that the pool of gasoline sold in the contiguous 48 states contains specific volumes of renewable fuel for each calendar year.[96] The requirement for calendar year 2007 was 4.7 billion gallons of renewable fuels being blended with gasoline.[97] The 2007 RFS rule also sets forth the responsibilities of refiners, importers, blenders, and other fuel producers, as well as creating a compliance trading program that allows parties to comply with the RFS requirements by purchasing renewable identification numbers.[98]

The RFS program was expanded by the Energy Independence and Security Act of 2007 by increasing the RFS volume standards starting in 2008 and adding diesel fuels.[99] The prior RFS standard of 5.4 billion gallons in 2008 was increased to 9.0 billion gallons, and Congress set an overall volume target of 36 billion gallons by 2022.[100] In addition, Congress established specific volume targets for cellulosic biofuel, biomass-based diesel, and total advanced renewable fuel.[101] In the Energy Independence and Security Act, Congress also established mandatory GHG reduction thresholds for four categories of renewable fuels to ensure that each category emits fewer GHG emissions than the petroleum fuel that is being displaced using a 2005 baseline.[102] The four categories are (1) renewable fuel (must reduce lifecycle GHG emissions by at least 20 percent to qualify), (2) advanced biofuel (must reduce lifecycle GHG emissions by at least 50 percent to qualify), (3) biomass-based diesel (must reduce lifecycle GHG emissions by at least 50 percent to qualify), and (4) cellulosic biofuel (must reduce lifecycle GHG emissions by at least 60 percent to qualify).[103] The GHG emission thresholds are based on a lifecycle analysis of the fuel, including feedstock production, distribution, and use by the consumer. In 2010, EPA promulgated revised RFS program standards to implement the provisions of the Energy Independence and Security Act.[104]

95. 72 Fed. Reg. 23,900 (May 1, 2007).
96. 72 Fed. Reg. at 23,903.
97. *Id.*
98. 72 Fed. Reg. at 23,909–10.
99. Pub. L. No. 110-140, 121 Stat. 1492 (2007).
100. Pub. L. No. 110-140, § 202(a)(2), 121 Stat. at 1522.
101. *Id.*
102. Pub. L. No. 110-140, § 202(c), 121 Stat. at 1524–25.
103. *Id.*
104. 75 Fed. Reg. 14,670 (Mar. 26, 2010).

13 Stratospheric Ozone

The stratospheric ozone layer protects the Earth and its inhabitants from harmful levels of ultraviolet radiation. Chemicals such as chlorofluorocarbons (CFCs), halons, carbon tetrachloride, and methyl chloroform destroy ozone molecules through a complex chemical reaction involving chlorine atoms released by these chemicals. Scientists have concluded that destruction of the ozone layer from the presence of chlorine atoms is particularly acute in the polar region over Antarctica (this causes the Antarctic "ozone hole" discovered in 1985). If left unchecked, the destruction of the ozone layer could result in serious harm to human health and the environment through the increased presence of ultraviolet radiation.

In an effort to combat and reverse global stratospheric ozone destruction, the U.S. government and other governments forged an international treaty, the Vienna Convention for the Protection of the Ozone Layer, which was adopted in 1985. The signatories to the Vienna Convention committed themselves to protect the ozone layer and to cooperate with each other in conducting scientific research to better understand the risks of ozone depletion. In 1987, the Vienna Convention signatories adopted the Montreal Protocol on Substances That Deplete the Ozone Layer, which is intended to implement the principles set forth in the Vienna Convention. Signatories to the Montreal Protocol agreed to adopt domestic regulatory measures to ban and control substances that cause depletion of the ozone layer. In the Clean Air Act Amendments of 1990, Congress crafted Title VI, which largely incorporates the goals of the Montreal Protocol and requires implementation of controls at least as restrictive as the Protocol; however, in several areas the 1990 amendments go beyond the requirements of the Protocol.

13.1 The Montreal Protocol

The Montreal Protocol initially took effect on January 1, 1989, and the United States was one of the original 29 signatories.[1] The Protocol has been amended four times and there have been five "adjustments," with the most significant changes in the various amendments and adjustments resulting in an acceleration of the phaseout dates of certain ozone-depleting substances (ODS).[2] Many of these substances are used in refrigeration and air-conditioning systems. Other uses of ODS include propellants, fire suppression, solvent cleaning, aerosols, fumigants, and foams. The Protocol generally requires the signatory nations to restrict the "production" and "consumption" of seven categories of ODS: CFCs, halons, carbon tetrachloride, methyl chloroform, methyl bromide, hydrobromofluorocarbons (HBFCs), and hydrochlorofluorocarbons (HCFCs). The term *production* under the Protocol does not include amounts recycled, reclaimed, or reused; amounts used as a feedstock to manufacture chemicals; or amounts destroyed by certain approved technologies. The term *consumption*, in contrast, was defined as "production plus imports minus exports." Thus, use of ODS per se was not banned by the Protocol. Under the Protocol, halons were scheduled for phaseout in 1994, followed by CFCs, methyl chloroform, carbon tetrachloride, and HBFCs in 1996. Methyl bromide was required to be phased out by January 2005,[3] although critical use exemptions for soil fumigation to control pests for agricultural products (e.g., fruits and vegetables) have continued.[4] The phaseout of HCFCs is scheduled for 2030.[5]

---

1. The status of the ratification of the Montreal Protocol on Substances That Deplete the Ozone Layer and its amendments is available at U.N. Env't Programme, Evolution of the Montreal Protocol: Status of Ratification, http://ozone.unep.org/Ratification_status/.

2. The amendments were adopted at the following meetings: London (1990), Copenhagen (1992), Montreal (1997), and Beijing (1999). Adjustments to the reduction schedules for the production and consumption of controlled substances were effective in 1991, 1993, 1996, 1998, and 2000. A summary of the various amendments and adjustments to the Montreal Protocol are available at U.N. Env't Programme, Evolution of the Montreal Protocol, http://ozone.unep.org/Ratification_status/evolution_of_mp.shtml.

3. *See* EPA, Ozone Layer Protection—Regulatory Programs, The Phaseout of Methyl Bromide, http://www.epa.gov/ozone/mbr/.

4. *See* EPA, Ozone Layer Protection—Regulatory Programs, Critical Use Exemption Information, http://www.epa.gov/ozone/mbr/cueinfo.html.

5. In September 2009, at the 19th Meeting of the Parties to the Montreal Protocol, a more aggressive phasedown of HCFCs in both developing and developed

Article 4 of the Protocol also bans the importation of CFCs, halons, carbon tetrachloride, methyl chloroform, and HBFCs from nonsignatory countries. Exportation to nonsignatory countries of these substances is similarly banned.[6]

The parties to the Montreal Protocol meet annually, and at the twenty-second meeting of the parties in 2010, the United States, Mexico, and Canada jointly submitted a proposed amendment to phase down hydrofluorocarbon (HFC) consumption as a means to mitigate potential climate change impacts due from the increased use of HFCs as a substitute for HCFCs and other ODS.[7] The amendment did not secure enough support to be adopted at the twenty-second meeting of the parties, and the proposal was resubmitted in May 2011.

Signatories to the Montreal Protocol may exempt certain "essential uses" of ODS.[8] Generally a use is essential only if (1) it is necessary for health or safety or is critical for the functioning of society, and (2) there are no environmentally acceptable alternatives that are technically and economically feasible.[9] If the use is deemed essential, production and consumption can occur only if (1) all economically feasible steps have been taken to minimize the essential use and any associated emissions and (2) the substance is not available in sufficient quantity and quality from existing stocks of banked or recycled ODS.[10] If a company seeks an essential use exemption, it must first convince its government to submit an exemption request, which is evaluated by a special committee created by the Protocol. This special technical committee will review and make a recommendation on the request. An essential use request must ultimately be approved by the signatory countries during the annual meeting of the Protocol parties.

---

countries was approved, which reduced the 100 percent phasedown date from 2040 to 2030. The phaseout schedule can be accessed at EPA, Ozone Layer Protection—Regulatory Programs, HCFCs Phaseout Schedule, http://www.epa.gov/ozone/title6/phaseout/hcfc.html.

6. Montreal Protocol, art. 4 ¶ 3-4 ter.

7. EPA reports that the amendment would yield a benefit of reducing about four gigatons of CO_2e emissions through 2020 and 98 gigatons of CO_2e emissions through 2050. *See* EPA, Ozone Layer Protection, Recent International Developments in Saving the Ozone Layer, http://www.epa.gov/ozone/intpol/mpagreement .html. A gigaton is equal to one billion metric tons of carbon. The U.S. CO_2e emission rate in 2009 was approximately 6.6 gigatons. EPA, EPA 430-R-11-005, INVENTORY OF U.S. GREENHOUSE GAS EMISSIONS AND SINKS: 1990–2009, at ES-6 (Apr. 15, 2011).

8. Montreal Protocol, art. 2A ¶ 4.

9. Fourth Meeting of the Parties, Decision IV/25(1)(a).

10. *Id.* at Decision IV/25(1)(b).

The Environmental Protection Agency publishes a notice each year requesting applications for essential use allowances that will be submitted to the Protocol parties for consideration. For example, CFCs used as a propellant in metered-dose inhalers have been granted essential use allowances.[11] Another essential use that currently qualifies for an exemption is the production of Class I ODS for laboratory and analytical uses. In 2007, consistent with Decision XIX/18 of the Protocol parties, EPA extended the exemption period for laboratory and analytical uses until December 31, 2011.[12]

For initial compliance with the Montreal Protocol, EPA promulgated regulations in 1987 and 1988.[13] EPA's regulations allocated production and consumption allowances—similar to SO$_2$ allowances under the acid rain program—according to the amount of controlled substances each company had produced or imported in 1986. The rules also implemented the phaseout schedule for ODS covered under the Protocol. These rules were subsequently substantially revised after Congress enacted the 1990 amendments to the CAA.[14]

13.2   1990 Clean Air Act Amendments

As noted earlier, Title VI of the 1990 amendments was intended to statutorily embrace the goals of and to implement the Montreal Protocol. Congress also recognized that reductions in ODS would have the collateral benefit of potentially lessening the impact of CFCs and HCFCs on global warming. Some members of the scientific community have concluded that CFCs and HCFCs qualify as *greenhouse gases*, which contribute to global climate change by trapping heat in the lower atmosphere.

In adopting the provisions of the Protocol, Title VI does not utilize traditional "command and control" abatement schemes, but instead focuses on the control, replacement, and eventual elimination of specific ozone-depleting substances from commerce. Title VI requires EPA to issue regulations implementing

---

11. See EPA, Ozone Layer Protection—Regulatory Programs, Essential Uses of CFCs for Metered-Dose Inhalers, http://www.epa.gov/ozone/title6/exemptions/essential.html, for copies of the annual EPA notices requesting applications for essential use allowances.
12.   72 Fed. Reg. 73,264 (Dec. 27, 2007).
13.   52 Fed. Reg. 47,486 (Dec. 14, 1987), 53 Fed. Reg. 30,598 (Aug. 12, 1998).
14.   See 40 C.F.R. §§ 82.1–82.24.

production and consumption phaseout target dates for ODS, new allowance trading rules, a recycling program, labeling requirements, and a safe alternatives program. The following sections briefly review some of the more pertinent provisions of the statute and EPA's implementing regulations.

13.3   Phaseout of Ozone-Depleting Substances

Title VI directs EPA to list "Class I" and "Class II" ODS, and CAA section 602 sets forth specific Class I and Class II substances. *Class I substances* are those that have an "ozone depletion potential of 0.2 or greater."[15] *Class II substances* are those that are "known or may reasonably be anticipated to cause or contribute to harmful effects on the stratospheric ozone layer."[16] EPA is authorized to add substances to either the Class I or II lists after a rulemaking procedure; however, no Class I or II substances may be removed from the respective lists, except a Class II substance may be advanced to Class I. Individuals may also petition to add substances to the list. Since 1990, methyl bromide and HBFCs have been added to the Class I list.[17] The Class I list includes CFCs, halons, carbon tetrachloride, methyl chloroform, methyl bromide, and HBFCs. HCFCs are listed as Class II substances.

CAA section 606(a)(3) authorizes EPA to synchronize the phaseout schedules in Title VI with subsequently adopted timetables accelerating ODS phaseouts adopted under the Montreal Protocol process. Consequently, a number of the original phaseout dates in CAA Title VI have been adjusted to reflect changes in the Montreal Protocol schedules.

CAA section 604(a) sets production phaseout deadlines for Class I substances. EPA regulations implementing the phaseout schedule for the production and consumption of ODS are set forth in 40 C.F.R. part 82, subpart A. CAA section 606 authorizes EPA to accelerate the phaseout dates under the 1990 amendments if (1) based on credible current scientific information, the EPA administrator determines that a more stringent schedule is needed to protect human health and the environment, (2) the EPA administrator determines that a more stringent schedule is practicable taking into account technological achievability, safety, and other

---

15. CAA § 602(a); 42 U.S.C. § 7671a(a).
16. CAA § 602(b); 42 U.S.C. § 7671a(b).
17. 58 Fed. Reg. 65,017 (Dec. 10, 1993).

factors, and (3) the Montreal Protocol schedule was also modified to provide a faster phaseout schedule.[18]

CAA section 604 provides that, effective January 1, 2000 (January 1, 2002, in the case of methyl chloroform), it is unlawful to produce any amount of a Class I substance.[19] However, EPA accelerated this phaseout schedule for most Class I substances. In 1993, EPA promulgated a final rule requiring the phaseout of all listed Class I substances except methyl bromide by January 1, 1996.[20] Production of methyl bromide was required to cease by January 1, 2001, in conformance with CAA section 602(d), but this date was extended by Congress to coincide with the Montreal Protocol phaseout date of January 1, 2005.[21] The phaseout schedule for Class II HCFCs is set by regulation with a prohibition on the production or consumption of certain HCFCs ranging from January 1, 2003, to January 1, 2030.[22] Halons were subject to a December 31, 1993, phaseout under the Protocol and the CAA, although the purchase and use of recycled halons remains permissible.

Similar to the Montreal Protocol, CAA section 604(d) contains limited exceptions for certain essential uses of ODS. Limited exemptions were established for essential uses of methyl chloroform in aviation applications and medical devices; for essential uses of Class I substances in medical devices; for essential uses of halon in aviation safety; and for the use of methyl bromide in compliance with sanitation, agricultural, and food protection standards.[23] The EPA administrator may also grant limited exceptions for production solely for export to developing countries that are signatories to the Protocol for national security (CFC-114 and halons), and for fire suppression and explosion prevention (halons).[24] The agency allocates essential use allowances on a calendar-year basis through a rulemaking process.[25]

18. CAA § 606(a); 42 U.S.C. § 7671e(a).
19. CAA § 604(b); 42 U.S.C. § 7671c(b).
20. 40 C.F.R. § 82.4.
21. Pub. L. No. 105-277, § 764 (1998).
22. 40 C.F.R. § 82.4(n)–(s). HCFC-141b was banned as of January 1, 2003; certain uses of HCFC-142b and HCFC-22 were banned effective January 1, 2010, and use of other HCFCs is being phased out from 2015 to a complete phaseout by 2030. Additional detail on EPA's regulations phasing out HCFCs is available at EPA, Ozone Layer Protection—Regulatory Programs, Phaseout of HCFCs, http://www.epa.gov/ozone/title6/phaseout/classtwo.html.
23. CAA § 604(d); 42 U.S.C. § 7671c(d).
24. CAA § 604(e), (f), (g); 42 U.S.C. § 7671c(e), (f), (g).
25. EPA final rules authorizing essential use allowance allocations are available at EPA, Ozone Layer Protection—Regulatory Programs, Essential Uses of CFCs for Metered-Dose Inhalers, http://www.epa.gov/ozone/title6/exemptions/essential.html.

Title VI authorizes the creation and transfer of both production and consumption allowances for Class I and Class II substances.[26] Under the implementing regulations, EPA allocated each company that was producing or consuming a listed Class I substance production or consumption allowances.[27] Most of the Class I allowance allocations expired on January 1, 1996, when the phaseout took effect; however, allocations for methyl bromide remained in effect until the January 1, 2005, phaseout date for that chemical. As of January 1, 2005, no further production and consumption allowances for Class I substances were available. The allowance system for Class II ODS will remain in effect until 2030 when the last categories of HCFCs are phased out. In 2009, EPA promulgated a rule that allocated production and consumption allowances for HCFC-22, HCFC-142b, and other HCFCs for the control period of 2010 to 2014.[28] Under CAA section 607, allowance transfers, including interpollutant transfers, can occur between companies within the United States.[29] CAA section 616 authorizes transfers between the United States and another signatory country to the Montreal Protocol.

13.4 Refrigerant Recycling

CAA section 608 of the Act sets forth the requirements for a national recycling and emission reduction program for appliances using Class I or Class II substances. It provided that, effective July 1, 1992, it shall be unlawful for any person to knowingly vent or otherwise knowingly release or dispose of any Class I or Class II substances. De minimis releases during recovery and recycling procedures are exempt.

On May 14, 1993, EPA promulgated rules to reduce emissions of Class I and Class II refrigerants during the service, maintenance, and repair of appliances and industrial process refrigeration to meet the requirements of CAA section 608.[30] CAA section 608

---

26. CAA § 607(a); 42 U.S.C. § 7671f(a).
27. 40 C.F.R. § 82.5 (production allowances); 40 C.F.R. § 82.6 (consumption allowances).
28. 74 Fed. Reg. 66,412 (Dec. 15, 2009).
29. CAA § 607(b), (c); 42 U.S.C. § 7671f(b), (c).
30. 58 Fed, Reg. 28,660 (May 14, 1993) (codified at 40 C.F.R. §§ 82.150–82.166). EPA's refrigerant recycling regulations were amended in 1994 and 2003 (see 59 Fed. Reg. 42,950 (Aug. 19, 1994), 59 Fed. Reg. 55,912 (Nov. 9, 1994), and 68 Fed. Reg. 43,786 (July 24, 2003)). An overview of EPA's refrigerant recycling program is available at EPA, Ozone Layer Protection—Regulatory Programs,

requires that emissions from appliances be reduced to the lowest achievable level and that recapture and recycling of such substances be maximized.[31] CAA section 608 also mandates that all ODS contained in bulk appliances be removed before disposal or delivery for recycling.[32] The EPA refrigerant recycling regulations affect the servicing and disposal of most air-conditioning and refrigeration equipment, including household air-conditioners and refrigerators, commercial air-conditioners and chillers, commercial refrigeration, industrial process refrigeration, refrigerated transport, and air-conditioning in vehicles not covered by CAA section 609.[33] The EPA regulations require that any such equipment used during the maintenance, service, repair, or disposal of appliances be certified by an approved equipment-testing organization.[34] Only certified technicians may open appliances for maintenance, service, or repair, and only certified individuals or companies may sell or distribute any Class I or Class II substance for use as a refrigerant.[35] All technicians must pass an exam administered by an EPA-testing program. EPA has taken actions to revoke certifications for certain refrigerant reclaimers and technician certification programs that have failed to comply with the requirements of 40 C.F.R. part 82, subpart F.

13.5   Motor Vehicle Air-Conditioning

CAA section 609 mandates the regulation of CFCs used in the servicing of motor vehicle air-conditioners (MVACs). EPA issued regulations in July 1992 that set forth the standards and requirements for servicing, repairing, maintaining, and disposing of MVACs.[36] These standards were further supplemented with rules promulgated in 1995 and 1997 addressing the standards for CFC-12 recovery equipment and the handling of CFC-12 substitutes.[37]

Stationary Refrigeration and Air-Conditioning, http://www.epa.gov/ozone/title6/608/index.html.
  31. CAA § 608(a)(3); 42 U.S.C. § 7671g(a)(3).
  32. CAA § 608(b)(1); 42 U.S.C. § 7671g(b)(1).
  33. 40 C.F.R. § 82.154.
  34. 40 C.F.R. § 82.158(a).
  35. 40 C.F.R. § 82.154(e), (m).
  36. 57 Fed. Reg. 31.242 (July 14, 1992).
  37. 60 Fed. Reg. 21,682 (May 2, 1995), 62 Fed. Reg. 68,025 (Dec. 30, 1997).

Since 1992, facilities servicing MVACs must generally comply with the following requirements:

- The refrigerant must be processed with approved recovery and recycling equipment.
- All technicians must be properly trained and certified, and must use approved equipment.
- MVAC refrigerant must be properly disposed, recycled, or reclaimed.
- Proper records must be kept by all repair and service facilities.[38]

The EPA MVAC regulations also require that any person selling a Class I or II refrigerant that is suitable for use in a motor vehicle air-conditioner is required to prominently post a sign that states: "It is a violation of federal law to sell containers of Class I or Class II refrigerant of less than 20 pounds of such refrigerant to anyone who is not properly trained and certified to operate approved refrigerant recycling equipment."[39]

13.6   # Ban on Nonessential Products

Pursuant to CAA section 610, EPA is required to promulgate rules that identify and prohibit the sale or distribution of nonessential products that release Class I substances into the environment.[40] In 1993, EPA promulgated regulations implementing the CAA section 610 requirements, which contain a list of banned CFC-containing products, including certain plastic party streamers and noise horns, cleaning fluids for electronic and photographic equipment, plastic flexible or packaging foam, and aerosol products.[41] CAA section 610(d) also authorizes the prohibition of the sale or distribution of any aerosol product or other pressurized dispenser that contains a Class II substance, or any plastic foam product that contains or is manufactured with a Class II substance.[42]

---

38. 40 C.F.R. §§ 82.34, 82.42.
39. 40 C.F.R. § 82.42(c). Additional guidance on EPA's MVAC program is available at EPA, Ozone Layer Protection, Motor Vehicle Air Conditioning, http://www.epa.gov/ozone/title6/609/index.html.
40. CAA § 610(b); 42 U.S.C. § 7671i(b).
41. 58 Fed. Reg. 4768 (Jan. 15, 1993) (codified at 40 C.F.R. § 82.66); *see also* 58 Fed. Reg. 69,638 (Dec. 30, 1993) and 58 Fed. Reg. 69,672 (Dec. 30, 1993).
42. CAA § 610(d); 42 U.S.C. § 7671i(d).

The agency is also authorized to grant certain exceptions to the Class I and Class II substances ban, and various products have in fact been exempted, such as certain medical devices identified as essential by the U.S. Food and Drug Administration and portable fire extinguishers for certain uses.[43]

13.7   Labeling

As of May 15, 1993, a warning label must be placed on containers containing Class I or Class II substance, products containing Class I substances, and products directly manufactured with Class I substances.[44] CAA section 611 provides that the warning label must be clearly legible and conspicuous and state as follows:

> Warning: Contains [or Manufactured with] [insert name of substance], a substance which harms public health and environment by destroying ozone in the upper atmosphere.[45]

After January 1, 2015, labels must be placed on all products containing or manufactured with a Class II substance.[46] The EPA regulations also provide that the warning statement must be placed on the display panel of a product, or outer packaging, or other prominent place, so that it is readily available to the person purchasing the product.[47] Importers of foreign products containing or made with Class I or Class II substances must label items before the products enter into the United States.[48]

The determination of what constitutes "containing" or "manufactured with" a Class I or II substance is not always easy, and EPA's Stratospheric Ozone Protection Division has issued regulatory guidance for such determinations.[49] In addition, there are sev-

---

43. 40 C.F.R. §§ 82.66, 82.70. A summary of the product exemptions issued by EPA under the nonessential products rules is available at EPA, Ozone Layer Protection—Regulatory Programs, The Nonessential Products Ban, http://www.epa.gov/ozone/title6/noness/index.html.

44. 40 C.F.R. § 82.102. The labeling rule became applicable to methyl bromide on January 1, 1995, one year after the effective date of methyl bromide becoming a Class I ODS.

45. CAA § 611(b), (d); 42 U.S.C. § 7671j(b), (d).

46. CAA § 611(c), (d); 42 U.S.C. § 7671j(c), (d). EPA has the authority to require that products manufactured with a Class II substance be subject to the labeling rule before January 1, 2015; however, to date, EPA has not exercised that authority.

47. 40 C.F.R. § 82.108.

48. 40 C.F.R. §§ 82.114, 82.116.

49. 58 Fed. Reg. 8136 (Feb. 11, 1993).

eral exceptions to the definition of "manufactured with a controlled substance" that may apply, including instances where the product has not had physical contact with the controlled substance.[50] Moreover, a number of specific exemptions from the labeling requirements are spelled out in the regulations, including an exemption for products containing trace quantities of a controlled substance.[51]

13.8   Significant New Alternatives Policy Program

EPA's Significant New Alternatives Policy (SNAP) program implements CAA section 612, which calls for the replacement of listed ODS with "chemicals, product substitutes, or alternative manufacturing processes that reduce overall risks to human health or the environment" to the maximum extent practicable.[52] The SNAP program, promulgated on March 18, 1994, identifies and classifies substitutes for existing applications of ODS and evaluates whether they are acceptable substitutes.[53] In general, the substitutes must generally present a lower overall risk to human health and the environment than the Class I and II compounds being replaced.

Producers must submit a SNAP notification to EPA 90 days before introducing new or existing chemicals into interstate commerce for any significant new uses as substitutes for Class I substances.[54] EPA has, by regulation, extended these requirements to Class II substances as well.[55] When reviewing a submission of a new chemical into interstate commerce as a substitute for a Class I or Class II ODS, EPA uses a comparative risk assessment analysis. EPA's review criteria include

- atmospheric effects and related health and environmental impacts
- ecosystem risks
- occupational risks
- consumer risks

---

50. 40 C.F.R. § 82.104(b).
51. 40 C.F.R. § 82.106; *see also* 60 Fed. Reg. 4010 (Jan. 19, 1995).
52. CAA § 612(a); 42 U.S.C. § 7671k(a).
53. 59 Fed. Reg. 13,044 (Mar. 18, 1994).
54. 40 C.F.R. § 82.174.
55. 40 C.F.R. § 82.176(a).

- general population risks from ambient exposure to substitutes with direct toxicity and to increased ground-level ozone
- flammability
- the cost and availability of the substitute[56]

EPA publishes its acceptability determinations in the *Federal Register*. There are generally five types of determinations: (1) acceptable, (2) acceptable subject to use conditions, (3) acceptable subject to narrowed use limits, (4) unacceptable, and (5) pending. The Code of Federal Regulations also contains a list of acceptable and unacceptable substitutes for Class I and Class II substances in appendix A to 40 C.F.R. part 82.

13.9   Title VI Enforcement Action

Since the mid-1990s, EPA has initiated a number of enforcement actions against individuals and companies to enforce the Title VI requirements, with a particular focus on illegal imports of CFCs. EPA's enforcement efforts have also targeted the improper recovery and disposal of ODS. Significant civil and criminal penalties have been assessed in certain cases, and ODS enforcement has remained a high priority for the agency.[57]

In the 1990s, EPA also issued three civil penalty policies that address specific types of Title VI violations, including illegal importation, improper MVAC services, and noncompliant maintenance, service, repair, and disposal of appliances containing refrigerant.[58]

---

56.   40 C.F.R. § 82.180.

57.   A summary of recent EPA ODS enforcement cases is available at EPA, Ozone Layer Protection—Regulatory Programs, Enforcement Actions Under Title VI of the Clean Air Act, http://www.epa.gov/ozone/enforce/index.html.

58.   *See* EPA, Clean Air Act Stationary Source Civil Penalty Policy, at apps. VIII, IX, and X (Oct. 25, 1991), http://www.epa.gov/compliance/resources/policies/civil/caa/stationary/penpol.pdf.

14 Enforcement and Judicial Review

The Environmental Protection Agency has broad authority under the Clean Air Act to pursue alleged violators of the statute and implementing regulations. Under the CAA, EPA has sweeping investigative powers and is authorized to seek both injunctive relief and civil penalties. Moreover, the federal government is empowered to seek criminal penalties and jail time for knowing violations of the CAA. The 1990 CAA amendments expanded the scope of criminal liability to almost all key substantive requirements of the CAA. In addition, under the CAA, citizens are granted authority to act as private attorneys general and may file citizen suits seeking to enforce the CAA provisions where EPA or a state is not diligently prosecuting a civil action in a court.

In December 2010, for example, EPA announced its civil and criminal enforcement results for fiscal year 2010, and highlighted that it resolved 21 Prevention of Significant Deterioration/New Source Review (PSD/NSR) and air toxics civil enforcement actions via consent orders or other compliance orders with a total projected required investment in pollution controls of over $1.4 billion.[1] EPA states that its CAA enforcement actions in fiscal year 2010 will result in projected emission reductions of over 370 million tons of pollutants, such as SO_2, NO_x, volatile organic compounds (VOCs), and ammonia (NH_3).[2] In one high-priority enforcement area, EPA announced three major settlements with coal-fired utility companies in 2010 resolving alleged violations of the PSD/NSR program. In each of the settlements, EPA assessed

---

1. *See* EPA, Fiscal Year 2010 EPA Enforcement & Compliance Annual Results 10 (Dec. 2, 2010), http://www.epa.gov/compliance/resources/reports/endofyear/eoy2010/fy2010results.pdf#page=3.
2. *Id.*

significant civil penalties ($850,000, $950,000, and $3 million) in addition to substantial payments for the installation of pollution controls and the implementation of environmental mitigation projects.[3] In short, these numbers indicate that the agency pursues a significant number of alleged CAA violators and the resulting penalties, pollution control technology requirements, and other environmental mitigation costs are often substantial.

EPA has used its broad enforcement authority to initiate a number of high-profile enforcement actions against different industry sectors, including electric generating utilities, pulp and paper mills, petroleum refineries, ethanol production facilities, cement manufacturing plants, and diesel engine manufacturers.[4] EPA has effectively used its authority to force older stationary sources to install pollution controls through a series of enforcement initiatives under the PSD/NSR program. As discussed in section 5.4, one of EPA's primary enforcement initiatives has focused on coal-fired power plants, and as of mid-2011 EPA had settled 23 major NSR cases with the electric utility owners covering over 70 coal-fired plants.[5]

CAA section 307 provides for judicial review of administrative compliance and penalty orders. This section also authorizes any person to request review of an EPA rule, federal permit, National Ambient Air Quality Standard, New Source Performance Standard (NSPS), National Emissions Standard for Hazardous Air Pollutants (NESHAP), or any other final agency action.

14.1   Inspections and Evidence Gathering

EPA has expansive authority under CAA section 114 to request any information it may reasonably require for the purpose of (1) developing emission standards, (2) determining whether any person is in violation of a state implementation plan (SIP) require-

---

3. *See* EPA Civil Enforcement, Coal-Fired Power Plant Enforcement Initiative, http://www.epa.gov/compliance/resources/cases/civil/caa/coal/index.html.
4. EPA has highlighted some of its key stationary source and mobile source enforcement priorities at EPA Civil Enforcement, Clean Air Act National Enforcement Initiatives, http://www.epa.gov/compliance/civil/caa/caaenfpriority.html.
5. A summary of the settlements is available at EPA Civil Enforcement, Coal-Fired Power Plant Enforcement Initiative, http://www.epa.gov/compliance/resources/cases/civil/caa/coal/index.html

ment or a CAA standard, or (3) carrying out any provision of the CAA except Title II regarding mobile sources.[6] EPA will use its CAA section 114 authority to develop a factual record for its rule-makings as well as for enforcement purposes. Under CAA section 114, EPA may require a source to sample emissions and report the results, submit compliance certifications, install and use monitoring equipment, and provide any other information that the agency deems reasonably necessary. During inspections, EPA may also sample emissions, copy records, and inspect monitoring equipment or methods. For mobile sources, CAA section 208 sets out a separate information collection regime, but it is substantially similar to the provisions under CAA section 114.[7]

Generally, any nonconfidential business information may be released to the public pursuant to the Freedom of Information Act process.[8] To protect confidential business information (CBI) and trade secrets from release, a person must specifically request that such information be treated as CBI. EPA has adopted regulations addressing how CBI submittals are handled.[9]

Issuance of a CAA section 114 information request letter is often the first indication that EPA suspects a regulated entity of noncompliance with the CAA.[10] Failure to respond to a CAA section 114 request within the allotted time potentially subjects the regulated entity to civil penalties of up to $25,000 per day per violation pursuant to section 113.[11] The maximum penalty is now indexed for inflation and is currently $37,500 per day per violation.[12] EPA may also couple the CAA section 114 letter with an on-site inspection.

After presenting their credentials, EPA staff or an "authorized representative" may at "reasonable times" inspect an emission source or review records and information maintained by any

---

6. CAA § 114(a); 42 U.S.C. § 7414(a).
7. CAA § 208; 42 U.S.C. § 7542.
8. CAA § 114(c); 42 U.S.C. § 7414(c); 5 U.S.C. § 552.
9. 40 C.F.R. §§ 2.201 et seq.
10. Under CAA section 114, EPA may request that any "person" owning or operating an emission source comply with an information request. Similarly, under CAA section 113, EPA may find that any "person" has violated or is in violation of the CAA. The term *person* is broadly defined under the CAA to generally include an individual, corporation, partnership, state, and municipality. CAA § 302(e); 42 U.S.C. § 7602(e). For ease of reference, this chapter uses the phrase "regulated entity" to refer to the term "person."
11. CAA § 113(b)(2), (d)(1)(B); 42 U.S.C. § 7413(b)(2), (d)(1)(B).
12. 40 C.F.R. § 19.4, tbl.1. Effective January 12, 2009, the maximum penalty per day per violation was increased from $32,500 to $37,500. See 73 Fed. Reg. 75,340 (Dec. 11, 2008); 74 Fed. Reg. 626 (Jan. 7, 2009).

regulated entity that the agency believes has information relevant to an enforcement action or implementation of the CAA.[13] EPA often uses its inspection authority to fully review a regulated entity's compliance status. If the agency's inspection relates to SIP requirements, it must first provide notice to the state where the regulated entity is located unless the agency believes that the state will give the targeted entity advance warning.

EPA typically seeks consent to enter and inspect a facility. If consent is denied, the agency will attempt to obtain a search warrant from a federal district court to enforce the request. CAA section 114 allows the agency or its "authorized representative" to perform inspections.[14] EPA interprets this phrase to permit the hiring of contractors to conduct inspections on behalf of the agency. Two U.S. courts of appeal (the Sixth and Tenth Circuits) have disagreed with this assertion, but one has embraced it (the Ninth Circuit).[15] However, EPA generally takes the position that it may continue to use contractors in the circuits where there is no binding precedent prohibiting it.

EPA has substantial administrative subpoena authority to compel the disclosure of information, production of documents, or witness testimony in an enforcement proceeding. EPA may seek to enforce compliance with a subpoena in a federal district court. Failure to comply with a subpoena could subject a person to contempt sanctions.[16]

14.2   Monitoring, Record Keeping, and Reporting

The CAA and its implementing regulations are replete with various monitoring, record-keeping, and reporting requirements. Individual NSPS and NESHAPs also typically set out detailed monitoring, record-keeping, and reporting requirements. For example, the asbestos NESHAP requires notice before the start of demolition activities and the submission of a report after the remediation is

---

13. CAA § 114(a)(2); 42 U.S.C. § 7414(a)(2).
14. CAA § 114(a)(2); 42 U.S.C. § 7414(a)(2).
15. *See* Stauffer Chem. Co. v. EPA, 647 F.2d 1075 (10th Cir. 1981); United States v. Stauffer Chem. Co., 684 F.2d 1174 (6th Cir. 1982), *aff'd on other grounds*, 464 U.S. 165 (1984); Bunker Hill Co. v. EPA, 658 F.2d 1280 (9th Cir. 1981).
16. CAA § 307(a); 42 U.S.C. § 7607(a).

complete.[17] In addition, for sources subject to Title V (operating permits) and Title IV (acid rain program), the 1990 amendments to the CAA now compel submission of "compliance certifications," which require a responsible official (Title V) or a designated representative (Title IV) to certify the compliance status of a stationary source. Most SIP rules also require extensive monitoring, record keeping, and reporting.

EPA's credible evidence rule, promulgated in 1997, dramatically increased the potential use of such monitoring data and records in enforcement actions.[18] The rule provides that "any credible evidence or information" may be used to prove that a facility has violated the CAA. Thus, for example, if a particular EPA regulation previously stated that compliance with an emission standard would be calculated by a particular test method, EPA's credible evidence rule broadened the type of information that can be used to demonstrate a violation, such as operating log data or monitoring data. The credible evidence rule particularly affects compliance with NSPS, NESHAPs, SIP rules, PSD/NSR permits, and Title V operating permits where facilities may routinely record information that is used to optimize operations, but that is not explicitly retained for CAA compliance purposes. As discussed in chapter 10, EPA takes the position that a Title V permit shield will not relieve a source of complying with its applicable requirements even if a regulated entity's monitoring results did not detect a violation.[19]

14.3 Enforcement Authority

EPA's enforcement authority pursuant to CAA section 113 was substantially revised and expanded by the 1990 CAA amendments. Specifically, the 1990 amendments provide clear authority for the agency to assess civil and administrative penalties for both past and current violations of Title I (SIPs, NSPS, NESHAPs, PSD/NSR), Title IV (acid rain program), Title V (operating permits), and Title VI (stratospheric ozone protection).[20] The 1990 amendments

---

17. 40 C.F.R. § 61.145.
18. 62 Fed. Reg. 8314 (Feb. 13, 1997).
19. 62 Fed. Reg. at 8320.
20. See CAA § 113(a)(3), (b), (d); § 42 U.S.C. § 7413(a)(3), (b), (d).

also authorized EPA to issue administrative penalty orders for up to $25,000 per day per violation and "field citations" for up to $5,000 per day of violation.[21] EPA regulations have increased these statutory penalty amounts up to $37,500 per day per violation and up to $7,500 per day per violation, respectively, to account for inflation.[22] Criminal penalties for knowing violations were also expanded under the 1990 amendments.

In general, the agency may file civil enforcement actions in federal or state courts seeking injunctive relief, penalties, or both. As noted earlier, EPA also has a fairly broad authority to pursue administration enforcement actions. Furthermore, EPA may request that the Attorney General commence a criminal action if a person knowingly violates any requirement or prohibition of CAA Title I, an emergency order under CAA section 303, Title IV, Title V, or Title VI. Moreover, as explained in section 14.4, the CAA authorizes citizens to file civil suits seeking injunctive relief and penalties for alleged violations.

14.3.1   Administrative Enforcement Tools

CAA section 113(a) authorizes EPA to issue an administrative compliance order if a person has violated or is in violation of any requirement or prohibition of Title I, CAA section 303 emergency orders, Title IV, Title V, or Title VI contained in any "rule, plan, order, waiver, or permit" or for any nonpayment of a required fee.[23] A CAA section 113 administrative order cannot become effective until the alleged violator has had a chance to confer with the agency, except for a CAA section 112 violation concerning hazardous air pollutants. Failure to comply with the terms of a compliance order is itself a violation of the CAA that may trigger civil penalties. However, EPA must initiate a separate administrative penalty action or civil action in a court to collect penalties. In instances of alleged SIP violations, EPA must give the regulated entity and the applicable state 30 days' notice before a compliance order is issued.[24] This notice period provides the state with

---

21. 42 U.S.C. § 7413(b), (d)(3).

22. 40 C.F.R. § 19.4, tbl.1; see also 73 Fed. Reg. 75,340 (Dec. 11, 2008); 74 Fed. Reg. 626 (Jan. 7, 2009).

23. CAA § 113(a); 42 U.S.C. § 7413(a).

24. CAA § 113(a)(1); 42 U.S.C. § 7413(a)(1).

an opportunity to bring its own enforcement action first. If the state is not enforcing its PSD/NSR permitting requirements, then EPA may issue a finding of violation that the state is not complying with federal PSD/NSR requirements, as well as issuing an order prohibiting construction of the new stationary source.[25]

EPA's administrative penalty authority provides the agency with significant leeway to initiate an enforcement action more quickly than taking the costly and often uncertain route of filing a civil complaint in a federal district court. Moreover, once a matter is referred to the U.S. Department of Justice, EPA lawyers are typically no longer in a lead role on the case. While the federal-state partnership envisioned by the CAA promotes the states taking a lead role in enforcement, the CAA accords EPA with concurrent enforcement authority. EPA interprets CAA authority as authorizing it to file a separate federal enforcement action (also known as "overfiling") if the agency does not agree with a state's enforcement action or permitting decision.

EPA's authority to check or second-guess a state agency's PSD/NSR permitting decision was before the U.S. Supreme Court in 2003, and in *Alaska Department of Environmental Conservation v. EPA*, the Court affirmed that EPA has the authority under CAA sections 113(a)(5) and 167 to issue stop-work orders prohibiting a stationary source from beginning construction or modification activities.[26] The *Alaska* case involved a challenge by EPA to a best available control technology (BACT) determination made by the state agency that was authorized to issue PSD permits under an EPA SIP-approved permitting program. The Supreme Court concluded that EPA can overrule a state BACT determination when the decision is not reasonable.[27] The court did not address how long EPA may take before it issues a stop-work order under CAA

25. CAA § 113(a)(5); 42 U.S.C. § 7413(a)(5).
26. Alaska Dep't of Envtl. Conservation v. EPA, 540 U.S. 461 (2004). CAA section 113(a)(5) provides that "Whenever, on the basis of any available information, the Administrator finds that a State is not acting in compliance with any requirement or prohibition of the chapter relating to the construction of new sources or the modification of existing sources, the Administrator may—(A) issue an order prohibiting the construction or modification of any major stationary source in any area to which such requirement applies, (B) issue an administrative penalty order in accordance with subsection (d) of this section, or (C) bring a civil action under subsection (b) of this section." CAA § 113(a)(5); 42 U.S.C. § 7413(a)(5). CAA section 167 refers specifically to the PSD program, and states that the "Administrator shall, and a State may, take such measure, including issuance of an order, or seeking injunctive relief, as necessary to prevent the construction or modification of a major emitting facility which does not conform to the [PSD] requirements. . . ." CAA § 167; 42 U.S.C. § 7477.
27. 540 U.S. at 502.

sections 113(a)(5) and 167, and the CAA does not establish a time limit. Historically, EPA has exercised its authority to issue orders under CAA sections 113(a)(5) and 167 in very few instances.

Other federal courts have generally been skeptical of EPA efforts to challenge state PSD/NSR permitting decisions issued pursuant to a SIP-approved PSD program, particularly when construction or modification was commenced in reliance on a validly issued state PSD permit. For example, in *United States v. Solar Turbines*, the district court dismissed an EPA action for injunction and penalties because the source was in compliance with its state-issued PSD permit.[28] In *United States v. AM General Corp.*, the court held that a source is not liable for operating under the auspices of a facially valid state-issued PSD permit when EPA failed to make a finding of violation prior to issuance of the permit.[29] However, in *United States v. Campbell Soup Co.*, a California federal district court held that a state's decision to grant a state permit did not necessarily bar a federal enforcement action based on a SIP violation for failure to go through the applicable PSD permit proceedings for a major modification.[30]

As discussed earlier, EPA has authority under CAA section 167 to stop construction or modification of a source that does not meet the PSD program requirements. CAA section 167 orders, however, do not require prior notice to the source or state, nor do they require a conference with the agency before the order becomes effective.

CAA section 113(d) authorizes the EPA administrator to issue an administrative penalty order for up to $25,000 per day per violation (now $37,500 as indexed for inflation) with a cap of $200,000 (now $295,000 indexed for inflation) against any person who violates any requirement or prohibition of any rule, order, waiver, permit, or plan, or fails to pay any required fee, under the CAA except for Title II.[31] The administrative penalty authority was added by the 1990 amendments, and it provides a simplified and often more viable alternative to seeking enforcement of the CAA in a civil suit. The EPA administrator's authority under this section is limited to the 12-month period prior to ini-

---

28. United State v. Solar Turbines, 732 F. Supp. 535, 538–40 (M.D. Pa. 1989).
29. United States v. AM Gen. Corp., 34 F.3d 472 (7th Cir. 1994).
30. United States v. Campbell Soup Co., Civ-S-95-1854 DFL, 1997 U.S. Dist. LEXIS 3211 (E.D. Cal. Mar. 11, 1997).
31. CAA § 113(d)(1); 42 U.S.C. § 7413(d)(1); *see also* 40 C.F.R. § 19.4, tbl.1; 73 Fed. Reg. 75,340 (Dec. 11, 2008); 74 Fed. Reg. 626 (Jan. 7, 2009).

tiation of the administrative action (counted from the first alleged date of the violation), unless the administrator and Attorney General jointly determine that a larger penalty amount or longer period of violation is appropriate. An extension determination is not subject to judicial review. An alleged violator has 30 days to file a request for a hearing before an EPA administrative law judge (ALJ) after receiving notice that an administrative penalty order will be issued.

CAA section 205(c) provides a similar authority to issue administrative penalties for violations of certain mobile source requirements (including CAA sections 205(a) (new motor vehicles and engines), 211(d) (fuels), and 213(d) (nonroad vehicles and engines)).

EPA has several other administrative enforcement tools at its disposal as well. CAA section 113(d) authorizes EPA to create a field citation program to address minor violations. This authority is similar to issuing a traffic ticket for motor vehicle violations. Under the field citation authority, EPA inspectors may issue penalty citations on-site in the amount not to exceed $5,000 per day per violation (now $7,500 as indexed for inflation).[32] A person who receives a field citation may petition EPA for a hearing to contest the alleged violation and penalty.

EPA may also issue CAA section 303 "emergency" administrative orders to abate a danger to human health or the environment caused by any source of air pollution, without a showing of noncompliance with the CAA. CAA section 303 authorizes EPA to issue an emergency administrative order after it consults with the relevant state authorities and attempts to confirm the accuracy of the information upon which the order is based. The order could require cessation of the pollution (including plant shutdown) or any other action necessary to abate the endangerment to public health and the environment.

In addition, pursuant to CAA section 120, EPA may assess noncompliance penalties after it notifies the source of an alleged CAA violation. CAA section 120 noncompliance penalty assessments can be asserted only for ongoing violations; the intent is to recover the economic advantage that might otherwise accrue to a source by reason of its failure to comply.

---

32. CAA § 113(d)(3); 42 U.S.C. § 7413(d)(3); *see also* 40 C.F.R. § 19.4, tbl.1; 73 Fed. Reg. 75,340 (Dec. 11, 2008); 74 Fed. Reg. 626 (Jan. 7, 2009).

14.3.2   Civil Penalty Authority

CAA section 113(b) allows EPA to bring a suit in a U.S. district court seeking injunctive relief and/or civil penalties against any person who owns or operates a stationary source, and the agency may commence any action against any other person who violates provisions of the CAA.[33] This authority spans the requirements of any rule, order, waiver, or permit issued pursuant to the CAA and includes any nonpayment of a fee required under the CAA. Enforcement of SIP provisions must be preceded by a 30-day notice to the state of the alleged violation. Under CAA sections 113(b) and 113(d), EPA may seek civil penalties of up to $25,000 per day per violation (now $37,500 as indexed for inflation).[34] Civil complaints are referred by EPA to the U.S. Department of Justice (DOJ) for filing with the appropriate court.

Before filing a civil complaint, the DOJ is required, pursuant to Executive Order 12,778, to make a "reasonable effort" to contact the alleged violator, to attempt to settle the case before the complaint is filed.[35] The Executive Order procedure is designed to encourage early settlement. EPA has prepared guidance on civil penalty policies for stationary sources[36] and mobile sources.[37] Typically, before initiation of prefiling discussions with the alleged violator, EPA or DOJ will have calculated an acceptable penalty amount to settle the case pursuant to EPA's CAA civil penalty guidance.[38] In general, the civil penalty policy provides that the minimum acceptable penalty must recover the economic benefit that the violator gained by noncompliance with the CAA. In addition, a penalty amount is usually added to address the gravity or seriousness of the violation, for deterrence purposes. It is important to note that once a complaint has been filed, EPA/DOJ will typically seek the maximum penalties allowed under the CAA and will no longer be restricted by the penalty policy guidance.

---

33. CAA § 113(b); 42 U.S.C. § 7413(b).

34. CAA § 113(b); 42 U.S.C. § 7413(b); *see also* 40 C.F.R. § 19.4, tbl.1; 73 Fed. Reg. 75,340 (Dec. 11, 2008); 74 Fed. Reg. 626 (Jan. 7, 2009).

35. Exec. Order 12,778, 3 C.F.R. § 359 (1991).

36. Clean Air Stationary Source Civil Penalty Policy (Oct. 25, 1991, amended May 11, 1992, Dec. 28, 1992, July 19, 1993, June 1, 1994, July 23, 1995, May 18, 1999).

37. *See, e.g.,* U.S. EPA Office of Enforcement and Compliance, Clean Air Act Mobile Source Civil Penalty Policy—Vehicle and Engine Certifications (Jan. 16, 2009); U.S. EPA Office of Air and Radiation, Interim Diesel Civil Penalty Policy (Feb. 8, 1994).

38. *See* EPA Civil Enforcement, Civil Penalty Policies, http://cfpub.epa.gov/compliance/resources/policies/civil/penalty/.

If a settlement resolving an enforcement matter is achieved, the agreement between the parties will be embodied in a consent decree. The DOJ will lodge the proposed consent decree and a complaint with the applicable federal district court, and petition the court for approval after a time period for public comment (typically, a minimum of 30 days is required). Notice of the availability for public comment on the draft consent decree will be published in the *Federal Register*.

CAA section 113(e) sets out mandatory criteria that courts and EPA must address when setting penalties to resolve enforcement actions in the federal courts and in EPA administrative proceedings. In general, the following factors are considered: the size of the violator's business; the economic impact of the penalty on the business; the violator's full compliance history and any good faith efforts to comply; the duration of the penalty, as established by any credible evidence (including evidence of any applicable test method); the violator's payment of penalties previously assessed for the same violation; the economic benefit the violator gained from noncompliance; the seriousness of the violation; and any other factors justice may require.[39]

CAA section 113(f) also authorizes a "bounty hunter" provision whereby the EPA administrator may pay up to $10,000 to any person who provides information leading to a criminal conviction or civil penalty.[40]

14.3.3 Criminal Penalty Authority

CAA section 113(c) provides criminal penalties for a variety of CAA violations. The section states that "any person who knowingly violates any requirement or prohibition" of a SIP, any orders under Title I, section 303, Title IV, or any requirement of Title V or Title VI shall be punished by a fine pursuant to Title 18 of the U.S. Code (the federal penal code), or imprisonment of not more than five years, or both.[41]

---

39. CAA § 113(e); 42 U.S.C. § 7413(e). Administrative penalty assessments under CAA section 113(d)(1) and field citations under CAA section 113(d)(3) are subject to the CAA section 113(e) penalty assessment factors. Administrative and civil penalties issued pursuant to CAA section 205(b) for mobile sources are also governed by the penalty assessment factors set forth in CAA section 113(e).
40. CAA § 113(f); 42 U.S.C. § 7413(f).
41. CAA § 113(c)(1); 42 U.S.C. § 7413(c)(1).

CAA section 113 also establishes criminal penalties for a person who (1) knowingly makes a false material statement, representation, or certification or falsifies any monitoring device or test method; (2) knowingly fails to pay a fee; or (3) negligently or knowingly releases a hazardous air pollutant (HAP) listed under CAA section 112 or an extremely hazardous pollutant under the Superfund statute that places another person in imminent danger of death or serious bodily injury.[42]

Fines for individuals convicted of knowing violations of the CAA can reach a maximum of $250,000 per conviction, or twice the gross pecuniary gain derived from the violation.[43] Generally, organizational entities convicted of knowing violations can face fines of up to $500,000, or twice the pecuniary gain from the noncompliance.[44] Filing a false statement, document, or certification, or tampering with or falsifying any monitoring device or test method, are also subject to criminal fines pursuant to U.S. Code Title 18, potentially up to two years in prison, or both.[45] A person who knowingly fails to pay a fee or negligently releases a HAP that places another person in imminent danger of death or serious bodily injury is subject to misdemeanor penalties and up to one year in prison, or both.[46]

A person who knowingly releases a HAP that places another person in imminent danger of death or serious bodily injury is subject to severe punishment: imprisonment for up to 15 years, or a fine pursuant to U.S. Code Title 18, or both.[47] If convicted, an organization is potentially subject to a fine of up to $1 million for each offense. In addition, the criminal provisions of the CAA generally provide that after the first conviction, the maximum punishment shall be doubled with respect to both fine and imprisonment.

The section on criminal penalties covers a broad range of CAA violations and is primarily limited to "knowing" violations. There is no discussion in CAA section 113(c) or its legislative history that indicates whether the section applies to past violations

---

42. CAA § 113(c)(2), (3), (4), (5); 42 U.S.C. § 7413(c)(2), (3), (4), (5).
43. 18 U.S.C. § 3571(b)(3), (d).
44. As defined under CAA section 113(c)(5), organizational defendants include "a corporation, company, association, firm, partnership, joint stock company, foundation, institution, trust, society, union, or any other association of persons."
45. CAA § 113(c)(2); 42 U.S.C. § 7413(c)(2).
46. CAA § 113(c)(3), (4); 42 U.S.C. § 7413(c)(3), (4).
47. CAA § 113(c)(5); 42 U.S.C. § 7413(c)(5).

as well as present violations. Nevertheless, the plain language of the section indicates that it applies to a person who "knowingly violates" certain requirements of the CAA. Thus, a past "knowing" violation of the CAA would appear to possibly subject a facility to potential criminal penalties.

The 1990 amendments also extended criminal liability to "responsible corporate officers."[48] Lower-level employees, when directly following management orders or implementing their ordinary duties, are shielded from criminal liability unless their conduct was "knowing and willful.[49] Similar to other environmental statutes, the evidentiary burden of proof standard requires that the alleged criminal violations be proved beyond a reasonable doubt.

14.3.4   **Statutes of Limitations**

CAA sections 113 and 167 give no clear indication of the statute of limitations for violation of the CAA. There is a split in the U.S. courts of appeal on whether a five-year statute of limitations will apply to CAA violations in the context of PSD/NSR program violations. Further complicating the analysis is the fact that some of the decisions have turned on the specific provisions in the applicable SIP. Moreover, the federal courts have often reached divergent conclusions on whether the five-year statute of limitations bars just penalties or whether injunctive relief is also potentially time-barred.[50]

In *National Parks & Conservation Ass'n, Inc. v. Tennessee Valley Authority*, the U.S. Court of Appeals for the Eleventh Circuit held that the alleged failure to obtain a PSD permit and undergo a BACT analysis for a project completed in 1983 was not an ongoing violation, and was time-barred under the five-year statute of limitations set forth in 28 U.S.C. § 2462.[51] The court also denied the plaintiffs' request for injunctive relief requiring application of

---

48. CAA § 113(c)(6); 42 U.S.C. § 7413(c)(6).

49. CAA § 113(h); 42 U.S.C. § 7413(h).

50. The plain language of 28 U.S.C. § 2462 applies to claims for legal relief, and it is silent on whether it applies to equitable remedies. Section 2462 provides that "an action, suit or proceeding for enforcement of any civil fine, penalty, or forfeiture . . . shall not be entertained unless commenced within five years from the date when the claim first accrued."

51. Nat'l Parks & Conservation Ass'n, Inc. v. Tenn. Valley Auth., 502 F.3d 1316 (11th Cir. 2007).

BACT, holding that where a party's legal remedies (penalties) are time-barred, the party's concurrent equitable claims are barred under the "concurrent remedy doctrine."[52] In *Sierra Club v. Otter Tail Power Co.,* the U.S. Court of Appeals for the Eighth Circuit also applied a five-year statute of limitations.[53] The court held that the failure to obtain a PSD permit for alleged major modifications that were initiated in 1995, 1998, and 2001 was time-barred because the modifications occurred more than five years before the suit was filed.[54]

In contrast, the U.S. Court of Appeals for the Sixth Circuit reached a different conclusion in *National Parks & Conservation Ass'n, Inc. v. Tennessee Valley Authority.*[55] In a lawsuit involving the same parties as the Eleventh Circuit decision discussed earlier, but a different Tennessee Valley Authority plant, the court held that the alleged PSD program violations were ongoing because a provision in the Tennessee SIP allowed for the issuance of a PSD permit even after construction had been completed.[56]

Several federal district courts have addressed the issue of whether civil penalty claims for PSD violations are barred by the statute of limitations if the alleged modifications occurred more than five years before the enforcement action was initiated. The majority of these lower courts have held that PSD permit violations are one-time events, and are subject to the five-year statute of limitations in 28 U.S.C. § 2462.[57] A minority of federal district courts have recognized that PSD permit violations are ongoing events.[58]

At least one federal district court has applied the five-year statute of limitations in 28 U.S.C. § 2462 for violations of SIP provisions. In *United States v. SCM Corp.,*[59] the court held

---

52. 502 F.3d at 1326–27.
53. Sierra Club v. Otter Tail Power Co., 615 F.3d 1008 (8th Cir. 2010).
54. 615 F.3d at 1018.
55. Nat'l Parks & Conservation Ass'n, Inc. v. Tenn. Valley Auth., 480 F.3d 410 (6th Cir. 2007).
56. 480 F.3d at 419.
57. *See, e.g.,* United States v. Midwest Generation, 694 F. Supp. 2d 999 (N.D. Ill. 2010); United States v. Cinergy Corp., 397 F. Supp. 2d 1025 (S.D. Ill. 2005); New York v. Niagara Mohawk Power Corp., 263 F. Supp. 2d 650 (W.D.N.Y. 2003); United States v. Westvaco Corp., 144 F. Supp. 2d 439 (D. Md. 2001); United States v. Campbell Soup Co., No. Civ-S-95-1854 DFL, 1997 U.S. Dist. LEXIS 3211 (E.D. Cal. Mar. 11, 1997).
58. *See, e.g.,* Sierra Club v. Portland Gen. Elec. Co, 663 F. Supp. 2d 983 (D. Or. 2009); United States v. Duke Energy Corp., 278 F. Supp. 2d 619 (M.D.N.C. 2003), *aff'd on other grounds,* 411 F.3d 539 (4th Cir. 2005), *vacated sub nom.* Envtl. Def. v. Duke Energy Corp., 549 U.S. 561 (2007); United States v. Am. Elec. Power Serv. Corp., 137 F. Supp. 2d 1060 (S.D. Ohio 2001).
59. 667 F. Supp. 1110 (D. Md. 1987).

that civil penalties are available for violations occurring within the five years prior to the filing of the action. In the *SCM* case, EPA argued that SCM had violated Maryland's SIP each day from August 7, 1977, to early 1987. The court held that penalties may be assessed for days of violation occurring prior to the issuance of a notice of violation; however, EPA could only assess penalties for violations occurring within the five years preceding the date the complaint was filed (i.e., January 2, 1980, to January 2, 1985).

14.4   Citizen Suits

All major environmental statutes provide for citizen suit provisions, and the CAA is no exception. The 1990 amendments significantly revamped the CAA citizen suit provisions.[60] CAA section 304 authorizes citizens to file a civil complaint in a federal district court against persons alleged to have violated (if there is evidence that the alleged violation has been repeated) or persons currently violating a federally enforceable emission standard or limitation or order.[61] The term *emission standard or limitation* is broadly defined to encompass SIP requirements, PSD/NSR requirements, NSPS, NESHAPs, Title IV requirements, Title V permitting requirements, and Title VI stratospheric ozone protection requirements. Citizen suits can seek injunctive relief as well as civil penalties, although the civil penalties are paid directly to a special fund in the U.S. Treasury established to provide for air quality compliance and enforcement activities. Most citizen suits are ultimately settled before the case goes to trial. In general, many citizen groups have successfully obtained settlements that provide for payment of penalties to the U.S. Treasury, an award of attorney's fees to the citizen group, and a substantial payment for a mitigation project or supplemental environmental project (such as land preservation).

Under the CAA, before commencing a citizen suit citizens must serve a letter of notice on the alleged violator, the EPA administrator, and the state in which the alleged violation

---

60. *See generally* Roy S. Belden, *Preparing for the Onslaught of Clean Air Act Citizen Suits: A Review of Strategies and Defenses*, 1 ENVTL. LAW. 377 (1995).

61. CAA § 304(a); 42 U.S.C. § 7604(a). Citizen suits may also be filed against EPA when it allegedly fails to perform a nondiscretionary duty under the CAA (e.g., promulgate regulations by a certain statutorily mandated date.).

occurred or is occurring.[62] The notice letter must be sent at least 60 days before the complaint is filed. In theory, this prefiling notice obligation gives the alleged violator an opportunity to correct the problem as well as allows time for the applicable permitting agency to take action. CAA section 304(b) provides that citizen suits may not be initiated when either EPA or the state has commenced and is diligently prosecuting a civil action in either a federal or state court. The diligent prosecution provision was designed to prevent duplicative litigation.

Citizen groups acting as private attorneys general can wield a significant amount of enforcement authority. Often, EPA and the state environmental agencies do not have sufficient resources or the inclination to pursue all alleged violators. Citizen groups have often donned the mantel of authority and used this power very effectively. In particular, new construction and development are often magnets for citizen group involvement and monitoring.

14.5 Judicial Review

The judicial review of an administrative penalty orders may be obtained by filing a petition for review in the appropriate U.S. district court within 30 days from the date the administrative penalty order becomes final.[63] Jurisdiction for review of an administrative penalty assessment will lie either in the U.S. District Court for the District of Columbia or in the federal district where the violation is alleged to have occurred, where the alleged violator resides, or where the alleged violator's principal place of business is located. EPA regulations provide that an administrative penalty order is not final until all of the available administrative remedies have been exhausted.[64] Generally, a challenge to an EPA administrative penalty order must first exhaust all administrative review remedies before an appeal may be filed with a federal district court. A challenge to an administrative penalty order is initially brought before an EPA ALJ. The ALJ's decision can then be appealed to EPA's Environmental Appeals Board. Courts will review the agency's penalty order decision to determine if there is substantial evi-

---

62. CAA § 304(b)(1)(A); 42 U.S.C. § 7604(b)(1)(A).
63. CAA § 113(d)(4); 42 U.S.C. § 7413(d)(4).
64. See generally 40 C.F.R. § 22.

dence in the record to support the finding of a violation, and they will analyze whether the agency's finding constitutes an abuse of discretion.[65]

EPA takes the position that agency-issued administrative compliance orders are not "final agency actions," and review of an EPA administrative compliance order has generally been held to not constitute a final agency action within the meaning of CAA section 307(b).[66] Nevertheless, at least one court held that an administrative stop-work order issued under CAA sections 113(a)(5) and 167 imposed such a severe burden on the defendant that it constituted a final agency action.[67]

The CAA provides that agency rulemaking proceedings are subject to judicial review. CAA section 307(b) governs judicial review of most EPA rules and accords exclusive jurisdiction to the Court of Appeals for the D.C. Circuit, if it is a nationally applicable rule, or to the court of appeals for the circuit where a locally applicable rule has its impact. Petitions for review of a rule must be filed within 60 days of publication of the rule in the *Federal Register*.[68] However, CAA section 307(b) does accord review in instances where grounds arise after the sixtieth day. In a "grounds arising after" situation, a petition must be filed within 60 days after such grounds arise.

Judicial review is limited to items in the administrative record, and the CAA provides that only an objection that was raised with reasonable specificity during the public comment period (including any public hearing) may be raised during judicial review of an EPA rule.[69] Therefore, in a challenge to a rule, a judicial panel ordinarily may not consider facts or data that are not part of the agency's rulemaking record.[70] A limited exception applies when a proposed rule failed to put the regulated community on notice of a position that EPA took in the final rule.[71]

Even if a party submits information that contradicts or detracts from EPA's conclusions, a court need not necessarily set EPA's

---

65. CAA § 113(d)(4); 42 U.S.C. § 7413(d)(4).
66. *See* Lloyd A. Fry Roofing Co. v. EPA, 554 F.2d 885 (8th Cir. 1977); Asbetec Constr. Servs. Inc. v. EPA, 849 F.2d 765 (2d Cir. 1988).
67. Allsteel v. EPA, 25 F.3d 312 (6th Cir. 1994).
68. CAA § 307(b); 42 U.S.C. § 7607(b).
69. *Id.*
70. *See* Envtl. Def. Fund v. Costle, 657 F.2d 275, 284 (D.C. Cir. 1987).
71. *See generally* Small Refiner Lead Phase-Down Task Force v. EPA, 705 F.2d 506, 546 (D.C. Cir. 1983); PPG Indus. v. Costle, 659 F.2d 1239, 1249–50 (D.C. Cir. 1981).

rule aside. Courts review EPA's rulemaking under the standard of "arbitrary, capricious, abuse of the agency's discretion, or otherwise not in accordance with the law."[72] Usually, the application of the arbitrary and capricious standard focuses on whether the agency's decision making responded to the comment at all or otherwise offered a reasoned explanation for its ultimate course of action.[73] Policy judgments, however, are difficult to reverse under the arbitrary and capricious standard. In general, a court may not substitute its own policy judgments for those of the agency.[74]

The U.S. Supreme Court reviewed the issue of when deference should be accorded to agency interpretations. In *Chevron U.S.A. v. Natural Resources Defense Council*, the Court reviewed whether EPA's plantwide definition is a permissible construction of the term "stationary source."[75] In *Chevron*, the Court set out a two-step review process. In step one, the reviewing court will review the plain language of the statute to determine whether Congress has "directly spoken to the precise question at issue."[76] If the intent is clear, then the court will give effect to the plain language of the statute. If the statute is silent or ambiguous, the court will move to step two, and determine whether "the agency's answer is based on a permissible construction of the statute."[77] If the construction is permissible, then the court should accord the agency's interpretation considerable weight.[78]

If there is an agency action under the CAA, which is not subject to review under CAA section 307(b), review may still be had under the Administrative Procedure Act (APA).[79] Pursuant to the APA, "(a) person suffering legal wrong because of agency action, or adversely affected or aggrieved by agency action within the meaning of the relevant statute" is permitted to obtain judicial review.[80] The APA applies not only to an agency action made reviewable by statute, but also to any other final agency action for which there is no other adequate remedy in a court.

---

72. CAA § 307(d)(9); 42 U.S.C. § 7607(d)(a).
73. *See* Motor Vehicle Mfr.'s Ass'n v. State Farm Mut. Auto Ins. Co., 463 U.S. 26, 48–49 (1983).
74. *See* Vt. Yankee Nuclear Power Corp. v. Nat. Res. Def. Council, 435 U.S. 519, 557–58 (1978); Weyerhaeuser Co. v. Costle, 590 F.2d 1011 (D.C. Cir. 1981).
75. Chevron U.S.A. v. Nat. Res. Def. Council, 467 U.S. 837 (1984).
76. 467 U.S. at 842–43.
77. 467 U.S. at 843.
78. 467 U.S. at 843–44.
79. 5 U.S.C. § 701 *et seq.*
80. 5 U.S.C. § 702.

Frequently Asked Questions

National Ambient Air Quality Standards

1. What is ambient air?

Ambient air is defined in 40 C.F.R. § 50.1(e) as "that portion of the atmosphere, external to buildings, to which the general public has access." In other words, all outdoor air is considered ambient air.

2. What is an air pollutant?

Air pollutants are gases and vapors or other tiny particles such as liquid droplets, dust, smoke, or soot found in the air. Pollutants can harm health, the environment, and property.

3. What is a criteria pollutant?

Criteria pollutants are a group of six very common air pollutants regulated by the Environmental Protection Agency (EPA) on the basis of scientific and technical criteria regarding the public health and environmental effects of those pollutants. The criteria pollutants are ozone (O_3), carbon monoxide (CO), sulfur dioxide (SO_2), nitrogen dioxide (NO_2), particulate matter (PM), and lead (Pb).

4. What are volatile organic compounds?

Volatile organic compounds (VOCs) are organic chemicals that all contain the element carbon. Organic chemicals are the basic chemicals found in living things, and in products derived from what once were living things. VOCs include gasoline and petroleum products as well as industrial chemicals such as various solvents. These compounds typically produce vapors at room temperature and normal atmospheric pressure. VOCs, along with nitrogen oxide, are precursors of O_3. Ground level or stratospheric O_3 is also commonly known as *smog*.

5. How are the primary and secondary National Ambient Air Quality Standards (NAAQS) different?

The primary standards are intended to protect public health, and theoretically may be set at more stringent levels than secondary standards. Secondary standards are intended to protect public welfare, a broad concept that includes effects on soils, water, crops, vegetation, man-made materials, animals, wildlife, weather, visibility, and the climate. *Public welfare* is also defined to include damage to property, hazards to transportation, and effects on personal comfort and well-being. In reality, there is little practical difference, as four of the five secondary NAAQS are set at the same levels as the primary NAAQS.

6. How are the NAAQS established?

Pursuant to CAA section 108, EPA is required to list those air pollutants that may be reasonably anticipated to endanger public health or welfare. Once EPA has made this listing determination, EPA must then issue air quality criteria for such pollutants. The air quality criteria must reflect the latest scientific knowledge that identifies the effects of such pollutants on public health or welfare. CAA section 109 requires EPA to publish proposed regulations prescribing primary and secondary NAAQS for each air pollutant for which air quality criteria have been issued. For any air pollutants for which air quality criteria are issued after December 31, 1970, EPA is required to publish the proposed primary and secondary NAAQS simultaneously with the issuance of such air quality criteria. After a reasonable period for the submission of comments, EPA is required to finalize the standards.

7. How are the NAAQS enforced?

The NAAQS are theoretically not directly enforceable; however, they do set ambient air quality levels that should not be exceeded and thus serve as the basis for emission standards in applicable SIP rules and emission limits in air permits. The potential air quality impacts from new source construction and major modifications to existing major sources are modeled prior to submittal of a PSD/NSR permit application. Permitting agencies are required to consider the modeling results from such air emission sources on the NAAQS for the particular area, and the potential impacts are factored into the applicable permit conditions.

State Implementation Plans

8. What is the difference between an attainment and a nonattainment area?

The country is generally divided into areas that are in attainment or in nonattainment with each NAAQS. States or areas within two or more states are divided into geographic areas, for air quality planning purposes called *air quality control regions* (AQCRs). More than 260 AQCRs are listed in the Code of Federal Regulations. Each AQCR is designated as being either in attainment or nonattainment for each criteria pollutant.

There are also "unclassifiable" areas, which generally are not subject to the more rigorous nonattainment area requirements, but instead are subject to attainment area provisions.

9. What is a state implementation plan?

A *state implementation plan* (SIP) is a collection of state emission control strategies and regulations, including state statutes, rules, transportation control measures, emission inventories, or local ordinances (collectively "SIP rules"), that are used by a state or local regulatory agency to reduce air pollution and carry out its responsibilities under the federal Clean Air Act. Once approved by EPA, these control strategies and regulations become part of the federally enforceable SIP. The federally approved SIPs are set forth in the state-specific subparts of 40 C.F.R. part 52. The CAA requires that each control strategy and regulation be approved by EPA before it can be considered part of a SIP. As a practical matter, states submit individual control strategies and regulations (as well as revisions to such strategies and regulations) to EPA on a rolling basis for approval. Thus, a SIP is a continually changing collection of federally approved state emission control strategies and regulations.

10. How does one know what is in a SIP?

Pursuant to the Clean Air Act Amendments of 1990, Congress directed EPA to collect EPA-approved state SIP control strategies and regulations for each state and make them available from the applicable EPA regions. Some EPA regions have put this data on their web pages.[1] Although EPA has identified all the applicable SIP rules for each state, practitioners will still need to confirm whether a particular state strategy or regulation was approved in its entirety by EPA. On occasion, EPA will approve only part of a state SIP submittal. After approval of a SIP rule, EPA will publish its approval finding in the *Federal Register*. The *Federal Register* notice should include references to each EPA-approved SIP rule.

11. How long does it take to amend a SIP?

After a SIP submittal is deemed complete, EPA is required to approve or disapprove (or partially approve and disapprove) the SIP submittal. EPA generally has 60 days to make a determination on the completeness of a SIP submittal; if the agency has not made a decision within six months after receipt of the submittal, then the submittal is deemed by operation of law to meet the minimum criteria. Once a SIP submittal is complete, EPA is generally required to approve or disapprove it within 12 months. Nevertheless, this deadline is frequently missed. States and other interested

---

1. *See* Availability of Federally Enforceable State Implementation Plans for All States, 63 Fed. Reg. 63,986 (Nov. 18, 1998).

parties have the option of suing EPA to force a decision on a SIP submittal; however, this course of action is rarely taken. As a result, it may take several years for EPA to finally make a decision on some SIP submittals.

12.   What rules apply if the state has adopted new SIP rules but EPA has not yet approved them?

Prior to submitting a rule to EPA for approval, the state must approve the rule through its own rulemaking process. Thus, the rule will be applicable to a source as a state-only enforceable standard until EPA has approved the standard. Once it is approved by EPA, a rule also becomes federally enforceable. If a SIP submittal is revising an existing EPA-approved SIP rule, then both the SIP submittal and the previously approved SIP rule will be in effect. Until EPA approves the new SIP submittal, both standards will apply to the source, but only the older EPA-approved rule will be federally enforceable.

13.   What is a federal implementation plan?

If a state fails to make a required SIP submittal, or if EPA determines that a submittal is either incomplete, or if EPA disapproves a submittal, then EPA must promulgate its own rules that will apply to sources in the state. These EPA-issued rules constitute a *federal implementation plan* (FIP). EPA is required to issue a FIP within two years if the state has not rectified the SIP deficiency. If a state submits an approvable SIP submittal prior to the expiration of the two-year period, a FIP is not needed. In addition, EPA is required to impose sanctions pursuant to CAA section 179 within 18 months after issuing a finding disapproving a SIP submittal. Sanctions may include either a loss of highway funding or a requirement that emissions offsets (on at least a 2 to 1 basis) be obtained for new or modified sources major sources.

14.   What happens if a nonattainment area does not reach attainment by the statutorily required date?

If a nonattainment area fails to meet the applicable NAAQS by the attainment date, then EPA will issue a failure-to-attain determination in the *Federal Register*. CAA section 179(c) requires that such a determination be based on the area's air quality at the time of the attainment date, and the decision must be made as expeditiously as practical, but not later than six months after the attainment date. Failure to reach attainment by the prescribed date will trigger the requirement to submit additional emission reduction measures, as part of the SIP, that can be feasibly implemented in light of technological availability, costs, and any non-air-quality and other air-quality-related health and environmental impacts. The SIP revision must be submitted within one year of the EPA notice of failure to attain. EPA may set a new attainment date pursuant to CAA section 172. In addition, two one-year extensions of the attainment date may be possible pursuant to CAA section 172(a)(2). For ozone nonattainment areas, failure to meet the statutorily prescribed attainment dates will trigger an automatic bump-up to the next highest classification or the classification applicable to the area's design value. No ozone nonattainment area may be reclassified as extreme under the bump-up provisions of CAA section 181.

Prevention of Significant Deterioration and New Source Review

15. What is New Source Review?

The New Source Review (NSR) program contains two components: the Prevention of Significant Deterioration (PSD) program for attainment areas and the nonattainment area NSR program. *New Source Review* generally refers to the process by which new major sources and major modifications of existing major sources are permitted. A stationary source undergoing the NSR process generally must apply either best available control technology (BACT) (for attainment areas) or lowest achievable emission rate (LAER) technology (for nonattainment areas), as well as undertaking a detailed air modeling and impacts analysis. In addition, major stationary sources undergoing PSD review must analyze potential impacts on nearby Class 1 areas and evaluate the potential consumption of PSD increments. For nonattainment areas, major stationary sources undergoing NSR permitting generally must also obtain emission offsets.

16. What is the difference between a major PSD/NSR source and a minor PSD/NSR source?

A major stationery source under the PSD program is any source belonging to a list of 28 source categories that emits or has the potential to emit 100 tons per year or more of any pollutant regulated under the CAA (except for HAPs regulated under CAA section 112), or any other stationary source that emits or has the potential to emit regulated pollutants in an amount equal to or greater to 250 tons per year. A major stationary source in a nonattainment area is generally defined the same as in the PSD program; however, the emission cutoffs for determining major sources are usually 100 tons per year or lower. Certain nonattainment areas (i.e., O_3, CO, and PM_{10}), have lower major source applicability thresholds. For example, the major source trigger for serious ozone nonattainment areas is 50 tons per year or more of VOCs or NO_x, and the major source threshold for severe ozone nonattainment areas is 25 tons per year of VOCs or NO_x. A minor PSD/NSR source is a stationary source with emissions that are below the applicable major source cutoffs for PSD and nonattainment NSR areas.

17. What constitutes best available control technology?

BACT is a technology standard that is determined on a case-by-case basis for new major sources and major modifications to existing major sources in attainment areas. *BACT* is defined as the most effective control technology available for a pollutant emitted by a particular type of source, taking into account energy and economic considerations and other environmental impacts. BACT is determined by a "top-down" review consisting of the following five steps: (1) identify all available control technologies, (2) eliminate technically infeasible options, (3) rank all remaining control technologies by control effectiveness (including cost effectiveness), (4) evaluate the most effective controls and document results, and (5) select BACT (i.e., the most effective control option not eliminated in steps 1–4).

18. What is the lowest achievable emission rate?

LAER is a technology standard that is determined on a case-by-case basis for new major sources and major modifications to existing major sources in nonattainment areas. At a minimum, LAER must be equivalent to BACT. *LAER* is generally defined as the most stringent emission limitation contained in a SIP rule of any state for the applicable category of sources or the most stringent emission limitation achieved in practice by a source in the same source category as the applicant.

19. What is an emission offset?

Emission offsets may be required for new major source construction or major modifications to an existing major source in certain nonattainment areas. Offsets are a right to emit certain pollutants and are created from emission reductions due to source shut downs, the addition of pollution controls, or enforceable emission limitations. Offsets must be real, quantifiable, permanent, enforceable, and surplus, and may be bought and sold as well as "banked" for future use.

20. What is the difference between SIP-approved PSD authority and delegated PSD authority?

SIP-approved PSD authority arises when EPA specifically approves a state's PSD program that contains the minimum elements listed in 40 C.F.R. § 51.166. In a SIP-approved PSD program, the state is the permitting authority. In a delegated PSD program, EPA has not specifically approved a separate state PSD program, but has authorized the state to implement EPA's federal program contained in 40 C.F.R. § 52.21. Under delegated PSD authority, the state issues a PSD permit; however, EPA has the authority to review and veto issuance of a PSD permit.

21. What is an increment?

PSD increments are based on the maximum allowable increase in ambient air quality concentrations for a particular criteria pollutant that may occur above a baseline concentration level. Baseline areas generally include those portions of an attainment or an unclassifiable area where the new major source or major modification will be located, as well as any attainment or unclassified area where potential emissions from the new or modified major source will have a significant impact. The PSD increments apply to three criteria pollutants: NO_2, SO_2, and PM (both PM_{10} and $PM_{2.5}$). Three classes of increments are applicable to the three classes of air quality areas: Class I (national parks and federal wilderness areas), Class II, and Class III. After all the increments for a particular area have been consumed, no additional new major sources or major modifications to existing major sources may be constructed in that area.

New Source Performance Standards

22. What is a New Source Performance Standard?

New Source Performance Standards (NSPS) are technology-based standards that establish a minimum floor of emission limitations or work practice standards applicable to certain categories of industrial sources such as electric utility steam generating units, petroleum refiners, and lead smelters. NSPS are applied to new, modified, and reconstructed pieces of equipment (i.e., the "affected facility").

23. What is best demonstrated technology?

Best demonstrated technology is the level at which NSPS standards are established. NSPS are intended to reflect the degree of emission limitation achievable through application of the best system of emission reduction that has been "adequately demonstrated," while considering the costs of achieving the reductions and any non-air-quality health and environmental impact and energy requirements. NSPS is generally not as stringent as BACT and LAER technology requirements imposed during a PSD/NSR permitting procedure.

24. What is the difference between a modification under the PSD/NSR program and under the NSPS program?

Both the PSD/NSR program and the NSPS program use the same definition of *modification* set forth in section 111(a)(4) of the CAA. A *modification* is defined under the CAA as "any physical change in, or change in the method of operation of, a stationary source which increases the amount of any air pollutant emitted by such source or which results in the emission of any air pollutant not previously emitted." By regulation, EPA has limited the application of PSD/NSR review to only those major modifications of existing major sources that constitute a physical or operational change that results in a significant net increase in emissions. As modified in 2002, the PSD/NSR program generally compares past actual emissions, on a tons-per-year basis, to the future projected actual annual emissions resulting from the physical or operational change to determine whether there will be a significant net increase in emissions. The emissions increase step of the NSPS modification analysis differs significantly from the PSD/NSR rules. Under the NSPS program, emission increases are calculated by comparing the hourly potential emission rate, at a maximum physical capacity, before and after the physical or operational change. The U.S. Supreme Court in *Environmental Defense v. Duke Energy Corp.*[2] addressed the issue of how a *modification* is determined under the PSD/NSR program. The Court upheld EPA's interpretation and concluded that the agency was authorized to apply different emissions tests under the PSD/NSR program and the NSPS program.

Control of Hazardous Air Pollutants

25. What is a maximum achievable control technology standard?

A *maximum achievable control technology* (MACT) standard is a technology-based emission limitation that applies to sources of hazardous air pollutants (HAPs). CAA section 112(d) specifies how MACT standards for new and existing sources are determined. MACT standards for existing and new sources must be based on the maximum degree of reduction achievable, taking into consideration certain factors prescribed by the CAA.

26. How are MACT standards developed for new and existing sources?

CAA section 112(d) specifies that EPA shall establish HAP emission standards for existing and new sources based on the maximum degree of reduction achievable "taking into consideration the cost of achieving such emission reduction, and any non-air quality health and environmental impacts and energy requirements." However, Congress also imposed minimum stringency requirements, which EPA calls "MACT floors," that "apply without regard to either costs or the other factors and methods listed in section 7412(d)(2)." MACT for new sources is based on a level of control that shall be set at a level no less stringent than the emission control that is achieved in practice by the best-controlled similar source. Setting MACT for existing sources is somewhat less stringent and is based on the following formula: the average emission limitation achieved by the best-performing 12 percent of existing sources for categories or subcategories with 30 or more sources. For categories or subcategories with less than 30 sources, the average limitation shall be based on the five best-performing existing sources. EPA also has authority to go "beyond the floor" for new and existing sources and set more stringent standards than suggested by a MACT floor analysis. In general, EPA must demonstrate that costs to achieve beyond-the-floor MACT standards are reasonable.

---

2. 549 U.S. 561 (2007).

27. What is a generally available control technology?

EPA may promulgate HAP standards for area sources based on *generally available control technology* (GACT). *Area sources* are nonmajor HAP emitters. GACT is generally a less rigorous emission standard than MACT and does not involve a MACT floor-type evaluation.

28. What is a residual risk standard?

CAA section 112(f) directs EPA to promulgate residual risk standards within eight years after promulgation of applicable MACT standards if EPA determines that residual risks remain following implementation of the applicable MACT standards for various source categories and subcategories. Residual risk standards are established to provide an ample margin of safety to protect public health or to prevent an adverse environmental effect (taking into consideration costs, energy, safety, and other relevant factors). If MACT standards applicable to sources emitting a known, probable, or possible human carcinogen do not reduce lifetime excess cancer risks to a level of less than one in one million, EPA is generally required to establish residual risk standards for such source categories or subcategories.

29. What is a risk management plan?

A *risk management plan* (RMP) is a document that must be prepared if the owner or operator of a stationary source has more than a threshold quantity of regulated HAP substances in a "process" on-site. A *process* is generally defined to include any activity involving a regulated substance, including any use, storage, manufacturing, handling, or on-site movement of such substance. A RMP generally includes a hazard assessment, a prevention program, and an emergency response program; it requires a fairly detailed discussion of the regulated substances that are stored or used on-site and typically also requires the development of a worse-case release scenario as part of the hazard assessment. An RMP also must include instructions on safety and handling precautions and a thorough emergency response plan setting forth procedures that will be employed during an accidental release.

Visibility Protection

30. What is a Class I area?

CAA section 162(a) specifically lists Class I areas that are required to be protected under the visibility program. Class I areas include (1) international parks, (2) national wilderness areas exceeding 5,000 acres in size, (3) national memorial parks exceeding 5,000 acres in size, and (4) national parks exceeding 6,000 acres in size. A total of 156 Class I areas have been identified in the EPA regulations at 40 C.F.R. §§ 81.400 *et seq.*

31. What is an air-quality-related value?

Air-quality-related values (AQRVs) are not specifically defined by the CAA or the EPA regulations. CAA section 165 indicates that AQRVs include visibility, and in a 1996 proposed rule, EPA defined AQRVs to include visibility or a scenic, cultural, physical, biological, ecological, or recreational resource that may be affected by a change in air quality. This definition has not yet been formally adopted.

32. What is the role of a federal land manager?

The federal land manager (FLM) is responsible for overseeing air quality in Class I areas that may affected by emissions from a proposed new major source or a major modification to an existing major source. FLMs include the secretary of the federal department with responsibility over a Class I area, or the secretary's designate. The FLMs include the Department of Interior/National Park Service (national parks and monuments), the Department of Interior/U.S. Fish and Wildlife Service (national wildlife refuges), and the Department of Agriculture/National Forest Service (national wilderness areas). The FLM will consider whether a PSD increment will be violated by emissions from a proposed project and review the overall potential impact of the proposed project's air emissions on the nearby Class I area. The FLM may file comments on the proposed project. In general, the burden is on the FLM to demonstrate to the satisfaction of the permitting authority that potential emissions from the proposed project will have an adverse impact on an AQRV for a particular Class I area.

Acid Rain Control

33. How is acid rain formed?

Acid rain is formed when SO_2 and NO_x, which are emitted by many stationary and mobile sources, such as power plants and cars, react with water, oxygen, and oxidants to form sulfuric acid and nitric acid. Rainwater, snow, fog, and other precipitation containing sulfuric acid and nitric acid fall to the earth as acid rain. Acid rain is more acidic than normal precipitation and causes acidification of lakes and streams and contributes to the damage of trees, plants, and soils.

34. What is an SO_2 allowance?

An SO_2 allowance authorizes the emission of one ton of SO_2 during a particular year for sources subject to the CAA's Title IV acid rain program. Title IV generally applies to fossil-fuel-fired electric generating units that produce electricity for sale. An affected source must have allowances that equal or exceed its SO_2 emissions for each calendar year.

35. What is a continuous emissions monitoring system?

A *continuous emissions monitoring system* (CEMS) is a piece of equipment, generally attached via a probe to an emissions stack or vent, that continuously measures air emissions from a stationary combustion source, such as a boiler or combustion turbine. Continuous emission monitoring systems under the acid rain program measure SO_2, NO_x, carbon dioxide (CO_2), and opacity. Certain NSPS also impose requirements to install CEMS and continuously monitor air emissions. However, the acid rain program CEMS rule generally imposes more stringent monitoring requirements than the NSPS CEMS provisions.

Title V Operating Permits

36. What is a Title V operating permit?

A Title V operating permit is intended to bring together all applicable federally required and/or federally approved air emission limitations, work practice standards, and monitoring, record-keeping, and reporting requirements for a facility into one document. By including all federal requirements in a single permit, it is typically much easier for EPA, state agencies, and citizen groups to identify the applicable regulatory limits and initiate an enforcement action. A Title V operating permit may also include state-only enforceable provisions.

37. What is a permit shield?

EPA's Title V rules provide that a permit shield may be included in a Title V operating permit. A permit shield generally provides that compliance with the terms and conditions of the permit shall be deemed compliance with any applicable federal requirements as of the date of permit issuance, as long as the applicable requirements are specifically identified in the permit or the permitting agency determines in writing that such requirements do not apply. In other words, if a state permitting agency incorrectly determines that a standard is not applicable, the permittee will generally be shielded from an enforcement action, during the term of the permit, for a violation of that standard. There are exceptions to a permit shield, including a prohibition on shielding permittees from complying with emergency orders. In addition, an "application shield" may be provided when a source submits a timely and complete Title V permit application. The facility is allowed to continue operations in compliance with application terms during the pendency of the Title V permit application review.

38. What is enhanced monitoring?

CAA section 114(a)(3) allows EPA to require enhanced monitoring from major stationary sources. In connection with the Title V program, EPA has generally required two types of monitoring to satisfy the enhanced monitoring requirement. The first type of enhanced monitoring is *compliance assurance monitoring* (CAM) for certain major sources. CAM applies to pollutant-specific emission units that use a control device to achieve compliance and have a precontrol potential to emit that is equal to or greater than the major source cutoff levels. For example, a coal-fired boiler would be viewed as a pollutant-specific emission unit for NO_x, SO_2, VOCs, PM_{10}, and CO. The CAM rule generally requires additional monitoring of indicator parameters to help determine whether a piece of equipment is in compliance with the applicable emission limits and standards. Indicator parameters might include monitoring pressure drop in a baghouse (a particulate matter control device) or monitoring oxygen flow in a boiler. The second type of monitoring that may satisfy enhanced monitoring requirements is *periodic monitoring*, which may be required pursuant to the Title V rules. If an applicable emission limit or emission standard does not require periodic testing or instrumental or noninstrumental monitoring, EPA's Title V rules require that periodic monitoring sufficient to yield reliable data to determine compliance must be incorporated into the Title V permit. In other words, periodic monitoring may be used as a gap filler when the underlying standard contains only a one-time compliance test, or does not provide for testing or monitoring, or specifies no monitoring frequency.

Greenhouse Gas Emissions

39. What are greenhouse gas emissions?

EPA's greenhouse gas (GHG) emissions rulemaking efforts have primarily focused on six types of greenhouse gas emissions: CO_2, methane (CH_4), nitrous oxide (N_2O), hydrofluorocarbons (HFCs), perfluorocarbons (PFCs), and sulfur hexafluoride (SF_6). EPA's mandatory greenhouse gas reporting rule codified at 40 C.F.R. part 98 defines greenhouse gas emissions as the six primary GHGs and other "fluorinated greenhouse gases." EPA's complete list of GHGs and their global warming potential is set forth at 40 C.F.R. part 98, subpart A, table A.

Mobile Sources and the Regulation of Fuels

40. What is the difference between tailpipe standards and evaporative standards?

Tailpipe standards apply to the emissions from mobile source engines, such as automobiles, trucks, and buses. In other words, the tailpipe standards apply to the emissions directly emitted by the mobile source when it is running. Evaporative standards apply to evaporative emissions that are caused during operation, during vehicle refueling, and during nonoperation (e.g., when the vehicle is out in the hot sun or high heat). Evaporative standards include the Stage II gasoline fuel-pump recovery systems used in ozone nonattainment areas, and on-board refueling vapor recovery canisters for light-duty vehicles and trucks.

41. What qualifies as a transportation control measure?

Transportation control measures (TCMs) are required as part of the state implementation plan for severe and extreme ozone nonattainment areas. TCMs include programs designed to encourage carpooling, greater use of mass transit, and similar measures to reduce work-related vehicle trips.

42. What is reformulated gasoline?

Reformulated gasoline (RFG) standards are set by the 1990 amendments. The goal of the RFG program is to foster cleaner-burning gasoline to reduce air emissions in ozone nonattainment areas. CAA section 211(k) sets the following compositional specifications for reformulated gasoline: (1) a 2.0 weight percent oxygen minimum, (2) a 1.0 volume percent benzene maximum, (3) a prohibition on heavy metals, (4) a prohibition on an increase in NO_x emissions, and (5) achievement of required toxics and VOC reductions.

43. What is oxygenated gasoline?

Oxygenated gasoline is required in areas in nonattainment with the CO NAAQS. In cold temperatures, motor vehicles emit more CO, and the addition of an oxygenate to motor fuels helps car engines burn cleaner and emit less CO. Oxygenates include ethanol, methyl tertiary butyl ether, and ethyl tertiary butyl ether.

Stratospheric Ozone

44. What is the difference between tropospheric ozone and stratospheric ozone?

Tropospheric ozone, or ground level ozone, is also known as smog. It is formed when VOCs and NO_x react in the presence of sunlight. Heavy concentrations of ground-level ozone may cause health problems for humans and affect plant life. *Stratospheric ozone* occurs approximately 6 to 30 miles (10 to 48 kilometers) above the Earth's surface, in the stratosphere. The ozone layer consists of high concentrations of ozone and it protects the Earth's surface from ultraviolet radiation from the sun.

45. What is the Montreal Protocol?

The *Montreal Protocol on Substances That Deplete the Ozone Layer* is an international treaty implementing the principles of the Vienna Convention for the Protection of the Ozone Layer. The Vienna Convention, entered in 1985, committed the signatory countries to protect the ozone layer and to cooperate with each other in scientific research on ozone depletion. As of mid-2011, 196 nations have signed the Montreal Protocol, which aims to reduce and eventually eliminate man-made ozone-depleting substances. The Montreal Protocol initially took effect on January 1, 1989, and has been amended four times. The signatories to the Montreal Protocol agreed to implement domestic regulatory measures to ban and control substances that deplete the ozone layer.

Enforcement and Judicial Review

46. If a source violates the CAA, what penalties may apply?

Under CAA sections 113(b) and (d), EPA may assess civil and administrative penalties for up to $25,000 per day, per violation. The penalty amount has increased to the current $37,500 per day, per violation, to account for inflation. Criminal penalties for knowing violations may also be assessed. In addition, EPA has authority to seek injunctive relief, including ordering compliance with specific emission limitations or prohibitions or ordering a facility to cease violating the CAA. Further, EPA has emergency authority to order the abatement of a danger to human health or the environment. An emergency order could require cessation of the pollution (including plant shutdown) or any other action necessary to abate the danger to public health or the environment.

47. What is a field citation?

CAA section 113(d) authorizes EPA to issue field citations to address minor violations of the CAA. Under the field citation authority, EPA inspectors may issue penalties at the time of the inspection in an amount not to exceed $5,000 per day, per violation. (This amount is now set at $7,500 per day, per violation, to account for inflation). A field citation is similar to a traffic ticket for a motor vehicle violation.

48. What constitutes credible evidence of a violation?

EPA's "credible evidence" rule, promulgated in 1997, modifies the NSPS and National Emissions Standards for Hazardous Air Pollutants (NES-HAP) general provisions and the federal rules governing SIP approvals to add language stating that for purposes of determining a "violation of any standard . . . nothing shall preclude the use, including the exclusive use, of any credible evidence or information relevant to whether a source would have been in compliance with the applicable requirements if the appropriate performance or compliance test or procedure had been performed." Credible evidence may include continuous emission monitoring data, emission factor calculations, parameter monitoring, and essentially any data that can somehow relate back to the specific rule's reference test method procedures for determining compliance.

49. Under what circumstances can a citizen suit be filed?

CAA section 304 authorizes citizens to file a civil complaint in a federal district court against persons or entities alleged to have violated or to currently be violating an emissions standard or limitation or an order issued by EPA or a state. Citizen suits may also be filed against EPA when the agency has allegedly failed to perform any nondiscretionary duty under the CAA. In general, citizens may allege violations of SIP requirements, PSD/NSR requirements, NSPS, NESHAPs, Title IV requirements, Title V permitting requirements, and stratospheric ozone protection requirements. Citizen suits typically may not be initiated when either EPA or a state has commenced and is diligently prosecuting a civil action against the alleged violator in either a federal or state court.

50. What does it mean to be federally enforceable?

Federally enforceable requirements include those emission standards or limitations or work practice conditions implemented pursuant to the federal CAA or EPA regulations implementing the CAA. EPA-approved state statutes, regulations, and control strategies, (i.e., SIP rules) are also considered federally enforceable requirements. Federally enforceable air emission limitations, work practice standards, and other requirements may be enforced by either EPA, states, or citizen groups.

Key Cases

National Ambient Air Quality Standards (NAAQS)

How NAAQS Are Set

Natural Resources Defense Council v. Train, 411 F. Supp. 864 (S.D.N.Y.), *aff'd*, 545 F.2d 320 (2d Cir. 1976). The Natural Resources Defense Council (NRDC) filed suit against the Environmental Protection Agency for its failure to list lead as a criteria pollutant. NRDC argued that once EPA has found that a pollutant "has an adverse effect on public health and welfare," EPA must regulate that criteria pollutant. EPA countered that it has the sole discretion in the initial decision on whether to list a criteria pollutant. The court held that EPA must list a pollutant as a criteria pollutant once EPA has found that such pollutant potentially has an adverse effect on public health and welfare.

American Petroleum Institute v. Costle, 665 F.2d 1176 (D.C. Cir. 1981), *cert. denied sub nom. American Petroleum Institute v. Gorsuch*, 455 U.S. 1034 (1982). Industry groups and environmental and health nongovernmental organizations challenged EPA's promulgation of the ozone NAAQS. The court determined that some procedural errors had been made (specifically failing to seek the Science Advisory Board's advice and comment); nevertheless, the court upheld the final standards, concluding that the administrative record provided a rational basis for EPA's conclusions.

American Lung Ass'n v. EPA, 134 F.3d 388 (D.C. Cir. 1998). The American Lung Association and other nongovernmental organizations challenged EPA's determination that it would not revise the SO_2 NAAQS. The D.C. Circuit held that EPA failed to adequately explain its decision not to revise the SO_2 NAAQS, and remanded the EPA SO_2 determination to the agency for further proceedings.

Whitman v. American Trucking Ass'n, 531 U.S. 457 (2001). The U.S. Supreme Court reviewed EPA's new eight-hour ozone NAAQS and "fine" particulate matter ($PM_{2.5}$) NAAQS, and affirmed in part, reversed in part, and remanded the D.C. Circuit decision that had held that EPA's interpretation of Clean Air Act section 109, which requires EPA to periodically review and revise NAAQS, was unconstitutional. The Court reversed the D.C. Circuit's conclusion that

EPA's interpretation of its standard-setting authority ran afoul of the nondelegation doctrine of the U.S. Constitution, and determined that CAA section 109(b)(1) does not impermissibly delegate legislative powers to EPA. The Court also affirmed that CAA section 109(b) does not permit the EPA administrator to consider implementation costs in setting NAAQS. Further, the Court recognized that EPA's implementation policy was unlawful in that the agency could not construe the interaction between the subpart 1 and subpart 2 ozone NAAQS provisions to render the more prescriptive subpart 2 provisions a nullity. The Supreme Court concluded that the interplay between subpart 1 and subpart 2 was ambiguous, and remanded the ozone NAAQS to EPA to develop a reasonable interpretation of how the gaps in subpart 2's requirements are to be given effect under the subpart 1 provisions in implementing the new eight-hour ozone NAAQS.

How NAAQS Are Revised

Environmental Defense Fund v. Thomas, 870 F.2d 892 (2d Cir.), *cert. denied sub nom. Alabama Power Co. v. Environmental Defense Fund*, 493 U.S. 991 (1989). The Environmental Defense Fund filed suit against EPA for not reviewing and revising the SO_2 NAAQS. EPA claimed that it had discretion as to whether or not it should review and revise the SO_2 NAAQS. The Second Circuit held that EPA has a mandatory duty to review air quality criteria every five years.

Natural Resources Defense Council v. EPA, 902 F.2d 962 (D.C. Cir. 1990), *vacated in part on other grounds*, 921 F.2d 326 (D.C. Cir. 1991), *cert. dismissed sub nom. Alabama Power Co. v. Natural Resources Defense Council*, 498 U.S. 1075 (1991), and *cert. dismissed sub nom. National Coal Ass'n v. Natural Resources Defense Council*, 498 U.S. 1075 (1991), and *cert. denied sub nom. American Iron & Steel Institute v. EPA*, 498 U.S. 1082 (1991). Several industry groups challenged EPA's revision of the NAAQS for particulate matter from total suspended particulates to particles with a diameter of 10 microns or less (PM_{10}). The court upheld the revision as not arbitrary or capricious, holding that EPA was acting within its expertise when it partially based its decisions on conflicting or uncertain data.

American Trucking Ass'ns, Inc. v. EPA, 283 F.3d 355 (D.C. Cir. 2002). Petitioners challenged various aspects of the revised National Ambient Air Quality Standards for ozone and particulate matter (PM) that were promulgated by EPA in 1997. In a prior decision, the Supreme Court (531 U.S. 457 (2001)) affirmed in part, reversed in part, and remanded part of the case to the D.C. Circuit for further proceedings. On remand, the D.C. Circuit held that EPA's adoption of the NAAQS for ozone and $PM_{2.5}$ was not arbitrary or capricious. Certain State and industry petitioners argued that in setting the primary NAAQS for ozone and $PM_{2.5}$, EPA "did not apply any legal standard," and the petitioners asserted that EPA failed to set the primary ozone and $PM_{2.5}$ NAAQS at levels " 'requisite' . . . to protect the public health with an adequate margin of safety." EPA responded that it had no obligation to determine a "safe level" of ozone or $PM_{2.5}$ prior to adopting a primary NAAQS. The court agreed and concluded that "EPA has no obligation either to identify an accurate "safe level" of a pollutant or to quantify precisely the pollutant's risks prior to setting primary NAAQS." The court noted that "EPA must err on the side of caution . . . [in] setting the NAAQS at whatever level it deems necessary and sufficient to protect the public health with an adequate margin of safety, taking into account both the available evidence and the inevitable scientific uncertainties."

South Coast Air Quality Management District v. EPA, 472 F.3d 882 (D.C. Cir. 2006), *decision clarified on denial of reh'g*, 489 F.3d 1245 (D.C. Cir. 2007), *cert. denied sub nom. National Petrochemical & Refiners Ass'n v. South Coast Air Quality Management District*, 552 U.S. 1140 (2008), and *cert. denied sub nom. Chamber of Greater Baton Rouge v. South Coast Air Quality Management District*, 552 U.S. 1140 (2008). The D.C. Circuit vacated EPA's Phase 1 Implementation Rule for the eight-hour ozone NAAQS. The court rejected EPA's reasons for implementing the eight-hour standard in certain nonattainment areas under subpart 1 instead of the more prescriptive subpart 2. The court also concluded that EPA had the authority to revoke the one-hour ozone NAAQS provided that adequate antibacksliding provisions are in place. By limiting the vacatur, the court let stand EPA's revocation of the one-hour ozone NAAQS and the antibacksliding provisions of the Phase 1 Implementation Rule.

American Farm Bureau Federation v. EPA, 559 F.3d 512 (D.C. Cir. 2009) (per curiam). Several states and state agencies, industry groups, and environmental groups filed challenges to EPA's final rule to review the $PM_{2.5}$ and PM_{10} NAAQS. The D.C. Circuit granted the petitions for review of the $PM_{2.5}$ NAAQS, holding that EPA improperly relied on only long-term studies and failed to adequately explain why an annual level of 15 $\mu g/m^3$ is "requisite to protect the public health" including vulnerable subpopulations, while providing an "adequate margin of safety." The court remanded the primary $PM_{2.5}$ NAAQS to EPA for reconsideration. Further, the court ruled that the EPA unreasonably concluded that the secondary $PM_{2.5}$ NAAQS was adequate to protect the public welfare from adverse effects on visibility. In addition, the D.C. Circuit rejected the petition seeking review of the primary PM_{10} daily standard and denied the petition challenging the revocation of the PM_{10} annual NAAQS.

Cost and Technological Feasibility

Lead Industries Ass'n v. EPA, 647 F.2d 1130 (D.C. Cir.), *cert. denied*, 449 U.S. 1042 (1980). Lead Industries Association challenged EPA over the ambient air quality standards that EPA set for lead, claiming that the NAAQS was too stringent because of its likely severe adverse economic impacts. The D.C. Circuit held that the EPA standard was reasonable and that the agency was not to consider economic or technological feasibility when setting the standards. The court also held that EPA, to ensure an absence of adverse health effects, must leave an adequate margin of safety (in other words, err on the side of caution) when setting the NAAQS.

State Implementation Plans (SIPs)

Cost and Technological Feasibility

Union Electric Co. v. EPA, 427 U.S. 246, *reh'g denied*, 429 U.S. 873 (1976). Missouri adopted a SIP that required air emission reductions from three of Union Electric's power plants. Union Electric obtained variance permits that allowed them to continue to emit the same amount of air emissions for a specific amount of time. Once the permits expired, Union Electric challenged EPA's prior approval of Missouri's SIP. Union Electric claimed that the reductions called for in the SIP were not technologically or economically feasible and that the company would have to shut down those offending plants and reduce its electric service. The Supreme Court held that Congress did not intend EPA to consider claims of technological or economic feasibility when reviewing and approving a SIP. The Court said that compliance was always possible by shutting down the polluting source entirely.

Navistar International Transportation Corp. v. EPA, 941 F.2d 1339 (6th Cir. 1991), *cert. denied*, 490 U.S. 1039 (1989). Navistar petitioned for review of EPA's disapproval of a SIP revision applicable to facilities operated by Navistar. The surface coating lines at the manufacturer's plants used paints containing volatile organic compounds (VOCs) that contributed to ozone formation. The court declined to rule that EPA had acted arbitrarily or capriciously in finding that the revision was inconsistent with the statutory requirement that nonattainment area SIPs provide for the implementation of all reasonably available control measures as expeditiously as possible. The court held that EPA neither overstepped the bounds of its authority nor acted unreasonably when it found that the company had failed to demonstrate that compliance was not technically and economically feasible.

State Flexibility to Develop SIP Rules

Train v. Natural Resources Defense Council, 421 U.S. 60 (1975). NRDC filed suit against EPA for approving Georgia's SIP rule as per CAA section 110(a). The Court held that Georgia's rule, granting a variance to an individual pollution source, must be approved by EPA.

Under CAA section 110(a)(2), the agency is required to approve a SIP rule that provides for the timely attainment and subsequent maintenance of ambient air standards, and that also satisfies that section's other general requirements. The agency may devise and promulgate a specific federal implementation plan of its own only if a state fails to submit a SIP rule(s) that satisfies those requirements.

Bethlehem Steel v. Gorsuch, 742 F.2d 1028 (7th Cir. 1984). Indiana submitted a proposed SIP rule to EPA for approval; the rule included specific emission standards and a compliance schedule applicable to Bethlehem Steel. EPA partially approved the SIP submittal and set aside the state's specific timetable for Bethlehem Steel. The court held that EPA's disapproval of the compliance schedule applicable to Bethlehem Steel was invalid. The court determined that EPA could not, in the guise of a partial approval, remove words of limitation to make a state standard more stringent without following the specific procedures of the CAA approval process for SIP submittals. The court noted, though, that the CAA does allow EPA to approve some portions and disapprove other portions of SIP submittals.

Virginia v. EPA, 108 F.3d 1397, *modified on other grounds*, 116 F.3d 499 (D.C. Cir. 1997). The D.C. Circuit struck down EPA's final rule requiring 12 northeastern states and the District of Columbia to revise their SIPs to adopt what is essentially the California Low Emission Vehicle (LEV) program to reduce NO_x and VOCs. In response to a finding by the Ozone Transport Commission recommending the implementation of additional ozone controls (namely the California LEV program), EPA issued a SIP call declaring each northeastern state's SIP inadequate and directing those states to adopt new control measures. The court reviewed the scope of EPA's authority under CAA section 110, and concluded that each state has the liberty "to adopt whatever mix of emission limitations it deems best suited to its particular situation." The court determined that EPA's two alternatives were essentially a pretext, and as a practical matter, EPA required the northeastern states to adopt the California LEV program because no state would seriously entertain the notion of adopting the more stringent requirements of the substitute program.

Kentucky Resources Council, Inc. v. EPA, 467 F.3d 986 (6th Cir. 2006). The Sixth Circuit reviewed a challenge to EPA's approval of a revision to the Kentucky State Implementation Plan (SIP) that would allow the state's vehicle inspection and maintenance program to be reclassified as a contingency measure in the SIP. The court concluded that the change did not violate the CAA's antibacksliding requirements, and upheld the SIP revision. The court also determined that the substitute control measures, which included the use of high transfer efficiency spray guns and limitations on solvent use in cold cleaning degreasing operations, were sufficient to sustain the anticipated improvements in the Northern Kentucky nonattainment area's air quality.

SIP Revision Timetables

General Motors Corp. v. United States, 496 U.S. 530 (1990). General
Motors (GM) filed an action against EPA claiming that the agency
is barred from enforcing an existing SIP if EPA fails to take action
on a proposed SIP revision within four months. EPA claimed that
an enforcement bar was a drastic remedy for EPA's delay and that
GM could have brought an action to compel agency action. The
Supreme Court held that the current approved SIP is the applicable
SIP under which enforcement can be brought until the revised SIP is
approved. The Court further found that there are other statutory remedies available when EPA delays in acting on a SIP revision.

Conditional Approval

Natural Resources Defense Council v. EPA, 22 F.3d 1125 (D.C. Cir.
1994). NRDC and trade associations representing automobile dealers filed petitions for review of EPA's action addressing SIP rules providing for reductions in automobile emissions. The court held that a
SIP or SIP revision, even if not approvable in its present form, can be
made so if the state adopts specific EPA-required changes within the
prescribed conditional period. A SIP revision must already contain
some specific enforceable measures before it can be conditionally
approved, and it must be submitted by the statutory deadlines. The
court further determined that EPA cannot use committal SIPs to postpone statutory deadlines.

Reasonably Available Control Technology (RACT) Determinations

National Steel Corp. v. Gorsuch, 700 F.2d 314 (6th Cir. 1983). National
Steel sought review of EPA's approval, conditional approval, and
disapproval of various provisions of Michigan's SIP. National Steel
claimed that EPA's decision was arbitrary and capricious in that it
imposed its own standards for RACT, and that achieving the EPA
standards was not feasible. The court held that in reviewing a proposed SIP revision to determine its adequacy, EPA can verify inde-
pendently that the provisions in the state plan represent RACT.
Sources could be required to meet RACT requirements without the
need for showing that the source contributes to nonattainment.

NO$_x$ SIP Call

Michigan v. EPA, 213 F.3d 663 (D.C. Cir. 2000). The D.C. Circuit largely
affirmed EPA's requirement that 19 of the 22 SIP call states implement emission controls to reduce NO$_x$ emissions to a specified budget level by 2007. In 1998, EPA promulgated the NO$_x$ SIP call rule,
which concluded that NO$_x$ emissions from certain states in the east-

ern portion of the United States contributed significantly to the non-attainment of or interfere with the maintenance of the ozone NAAQS in downwind states. The court upheld EPA's interpretation of how to determine whether upwind states "significantly contribute" to ozone NAAQS compliance problems in downwind states. It also upheld EPA's authority and methodology to calculate state NO_x budgets. The court did vacate the inclusion of Georgia, Missouri, and Wisconsin in the NO_x SIP call, holding that there was a lack of evidence indicating that NO_x emissions from these states contributed to ozone nonattainment in downwind states. The court also remanded limited portions of the rule to EPA for further proceedings.

Section 126

Appalachian Power Co. v. EPA, 249 F.3d 1032 (D.C. Cir. 2001). EPA finalized its CAA section 126 rule in January 2000, finding that stationary sources of NO_x emissions in twelve upwind states and the District of Columbia contribute significantly to ozone nonattainment in northeastern states. The EPA section 126 rule imposed controls on various downwind sources, and a number of the affected plants petitioned for judicial review. The D.C. Circuit largely upheld the CAA section 126 rule, concluding that (1) EPA was not required to postpone its final action on downwind states' contribution petitions pending approval of state implementation plan (SIP) revisions that had been requested by upwind states, (2) EPA reasonably looked to an entire upwind state's NO_x emissions contribution, rather than to emissions of specified stationary sources in upwind state when determining whether the emissions resulted in a "significant contribution" to downwind states' nonattainment, (3) EPA's NO_x emissions growth projections were arbitrary to the extent its model assumed a baseline of negative growth in electric power generation over the next ten years, and (4) EPA failed to adequately justify its change in classification of cogenerators that sell electricity to the electric grid as EGUs. The last two findings were remanded to EPA for reconsideration.

Clean Air Interstate Rule

North Carolina v. EPA, 531 F.3d 896 (per curiam), *on reh'g in part,* 550 F.3d 1176 (D.C. Cir. 2008). The D.C. Circuit vacated the Clean Air Interstate Rule (CAIR), holding that the rule was fundamentally flawed. On rehearing, CAIR was temporarily reinstated in order to maintaining the environmental benefits of implementing CAIR while allowing EPA sufficient time to address the flaws in the rule. The court held that CAA section 110 requires an analysis of sources that contribute significantly to downwind nonattainment or interfere with the maintenance of attainment areas, and the CAIR cap-and-trade requirements were region-wide programs that were not based on individual source contributions. Another key finding was that the allocation of NO_x and SO_2 allowances under CAIR was not based on each upwind state's contribution to down-wind nonattainment or interference with maintenance of attainment areas. Further, the court concluded that EPA did not have the statutory authority to require the retirement of SO_2 allowances under the acid rain program to satisfy the requirements of the CAIR SO_2 program.

EPA Authority to Withhold Federal Funds

Natural Resources Defense Council v. Browner, 57 F.3d 1122 (D.C. Cir. 1995). EPA promulgated a final rule that permits a state to halt the 18-month sanctions clock for failing to submit an approvable SIP. EPA's rule allows states to halt the running of the sanctions clock by submitting a complete plan, even if that plan is ultimately unapprovable due to substantive inadequacies. The court held that the CAA authorizes states to halt the 18-month sanctions clock by submitting a complete plan, regardless of whether it is ultimately approvable.

Virginia v. Browner, 80 F.3d 869 (4th Cir. 1996), *cert. denied*, 519 U.S. 1090 (1997). Virginia petitioned review of EPA's denial of its air permit program. EPA denied the program because Virginia's proposal lacked adequate provisions for judicial review of the permitting decisions. Virginia claimed that EPA overstepped its authority because a mandate of these provisions improperly commandeered the legislative process of the state, in violation of the Tenth Amendment and the Commerce Clause to the U.S. Constitution. The court held that EPA did not commandeer the legislative process, but simply induced Virginia to comply with EPA's judicial standing provisions. The court also said that EPA's withholding of federal highway funds was appropriate because Congress may ensure that funds it allocates are not used to exacerbate the overall problem of air pollution.

Tribal Lands

Arizona Public Service Co. v. EPA, 211 F.3d 1280 (D.C. Cir. 2000). Several industry groups challenged EPA's tribal authority rule, which authorizes Indian tribes to seek agency approval to implement air quality programs (e.g., Title V operating permit program) for Indian reservation lands, allotted lands, and dependent Indian communities through tribal implementation plans (similar to SIPs). The petitioners also alleged that EPA improperly exempted Indian tribes from certain CAA judicial review requirements. The court held that EPA did not err in authorizing Indian tribes to regulate air quality within reservation lands, including land owned by non-tribal members. The court also held that judicial review provisions applicable to tribal air permitting decisions were reasonable.

Transportation Control Measures

Bayview Hunters Point Community Advocates v. Metropolitan Transportation Commission (MTC), 366 F.3d 692 (9th Cir. 2004). Community groups brought a CAA citizen suit action, alleging that Transportation Control Measure 2 (TCM 2) imposed an enforceable obligation upon the Metropolitan Transportation Commission (MTC) to increase ridership by 15 percent over 1982–1983 levels. The Ninth Circuit reversed the district court's ruling, holding that the CAA and TCM 2 did not impose an enforceable obligation on MTC to increase public transit ridership. The court concluded that "[t]he expected ridership increase was never described as anything more than a 'target,'" and the plain language of TCM 2 did not establish a binding obligation to achieve a specific increase in public transit ridership.

Prevention of Significant Deterioration (PSD) and New Source Review (NSR)

PSD SIP Provisions

Sierra Club v. Ruckelshaus, 344 F. Supp. 253 (D.D.C.), *aff'd*, 4 Env't Rep. Cas. (BNA) 1815 (D.C. Cir. 1972). The Sierra Club sued EPA to prevent air quality that was better than required from being allowed to deteriorate. The court, relying on pertinent legislative history and the statement of purpose in CAA section 101(b)(1) (to protect and enhance the quality of the nation's air resources so as to promote the public health and welfare and the productive capacity of the population), held that EPA was required to disapprove state plans insofar as they did not prevent the significant deterioration of air quality.

PSD Applicability

Alabama Power Co. v. Costle, 636 F.2d 323 (D.C. Cir. 1979). In 1977, Congress added a new Part C to the CAA, which codified the creation of the PSD program. *Alabama Power* is the first case involving a challenge to EPA's initial set of regulations for the PSD program. In a per curiam opinion, the D.C. Circuit held that (1) contrary to EPA's position, an analysis of a source's "potential to emit" must include beneficial effects of air pollution control equipment; (2) EPA's modeling regulations were valid; (3) the NSPS definition of *source* applies to the PSD program; (4) the "bubble" concept may apply when determining if an emissions increase has occurred for purposes of a modification; and (5) the visible emission standards may be considered by the PSD permitting authority in applying best available control technology (BACT).

Chevron U.S.A., Inc. v. Natural Resources Defense Council, 467 U.S. 837 (1984). The CAA, in and of itself, does not define *stationary source*.

Therefore, EPA initially interpreted *stationary source* to include all pieces of pollution-emitting equipment within a facility. Later, EPA replaced its earlier definition with one based on a more permissive bubble theory. The Supreme Court held that the agency's construction of the statute is accorded deference when the statute in question is ambiguous as to the precise question at issue.

New York v. EPA, 413 F.3d 3 (D.C. Cir. 2005). The D.C. Circuit largely upheld EPA's final NSR reform rule that made changes to the applicability provisions of the PSD/NSR program. The court upheld EPA's approach to calculating baseline emissions and measuring a significant net emissions increase. The D.C. Circuit also agreed that EPA's plantwide applicability limitation provision was not arbitrary and capricious. The court vacated EPA's provisions allowing "clean units" and "pollution control projects" to avoid PSD/NSR permitting. The court held that these regulatory exceptions to the PSD/NSR program were not authorized by the CAA.

Sierra Club v. EPA, 499 F.3d 653 (7th Cir. 2007). Sierra Club challenged the PSD permit issued to a 1,500 megawatt coal-fired power plant, alleging that the state permitting agency should have considered low sulfur coal in the BACT analysis for SO_2. The Sierra Club also asserted that the plant should demonstate compliance with the old one-hour ozone NAAQS as well as the eight-hour ozone NAAQS that was in the process of being implemented at the time. The court held that a BACT analysis was not required for low sulfur coal at a mine mouth facility because a change in the fuel would be a redesign of the source. The Seventh Circuit also ruled that the state permitting agency was entitled to rely on compliance measures demonstrating that the plant would meet the one-hour ozone NAAQS as a surrogate for concluding the plant would be unlikely to violate the new eight-hour ozone standard.

PSD/NSR Modifications

Puerto Rican Cement Co. v. EPA, 889 F.2d 292 (1st Cir. 1989). The Puerto Rican Cement Company wanted to convert a cement kiln from a "wet" to a "dry" process and combine it with another kiln. Both kilns were previously operating at 60 percent of their capacity. The converted kiln, if operated at the same level as the old kilns, would produce far less pollution than the old kilns. However, if the company were to operate the converted kiln at higher levels of production, it would emit more pollutants than the old kilns. Puerto Rican Cement sought a determination from EPA that the PSD major modification requirements would not be triggered. EPA denied the company's nonapplicability determination request, finding that the emissions would trigger the need for a PSD permit; it based the finding on a comparison of the old kilns' past actual emissions against future potential emissions for the converted kiln. Puerto Rican

Cement argued that EPA's decision was arbitrary because the agency's regulation would discourage the company from installing more efficient equipment that emits less pollution. The First Circuit upheld EPA's interpretation of its regulations.

Wisconsin Electric Power Co. v. Reilly, 893 F.2d 901 (7th Cir. 1990). A Wisconsin Electric Power Company's (WEPCO) plant in Port Washington, Wisconsin, contained five coal-fired steam generating units that had been in operation since 1950. In a plant availability study conducted in 1983, WEPCO found that the five steam generators needed extensive renovation if the plant was to continue operation. WEPCO proposed a plan whereby each steam generator would be taken out of service for nine months for renovation. WEPCO claimed that these changes should be considered "routine maintenance, repair and replacement," which is exempt from PSD review. However, EPA argued that because these changes would extend the life of the steam generators, the plant should then be subject to new source review under the PSD major modification trigger. EPA claimed that WEPCO's renovations did not fall within the "routine" exception because, to be routine, proposed work must be completed during normal plant outages and must not result in extending the life of the facility. The court held that deference should be given to EPA in determining what *routine* means. The Seventh Circuit court also held that EPA's analysis of the factors, which led it to determine that WEPCO's work was not routine, was not arbitrary and capricious.

   A second issue in the case was EPA's determination that WEPCO's emissions increase should be based on a comparison of past actual emissions to future potential emissions. WEPCO argued that its modification was a "like-kind" modification (replacement of equipment with equipment of similar design), and therefore EPA should compare past actual emissions against expected future actual emissions. The court held that EPA could not rely on future potential emissions and that the agency should compare past actual emissions against expected future actual emissions when a source has "begun normal operations."

Alaska Department of Environmental Conservation v. EPA, 540 U.S. 461 (2004). The U.S. Supreme Court upheld EPA's ability to issue an administrative order under CAA sections 113(a)(5) and 167 prohibiting modification of a mine based on the agency's conclusion that the state-issued PSD permit did not comply with the CAA's BACT requirements. In a 5–4 decision, the U.S. Supreme Court upheld the Ninth Circuit's ruling that rejected the Alaska Department of Environmental Conservation's claim that EPA lacked the authority to issue an administrative order halting the state-permitted modifications planned by the mine. The Supreme Court concluded that EPA may issue an order in situations where a state agency's permitting decision is not based on a "reasoned analysis."

New York v. EPA, 443 F.3d 880 (D.C. Cir. 2006), *cert. denied*, 550 U.S. 928 (2007) and *cert. denied sub nom. Utility Air Regulatory Group*

v. *New York,* 550 U.S. 928 (2007). The D.C. Circuit vacated EPA's Equipment Replacement Provision (ERP) rule that was intended to create a bright line safe harbor for projects that qualify as routine replacement of equipment. Under the ERP rule, EPA categorized equipment replacement projects as those projects costing 20 percent or less of an emissions unit so long as the parts were identical or the functional equivalent of the replaced part. The court held that EPA's ERP rule violated CAA section 111(a)(4) because the use of "any" in referring to "any physical change" that results in an emissions increase constitutes a *modification.* The ERP rule would have allowed non–de minimis increases in emissions to avoid NSR, and therefore the rule was contrary to the CAA.

Natural Resources Defense Council v. Jackson, ___ F.3d __, 2011 WL 2410398 (7th Cir. 2011). NRDC and the Sierra Club challenged EPA's approval of Wisconsin's adoption of the 2002 NSR reform rule. The petitioners alleged that EPA's approval of Wisconsin's SIP revision would violate the CAA's "antibacksliding" provisions by arguably allowing more air pollution to result from implementation of a "past actual" emissions to "projected actual" emissions test, use of a longer emissions baseline period, and use of plantwide applicability limitations. The Seventh Circuit disagreed with the petitioners, and denied the petitions.

PSD/NSR Commence Construction

Sierra Club v. Franklin County Power of Illinois, 546 F.3d 918 (7th Cir.), *cert. denied,* 129 S. Ct. 2866 (2009). The Sierra Club filed a citizen suit seeking to enjoin Franklin County Power of Illinois from building a coal-fired power plant, alleging that the plant's PSD permit had expired and was invalid. The Seventh Circuit affirmed the district court's permanent injunction in favor of the Sierra Club, holding that the company had not "commenced construction" of the plant within 18 months after receipt of the PSD permit. The Seventh Circuit concluded that the company had not engaged in any kind of permanent construction, such as laying foundation or constructing building supports, underground piping, or permanent storage structures. The only construction which took place was the digging of a hole, which did not constitute the start of a "continuous program" of actual construction. Further, the court held that a construction memorandum was not sufficient to satisfy the commencement of construction requirement. The construction memorandum was merely a preliminary commitment to enter into an engineering, construction, and procurement contract.

Nonattainment Areas—Offsets

Citizens Against Refinery's Effects v. EPA, 643 F.2d 183 (4th Cir. 1981). Citizens Against Refinery's Effects (CARE) challenged EPA's approval of Virginia's SIP for reducing hydrocarbons. The Virginia SIP required the Virginia Highway Department to use a different type of asphalt in some areas, so as to reduce hydrocarbon emissions and offset future emissions from the Hampton Roads Energy Company's proposed refinery. CARE argued that the area used to determine the base level of the offset was artificially developed by the state. EPA contended that Congress intended to give EPA and the states flexibility in designing and implementing SIPs, including the flexibility to determine which areas should be used to offset new emissions. The Fourth Circuit held that an owner/operator can satisfy the offset requirement by reducing emissions at other sources within the same nonattainment area. An owner/operator can also meet the offset requirement by obtaining emissions reductions in another nonattainment area, as long as the other area has an equal or higher nonattainment classification than the area in which the source is located.

Nonattainment Areas—Redesignation

Kentucky Natural Resources & Environmental Protection Cabinet v. EPA, 47 Env't Rep. Cas. (BNA) 1348, 1998 U.S. App. LEXIS 21686 (6th Cir. 1998). Kentucky appealed EPA's rejection of its petition requesting redesignation of the Kentucky portion of the Cincinnati-Northern Kentucky Moderate Ozone Nonattainment Area to "attainment" for ozone. The court affirmed EPA's decision and concluded that EPA's interpretation of the statute was reasonable. Kentucky argued that EPA's final ruling was arbitrary and capricious because the agency denied its redesignation request on the basis of one violation that occurred after the redesignation request was submitted. An area is designated as nonattainment with the one-hour ozone ambient air quality standard if there are more than three exceedances in a three-year period. The Sixth Circuit affirmed EPA's ruling, based in large part on the finding that the nonattainment requirements remain in full force and effect while a redesignation petition is pending, and that the agency is not constrained to look at only the three-year period specified in a redesignation petition. The court held that EPA was free to look at the most recent three-year period in which four exceedances were recorded.

Potential to Emit

Chemical Manufacturers Ass'n v. EPA, 70 F.3d 637 (D.C. Cir. 1995). The D.C. Circuit vacated the federal enforceability requirement of the "potential to emit" definition in the PSD/NSR program rules. *See also National Mining Ass'n v. EPA*, 59 F.3d 1351 (D.C. Cir. 1995), *infra* p. 236.

Class I Areas

Arizona v. EPA, 151 F.3d 1205 (9th Cir. 1998), *amended and reh'g denied*, 170 F.3d 870 (9th Cir. 1999). The state of Arizona sought to overturn

EPA's approval of the request by the Yavapai-Apache Tribal Council to redesignate five parcels as nonfederal Class I areas under the CAA. The Class I redesignation would allow the tribe to lower the allowable increases of certain ambient air pollutants on the tribe's land. Arizona contended that EPA abused its discretion by approving the redesignation of four of the five parcels because they were not actually part of the Indian reservation as the term is used in CAA section 164. Further, Arizona asserted that the tribe failed to meet certain procedural requirements and that EPA improperly promulgated the redesignation as part of a federal implementation plan (FIP) instead of a tribal implementation plan. The court held that there was insufficient evidence in the record to support a finding that four of the parcels were part of the reservation. Nevertheless, the court noted that this issue did not have to be definitively decided, because redesignation of the fifth parcel effectively achieved Class I status for the four surrounding parcels. The court also concluded that EPA did not abuse its discretion with respect to approving the redesignation request for the fifth parcel; however, EPA did ignore the dictates of the CAA in promulgating the redesignation as part of a FIP. The court remanded this portion of the case so that EPA could repromulgate its redesignation as part of a tribal implementation plan.

New Source Performance Standards (NSPS)

Applicability

PPG Industries v. Harrison, 660 F.2d 628 (5th Cir. 1981). PPG appealed EPA's action subjecting waste heat boilers at its newly constructed power plant to the NSPS for fossil-fuel-fired steam generating units. The court held that EPA exceeded its statutory authority in applying an emission limitation based on fossil fuel, rather than total heat input, to PPG's boilers, which were fueled with waste heat thrown off by gas turbine exhaust and the burning of fossil fuel. The manner in which EPA applied the emission limitations in effect required use of low-sulfur fuel in violation of then-existing law, under which performance standards could be established only in the form of emission limitations based on output, and not on the form of practice or operational requirements.

Cost and Technological Feasibility

Portland Cement Ass'n v. Ruckelshaus, 486 F.2d 375 (D.C. Cir. 1973), *cert. denied*, 417 U.S. 921 (1974). Portland Cement Association, along with other cement manufacturers, sought review of EPA's promulgation of the NSPS for portland cement plants, pursuant to CAA section 111. The court held that EPA was not required to compare the portland cement industry to other industry NSPS in taking into account the costs of achieving the emission reductions; the courts also rejected the claim that the CAA's requirement that emission limitations be "adequately demonstrated" necessarily implies that any cement plant now in existence would be able to meet the proposed standards.

National Asphalt Pavement Ass'n v. Train, 539 F.2d 775 (D.C. Cir. 1976). EPA listed asphalt concrete producers as a category of significant polluters that contribute to the endangerment of public health or welfare. National Asphalt claimed that EPA relied on a study that did not take into account the fact that many asphalt producers have equipped their plants with various control devices in response to state and local regulations. Additionally, National Asphalt claimed that EPA failed to conduct a proper cost-benefit analysis in determining the proper NSPS. The D.C. Circuit held that compliance with state and local regulations may enable a state to meet national standards, but it does not mean that EPA is prohibited from regulating industries meeting these standards even further in order to prevent deterioration of areas in attainment with the applicable NAAQS. The court also held that EPA properly analyzed cost as one of many factors in setting NSPS and was under no duty to do a cost-benefit analysis.

Sierra Club v. Costle, 657 F.2d 298 (D.C. Cir. 1981). The Sierra Club and other environmental groups, as well as electric utilities, filed petitions for review of EPA's standards limiting emissions of particulates and SO_2 by coal-burning power plants. The court upheld EPA's authority to issue a sliding scale or variable standard for the reduction of SO_2 based on the sulfur content of the coal burned.

Nationally Uniform and Nationally Achievable

National Lime Ass'n v. EPA, 627 F.2d 416 (D.C. Cir. 1980). The National Lime Association challenged EPA's NSPS for the lime industry on the ground that the agency conducted inadequate sampling tests to derive the NSPS. EPA contended that its testing was valid and that, therefore, the NSPS should stand. The D.C. Circuit held that because EPA did not conduct tests that are representative of the lime industry nationwide, the NSPS was based on inadequate data. The court also said that the NSPS have to be nationally uniform and nationally achievable standards for the particular industry category.

Control of Hazardous Air Pollutants (HAPs)

Cost and Technological Feasibility

Natural Resources Defense Council v. EPA, 824 F.2d 1146 (D.C. Cir. 1987). The NRDC petitioned the court for review of EPA's decision to abandon proposed amendments to the emission standards for vinyl chloride. The controversy over EPA's decision related to the use of cost and technological feasibility factors in establishing an emission standard for a HAP pursuant to CAA section 112. Under CAA section 112, EPA may consider cost and technological feasibility in selecting levels for hazardous pollutant standards. The court held that once EPA has determined a safe level of exposure, it may then consider cost and feasibility in providing for the ample margin of safety required by CAA section 112.

Potential to Emit

National Mining Ass'n v. EPA, 59 F.3d 1351 (D.C. Cir. 1995). The D.C. Circuit remanded the federal enforceability requirement of EPA's definition of "potential to emit" in the CAA section 112 air toxics program. EPA's "potential to emit" definition had required that a permit limit or other emission standard be federally enforceable in order to be considered an effective limitation on air emissions. The court recognized that "effective" state and local controls might also be sufficient to limit a source's potential to emit.

Maximum Achievable Control Technology (MACT) Standards

Sierra Club v. EPA, 167 F.3d 658 (D.C. Cir. 1999). The Sierra Club and the Natural Resources Defense Council challenged EPA's use of state permit and regulatory data to calculate the MACT standard for existing municipal waste incinerators. The petitioners also alleged that EPA improperly used uncontrolled test data to supplement the state permit and regulatory data in setting the MACT floor for existing sources. The petitioners also questioned EPA's methodology for setting the MACT floor for new municipal waste incinerators. The court held that EPA may use state permit and regulatory data instead of plant-specific performance data so long as the data supports a reasonable inference as to the performance of the top 12 percent of the existing units. However, the court remanded the rule to EPA for further explanation of its reasoning in determining why it was appropriate to use a combination of state regulatory data and uncontrolled test data in setting the MACT floor for existing sources. The court also remanded the MACT standard for new municipal waste combustors holding that EPA did not adequately explain the methodology it used to set the standard.

National Lime Ass'n v. EPA, 233 F.3d 625 (D.C. Cir. 2000). The National Lime Association and the Sierra Club separately challenged EPA's regulations establishing MACT standards for portland cement manufacturing facilities. The D.C. Circuit held that EPA's decision not to establish MACT standards for hydrogen chloride, mercury, and organic HAPs was a violation of the CAA. The court noted that EPA has a clear statutory obligation to set emission standards for each listed HAP. EPA considered only whether the portland cement manufacturing facilities had pollution controls in place to address HAP emissions. The court also held that EPA was statutorily required to evaluate process changes, substitution of materials, or other modifications as the basis for a potential MACT standard. In addition, the court concluded that that EPA's refusal to set beyond-the-floor MACT standards for HAP metals was not justified because the agency failed to consider non-air-quality health and environmental impacts in making the determination. Further, EPA rejected the National Lime Association's objection to EPA's use of particulate matter as a surrogate for nonvolatile HAP metals, concluding that EPA may use a surrogate to regulate HAPs if it is reasonable to do so.

Arteva Specialties S.A.R.L. v. EPA, 323 F.3d 1088 (D.C. Cir. 2003). Arteva Specialties and Eastman Chemical Company sought review of EPA's equipment-leak standard for the Group IV polymers and resins National Emissions Standard for Hazardous Air Pollutants, alleging that the required emission controls were not cost effective because EPA aggregated the cost and effectiveness on a facility-wide basis rather than disaggregating the cost effectiveness of the individual control technologies. EPA selected sensory leak detection and repair (LDAR) as the MACT floor for polyethylene terephthalate resin manufacturing facilities. However, for most of the equipment categories, EPA prescribed two beyond-the-floor technologies in lieu of or as an alternative to sensory LDAR. The two beyond-the-floor MACT standards were a one-time equipment modification, or Method 21 LDAR, which used portable organic vapor analyzers to monitor emissions. The petitioners contended that EPA inappropriately misrepresented the cost effectiveness for some types of control equipment because it aggregated and averaged the high-cost Method 21 LDAR with the costs of the two other controls. The D.C. Circuit agreed and held that although aggregating the cost effectiveness of different technologies may be a permissible approach to assessing a MACT standard's cost effectiveness, the record for establishing the equipment leak standard did not demonstrate that EPA's cost aggregation approach was reasonable. The court remanded the decision in order for EPA to clarify the equipment leak MACT standard after reconsidering its cost effectiveness.

Sierra Club v. EPA, 479 F.3d 875 (D.C. Cir. 2007). The D.C. Circuit reviewed a challenge to EPA's NESHAP for brick kilns, and held that the agency's failure to set technology floors for existing tunnel brick kilns and new periodic brick kilns violated CAA section 112(d)(3). The D.C. Circuit also concluded that EPA could not substitute work practice standards for a specific limitation to set the emission floors unless the measuring of emissions is "technologically or economically impracticable." EPA's conclusion that it lacked emissions data from ceramic kilns was not an adequate basis to use work practice standards as the emission floor. The court also rejected EPA's use of emission levels from the worst performing kilns to estimate the variability of the best performing kilns without adequately demonstrating how the variability was related.

New Jersey v. EPA, 517 F.3d 574 (D.C. Cir. 2008). The D.C. Circuit vacated EPA's rule to delist the electric generating units (EGUs) source category from regulation under CAA section 112 and the agency's Clean Air Mercury Rule (CAMR), concluding that EPA did not follow the proper procedural requirements in making its decision to delist EGUs from the CAA section 112 source category list. EPA's "delisting rule" violated the plain language of the CAA because the agency failed to make specific findings prior to removing EGUs from the source category list. As a result, EGUs remain a regulated source category under CAA section 112, and regulation under CAA section 111 is prohibited. The vacatur of the delisting rule effectively invalidated the CAMR cap-and-trade regulatory approach under CAA section 111. Accordingly, the court also vacated CAMR.

Sierra Club v. Sandy Creek Energy Assocs., 627 F.3d 134 (5th Cir. 2010), *cert. petition pending*, 79 U.S.L.W. 3636 (Apr. 26, 2011). Two environmental organizations filed a citizen suit alleging that construction of the Sandy Creek coal-fired power plant violated the requirement to comply with the case-by-case MACT determination provisions of CAA section 112(g). The plant had commenced construction at a time when EPA's rule delisting coal- and oil-fired electric utility steam generating units (EGUs) from the CAA section 112 HAP source categories list was in effect. After the delisting rule was vacated, coal-fired EGUs were once again subject to the requirements of CAA section 112. The Fifth Circuit reversed the district court decision, and held that the state permitting agency had relied on the delisting rule and not included a case-by-case MACT determination in its final order. Further, the ongoing construction of the power plant for which no case-by case MACT determination was obtained violated the plain language of CAA section 112(g)(2)(B), and the violation arose starting on March 14, 2008, the date the mandate vacating the delisting rule was entered.

Medical Waste Institute & Energy Recovery Council v. EPA, ___ F.3d ___, 2011 WL 2507842 (D.C. Cir. 2011). Trade associations representing the medical waste and waste-to-energy industries challenged EPA's rule setting MACT performance standards for new and existing medical waste incinerators. The petitioners alleged that the data set EPA used to establish the MACT floor for medical waste incinerators was flawed. EPA responded that it was merely correcting erroneous data developed for the first set of MACT standards for the medical waste incinerators that were promulgated in 1997. The D.C. Circuit remanded the 1997 rule to EPA for further explanation of the methodology used to set the standards. In 2009, after approximately 94 percent of the medical waste incinerators in operation in 1997 shut down, EPA repromulgated the rule based on data from the 57 current operating medical waste incinerators. The petitioners asserted that the recalculated MACT floors were improperly made more stringent, and EPA should have considered the costs of compliance pursuant to CAA sections 111(a)(1) and 129(a)(5). The court agreed with EPA that nothing in the CAA prohibits the agency from resetting the MACT floors in order to correct data errors. The court concluded that EPA's use of the data from the 57 remaining medical waste incinerators was reasonable.

Startup, Shutdown, and Malfunction

Sierra Club v. EPA, 551 F.3d 1019 (D.C. Cir. 2008), *cert. denied sub nom. American Chemistry Council v. Sierra Club,* 130 S. Ct. 1735 (2010). The Sierra Club challenged (1) the exemption in the CAA section 112 general provisions for emissions occurring during startup, shutdown, and malfunction events and (2) the imposition of the less onerous requirement of preparing a startup, shutdown, and malfunction plan instead of requiring continuous compliance with the emission standards during startup, shutdown and malfunction events. The Sierra Club asserted that the CAA required major HAP sources to demonstrate "continuous" compliance with an emission standard established pursuant to section 112. The D.C. Circuit agreed and vacated the startup, shutdown, and malfunction exemption under CAA section 112.

Visibility Protection

Vermont v. Thomas, 850 F.2d 99 (2d Cir. 1988). Vermont submitted a visibility SIP to EPA addressing visibility impairment at the Lyle Brook National Wilderness Area. Vermont determined that the visibility impairment—summertime haze—was due to SO_2 emissions from eight upwind states. Therefore, Vermont requested that EPA revise those eight states' SIPs so that they would have to reduce their SO_2 emissions, and thus resolve Lyle Brook's summertime haze problem. EPA, however, had promulgated rules only for plume-blight visibility issues, and had decided to wait until monitoring and other scientific techniques progressed to the point that EPA could develop a sufficient regulatory program before issuing regulations for summertime haze. The Second Circuit held that the CAA only makes reference to visibility issues in general and that there is no specific provision for summertime haze. Therefore, it is within EPA's discretion to promulgate rules as it finds reasonable to deal with visibility issues. The court also held that because EPA had identified haze as a future issue, it would be inappropriate for the court to fashion a remedy at this time.

Central Arizona Water Conservation District v. EPA, 990 F.2d 1531 (9th Cir.), *cert. denied*, 510 U.S. 828 (1993). Central Arizona Conservation District (CACD) challenged an EPA rule that required a 90 percent reduction in SO_2 emissions from the Navajo Generating Station (NGS) to reduce wintertime haze at the Grand Canyon. CACD argued that since EPA had not promulgated rules addressing regional haze, EPA has exceeded the scope of its regulatory authority. EPA responded by saying that EPA's Title I program is directed at controlling visibility impairment that can be reasonably traced to a single existing stationary facility. EPA, in a final rule, traced certain visibility impairment episodes at the Grand Canyon back to NGS. Therefore, EPA claimed that the visibility impairment was reasonably traceable to NGS, and thus was within their scope of authority. The court held that EPA acted within the scope of its authority by determining that the visibility impairment was traceable to NGS. The court distinguished this case from *Vermont v. Thomas* based on the different statutory provisions at issue. In *Thomas*, Vermont asked EPA to approve its SIP submittal; in *Central Arizona*, it was EPA, pursuant to its Title I rulemaking authority, that created the enforceable rule.

Utility Air Regulatory Group v. EPA, 471 F.3d 1333 (D.C. Cir. 2006). The D.C. Circuit considered challenges filed by industry and environmental groups to EPA's Regional Haze Rule, which requires the application of best available retrofit technology (BART) to certain types of stationary sources that may cause or contribute to visibility impairments in federal Class I areas. The D.C. Circuit rejected the environmental groups' arguments alleging that the rule failed to ensure "reasonable progress" at Class I areas by allowing BART alternatives to be used. The court concluded that the CAA provided EPA with wide discretion to determine what measures will achieve reasonable progress. EPA also rejected industry petitioners' arguments that EPA impermissibly issued mandatory BART guidelines for setting power plant emission limits and that EPA unreasonably allowed states to consider whether BART-eligible sources may collectively contribute to regional haze.

Title V Operating Permits

Program Approval

Public Citizen, Inc. v. EPA, 343 F.3d 449 (5th Cir. 2003). Several environmental groups sought review of EPA's decision to grant full approval to Texas's operating permit program pursuant to Title V of the CAA. EPA granted interim approval of the Texas Title V program in 1996, and identified numerous deficiencies that Texas was required to correct in order to obtain full approval. The petitioners commented that Texas failed to correct the initial deficiencies and that additional deficiencies existed that had not been previously identified. EPA determined that Texas's revisions addressed the deficiencies initially identified in the interim approval and granted Texas full approval of its Title V program in December 2001 because newly identified deficiencies did not prohibit full approval of a Title V program. EPA also issued a notice of deficiency that identified six other deficiencies, but not those claimed by petitioners. EPA responded separately to the petitioners in February 2002 and determined that it would not issue a notice of deficiency for the issues raised by the petitioners. The petitioners sought review of the December 2001 and February 2002 actions, claiming that EPA has no authority to grant Texas's Title V permit program full approval because Texas had not corrected all of the Title V programs deficiencies. The Fifth Circuit found that EPA's interpretation of its authority to approve Title V programs despite the existence of newly identified deficiencies was entitled to deference and was reasonable.

Enhanced Monitoring

Natural Resources Defense Council v. EPA, 194 F.3d 130 (D.C. Cir. 1999). NRDC challenged EPA's enhanced emission source monitoring rule, known as the compliance assurance monitoring (CAM) rule. NRDC asserted that the rule is contrary to the CAA because it exempts certain major sources from coverage and because CAM's "reasonable assurance of compliance" standard does not actually assure compliance with the CAA. In applying the two-step process of reviewing an agency's interpretation of a statute (set out in *Chevron U.S.A. v. Natural Resources Defense Council*, 467 U.S. 837 (1984)), the court held that EPA's enhanced monitoring system complies with the Clean Air Act Amendments of 1990 except for the portion of the rule pertaining to the continuous or intermittent compliance certification. In remanding this issue back to the agency, the court determined that the statute specifically requires that the CAM certification include an indication of whether compliance is continuous or intermittent, and not just a statement of whether data is continuous or intermittent.

Sierra Club v. EPA, 536 F.3d 673 (D.C. Cir. 2008). The D.C. Circuit vacated an EPA rule preventing state and local authorities from supplementing "inadequate monitoring requirements." The court found that the CAA requires each Title V operating permit to include adequate monitoring requirements. Further, the court held that the CAA allows states to supplement an inadequate monitoring requirement to "assure compliance with the permit terms and conditions."

Periodic Monitoring

Appalachian Power v. EPA, 208 F.3d 1015 (D.C. Cir. 2000). Electric power companies and trade associations representing the chemical and petroleum industry petitioned for review of an EPA guidance document addressing periodic monitoring requirements for incorporation in Title V operating permits. The D.C. Circuit held that the guidance document broadened the underlying EPA operating permit rule and the issuance of the guidance was thus improper, absent compliance with formal rulemaking procedures.

Utility Air Regulatory Group v. EPA, 320 F.3d 272 (D.C. Cir. 2003). The
Utility Air Regulatory Group (UARG), a trade association whose members include individual electric utilities, sought review of EPA's interpretation of its Title V permit program regulations to impose additional
monitoring requirements where the permit issuer determines that the
required monitoring is insufficient to assure compliance with the terms
and conditions of a Title V permit. UARG alleged that this interpretation was implemented in a Title V guidance document and in two per-
mit-related adjudications. UARG asserted that this interpretation was
an impermissible broadening of the Title V monitoring requirements.
The D.C. Circuit dismissed the petition, finding that the petitioner
lacked standing because it failed to identify that EPA's interpretation
has caused it or its members any concrete and particularized injury.
In addition, the court concluded that the agency's interpretation was a
nonbinding announcement of policy, which does not injure the petitioner or its members in any imminent or redressable manner.

Potential to Emit

Clean Air Implementation Project v. EPA, No. 96-1224, 1996 U.S. App.
LEXIS 18402 (D.C. Cir. June 28, 1996). The D.C. Circuit vacated
EPA's "potential to emit" definition used in the Title V operating per-
mit program. *See also National Mining Ass'n v. EPA*, 59 F.3d 1351
(D.C. Cir. 1995), *supra* p. 236.

Compliance Plans

New York Public Interest Research Group v. Whitman, 321 F.3d 316 (2d
Cir. 2003). An environmental group sought review of EPA's granting
of full approval of New York's Title V air operating permit program
and the agency's decision to deny the petitioner's request for a notice
of deficiency. The petitioner also challenged EPA's denial of a review
of three specific Title V permits even though the agency determined
that the identified noncompliance was "harmless error." The Second
Circuit concluded that EPA's interpretation of the CAA was reasonable and permissible in determining that once a state has received
interim approval of its Title V program, the state is only obligated to
make the changes specified at the time of interim approval in order
to obtain full approval of its Title V program. The court also held
that EPA has the discretion to determine whether to issue a notice of
deficiency to address identified deficiencies in a state's Title V program. EPA's decision not to issue a notice of deficiency was within
the agency's discretion. Finally, the Second Circuit concluded that
EPA had a statutory obligation to object to draft Title V permits where
a lack of compliance with the CAA was identified. The court struck
down EPA's application of a "harmless error rule," concluding that
the CAA does not provide for the excise of EPA discretion if a dem-

onstration of noncompliance in a draft Title V permit is made. The Second Circuit remanded the three draft Title V permits to the agency for further proceedings.

Failure to Object

Romoland School District v. Inland Empire Energy Center, LLC, 548 F.3d 738 (9th Cir. 2008). Romoland School District and other petitioners (Romoland) filed a CAA citizen suit seeking a preliminary injunction against the local air pollution control agency and power plant owner, challenging the construction of an 810-megawatt power plant. Inland Empire filed a motion to dismiss, contending that the district court lacked jurisdiction over the suit because the defendant had been granted a combined permit to construct/Title V permit, and since the permit was issued pursuant to the CAA's Title V procedures, it could not be challenged in civil or criminal enforcement proceedings in federal district court. In affirming the district court's dismissal of Romoland's claims, the Ninth Circuit concluded that the combined permit to construct/Title V permit could only be challenged pursuant to provisions of Title V of the CAA, not the CAA citizen suit provision.

Citizens Against Ruining the Environment v. EPA, 535 F.3d 670 (7th Cir. 2008). Several environmental organizations and the Attorney General of Illinois challenged the failure of EPA to object to Title V operating permits issued to six coal-fired power plants owned by Midwest Generation. The petitioners alleged that the EPA administrator was obligated to object to the permits when there was a demonstration that the permits were not in compliance with the CAA. The court held that the CAA provides the EPA with discretion in determining whether violations occurred, and it was reasonable for the agency to require further investigation and analysis.

Sierra Club v. EPA, 557 F.3d 401 (6th Cir. 2009). The Sierra Club sought review of EPA's denial of a petition to object to issuance of a Title V permit for a coal-fired power plant. The Sierra Club alleged that EPA was required to object to the issuance of a Title V permit if the petitioner "demonstrate[d]" that the permit did not comply with the CAA requirements. As support for its position, the Sierra Club pointed to a notice of violation and an enforcement action that were initiated by EPA. EPA concluded that its earlier notice of violation and enforcement action did not reflect its later conclusion about the plant's compliance status based on intervening events (i.e., the settlement of the enforcement action in 2007). The Sixth Circuit dismissed the Sierra Club's petition, holding that EPA's prior notice of violation and enforcement action did not require EPA to object to issuance of the Title V permit, and the agency could reasonably consider later developments in determining whether to object to the issuance of a Title V permit.

Startup, Shutdown, and Malfunction

Sierra Club v. Georgia Power Co., 443 F.3d 1346 (11th Cir. 2006). The Eleventh Circuit reviewed whether the startup, shutdown, and malfunction (SSM) provisions of a coal-fired power plant's Title V permit could be invoked in the defense of the plaintiff's allegation of approximately 4,000 opacity exceedances. The court reversed the district court's ruling that the SSM provisions could not be used in defense of the citizen suit claims. The Eleventh Circuit concluded that the SSM provisions in the plant's Title V permit were not at odds with EPA's SSM policy because that policy was not intended to alter the status of existing SIP rules.

Greenhouse Gas (GHG) Emissions

Massachusetts v. EPA, 549 U.S. 497 (2007). The Supreme Court concluded that CO_2 and other GHGs fall within the broad definition of "air pollutant" under the CAA. The Court also addressed whether the CAA authorizes EPA to regulate GHG emissions from new motor vehicles, and held that the CAA section 202(a)(1) requires EPA to make a "judgment" on whether an air pollutant "cause[s], or contributes[s] to, air pollution which may reasonably be anticipated to endanger public health or welfare." The Court remanded the issue to EPA for a decision on whether GHGs cause or contribute to climate change in accordance with the CAA.

American Electric Power v. Connecticut, 131 S. Ct. 2527, 2011 WL 2437011 (2011). The plaintiffs, including eight state attorneys general, New York City, and three public interest land trusts, sought to curtail the GHG emissions from six electric utilities. The Second Circuit reversed the lower court decision, concluding that the plaintiffs had stated claims under the common law of public nuisance and that the CAA had not displaced the public nuisance claim. The Supreme Court disagreed and held that the CAA and the EPA actions authorized by the CAA displace any federal common law right to seek the abatement of CO_2 emissions from fossil-fuel-fired power plants.

Mobile Sources and the Regulation of Fuel

Waivers

Ethyl Corp. v. EPA, 51 F.3d 1053 (D.C. Cir. 1995). Ethyl Corp. submitted a fuel additive to EPA, seeking a waiver pursuant to CAA section 211(f)(4) and claiming that the additive would not cause or contribute to a failure of any emission control device or system. EPA denied the waiver on public health grounds, based on the language of CAA section 211(f)(4). The D.C. Circuit held that CAA section 211(f)(4) does not authorize EPA to consider "other factors in the public interest," and thus concluded that the waiver should have been granted pursuant to CAA section 211(f)(4). The court noted that if EPA wanted to consider the health effects of the fuel additive's emissions, the agency could conduct proceedings pursuant to CAA section 211(c)(1) to determine whether the emissions of the fuel additive can reasonably endanger the public health.

Motor & Equipment Manufacturers Ass'n v. Nichols, 142 F.3d 449 (D.C. Cir. 1998). The D.C. Circuit reviewed challenges to EPA's regulations governing on-board emissions diagnostic devices (OBDs). The petitioners, a number of trade associations representing companies that manufacture, rebuild, and sell car parts that replace parts installed by the original automobile manufacturers, challenged EPA's decision to permit California to enforce its own OBD regulations pursuant to CAA section 209(b). They also challenged EPA's rule determining that the California diagnostic device regulations constitute compliance with the federal diagnostic device regulations. The D.C. Circuit concluded that EPA's decision to allow California to enforce its own OBD rules was not inconsistent with the CAA. The court also deferred to EPA's reasonable interpretation of the statute and held that EPA's rule, determining that the California diagnostic device regulations complied with the federal standards, was validly promulgated.

Reformulated Gasoline (RFG)

American Petroleum Institute v. EPA, 52 F.3d 1113 (D.C. Cir. 1995). The American Petroleum Institute (API) challenged EPA's renewable oxygen requirement (ROR) in its regulations for the RFG program under the CAA. API claimed the RFG program's overriding goal is the reduction of VOCs and toxic emissions, and argued that EPA overstepped its authority by requiring that 30 percent of the oxygen required to be used in RFG come from a renewable oxygenate, even though this requirement does nothing to further the reduction of VOCs and toxic emissions and may in fact worsen them. EPA rebutted by stating that the ROR is designed to ensure that emission requirements for RFG are achieved in a way that reasonably optimizes the impacts on costs, energy, and other health and environmental impacts. The D.C. Circuit held that the plain meaning of CAA section 7545(k)(1) precludes any of EPA's ROR rules that are not directed toward the reduction of VOCs and toxic emissions.

Enforcement and Judicial Review

Economic and Technology Defense

Union Electric Co. v. EPA, 593 F.2d 299 (8th Cir.), *cert. denied*, 444 U.S. 839 (1979). Union Electric filed a complaint asking the court to enjoin EPA from instituting enforcement proceedings under the CAA against the company while the company, in good faith, was pursuing a revision or variance of SO_2 regulations of the Missouri SIP in the administrative agencies and judicial courts of the State of Missouri. Union Electric claimed that that the regulations under the Missouri SIP were economically and technologically infeasible. EPA responded that CAA section 7413(b) specifically requires the administrator to commence a civil action for injunctive relief or for the assessment of civil penalties 30 days after notice of the violation has been given to the offending party. The court held that claims of infeasibility do not afford a basis for review, per the Supreme Court decision in *Union Electric Co. v. EPA*, 427 U.S. 246 (1976). However, Union Electric's claims of economic and technological infeasibility are relevant to fashioning an appropriate compliance order and can be raised as a defense in an enforcement proceeding.

Inspections

United States v. Tivian Laboratories, 589 F.2d 49 (1st Cir. 1978), *cert. denied*, 442 U.S. 942 (1979). Tivian Laboratories challenged the constitutionality of CAA provisions that authorized EPA to require the owner or operator of any emission source to provide EPA with information needed to carry out its responsibilities under the CAA. The court held that EPA can request and obtain any information if the subject is authorized by any pertinent statute and the documents are relevant. The burden is on the entity being inspected to prove that either EPA does not have the authority or that the material is not relevant. The court concluded that requiring Tivian Laboratories to provide the requested information did not violate the Fourth Amendment's prohibition on unreasonable searches and seizures, the Thirteenth Amendment's bar against involuntary servitude, and the Fifth Amendment's guarantee of due process.

Ced's, Inc. v. EPA, 745 F.2d 1092 (7th Cir. 1984), *cert. denied*, 471 U.S. 1015 (1985). Ced's manufactured and distributed automotive engine exhaust equipment that could be used to replace the catalytic converter in a car. Ced's was granted an injunction in the district court, which prevented EPA from making use of copies of business records it had obtained under an administrative warrant and which ordered EPA to return the copies to the company. In vacating the order, the Seventh Circuit held that the agency had statutory authority to carry out its inspection and to copy the company's records, even though it had never required the company to keep any records. The Seventh Circuit based its holding on its determination that EPA can require the owners and operators of emission sources, as well as any person who is subject to a requirement of the CAA, to do the same things, and that EPA has a right of entry to the premises of both types of persons.

Administrative Consent Orders

Tennessee Valley Authority v. Whitman, 336 F.2d 1236 (8th Cir. 2003).
The court evaluated whether it had jurisdiction to review an administrative consent order (ACO) issued by EPA directing the Tennessee Valley Authority (TVA) to identify major modifications to its
nine coal-fired power plants that were taken without CAA PSD/NSR
permits, obtain such PSD/NSR permits, and enter into a compliance
agreement requiring the installation of pollution control equipment
and other measures to reduce air emissions. TVA refused to comply with the ACO, and EPA's Environmental Appeals Board (EAB)
was delegated the task of reconsidering the ACO. The EAB largely
upheld EPA's ACO and concluded that TVA had violated the CAA.
TVA petitioned the Eleventh Circuit to set aside the EAB decision.
The Eleventh Circuit analyzed whether ACOs had the status of law
and whether noncompliance with an ACO could be a basis for
imposing penalties. The court declined to assert jurisdiction over
TVA's petition because it held that the ACO did not constitute a final
agency action. The court concluded that EPA must first prove the
existence of a CAA violation in district court before it may seek to
impose civil and criminal penalties on TVA.

Stay of Regulations

Natural Resources Defense Council v. EPA, 976 F.2d 36 (D.C. Cir. 1992).
The NRDC petitioned the court for a review of an EPA order that
stayed application of emission standards for radioactive pollutants.
EPA had stayed its application based on an alleged conflict with
Nuclear Regulatory Commission regulations. The court held that
EPA did not have authority to stay already promulgated emission
standards, and that the CAA's broad grant of authority to EPA did not
allow for any stay of a regulation promulgated pursuant to the CAA
except for one three-month period, pursuant to CAA section 307(d)
(7)(B), for postpetition reconsideration of a rule.

Calculation of Penalties

United States v. SCM Corp., 667 F. Supp. 1110 (D. Md. 1987). The
United States brought a civil action against SCM for violations of
the CAA. SCM argued that the court should take into consideration
the size of the business, the economic impact of the penalty on the
business, and the seriousness of the violation when determining the
appropriate remedy. The United States responded by showing that
SCM is a major corporation where only a substantial penalty would
have any economic impact or incentive to deter further noncompliance. The court held that because SCM is a major corporation a
large penalty was appropriate. However, because the United States
delayed 13 years in bringing this action, the penalty was cut in half.

The court also held that penalties could be assessed only for violations within five years of the filing of the complaint.

United States v. Trident Seafood Corp., 60 F.3d 556 (9th Cir. 1995). The court held that Trident's failure to provide notice of asbestos removal operations constituted a single violation occurring on a single day, rather than a continuous violation subject to multiday penalties. The Ninth Circuit thus reversed the district court, which had determined that the failure to give notice was a continuous violation that subjected Trident to a potential civil liability of $1.1 million. The Ninth Circuit concluded that Trident should not be subject to penalties for a continuous violation because the statute and implementing regulations did not specify that failure to give notice was a continuous violation.

PSD/NSR Violations

United States v. Solar Turbines, Inc., 732 F. Supp. 535 (M.D. Pa. 1989). EPA filed a claim for injunctive relief to prevent construction of a turbine. It subsequently amended its complaint to add a claim for civil penalties under CAA section 113(b). The state of Pennsylvania had issued Solar Turbines a PSD permit, which EPA determined did not include an accurate BACT analysis. The court held that EPA, as a matter of law, may not pursue an enforcement action against an owner/operator who has committed no violation and is acting in accordance with its state-issued PSD permit. In concluding that EPA's actions were unreasonable, the court determined that CAA section 113(b) reaches objective standards, such as failure to apply for a permit, failure to obtain a permit prior to construction, or failure to comply with quantifiable emission levels.

Allsteel Inc. v. EPA, 25 F.3d (6th Cir. 1994). Allsteel had received a PSD construction permit from the state of Tennessee. EPA issued a stop-work order for construction under CAA sections 113(a)(5) and 167 because it concluded that Tennessee had not issued the permit in accordance with the CAA. Without reaching the question of EPA's authority, the court determined that the order would be stayed, pending a decision on the merits, because the order would impose potentially severe consequences on Allsteel.

United States v. AM General Corp., 34 F.3d 472 (7th Cir. 1994). In interpreting CAA section 113(b)(3), the Seventh Circuit affirmed an Indiana district court's decision that EPA could not enjoin or impose penalties against a source operating under the auspices of a facially valid state-issued PSD permit.

United States v. Campbell Soup Co., Civ-95-1854, 1997 U.S. Dist. LEXIS 3211 (E.D. Cal. Mar. 11, 1997). EPA filed a complaint seeking civil penalties and injunctive relief for modifications Campbell Soup made to can-manufacturing machines at one of its plants between 1983 and 1988. EPA alleged that Campbell Soup failed to comply with local air quality management district regulations (i.e., the SIP), which required issuance of an Authority to Construct, a BACT analysis, and offsets for reactive organic compound (i.e., VOCs) emission increases above the applicable regulatory threshold. Campbell Soup claimed that compliance with state permits barred federal enforcement of BACT and offset claims. Campbell Soup also argued that the five-year statute of limitations barred the government's claims, because the violations were not continuing. The local air quality management district issued state operating permits to Campbell Soup in 1992, and the court considered whether compliance with the state permit constituted a "safe harbor" from federal enforcement. The court held that the statute of limitations barred the civil penalties claim. However, the court also found that a state's decision to grant a permit does not bar federal enforcement. The court reasoned that the "sweeping" language of CAA section 113 authorizes a compliance action by EPA whenever the agency finds that any person "has violated or is in violation" of an applicable SIP provision, and that a validly issued state permit does not prevent EPA from seeking penalties for SIP violations, including the failure to go through a PSD review.

United States v. Cinergy, 458 F.3d 705 (7th Cir. 2006), *cert. denied*, 549 U.S. 1338 (2007). EPA filed suit against Cinergy, alleging that a number of the company's coal-fired plants were modified without first obtaining a PSD permit. Cinergy argued that the applicable regulations did not require a permit for the modifications unless they increased the hourly emissions rate, even if the changes would have increased the plant's annual emissions by enabling the plant to operate for more hours during the year. The district court rejected Cinergy's interpretation and held that a PSD permit was required for major modifications that result in an increase in annual emissions. The Seventh Circuit agreed and affirmed the district court's holding.

Environmental Defense v. Duke Energy Corp., 549 U.S. 561 (2007). EPA and the Department of Justice filed a civil enforcement action against Duke Energy alleging that the company modified several of its coal-fired units at eight plants without first obtaining a PSD permit. The district court granted summary judgment in favor of Duke Energy, concluding that none of the projects was a major modification because there was no increase in hourly emission rates. The Fourth Circuit affirmed the lower court, reasoning that the CAA used identical definitions of *modification* under the NSPS and PSD provisions. The U.S. Supreme Court vacated and remanded the Fourth Circuit decision, concluding that EPA was not required to interpret the term "modification" the same for both the NSPS and PSD programs. The Court recognized that there was nothing in the CAA text or legislative history that suggested Congress meant to eliminate customary agency discretion to resolve questions about a statutory definition by looking to the surroundings in which the defined term appears. The Supreme Court also held that the Fourth Circuit's inter-pretation would have effectively invalidated the PSD regulations, which would run afoul of the CAA limits on the judicial review of agency regulations.

United States v. Cinergy, 623 F.3d 455 (7th Cir. 2010). In a decision related to the Seventh Circuit's 2006 opinion in *United States v. Cinergy,* 458 F.3d 705 (7th Cir. 2006), the court considered whether a PSD permit was required for SO_2 emission increases at Cinergy's Wabash plant that occurred between 1989 and 1992. Cinergy argued that the SIP rule in place at the time the alleged modifica-tions were made only looked to whether there was an increase in the plant's hourly rate of emissions and not the amount of an increase in annual emissions. The Indiana rule applicable to increases in SO_2 was modified to an annual emissions basis, but it was not submitted to EPA for approval until 1994. The Seventh Circuit reversed the dis-trict court's decision and held that the pre-1994 SIP standard, which used an hourly rate of emissions increase for SO_2, was applicable and that EPA could not rely on the later approved rule.

Sierra Club v. Otter Tail Power Co., 615 F.3d 1008 (8th Cir. 2010). The Sierra Club filed a citizen suit against the owners of a coal-fired power plant, alleging that the plant failed to obtain PSD permit modifications for a series of alleged equipment modifications and changes in the method of operation. The Sierra Club also alleged that the plant con-tinued to violate the CAA by operating without applicable PSD permits and abiding by BACT emission limits that would have been imposed as part of the PSD permitting process. The Eighth Circuit upheld the lower court's decision, holding that the PSD claims were time-barred by the applicable five-year statute of limitations (28 U.S.C. § 2462) because the last alleged modification occurred in 2001 and the suit was filed in 2008. The court concluded that the plain language of the CAA and applicable regulations prohibited only modification of the plant without a PSD permit or BACT review, but not its operation. The Eighth Circuit also dismissed the Sierra Club's claim that the plant trig-gered emission limits under NSPS due to the alleged equipment modi-fications and operational changes. The court agreed with the district court's holding that the Sierra Club's mechanism for challenging the alleged failure to include NSPS limits was through the Title V process, and further review of the claim was foreclosed.

Credible Evidence (CE)

Clean Air Implementation Project v. EPA, 150 F.3d 1200 (D.C. Cir. 1998), *cert. denied sub nom. Appalachian Power Co. v. EPA,* 527 U.S. 1021 (1999). The D.C. Circuit determined that the challenge to EPA's CE rule was not ripe for review because it failed to satisfy the requirements for judicial decision. The CE rule added language to five different sections of the agency's air regulations that permitted use of credible evidence to prove or disprove violations of the CAA. The petitioners argued that the CE rule was contrary to CAA sections 113(a) and (c) and that it was an unlawful revision of the various air regulations because it altered the means of compliance with and increased the stringency of certain standards without going through the requisite notice and comment rulemaking. The petitioners also argued that EPA did not have authority to require states to amend their SIPs to allow for the use of credible evidence. The court concluded that the petitioners' challenge was not ripe because it raised factual questions about how the CE rule had changed certain standards. The court found the issue would benefit from a "more concrete setting" and determined that there were "too many imponderables" to make a decision at this time. The court also held that nothing in the CE rule required states to revise their implementation plans, and even if it did, the issue was not ripe for a decision.

Jurisdiction

Harrison v. PPG Industries, 446 U.S. 578 (1980). PPG Industries sought review of an EPA decision subjecting certain equipment at a power plant to NSPS. PPG concurrently filed petitions for review in the Fifth Circuit, as well as seeking injunctive relief in the district court, because of uncertainty as to which court had jurisdiction. The Fifth Circuit dismissed petitioner's petition on the grounds that it had no jurisdiction. The Supreme Court reversed the Fifth Circuit's decision and held that CAA section 307 vests jurisdiction solely in the circuit courts for final agency actions by EPA, pursuant to the specific sections of the CAA enumerated by section 307.

Delaware Valley Citizens Council for Clean Air v. Davis, 932 F.2d 256 (3d Cir. 1991). A citizens' groups appealed a final district court order dismissing all four of its claims against the state of Pennsylvania for violating the CAA and its EPA-approved SIP. Three of the counts claimed that Pennsylvania's SIP failed to contain all of the provisions required under the CAA, and the fourth count charged Pennsylvania with failing to implement its SIP. In affirming the district court's order dismissing the first three counts, the court held that CAA section 304 "does not give the district court subject matter jurisdiction over the Citizens' private suit," because such claims fall under CAA section 307, which "allows groups such as the Citizens to hold the EPA to the Act's general standards in formulating and approving implementation plans by permitting them to petition for review of those plans in the courts of appeals." The Third Circuit, however, reversed the district court's order on the fourth count, which claimed that Pennsylvania violated the terms of its SIP by failing to take appropriate steps to decrease ozone emissions in the Philadelphia area before March 15, 1985. The Third Circuit held that "[w]e cannot eliminate, as a matter of law, the possibility that the Plan . . . requires Pennsylvania to undertake additional measures to improve air quality in the Philadelphia metropolitan area."

New Information

Group Against Smog & Pollution v. EPA, 665 F.2d 1284 (D.C. Cir. 1981). Various environmental groups challenged EPA's standards of performance for basic oxygen process furnaces (BOPF) used in the production of steel. The court held that the challenge was not timely because, in effect, it was a petition to revise and broaden a preexisting BOPF standard on the basis of new information. The court concluded that the petitioners' failure to mount a judicial challenge to the exclusion of fugitive emissions from the original BOPF rule did not preclude them from later seeking judicial review of the agency's subsequent refusal to revise the standard on the basis of new information.

Criminal Penalties

United States v. Thorn, 317 F.3d 107 (2d Cir. 2003). The defendant, an owner and operator of an asbestos abatement company, was convicted of nine counts of violating the CAA asbestos abatement standards. The defendant allegedly denied safety equipment to employees, hired minors to engage in asbestos removal without protective equipment, directed employees to undertake environmentally unsound removal processes, and falsified documents relating to compliance with the safety standards. The jury found the defendant guilty and the district court imposed a sentence of 65 months as well as forfeiture and restitution of fees collected for asbestos remediation projects. The government appealed and argued that the district court erred in not considering the nine-level enhancement for a CAA violation if the offense resulted in a substantial likelihood of death or serious bodily injury. The Second Circuit reversed the district court, holding that the "nine-level enhancement applies when the offense resulted in a substantial likelihood of death or serious bodily injury and not only when the offense actually caused such illness or death." Further, the Second Circuit found that the evidence was sufficient to support a finding that due to the defendant's violative acts, the defendant's workers were considerably more likely to develop asbestos-related diseases than if they had performed abatement under lawful conditions.

Clean Air Act (42 U.S.C. §§ 7401 to 7671q)

Chapter 85—Air Pollution Prevention and Control

Subchapter I—Programs and Activities

Part A—Air Quality and Emission Limitations

Subchapter II—Emission Standards for Moving Sources

Part A—Motor Vehicle Emission and Fuel Standards

Subchapter IV—Noise Pollution

Subchapter IV-A—Acid Deposition Control

Subchapter V—Permits

Subchapter VI—Stratospheric Ozone Protection

Code of Federal Regulations Air Programs: Index

Part 49—Tribal Clean Air Act Authority

Subpart K—Implementation Plans for Region VIII (starts at § 49.4161)

Subpart L—Implementation Plans for Region IX (starts at § 49.5511)

Subpart M—Implementation Plans for Region X (starts at § 49.9861)

Part 50—National Primary and Secondary Ambient Air Quality Standards

Part 51—Requirements for Preparation, Adoption, and Submittal of Implementation Plans

Subpart A—Air Emissions Reporting Requirements

Subpart F—Procedural Requirements (starts at § 51.100)

Subpart G—Control Strategy

Part 52—Approval and Promulgation of Implementation Plans

Subpart R—Kansas (starts at § 52.869)

Subpart S—Kentucky (starts at § 52.919)

Subpart T—Louisiana (starts at § 52.970)

Subpart U—Maine (starts at § 52.1019)

Subpart V—Maryland (starts at § 52.1070)

Subpart W—Massachusetts (starts at § 52.1119)

Subpart X—Michigan (starts at § 52.1170)

Subpart Y—Minnesota (starts at § 52.1219)

Subpart Z—Mississippi (starts at § 52.1270)

Subpart AA—Missouri (starts at § 52.1319)

Subpart BB—Montana (starts at § 52.1370)

Subpart CC—Nebraska (starts at § 52.1420)

Subpart DD—Nevada (starts at § 52.1470)

Subpart EE—New Hampshire (starts at § 52.1519)

Subpart FF—New Jersey (starts at § 52.1570)

Subpart GG—New Mexico (starts at § 52.1620)

Subpart HH—New York (starts at § 52.1670)

Subpart II—North Carolina (starts at § 52.1770)

Subpart JJ—North Dakota (starts at § 52.1820)

Subpart KK—Ohio (starts at § 52.1870)

Subpart LL—Oklahoma (starts at § 52.1920)

Subpart MM—Oregon (starts at § 52.1970)

Subpart NN—Pennsylvania (starts at § 52.2020)

Subpart OO—Rhode Island (starts at § 52.2070)

Subpart PP—South Carolina (starts at § 52.2119)

Subpart QQ—South Dakota (starts at § 52.2170)

Subpart RR—Tennessee (starts at § 52.2219)

Subpart SS—Texas (starts at § 52.2270)

Subpart TT—Utah (starts at § 52.2320)

Subpart UU—Vermont (starts at § 52.2370)

Subpart VV—Virginia (starts at § 52.2420)

Subpart WW—Washington (starts at § 52.2470)

Subpart XX—West Virginia (starts at § 52.2520)

Subpart YY—Wisconsin (starts at § 52.2569)

Subpart ZZ—Wyoming (starts at § 52.2620)

Subpart AAA—Guam (starts at § 52.2670)

Subpart BBB—Puerto Rico (starts at § 52.2720)

Subpart CCC—Virgin Islands (starts at § 52.2770)

Subpart DDD—American Samoa (starts at § 52.2820)

Subpart EEE—Approval and Promulgation of Plans (starts at § 52.2850)

Subpart FFF—Commonwealth of the Northern Mariana Islands
(starts at § 52.2900)

Part 53—Ambient Air Monitoring Reference and Equivalent Methods

Subpart A—General Provisions (starts at § 53.1)

Subpart B—Procedures for Testing Performance Characteristics of
Automated Methods for SO_2, CO, O_3, and NO_2 (starts at § 53.20)

Subpart C—Procedures for Determining Comparability between
Candidate Methods and Reference Methods (starts at § 53.30)

Subpart D—Procedures for Testing Performance Characteristics of
Methods for PM_{10} (starts at § 53.40)

Subpart E—Procedures for Testing Physical (Design) and Performance
Characteristics of Reference Methods and Class I Equivalent Methods for
$PM_{2.5}$ (starts at § 53.50)

Subpart F—Procedures for Testing Performance Characteristics of Class
II Equivalent Methods for $PM_{2.5}$ (starts at § 53.60)

Part 54—Prior Notice of Citizen Suits

Part 55—Outer Continental Shelf Air Regulations

Part 56—Regional Consistency

Part 57—Primary Nonferrous Smelter Orders

Part 58—Ambient Air Quality Surveillance

Subpart A—General Provisions (starts at § 58.1)

Subpart B—Monitoring Network (starts at § 58.10)

Subpart C—Special Purpose Monitors (starts at § 58.20)

Subpart D—Comparability of Ambient Data to NAAQS (starts at § 58.30)

Subpart F—Air Quality Index Reporting (starts at § 58.50)

Subpart G—Federal Monitoring (starts at § 58.60)

Appendix A to Part 58—Quality Assurance Requirements for State and
Local Air Monitoring Stations (SLAMS)

Appendix C to Part 58—Ambient Air Quality Monitoring Methodology

Appendix D to Part 58—Network Design Criteria for Ambient Air Quality Monitoring

Appendix E to Part 58—Probe and Monitoring Path Siting Criteria for Ambient Air Quality Monitoring

Appendix G to Part 58—Uniform Air Quality Index (AQI) and Daily Reporting

Part 59—National Volatile Organic Compound Emission Standards for Consumer and Commercial Products

Subpart A—General (starts at § 59.1)

Subpart B—National Volatile Organic Compound Emission Standards for Automobile Refinish Coatings (starts at § 59.100)

Subpart C—National Volatile Organic Compound Emission Standards for Consumer Products (starts at § 59.201)

Subpart D—National Volatile Organic Compound Emission Standards for Architectural Coatings (starts at § 59.400)

Subpart E—National Volatile Organic Compound Emission Standards for Aerosol Coatings (starts at § 59.500)

Subpart F—Control of Evaporative Emissions from New and In-Use Portable Fuel Containers (starts at § 59.600)

Part 60—Standards of Performance for New Stationary Sources

Subpart A—General Provisions
§ 60.1	Applicability
§ 60.2	Definitions
§ 60.3	Units and abbreviations
§ 60.4	Address
§ 60.5	Determination of construction or modification
§ 60.6	Review of plans
§ 60.7	Notification of recordkeeping
§ 60.8	Performance tests
§ 60.9	Availability of information
§ 60.10	State authority
§ 60.11	Compliance with standards and maintenance requirements
§ 60.12	Circumvention
§ 60.13	Monitoring requirements
§ 60.14	Modification
§ 60.15	Reconstruction
§ 60.16	Priority list
§ 60.17	Incorporations by reference
§ 60.18	General control device and work practice requirements
§ 60.19	General notification and reporting requirements

Subpart B—Adoption and Submittal of State Plans for Designated Facilities (starts at § 60.20)

Subpart C—Emission Guidelines and Compliance Times (starts at § 60.30)

Subpart Cb—Emission Guidelines and Compliance Times for Large Municipal Waste Combustors that are Constructed on or before September 20, 1994 (starts at § 60.30b)

Subpart Cc—Emission Guidelines and Compliance Times for Municipal Solid Waste Landfills (starts at § 60.30c)

Subpart Cd—Emissions Guidelines and Compliance Times for Sulfuric Acid Production Units (starts at § 60.30d)

Subpart Ce—Emission Guidelines and Compliance Times for Hospital/Medical/Infectious Waste Incinerators (starts at § 60.30e)

Subpart D—Standards of Performance for Fossil-Fuel-Fired Steam Generators for Which Construction Is Commenced after August 17, 1971 (starts at § 60.40)

Subpart Da—Standards of Performance of Electric Utility Steam Generating Units for Which Construction Is Commenced after September 18, 1978 (starts at § 60.40Da)

Subpart Db—Standards of Performance for Industrial-Commercial-Institutional Steam Generating Units (starts at § 60.40b)

Subpart Dc—Standards of Performance for Small Industrial-Commercial-Institutional Steam Generating Units (starts at § 60.40c)

Subpart Ea—Standards of Performance for Municipal Waste Combustors for Which Construction Is Commenced after December 20, 1989, and on or before September 20, 1994 (starts at § 60.50a)

Subpart Eb—Standards of Performance for Large Municipal Waste Combustors for Which Construction Is Commenced after September 20, 1994, or for which Modification or Reconstruction Is Commenced after June 19, 1996 (starts at § 60.50b)

Subpart Ec—Standards of Performance for Hospital/Medical/Infectious Waste Incinerators for Which Construction Is Commenced after June 20, 1996 (starts at § 60.50c)

Subpart F—Standards of Performance for Portland Cement Plants (starts at § 60.60)

Subpart G—Standards of Performance for Nitric Acid Plants (starts at § 60.70)

Subpart H—Standards of Performance for Sulfuric Acid Plants (starts at § 60.80)

Subpart I—Standards of Performance for Hot Mix Asphalt Facilities (starts at § 60.90)

Subpart J—Standards of Performance for Petroleum Refineries
(starts at § 60.100)

Subpart Ja—Standards of Performance for Petroleum Refineries for Which
Construction, Reconstruction, or Modification Commenced after May 14,
2007 (starts at § 60.100a)

Subpart K—Standards of Performance for Storage Vessels for Petroleum
Liquids for Which Construction, Reconstruction, or Modification
Commenced after June 11, 1973, and prior to May 19, 1978
(starts at § 60.110)

Subpart Ka—Standards of Performance for Storage Vessels for Petroleum
Liquids for Which Construction, Reconstruction, or Modification
Commenced after May 18, 1978, and prior to July 23, 1984
(starts at § 60.110a)

Subpart Kb—Standards of Performance for Volatile Organic Liquid
Storage Vessels (Including Petroleum Liquid Storage Vessels) for Which
Construction, Reconstruction, or Modification Commenced after July 23,
1984 (starts at § 60.110b)

Subpart L—Standards of Performance for Secondary Lead Smelters
(starts at § 60.120)

Subpart M—Standards of Performance for Secondary Brass and Bronze
Production Plants (starts at § 60.130)

Subpart N—Standards of Performance for Primary Emissions from Basic
Oxygen Process Furnaces for Which Construction Is Commenced after
June 11, 1973 (starts at § 60.140)

Subpart Na—Standards of Performance for Secondary Emissions from
Basic Oxygen Process Steelmaking Facilities for Which Construction Is
Commenced after January 20, 1983 (starts at § 60.140a)

Subpart O—Standards of Performance for Sewage Treatment Plants
(starts at § 60.150)

Subpart P—Standards of Performance for Primary Copper Smelters
(starts at § 60.160)

Subpart Q—Standards of Performance for Primary Zinc Smelters
(starts at § 60.170)

Subpart R—Standards of Performance for Primary Lead Smelters
(starts at § 60.180)

Subpart S—Standards of Performance for Primary Aluminum Reduction
Plants (starts at § 60.190)

Subpart T—Standards of Performance for the Phosphate Fertilizer
Industry: Wet-Process Phosphoric Acid Plants (starts at § 60.200)

Subpart U—Standards of Performance for the Phosphate Fertilizer
Industry: Superphosphoric Acid Plants (starts at § 60.210)

Subpart V—Standards of Performance for the Phosphate Fertilizer Industry: Diammonium Phosphate Plants (starts at § 60.220)

Subpart W—Standards of Performance for the Phosphate Fertilizer Industry: Triple Superphosphate Plants (starts at § 60.230)

Subpart X—Standards of Performance for the Phosphate Fertilizer Industry: Granular Triple Superphosphate Storage Facilities (starts at § 60.240)

Subpart Y—Standards of Performance for Coal Preparation Plants (starts at § 60.250)

Subpart Z—Standards of Performance for Ferroalloy Production Facilities (starts at § 60.260)

Subpart AA—Standards of Performance for Steel Plants: Electric Arc Furnaces Constructed after October 21, 1974, and on or before August 17, 1983 (starts at § 60.270)

Subpart AAa—Standards of Performance for Steel Plants: Electric Arc Furnaces and Argon-Oxygen Decarburization Vessels Constructed after August 7, 1983 (starts at § 60.270a)

Subpart BB—Standards of Performance for Kraft Pulp Mills (starts at § 60.280)

Subpart CC—Standards of Performance for Glass Manufacturing Plants (starts at § 60.290)

Subpart DD—Standards of Performance for Grain Elevators (starts at § 60.300)

Subpart EE—Standards of Performance for Surface Coating of Metal Furniture (starts at § 60.310)

Subpart GG—Standards of Performance for Stationary Gas Turbines (starts at § 60.330)

Subpart HH—Standards of Performance for Lime Manufacturing Plants (starts at § 60.340)

Subpart KK—Standards of Performance for Lead-Acid Battery Manufacturing Plants (starts at § 60.370)

Subpart LL—Standards of Performance for Metallic Mineral Processing Plants (starts at § 60.380)

Subpart MM—Standards of Performance for Automobile and Light-Duty Truck Surface Coating Operations (starts at § 60.390)

Subpart NN—Standards of Performance for Phosphate Rock Plants (starts at § 60.400)

Subpart PP—Standards of Performance for Ammonium Sulfate Manufacture (starts at § 60.420)

Subpart QQ—Standards of Performance for the Graphic Arts Industry; Publication Rotogravure Printing (starts at § 60.430)

Subpart RR—Standards of Performance for Pressure Sensitive Tape and Label Surface Coating Operations (starts at § 60.440)

Subpart SS—Standards of Performance for Industrial Surface Coating; Large Appliances (starts at § 60.450)

Subpart TT—Standards of Performance for Metal Coil Surface Coating (starts at § 60.460)

Subpart UU—Standards of Performance for Asphalt Processing and Asphalt Roofing Manufacture (starts at § 60.470)

Subpart VV—Standards of Performance for Equipment Leaks of VOC in the Synthetic Organic Chemicals Manufacturing Industry for Which Construction, Reconstruction, or Modification Commenced after January 5, 1981, and on or before November 7, 2006 (starts at § 60.480)

Subpart VVa—Standards of Performance for Equipment Leaks of VOC in the Synthetic Organic Chemicals Manufacturing Industry for Which Construction, Reconstruction, or Modification Commenced after November 7, 2006 (starts at § 60.480a)

Subpart WW—Standards of Performance for the Beverage Can Surface Coating Industry (starts at § 60.490)

Subpart XX—Standards of Performance for Bulk Gasoline Terminals (starts at § 60.500)

Subpart AAA—Standards of Performance for New Residential Wood Heaters (starts at § 60.530)

Subpart BBB—Standards of Performance for the Rubber Tire Manufacturing Industry (starts at § 60.540)

Subpart DDD—Standards of Performance for Volatile Organic Compound (VOC) Emissions from the Polymer Manufacturing Industry (starts at § 60.560)

Subpart FFF—Standards of Performance for Flexible Vinyl and Urethane Coating and Printing (starts at § 60.580)

Subpart GGG—Standards of Performance for Equipment Leaks of VOC in Petroleum Refineries (starts at § 60.590)

Subpart HHH—Standards of Performance for Synthetic Fiber Production Facilities (starts at § 60.600)

Subpart III—Standards of Performance for Volatile Organic Compound (VOC) Emissions from the Synthetic Organic Chemical Manufacturing Industry (SOCMI) Air Oxidation Unit Processes (starts at § 60.610)

Subpart JJJ—Standards of Performance for Petroleum Dry Cleaners (starts at § 60.620)

Subpart KKK—Standards of Performance for Equipment Leaks of VOC from Onshore Natural Gas Processing Plant (starts at § 60.630)

Subpart LLL—Standards of Performance for Onshore Natural Gas Processing; SO_2 Emissions (starts at § 60.640)

Subpart NNN—Standards of Performance for Volatile Organic Compound (VOC) Emissions from Synthetic Organic Chemical Manufacturing Industry (SOCMI) Distillation Operation (starts at § 60.660)

Subpart OOO—Standards of Performance for Nonmetallic Mineral Processing Plants (starts at § 60.670)

Subpart PPP—Standard of Performance for Wool Fiberglass Insulation Manufacturing Plants (starts at § 60.680)

Subpart QQQ—Standards of Performance for VOC Emissions from Petroleum Refinery Wastewater Systems (starts at § 60.690)

Subpart RRR—Standards of Performance for Volatile Organic Compound (VOC) Emissions from Synthetic Organic Chemical Manufacturing Industry (SOCMI) Reactor Processes (starts at § 60.700)

Subpart SSS—Standard of Performance for Magnetic Tape Coating Facilities (starts at § 60.710)

Subpart TTT—Standards of Performance for Industrial Surface Coating; Surface Coating of Plastic Parts for Business Machines (starts at § 60.720)

Subpart UUU—Standards of Performance for Calciners and Dryers in Mineral Industries (starts at § 60.730)

Subpart VVV—Standards of Performance for Polymeric Coating of Supporting Substrates Facilities (starts at § 60.740)

Subpart WWW—Standards of Performance for Municipal Solid Waste Landfills (starts at § 60.750)

Subpart AAAA—Standards of Performance for Small Municipal Waste Combustion Units for Which Construction Is Commenced after August 30, 1999 or for Which Modification or Reconstruction Is Commenced after June 6, 2001 (starts at § 60.1000)

Subpart BBBB—Emission Guidelines and Compliance Times for Small Municipal Waste Combustion Units Constructed on or before August 30, 1999 (starts at § 60.1500)

Subpart CCCC—Standards of Performance for Commercial and Industrial Solid Waste Incineration Units for Which Construction Is Commenced after November 30, 1999 or for Which Modification or Reconstruction Is Commenced after June 1, 2001 (starts at § 60.2000)

Subpart DDDD—Emission Guidelines and Compliance Times for Commercial and Industrial Solid Waste Incineration Units that Commenced Construction on or before November 30, 1999 (starts at § 60.2500)

Subpart EEEE—Standards of Performance for Other Solid Waste Incineration Units for Which Construction Is Commenced after December 9, 2004, or for Which Modification or Reconstruction Is Commenced on or after June 16, 2006 (starts at § 60.2880)

Subpart FFFF—Emission Guidelines and Compliance Times for Other Solid Waste Incineration Units that Commenced Construction on or before December 9, 2004 (starts at § 60.2980)

Subpart HHHH—Emission Guidelines and Compliance Times for Coal-Fired Electric Steam Generating Units (starts at § 60.4101)

Subpart IIII—Standards of Performance for Stationary Compression Ignition Internal Combustion Engines (starts at § 60.4200)

Subpart JJJJ—Standards of Performance for Stationary Spark Ignition Internal Combustion Engines (starts at § 60.4230)

Subpart KKKK—Standards of Performance for Stationary Combustion Turbines (starts at § 60.4300)

Appendix A to Part 60—Test Methods

Appendix B to Part 60—Performance Specifications

Appendix C to Part 60—Determination of Emission Rate Change

Appendix D to Part 60—Required Emission Inventory Information

Part 61—National Emission Standards for Hazardous Air Pollutants

Subpart A—General Provisions

§ 61.01	Lists of pollutants and applicability of part 61
§ 61.02	Definitions
§ 61.03	Units and abbreviations
§ 61.04	Address
§ 61.05	Prohibited activities
§ 61.06	Determination of construction or modification
§ 61.07	Application for approval of construction or modification
§ 61.08	Approval of construction or modification
§ 61.09	Notification of startup
§ 61.10	Source reporting and waiver request
§ 61.11	Waiver of compliance
§ 61.12	Compliance with standards and maintenance requirements
§ 61.13	Emission tests and waiver of emission tests
§ 61.14	Monitoring requirements
§ 61.15	Modification
§ 61.16	Availability of information
§ 61.17	State authority
§ 61.18	Incorporations by reference
§ 61.19	Circumvention

Subpart B—National Emission Standards for Random Emissions from Underground Uranium Mines (starts at § 61.20)

Subpart C—National Emission Standard for Beryllium (starts at § 61.30)

Subpart D—National Emission Standard for Beryllium Rocket Motor Firing (starts at § 61.40)

Subpart E—National Emission Standard for Mercury (starts at § 61.50)

Subpart F—National Emission Standard for Vinyl Chloride (starts at § 61.60)

Subpart H—National Emission Standard for Emissions of Radionuclides Other Than Radon from Department of Energy Facilities (starts at § 61.90)

Subpart I—National Emission Standards for Radionuclide Emissions from Federal Facilities Other Than Nuclear Regulatory Commission Licensees and Not Covered by Subpart H (starts at § 61.100)

Subpart J—National Emission Standard for Equipment Leaks (Fugitive Emission Sources) of Benzene (starts § 61.110)

Subpart K—National Emission Standards for Radionuclide Emissions from Elemental Phosphorus Plants (starts at § 61.120)

Subpart L—National Emission Standard for Benzene Emissions from Coke By-Product Recovery Plants (starts at § 6.130)

Subpart M—National Emission Standard for Asbestos (starts at § 61.140)

Subpart N—National Emission Standard for Inorganic Arsenic Emissions from Glass Manufacturing Plants (starts at § 61.160)

Subpart O—National Emission Standard for Inorganic Arsenic Emissions from Primary Copper Smelters (starts at § 61.170)

Subpart P—National Emission Standard for Inorganic Arsenic Emissions from Arsenic Trioxide and Metallic Arsenic Production Facilities (starts at § 61.180)

Subpart Q—National Emission Standards for Radon Emissions from Department of Energy Facilities (starts at § 61.190)

Subpart R—National Emission Standards for Radon Emissions from Phosphogypsum Stacks (starts at § 61.200)

Subpart T—National Emission Standards for Radon Emissions from the Disposal of Uranium Mill Tailings (starts at § 61.220)

Subpart V—National Emission Standard for Equipment Leaks (Fugitive Emission Sources) (starts at § 61.240)

Subpart W—National Emission Standards for Radon Emissions from Operating Mill Tailings (starts at § 61.250)

Subpart Y—National Emission Standard for Benzene Emissions from Benzene Storage Vessels (starts at § 61.270)

Subpart BB—National Emission Standard for Benzene Emissions from Benzene Transfer Operations (starts at § 61.300)

Subpart FF—National Emission Standard for Benzene Waste Operations (starts at § 61.340)

Part 62—Approval and Promulgation of State Plans for Designated Facilities and Pollutants

Subpart A—General Provisions (starts at § 62.01)

Subpart B to Subpart DDD (Covers the 50 states and U.S. Territories) (starts at § 62.100)

Subpart FFF—Federal Plan Requirements for Large Municipal Waste Combustors Constructed on or before September 20, 1994 (starts at § 62.14100)

Subpart GGG—Federal Plan Requirements for Municipal Solid Waste Landfills That Commenced Construction prior to May 30, 1991 and Have Not Been Modified or Reconstructed Since May 30, 1991 (starts at § 62.14350)

Subpart HHH—Federal Plan Requirements for Hospital/ Medical/ Infectious Waste Incinerators Constructed on or before June 20, 1996 (starts at § 62.14400)

Subpart III—Federal Plan Requirements for Commercial and Solid Waste Incineration Units That Commenced Construction on or before November 30, 1999 (starts at § 62.14500)

Subpart JJJ—Federal Plan Requirements for Small Municipal Waste Combustion Units Constructed on or before August 30, 1999 (starts at § 62.15000)

Part 63—National Emission Standards for Hazardous Air Pollutants for Source Categories

Subpart A—General Provisions
§ 63.1	Applicability
§ 63.2	Definitions
§ 63.3	Units and abbreviations
§ 63.4	Prohibited activities and circumvention
§ 63.5	Preconstruction review and notification requirements
§ 63.6	Compliance with standards and maintenance requirements
§ 63.7	Performance testing requirements
§ 63.8	Monitoring requirements
§ 63.9	Notification requirements
§ 63.10	Recordkeeping and reporting requirements
§ 63.11	Control device and work practice requirements
§ 63.12	State authority and delegations
§ 63.13	Addresses of State air pollution control agencies and EPA Regional Offices
§ 63.14	Incorporations by reference
§ 63.15	Availability of information and confidentiality
§ 63.16	Performance Track Provisions

Subpart B—Requirements for Control Technology Determinations for Major Sources in Accordance with Clean Air Act Sections, Sections 112(g) and 112(j)

§ 63.40	Applicability of §§ 63.40 through 63.44
§ 63.41	Definitions
§ 63.42	Program requirements governing construction or reconstruction of major sources
§ 63.43	Maximum achievable control technology (MACT) determinations for constructed and reconstructed major sources
§ 63.44	Requirements for constructed or reconstructed major sources subject to a subsequently promulgated MACT standard or MACT requirement
§ 63.50	Applicability
§ 63.51	Definitions
§ 63.52	Approval process for new and existing emission units
§ 63.53	Application content for case-by-case MACT determinations
§ 63.54	Preconstruction review procedures for new affected sources
§ 63.55	Maximum achievable control technology (MACT) determinations for affected sources subject to case-by-case determination of equivalent emission limitations
§ 63.56	Requirements for case-by-case determination of equivalent emission limitations after promulgation of subsequent MACT standard

Subpart C—List of Hazardous Air Pollutants, Petitions Process, Lesser Quantity Designations, Source Category List (starts at § 63.60)

Subpart D—Regulations Governing Compliance Extensions for Early Reductions of Hazardous Air Pollutants (starts at § 63.70)

Subpart E—Approval of State Programs and Delegation of Federal Authorities (starts at § 63.90)

Subpart F—National Emission Standards for Organic Hazardous Air Pollutants from the Synthetic Organic Chemical Manufacturing Industry (starts at § 63.100)

Subpart G—National Emission Standards for Organic Hazardous Air Pollutants from the Synthetic Organic Chemical Manufacturing Industry for Process Vents, Storage Vessels, Transfer Operations, and Wastewater (starts at § 63.110)

Subpart H—National Emission Standards for Organic Hazardous Air Pollutants for Equipment Leaks (starts at § 63.160)

Subpart I—National Emission Standards for Organic Hazardous Air Pollutants for Certain Processes Subject to the Negotiated Regulation for Equipment Leaks (starts at § 63.190)

Subpart J—National Emission Standards for Hazardous Air Pollutants for Polyvinyl Chloride and Copolymers Production (starts at § 63.210)

Subpart L—National Emission Standards for Coke Oven Batteries (starts at § 63.300)

Subpart M—National Perchloroethylene Air Emission Standards for Dry Cleaning Facilities (starts at § 63.320)

Subpart N—National Emission Standards for Chromium Emissions from Hard and Decorative Chromium Electroplating and Chromium Anodizing Tanks (starts at § 63.340)

Subpart O—Ethylene Oxide Emissions Standards for Sterilization Facilities (starts at § 63.360)

Subpart Q—National Emission Standards for Hazardous Air Pollutants for Industrial Process Cooling Towers (starts at § 63.400)

Subpart R—National Emission Standards for Gasoline Distribution Facilities (Bulk Gasoline Terminals and Pipeline Breakout Stations) (starts at § 63.420)

Subpart S—National Emission Standards for Hazardous Air Pollutants from the Pulp and Paper Industry (starts at § 63.440)

Subpart T—National Emission Standards for Halogenated Solvent Cleaning (starts at § 63.460)

Subpart U—National Emission Standards for Hazardous Air Pollutant Emissions: Group I Polymers and Resins (starts at § 63.480)

Subpart W—National Emission Standards for Hazardous Air Pollutants for Epoxy Resins Production and Non-Nylon Polyamides Production (starts at § 63.520)

Subpart X—National Emission Standards for Hazardous Air Pollutants from Secondary Lead Smelting (starts at § 63.541)

Subpart Y—National Emission Standards for Marine Tank Vessel Tank Loading Operations (starts at § 63.560)

Subpart AA—National Emission Standards for Hazardous Air Pollutants from Phosphoric Acid Manufacturing Plants (starts at § 63.600)

Subpart BB—National Emission Standards for Hazardous Air Pollutants from Phosphate Fertilizers Production Plants (starts at § 63.620)

Subpart CC—National Emission Standards for Hazardous Air Pollutants from Petroleum Refineries (starts at § 63.640)

Subpart DD—National Emission Standards for Hazardous Air Pollutants from Off-Site Waste and Recovery Operations (starts at § 63.680)

Subpart EE—National Emission Standards for Magnetic Tape Manufacturing Operations (starts at § 63.701)

Subpart GG—National Emission Standards for Aerospace Manufacturing and Rework Facilities (starts at § 63.741)

Subpart HH—National Emission Standards for Hazardous Air Pollutants from Oil and Natural Gas Production Facilities (starts at § 63.760)

Subpart II—National Emission Standards for Shipbuilding and Ship Repair (Surface Coating) (starts at § 63.780)

Subpart JJ—National Emission Standards for Wood Furniture Manufacturing Operations (starts at § 63.800)

Subpart KK—National Emission Standards for the Printing and Publishing Industry (starts at § 63.820)

Subpart LL—National Emission Standards for Hazardous Air Pollutants for Primary Aluminum Reduction Plants (starts at § 63.840)

Subpart MM—National Emission Standards for Hazardous Air Pollutants for Chemical Recovery Combustion Sources at Kraft, Soda, Sulfite, and Stand-Alone Semichemical Pulp Mills (starts at § 63.860)

Subpart OO—National Emission Standards for Tanks—Level 1 (starts at § 63.900)

Subpart PP—National Emission Standards for Containers (starts at § 63.920)

Subpart QQ—National Emission Standards for Surface Impoundments (starts at § 63.940)

Subpart RR—National Emission Standards for Individual Drain Systems (starts at § 63.960)

Subpart SS—National Emission Standards for Closed Vent Systems, Control Devices, Recovery Devices and Routing to a Fuel Gas System or a Process (starts at § 63.980)

Subpart TT—National Emission Standards for Equipment Leaks—Control Level 1 (starts at § 63.1000)

Subpart UU—National Emission Standards for Equipment Leaks—Control Level 2 Standards (starts at § 63.1019)

Subpart VV—National Emission Standards for Oil-Water Separators and Organic Water Separators (starts at § 63.1040)

Subpart WW—National Emission Standards for Storage Vessels (Tanks)—Control Level 2 (starts at § 63.1060)

Subpart XX—National Emission Standards for Ethylene Manufacturing Process Units: Heat Exchange Systems and Waste Operations (starts at § 63.1080)

Subpart YY—National Emission Standards for Hazardous Air Pollutants for Source Categories: Generic Maximum Achievable Control Technology Standards (starts at § 63.1100)

Subpart CCC— National Emission Standards for Hazardous Air Pollutants for Steel Pickling—HCL Process Facilities and Hydrochloric Acid Regeneration Plants (starts at § 63.1155)

Subpart DDD—National Emission Standards for Hazardous Air Pollutants for Mineral Wool Production (starts at § 63.1175)

Subpart EEE—National Emission Standards for Hazardous Air Pollutants from Hazardous Waste Combustors (starts at § 63.1211)

Subpart GGG—National Emission Standards for Pharmaceuticals Production (starts at § 63.1250)

Subpart HHH—National Emission Standards for Hazardous Air Pollutants from Natural Gas Transmission and Storage Facilities (starts at § 63.1270)

Subpart III—National Emission Standards for Hazardous Air Pollutants for Flexible Polyurethane Foam Production (starts at § 63.1290)

Subpart JJJ—National Emission Standards for Hazardous Air Pollutant Emissions: Group IV Polymers and Resins (starts at § 63.1310)

Subpart LLL—National Emission Standards for Hazardous Air Pollutants from the Portland Cement Manufacturing Industry (starts at § 63.1340)

Subpart MMM—National Emission Standards for Hazardous Air Pollutants for Pesticide Active Ingredient Production (starts at § 63.1360)

Subpart NNN—National Emission Standards for Hazardous Air Pollutants for Wool Fiberglass Manufacturing (starts at § 63.1380)

Subpart OOO—National Emission Standards for Hazardous Air Pollutant Emissions: Manufacture of Amino/Phenolic Resins (starts at § 63.1400)

Subpart PPP—National Emission Standards for Hazardous Air Pollutant Emissions for Polyether Polyols Production (starts at § 63.1420)

Subpart QQQ—National Emission Standards for Hazardous Air Pollutants for Primary Copper Smelting (starts at § 63.1440)

Subpart RRR—National Emission Standards for Hazardous Air Pollutants for Secondary Aluminum Production (starts at § 63.1500)

Subpart TTT—National Emission Standards for Hazardous Air Pollutants for Primary Lead Smelting (starts at § 63.1541)

Subpart QQQ—National Emission Standards for Hazardous Air Pollutants for Petroleum Refineries: Catalytic Cracking Units, Catalytic Reforming Units, and Sulfur Recovery Units (starts at § 63.1560)

Subpart VVV—National Emission Standards for Hazardous Air Pollutants: Publicly Owned Treatment Works (starts at § 63.1580)

Subpart XXX—National Emission Standards for Hazardous Air Pollutants for Ferroalloys Production: Ferromanganese and Silicomanganese (starts at § 63.1620)

Subpart AAAA—National Emission Standards for Hazardous Air Pollutants: Municipal Solid Waste Landfills (starts at § 63.1930)

Subpart CCCC—National Emission Standards for Hazardous Air Pollutants: Manufacturing of Nutritional Yeast (starts at § 63.2130)

Subpart DDDD—National Emission Standards for Hazardous Air Pollutants: Plywood and Composite Wood Products (starts at § 63.2230)

Subpart EEEE—National Emission Standards for Hazardous Air Pollutants: Organic Liquids Distribution (Non-Gasoline) (starts at § 63.2330)

Subpart FFFF—National Emission Standards for Hazardous Air Pollutants: Miscellaneous Organic Chemical Manufacturing (starts at § 63.2430)

Subpart GGGG—National Emission Standards for Hazardous Air Pollutants: Solvent Extraction for Vegetable Oil Production (starts at § 63.2830)

Subpart HHHH—National Emission Standards for Hazardous Air Pollutants for Wet-Formed Fiberglass Mat Production (starts at § 63.2980)

Subpart IIII—National Emission Standards for Hazardous Air Pollutants: Surface Coating of Automobiles and Light-Duty Trucks (starts at § 63.3080)

Subpart JJJJ—National Emission Standards for Hazardous Air Pollutants: Paper and Other Web Coating (starts at § 63.3280)

Subpart KKKK—National Emission Standards for Hazardous Air Pollutants: Surface Coating of Metal Cans (starts at § 63.3480)

Subpart MMMM—National Emission Standards for Hazardous Air Pollutants for Surface Coating of Miscellaneous Metal Parts and Products (starts at § 63.3880)

Subpart NNNN—National Emission Standards for Hazardous Air Pollutants: Surface Coating of Large Appliances (starts at § 63.4080)

Subpart OOOO—National Emission Standards for Hazardous Air Pollutants: Printing, Coating, and Dyeing of Fabrics and Other Textiles (starts at § 63.4280)

Subpart PPPP—National Emission Standards for Hazardous Air Pollutants for Surface Coating of Miscellaneous Plastic Parts and Products (starts at § 63.4480)

Subpart QQQQ—National Emission Standards for Hazardous Air Pollutants: Surface Coating of Wood Building Products (starts at § 63.4680)

Subpart RRRR—National Emission Standards for Hazardous Air Pollutants: Surface Coating of Metal Furniture (starts at § 63.4880)

Subpart SSSS—National Emission Standards for Hazardous Air Pollutants: Surface Coating of Metal Coil (starts at § 63.5080)

Subpart TTTT—National Emission Standards for Hazardous Air Pollutants for Leather Finishing Operations (starts at § 63.5280)

Subpart UUUU—National Emission Standards for Hazardous Air Pollutants for Cellulose Products Manufacturing (starts at § 63.5480)

Subpart VVVV—National Emission Standards for Hazardous Air Pollutants for Boat Manufacturing (starts at § 63.5680)

Subpart WWWW—National Emission Standards for Hazardous Air Pollutants: Reinforced Plastic Composites Production (starts at § 63.5780)

Subpart XXXX—National Emission Standards for Hazardous Air Pollutants: Rubber Tire Manufacturing (starts at § 63.5980)

Subpart YYYY—National Emission Standards for Hazardous Air Pollutants for Stationary Combustion Turbines (starts at § 63.6080)

Subpart ZZZZ—National Emission Standards for Hazardous Air Pollutants for Stationary Reciprocating Internal Combustion Engines (starts at § 63.6580)

Subpart AAAAA—National Emission Standards for Hazardous Air Pollutants for Lime Manufacturing Plants (starts at § 63.7080)

Subpart BBBBB—National Emission Standards for Hazardous Air Pollutants for Semiconductor Manufacturing (starts at § 63.7180)

Subpart CCCCC—National Emission Standards for Hazardous Air Pollutants for Coke Ovens: Pushing, Quenching, and Battery Stacks (starts at § 63.7280)

Subpart DDDDD—National Emission Standards for Hazardous Air Pollutants for Industrial, Commercial, and Institutional Boilers and Process Heaters (starts at § 63.7480)

Subpart EEEEE—National Emission Standards for Hazardous Air Pollutants for Iron and Steel Foundries (starts at § 63.7680)

Subpart FFFFF—National Emission Standards for Hazardous Air Pollutants for Integrated Iron and Steel Manufacturing Facilities (starts at § 63.7780)

Subpart GGGGG—National Emission Standards for Hazardous Air Pollutants: Site Remediation (starts at § 63.7880)

Subpart HHHHH—National Emission Standards for Hazardous Air Pollutants: Miscellaneous Coating Manufacturing (starts at § 63.7980)

Subpart IIIII—National Emission Standards for Hazardous Air Pollutants: Mercury Emissions from Mercury Cell Chlor-Alkali Plants (starts at § 63.8180)

Subpart JJJJJ—National Emission Standards for Hazardous Air Pollutants for Brick and Structural Clay Products Manufacturing (starts at § 63.8380)

Subpart KKKKK—National Emission Standards for Hazardous Air Pollutants for Clay Ceramics Manufacturing (starts at § 63.8530)

Subpart LLLLL—National Emission Standards for Hazardous Air Pollutants: Asphalt Processing and Asphalt Roofing Manufacturing (starts at § 63.8680)

Subpart MMMMM—National Emission Standards for Hazardous Air Pollutants: Flexible Polyurethane Foam Fabrication Operations (starts at § 63.8780)

Subpart NNNNN—National Emission Standards for Hazardous Air Pollutants: Hydrochloric Acid Production (starts at § 63.8980)

Subpart PPPPP—National Emission Standards for Hazardous Air Pollutants for Engine Test Cells/Stands (starts at § 63.9280)

Subpart QQQQQ—National Emission Standards for Hazardous Air Pollutants for Friction Materials Manufacturing Facilities (starts at § 63.9480)

Subpart RRRRR—National Emission Standards for Hazardous Air Pollutants: Taconite Iron Ore Processing (starts at § 63.9580)

Subpart SSSSS—National Emission Standards for Hazardous Air Pollutants for Refractory Products Manufacturing (starts at § 63.9780)

Subpart TTTTT—National Emission Standards for Hazardous Air Pollutants for Primary Magnesium Refining (starts at § 63.9880)

Subpart WWWWW—National Emission Standards for Hospital Ethylene Oxide Sterilizers (starts at § 63.10382)

Subpart YYYYY—National Emission Standards for Hazardous Air Pollutants for Area Sources: Electric Arc Furnace Steelmaking Facilities (starts at § 63.10680)

Subpart ZZZZZ—National Emission Standards for Hazardous Air Pollutants for Iron and Steel Foundries Area Sources (starts at § 63.10880)

Subpart BBBBBB—National Emission Standards for Hazardous Air Pollutants for Source Category: Gasoline Distribution Bulk Terminals, Bulk Plants, and Pipeline Facilities (starts at § 63.11080)

Subpart CCCCCC—National Emission Standards for Hazardous Air Pollutants for Source Category: Gasoline Dispensing Facilities (starts at § 63.11110)

Subpart DDDDDD—National Emission Standards for Hazardous Air Pollutants for Polyvinyl Chloride and Copolymers Production Area Sources (starts at § 63.11140)

Subpart EEEEEE—National Emission Standards for Hazardous Air Pollutants for Primary Copper Smelting Area Sources (starts at § 63.11146)

Subpart FFFFFF—National Emission Standards for Hazardous Air Pollutants for Secondary Copper Smelting Area Sources (starts at § 63.11153)

Subpart GGGGGG—National Emission Standards for Hazardous Air Pollutants for Primary Nonferrous Metals Area Sources—Zinc, Cadmium, and Beryllium (starts at § 63.11160)

Subpart HHHHHH—National Emission Standards for Hazardous Air Pollutants: Paint Stripping and Miscellaneous Surface Coating Operations at Area Sources (starts at § 63.11169)

Subpart LLLLLL—National Emission Standards for Hazardous Air Pollutants for Acrylic and Modacrylic Fibers Production Area Sources (starts at § 63.11393)

Subpart MMMMMM—National Emission Standards for Hazardous Air Pollutants for Carbon Black Production Area Sources (starts at § 63.11400)

Subpart NNNNNN—National Emission Standards for Hazardous Air Pollutants for Chemical Manufacturing Area Sources: Chromium Compounds (starts at § 63.11407)

Subpart OOOOOO—National Emission Standards for Hazardous Air Pollutants for Flexible Polyurethane Foam Production and Fabrication Area Sources (starts at § 63.11414)

Subpart PPPPPP—National Emission Standards for Hazardous Air Pollutants for Lead Acid Battery Manufacturing Area Sources (starts at § 63.11421)

Subpart QQQQQQ—National Emission Standards for Hazardous Air Pollutants for Wood Preserving Area Sources (starts at § 63.11428)

Subpart RRRRRR—National Emission Standards for Hazardous Air Pollutants for Clay Ceramics Manufacturing Area Sources (starts at § 63.11435)

Subpart SSSSSS—National Emission Standards for Hazardous Air Pollutants for Glass Manufacturing Area Sources (starts at § 63.11448)

Subpart TTTTTT—National Emission Standards for Hazardous Air Pollutants for Secondary Nonferrous Metals Processing Area Sources (starts at § 63.11462)

Subpart VVVVVV—National Emission Standards for Hazardous Air Pollutants for Chemical Manufacturing Area Sources (starts at § 63.11494)

Subpart WWWWWW—National Emission Standards for Hazardous Air Pollutants: Area Source Standards for Plating and Polishing Operations (starts at § 63.11504)

Subpart XXXXXX—National Emission Standards for Hazardous Air Pollutants Area Source Standards for Nine Metal Fabrication and Finishing Source Categories (starts at § 63.11514)

Subpart YYYYYY—National Emission Standards for Hazardous Air Pollutants for Area Sources: Ferroalloys Production Facilities (starts at § 63.11524)

Subpart ZZZZZZ—National Emission Standards for Hazardous Air Pollutants: Area Source Standards for Aluminum, Copper, and Other Nonferrous Foundries (starts at § 63.11544)

Subpart AAAAAAA—National Emission Standards for Hazardous Air Pollutants for Area Sources: Asphalt Processing and Asphalt Roofing Manufacturing (starts at § 63.11559)

Subpart BBBBBBB—National Emission Standards for Hazardous Air Pollutants for Area Sources: Chemical Preparations Industry (starts at § 63.11579)

Subpart CCCCCCC—National Emission Standards for Hazardous Air Pollutants for Area Sources: Paints and Allied Products Manufacturing (starts at § 63.11599)

Subpart DDDDDDD—National Emission Standards for Hazardous Air Pollutants for Area Sources: Prepared Feeds Manufacturing (starts at § 63.11619)

Part 64— Compliance Assurance Monitoring

§ 64.1   Definitions
§ 64.2   Applicability
§ 64.3   Monitoring design criteria
§ 64.4   Submittal requirements
§ 64.5   Deadlines for submittals
§ 64.6   Approval of monitoring
§ 64.7   Operation of approved monitoring
§ 64.8   Quality improvement plan (QIP) requirements
§ 64.9   Reporting and recordkeeping requirements
§ 64.10   Savings provisions

Part 65— Consolidated Federal Air Rule

Subpart A—General Provisions (starts at § 65.1)

Subpart C—Storage Vessels (starts at § 65.40)

Subpart D—Process Vents (starts at § 65.60)

Subpart E—Transfer Racks (starts at § 65.80)

Subpart F—Equipment Leaks (starts at § 65.100)

Subpart G—Closed Vent Systems, Control Devices, and Routing to a Fuel Gas System or a Process (starts at § 65.140)

Part 66— Assessment and Collection of Noncompliance Penalties by EPA

Part 67— EPA Approval of State Noncompliance Penalty Program

Part 68— Chemical Accident Prevention Provisions

Subpart A—General (starts at § 68.1)

Subpart B—Hazard Assessment (starts at § 68.20)

Subpart C—Program 2 Prevention Program (starts at § 68.48)

Subpart D—Program 3 Prevention Program (starts at § 68.65)

Subpart E—Emergency Response (starts at § 68.90)

Subpart F—Regulated Substances for Accidental Release Prevention (starts at § 68.100)

Subpart G—Risk Management Plan (starts at § 68.150)

Subpart H—Other Requirements (starts at § 68.200)

Part 69— Special Exemptions from Requirements of the Clean Air Act

Part 70 — State Operating Permit Programs

Part 71 — Federal Operating Permit Program

Part 72 — Permit Regulation

Part 73—Sulfur Dioxide Allowance System

Part 74—Sulfur Dioxide Opt-ins

Part 75—Continuous Emission Monitoring

Part 76—Acid Rain Nitrogen Oxides Emission Reduction Program

Part 77—Excess Emissions

Part 78—Appeal Procedures for Acid Rain Program

Part 79 — Registration of Fuels and Fuel Additives

Part 80 — Regulation of Fuels and Fuel Additives

Subpart B—Controls and Prohibitions (starts at § 80.20)

Subpart C—Oxygenated Gasoline (starts at § 80.35)

Subpart D—Reformulated Gasoline (starts at § 80.40)

Subpart E—Anti-Dumping (starts at § 80.90)

Subpart F—Attest Engagements (starts at § 80.125)

Subpart G—Detergent Gasoline (starts at § 80.140)

Subpart H—Gasoline Sulfur (starts at § 80.180)

Subpart I—Motor Vehicle Diesel Fuel; Nonroad, Locomotive, and Marine Diesel Fuel; and ECA Marine Fuel (starts at § 80.500)

Subpart J—Gasoline Toxics (starts at § 80.800)

Subpart K—Renewable Fuel Standard (starts at § 80.1100)

Subpart L—Gasoline Benzene (starts at § 80.1200)

Subpart M—Renewable Fuel Standard (starts at § 80.1400)

Part 81—Designation of Areas for Air Quality Planning Purposes

Subpart A—Meaning of Terms (starts at § 81.1)

Subpart B—Designation of Air Quality Control Regions (starts at § 81.11)

Subpart C—Section 107 Attainment Status Designations (starts at § 81.300)

Subpart D—Identification of Mandatory Class I Federal Areas Where Visibility Is an Important Value (starts at § 81.400)

Part 82—Protection of Stratospheric Ozone

Subpart A—Production and Consumption Controls (starts at § 82.1)

Subpart B—Servicing of Motor Vehicle Air Conditioners (starts at § 82.30)

Subpart C—Ban on Nonessential Products Containing Class I Substances and Ban on Nonessential Products Containing or Manufactured with Class II Substances (starts at § 82.60)

Subpart D—Federal Procurement (starts at § 82.80)

Subpart E—The Labeling of Products Using Ozone Depleting Substances (starts at § 82.100)

Subpart F—Recycling and Emissions Reduction (starts at § 82.150)

Subpart G—Significant New Alternatives Policy Program (starts at § 82.170)

Subpart H—Halon Emissions Reduction (starts at § 82.250)

Part 85—Control of Air Pollution from Mobile Sources

Subpart F—Exemption of Aftermarket Conversions from Tampering Prohibition (starts at § 85.501)

Subpart O—Urban Bus Rebuild Requirements (starts at § 85.1401)

Subpart P—Importation of Motor Vehicles and Motor Vehicle Engines (starts at § 85.1501)

Subpart R—Exclusion and Exemption of Motor Vehicles and Motor Vehicle Engines (starts at § 85.1701)

Subpart S—Recall Regulations (starts at § 85.1801)

Subpart T—Emission Defect Reporting Requirements (starts at § 85.1901)

Subpart V—Emissions Control System Performance Warranty Regulations and Voluntary Aftermarket Part Certification Program (starts at § 85.2101)

Subpart W—Emission Control System Performance Warranty Short Tests (starts at § 85.2201)

Subpart X—Determination of Model Year for Motor Vehicles and Engines Used in Motor Vehicles Under Section 177 and Part A of Title II of the Clean Air Act (starts at § 85.2301)

Subpart Y—Fees for the Motor Vehicle and Engine Compliance Program (starts at § 85.2401)

Part 86—Control of Emissions from New and In-Use Highway Vehicles and Engines

Subpart A—General Provisions for Emission Regulations for 1977 and Later Model Year New Light-Duty Vehicles, Light-Duty Trucks and Heavy-Duty Engines, and for 1985 and Later Model Year New Gasoline Fueled, Natural Gas-Fueled, Liquified Petroleum Gas-Fueled and Methanol-Fueled Heavy-Duty Vehicles (starts at § 86.000-2)

Subpart B—Emission Regulations for 1977 and Later Model Year New Light-Duty Vehicles and New Light-Duty Trucks and New Otto-Cycle Complete Heavy-Duty Vehicles; Test Procedures (starts at § 86.101)

Subpart C—Emission Regulations for 1994 and Later Model Year Gasoline-Fueled New Light-Duty Vehicles, New Light-Duty Vehicles and New Light-Duty Trucks; Cold Temperature Test Procedures (starts at § 86.201-94)

Subpart D—Emission Regulations for New Gasoline-Fueled and Diesel-Fueled Heavy-Duty Engines; Gaseous Exhaust Test Procedures (starts at § 86.301-79)

Subpart E—Emission Regulations for 1978 and Later New Motorcycles, General Provisions (starts at § 86.401-97)

Subpart F—Emission Regulations for 1978 and Later New Motorcycles, Test Procedures (starts at § 86.501-78)

Subpart G—Selective Enforcement Auditing of New Light-Duty Vehicles, Light-Duty Trucks, and Heavy-Duty Vehicles (starts at § 86.601-1)

Subpart H—General Provisions for In-Use Emission Regulations for 1994 and Later Model Year Light-Duty Vehicles and Light-Duty Trucks (starts at § 86.701-94)

Subpart I—Emission Regulations for New Diesel Heavy-Duty Engines; Smoke Exhaust Test Procedure (starts at § 86.884-1)

Subpart J—Fees for the Motor Vehicle and Engine Compliance Program (starts at § 86.901)

Subpart K—Selective Enforcement Auditing of New Heavy-Duty Engines, Heavy-Duty Vehicles, and Light-Duty Trucks (starts at § 86.1001-84)

Subpart L—Nonconformance Penalties for Gasoline-Fueled and Diesel Heavy-Duty Engines and Heavy-Duty Vehicles, including Light-Duty Trucks (starts at § 86.1101-87)

Subpart M—Evaporative Emission Test Procedures for New Gasoline-Fueled, Natural Gas-Fueled, Liquefied Petroleum Gas-Fueled and Methanol-Fueled Heavy-Duty Vehicles (starts at § 86.1201-90)

Subpart N—Emission Regulations for New Otto-Cycle and Diesel Heavy-Duty Engines; Gaseous and Particulates Exhaust Test Procedures (starts at § 86-1301-90)

Subpart O—Emission Regulations for New Gasoline-Fueled Otto-Cycle Light-Duty Vehicles and New Gasoline-Fueled Otto-Cycle Light-Duty Trucks; Certification Short Test Procedures (starts at § 86.1401)

Subpart P—Emission Regulations for Otto-Cycle Heavy-Duty Engines, New Methanol-Fueled Natural Gas-Fueled, and Liquefied Petroleum Gas-Fueled Diesel-Cycle Heavy-Duty Engines, New Otto-Cycle Light-Duty Trucks, and New Methanol-Fueled Natural Gas-Fueled and Liquefied Petroleum Gas-Fueled Diesel-Cycle Light-Duty Trucks; Idle Test Procedures (starts at § 86.1501)

Subpart Q—Regulations for Altitude Performance Adjustments for New and In-Use Motor Vehicles and Engines (starts at § 86.1601)

Subpart R—General Provisions for the Voluntary National Low Emission Vehicle Program for Light-Duty Vehicles and Light-Duty Trucks (starts at § 86.1701-99)

Subpart S—General Compliance Provisions for Control of Air Pollution from New and In-Use Light-Duty Vehicles, Light-Duty Trucks, and Complete Otto-Cycle Heavy-Duty Vehicles (starts at § 86.1801-01)

Subpart T—Manufacturer-Run In-Use Testing Program for Heavy-Duty Diesel Engines (starts at § 86.1901)

Part 87—Control of Air Pollution from Aircraft and Aircraft Engines

Part 88—Clean-Fuel Vehicles

Subpart A—Emission Standards for Clean-Fuel Vehicles (starts at § 88.101-94)

Subpart B—California Pilot Test Program (starts at § 88.201-94)

Subpart C—Clean-Fuel Fleet Program (starts at § 88.301-93)

Part 89—Control of Emissions from New and In-Use Nonroad Compression-Ignition Engines

Subpart A—General (starts at § 89.1)

Subpart B—Emission Standards and Certification Provisions (starts at § 89.101)

Subpart C—Averaging, Banking, and Trading Provisions (starts at § 89.201)

Subpart D—Emission Test Equipment Provisions (starts at § 89.301)

Subpart E—Exhaust Emission Test Procedures (starts at § 89.401)

Subpart F—Selective Enforcement Auditing (starts at § 89.501)

Subpart G—Importation of Nonconforming Nonroad Engines (starts at § 89.601)

Subpart H—Recall Regulations (starts at § 89.701)

Subpart I—Emission Defect Reporting Requirements (starts at § 89.801)

Subpart J—Exemption Provisions (starts at § 89.901)

Subpart K—General Enforcement Provisions and Prohibited Acts (starts at § 89.1001)

Part 90—Control of Emissions from Nonroad Spark-Ignition Engines At or Below 19 Kilowatts

Part 91—Control of Emissions from Marine Spark-Ignition Engines

Part 92—Control of Air Pollution from Locomotives and Locomotive Engines

Part 93—Determining Conformity of Federal Actions to State or Federal Implementation Plans

Part 94—Control of Emissions from Marine Compression-Ignition Engines

Part 96—NO$_x$ Budget Trading Program and CAIR NO$_x$ and SO$_2$ Trading Programs for State Implementation Plans

Subpart A—NO$_x$ Budget Trading Program General Provisions (starts at § 96.1)

Subpart B—Authorized Account Representative for NO$_x$ Budget Sources (starts at § 96.10)

Subpart C—Permits (starts at § 96.20)

Subpart D—Compliance Certification (starts at § 96.30)

Subpart E—NO$_x$ Allowance Allocations (starts at § 96.40)

Subpart F—NO$_x$ Allowance Tracking System (starts at § 96.50)

Subpart G—NO$_x$ Allowance Transfers (starts at § 96.60)

Subpart H—Monitoring and Reporting (starts at § 96.70)

Subpart I—Individual Unit Opt-ins (starts at § 96.80)

Subpart AA—CAIR NO$_x$ Annual Trading Program General Provisions (starts at § 96.80)

Subpart BB—CAIR Designated Representative for CAIR NOx Sources (starts at § 96.110)

Subpart CC—Permits (starts at § 96.120)

Subpart EE—CAIR NO$_x$ Allowance Allocations (starts at § 96.140)

Subpart FF—CAIR NO$_x$ Allowance Tracking System (starts at § 96.150)

Subpart GG—CAIR NO$_x$ Allowance Transfers (starts at § 96.160)

Subpart HH—Monitoring and Reporting (starts at § 96.170)

Subpart II—CAIR NO$_x$ Opt-in Units (starts at § 96.180)

Subpart AAA—CAIR SO$_2$ Trading Program General Provisions (starts at § 96.201)

Subpart BBB—CAIR Designated Representative for CAIR SO$_2$ Sources (starts at § 96.210)

Subpart CCC—Permits (starts at § 96.220)

Subpart FFF—CAIR SO$_2$ Allowance Tracking System (starts at § 96.250)

Subpart GGG—CAIR SO$_2$ Allowance Transfers (starts at § 96.260)

Subpart HHH—Monitoring and Reporting (starts at § 96.270)

Subpart III—CAIR SO$_2$ Opt-in Units (starts at § 96.280)

Subpart AAAA—CAIR NO$_x$ Ozone Season Trading Program General Provisions (starts at § 96.301)

Subpart BBBB—CAIR Designated Representative for CAIR NO$_x$ Ozone Season Sources (starts at § 96.310)

Subpart CCCC—Permits (starts at § 96.320)

Subpart EEEE—CAIR NO$_x$ Ozone Season Allowance Allocations (starts at § 96.340)

Subpart FFFF—CAIR NO$_x$ Ozone Season Allowance Tracking System (starts at § 96.350)

Subpart GGGG—CAIR NO$_x$ Ozone Season Allowance Transfers (starts at § 96.360)

Subpart HHHH—Monitoring and Reporting (starts at § 96.370)

Subpart IIII—CAIR NO$_x$ Ozone Season Opt-in Units (starts at § 96.380)

Part 97—Federal NO$_x$ Budget Trading Program

Subpart A—NO$_x$ Budget Trading Program General Provisions (starts at § 97.1)

Subpart B—NO$_x$ Authorized Account Representative for NO$_x$ Budget Sources (starts at § 97.10)

Subpart C—Permits (starts at § 97.20)

Subpart D—Compliance Certification (starts at § 97.30)

Subpart E—NO$_x$ Allowance Allocations (starts at § 97.40)

Subpart F—NO$_x$ Allowance Tracking System (starts at § 97.50)

Subpart G—NO$_x$ Allowance Transfers (starts at § 97.60)

Subpart H—Monitoring and Reporting (starts at § 97.70)

Subpart I—Individual Unit Opt-ins (starts at § 97.80)

Subpart J—Appeal Procedures (starts at § 97.90)

Subpart AA—CAIR NO$_x$ Annual Trading Program General Provisions (starts at § 97.101)

Subpart BB—CAIR Designated Representative for CAIR NO$_x$ Sources (starts at § 97.110)

Subpart CC—Permits (starts at § 97.120)

Subpart EE—CAIR NO$_x$ Allowance Allocations (starts at § 97.140)

Subpart FF—CAIR NO$_x$ Allowance Tracking System (starts at § 97.150)

Subpart GG—CAIR NO$_x$ Allowance Transfers (starts at § 97.160)

Subpart HH—Monitoring and Reporting (starts at § 97.170)

Subpart II—CAIR NO$_x$ Opt-in Units (starts at § 97.180)

Subpart AAA—CAIR SO$_2$ Trading Program General Provisions (starts at § 97.201)

Subpart BBB—CAIR Designated Representative for CAIR SO$_2$ Sources (starts at § 97.210)

Subpart CCC—Permits (starts at § 97.220)

Subpart FFF—CAIR SO$_2$ Allowance Tracking System (starts at § 97.250)

Subpart GGG—CAIR SO$_2$ Allowance Transfers (starts at § 97.260)

Subpart HHH—Monitoring and Reporting (starts at § 97.270)

Subpart III—CAIR SO$_2$ Opt-in Units (starts at § 97.280)

Subpart AAAA—CAIR NO$_x$ Ozone Season Trading Program General Provisions (starts at § 97.301)

Subpart BBBB—CAIR Designated Representative for CAIR NO$_x$ Ozone Season Sources (starts at § 97.310)

Subpart CCCC—Permits (starts at § 97.320)

Subpart EEEE—CAIR NO$_x$ Ozone Season Allowance Allocations (starts at § 97.340)

Subpart FFFF—CAIR NO$_x$ Ozone Season Allowance Tracking System (starts at § 97.350)

Subpart GGGG—CAIR NO$_x$ Ozone Season Allowance Transfers (starts at § 97.360)

Subpart HHHH—Monitoring and Reporting (starts at § 97.370)

Subpart IIII—CAIR NO$_x$ Ozone Season Opt-in Units (starts at § 97.380)

Subpart AAAAA—TR NO$_x$ Annual Trading Program

§ 97.401	Purpose
§ 97.402	Definitions
§ 97.403	Measurements, abbreviations, and acronyms
§ 97.404	Applicability
§ 97.405	Retired unit exemption
§ 97.406	Standard requirements
§ 97.407	Computation of time
§ 97.408	Administrative appeal procedures
§ 97.410	State NO$_x$ Annual trading budgets, new unit set-asides, Indian country new unit set-asides and variability limits
§ 97.411	Timing requirements for TR NO$_x$ Annual allowance allocations
§ 97.412	TR NO$_x$ Annual allowance allocations to new units
§ 97.413	Authorization of designated representative and alternate designated representative
§ 97.414	Responsibilities of designated representative and alternate designated representative
§ 97.415	Changing designated representative and alternate designated representative; changes in owners and operators
§ 97.416	Certificate of representation
§ 97.417	Objections concerning designated representative and alternate designated representative
§ 97.418	Delegation by designated representative and alternate designated representative
§ 97.420	Establishment of compliance accounts and general accounts

Part 98—Mandatory Greenhouse Gas Reporting

Subpart A—General Provisions (starts at § 98.1)

Subpart C—General Stationary Fuel Combustion Sources (starts at § 98.30)

Subpart D—Electricity Generation (starts at § 98.40)

Subpart E—Adipic Acid Production (starts at § 98.50)

Subpart F—Aluminum Production (starts at § 98.60)

Subpart G—Ammonia Manufacturing (starts at § 98.70)

Subpart H—Cement Production (starts at § 98.80)

Subpart K—Ferroalloy Production (starts at § 98.110)

Subpart N—Glass Production (starts at § 98.140)

Subpart O—HCFC-22 Production and HFC-23 Destruction (starts at § 98.150)

Subpart P—Hydrogen Production (starts at § 98.160)

Subpart Q—Iron and Steel Production (starts at § 98.170)

Subpart R—Lead Production (starts at § 98.180)

Subpart S—Lime Manufacturing (starts at § 98.190)

Subpart U—Miscellaneous Uses of Carbonate (starts at § 98.210)

Subpart V—Nitric Acid Production (starts at § 98.220)

Subpart X—Petrochemical Production (starts at § 98.240)

Subpart Y—Petroleum Refineries (starts at § 98.250)

Subpart Z—Phosphoric Act Production (starts at § 98.260)

Subpart AA—Pulp and Paper Manufacturing (starts at § 98.270)

Subpart BB—Silicon Carbide Production (starts at § 98.280)

Subpart CC—Soda Ash Manufacturing (starts at § 98.290)

Subpart EE—Titanium Dioxide Production (starts at § 98.310)

Subpart GG—Zinc Production (starts at § 98.330)

Subpart HH—Municipal Solid Waste Landfills (starts at § 98.340)

Subpart JJ—Manure Management (starts at § 98.360)

Subpart LL—Suppliers of Coal-based Liquid Fuels (starts at § 98.380)

Subpart MM—Suppliers of Petroleum Products (starts at § 98.390)

Subpart NN—Suppliers of Natural Gas and Natural Gas Liquids (starts at § 98.400)

Subpart OO—Suppliers of Industrial Greenhouse Gases (starts at § 98.410)

Subpart PP—Suppliers of Carbon Dioxide (starts at § 98.420)

PSD Source Categories with 100 Tons per Year Major Source Threshold

1. Fossil-fuel-fired steam electric plants of more than 250 million British thermal units per hour heat input

2. Coal cleaning plants (with thermal dryers)

3. Kraft pulp mills

4. Portland cement plants

5. Primary zinc smelters

6. Iron and steel mill plants

7. Primary aluminum ore reduction plants (with thermal dryers)

8. Primary copper smelters

9. Municipal incinerators capable of charging more than 250 tons of refuse per day

10. Hydrofluoric acid plants

11. Sulfuric acid plants

12. Nitric acid plants

13. Petroleum refineries

14. Lime plants

15. Phosphate rock processing plants

16. Coke oven batteries

17. Sulfur recovery plants

18. Carbon black plants (furnace process)

19. Primary lead smelters

20. Fuel conversion plants

21. Sintering plants

22. Secondary metal production plants

23. Chemical process plants (not including certain ethanol plants)

24.   Fossil-fuel boilers totaling more than 250 million British thermal units per hour heat input

25.   Petroleum storage and transfer units with a total storage capacity exceeding 300,000 barrels

26.   Taconite ore processing plants

27.   Glass fiber processing plants

28.   Charcoal production plants

Glossary

acid rain. Precipitation in the form of rain, snow, or fog with a pH of generally less than 5.5. Acid rain is primarily the combination of sulfuric acid and nitric acid produced in the atmosphere by the oxidation and hydrolysis of precursor SO_2 and NO_x that have been released during the combustion of fossil fuels.

air quality control region (AQCR). Geographic area for air quality planning, consisting of portions of states or areas within two or more states. More than 260 AQCRs are listed in 40 C.F.R. part 81. Each AQCR is classified according to its compliance status with the applicable NAAQS.

air-quality-related values (AQRV). AQRVs relate to the protection of visibility and other air emission impacts on Class I areas. AQRVs are considered in the PSD review of emission sources to be sited near Class I areas.

alternative control technique (ACT). Guidance issued by EPA to state and local air quality control agencies regarding air pollution control techniques to address the reduction of air emissions required in state implementation plans. ACTs generally do not provide a presumptive level of control, as do Control Technique Guideline documents, but may set forth a case-by-case review process. CAA section 183 requires EPA to issue ACTs for certain NO_x and VOC emission sources.

alternative fuels. Motor fuels that can replace gasoline and typically provide pollution reduction and/or energy efficiency benefits. Examples of alternative fuels include ethanol, biodiesel, and liquefied natural gas.

area source. For purposes of the CAA section 112 air toxics program, any stationary source that is not a major source.

attainment area. Geographic area in which levels of a criteria pollutant meet the National Ambient Air Quality Standard set by EPA.

best available control technologies (BACT). Applies to new and modified sources of air pollution in attainment areas. BACT is the maximum degree of emissions reduction achievable after taking into account energy, economic, and environmental impacts.

best available retrofit technologies (BART). Potentially applies to certain existing stationary sources located near large national parks or wilderness areas. BART is an emission limitation based on the degree of reduction achievable through the application of the best system of continuous emission reduction for each pollutant.

best demonstrated technology (BDT). The standard of performance for which New Source Performance Standards are to be established. The BDT standard is required to be set at the "degree of emission limitation achievable through the application of the best system of emission reduction which (taking into account the costs of achieving such reduction in any non-air-quality health and environmental impact and energy requirements) the Administrator determines has been adequately demonstrated." *See* CAA § 111(a)(1); 42 U.S.C. § 7411(a)(1).

carbon dioxide (CO$_2$). A colorless, odorless, nonpoisonous gas that results from fossil fuel combustion and is part of the ambient air. CO$_2$ is generated from the combustion of any carbon-based fuel.

carbon dioxide equivalent (CO$_2$e). Measurement of the functionally equivalent amount of CO$_2$ as a reference for greenhouse gas emissions of varying global warming potential. CO$_2$e is calculated by multiplying the GHG's GWP by the mass amount of emissions (tons per year) for the particular GHG.

carbon monoxide (CO). A colorless, odorless, poisonous gas, produced by incomplete burning of carbon-based fuels, such as natural gas, oil, and coal. CO is regulated as a criteria pollutant.

chlorofluorocarbons (CFCs). Typically found in refrigeration products, air conditioners, and aerosol products. CFCs, when released into the air, go through chemical reactions with other compounds that result in destruction of the stratospheric ozone layer.

Class I area. Includes international parks, national wilderness areas, memorial parks larger than 5,000 acres, and national parks larger than 6,000 acres.

Class II area. All other areas in a state that are not established as Class I areas.

Class III area. Areas where states are permitted to increase air quality deterioration to target industrial development. To date, no state has established a Class III area.

Clean Air Act Scientific Advisory Committee (CASAC). Provides independent advice to the EPA administrator on the technical basis for retaining or modifying EPA's NAAQS. CASAC also reviews and provides input to the EPA administrator on research related to air quality, sources of air pollution, and the strategies to attain and maintain air quality standards.

climate change. The alteration of Earth's climate caused by human activities that change the chemical composition of the atmosphere through the buildup of greenhouse gases (primarily CO_2, methane, and nitrous oxide).

compliance assurance monitoring (CAM). Enhanced emission source monitoring required to provide a reasonable assurance of compliance. Such monitoring is required to be incorporated into Title V operating permits for certain major sources.

continuous emissions monitoring system (CEMS). Equipment that measures, on a continuous basis, pollutants released by a source. CEMS measure emissions via a probe connected to a smokestack or other emissions conveyance system.

control technique guideline (CTG). Information that EPA is required to issue to state and local air quality control agencies concerning air emission control techniques for certain criteria pollutants. CTGs are considered presumptive norms for determining RACT controls that will be incorporated into the state SIPs. Though technically not binding, CTGs are intended to be adopted by states into the SIPs.

criteria pollutants. A group of air pollutants regulated by EPA on the basis of their health and environmental effects. Criteria air pollutants include SO_2, PM (including $PM_{2.5}$ and PM_{10}), CO, O_3, NO_2, and Pb. *See* chapter 3.

emission. The release of pollutants from a source into the air.

Environmental Appeals Board (EAB). Highest internal EPA administrative appeal authority. The EAB is the final agency decision maker on administrative appeals under the Clean Air Act. The EAB currently has four judges and hears cases involving PSD/NSR permit appeals, Title IV acid rain permit appeals, Title V permit appeals, and administrative penalty decisions.

Environmental Protection Agency (EPA). Federal agency with jurisdiction over implementation of the Clean Air Act.

E10. Gasohol; mixture of 10 percent ethanol and 90 percent gasoline.

E15. Gasohol; mixture of 15 percent ethanol and 85 percent gasoline.

federal implementation plan (FIP). Federal rules promulgated by EPA to implement Clean Air Act requirements when a particular state has failed to adopt approvable SIP rules.

federal land manager (FLM). The secretary of the federal agency with authority over Class I areas, including the Secretary of the Interior (for National Park Service and U.S. Fish and Wildlife Service lands) and the Secretary of Agriculture (for U.S. Forest Service lands). Designees of the secretary may be appointed as the FLM.

federally enforceable state operating permit (FESOP). Emission limits that are adopted pursuant to a federally approved permitting program or SIP rule. Federally enforceable emission limits are enforceable by both state and local regulatory agencies, EPA, and citizen groups.

fugitive emissions. Emissions that could not reasonably pass through a stack, chimney, vent, or other functionally equivalent opening.

generally available control technology (GACT). Emissions control technology that is currently and widely available. For area sources under the CAA section 112 air toxics program, EPA can promulgate standards requiring the application of generally available control technologies to reduce HAPs.

global warming. Climate change predicted to occur as increasing concentrations of greenhouse gases accelerate the rate of atmospheric heat trapping.

global warming potential (GWP). The GWP reflects both the instantaneous heat-trapping intensity of the gas and the time it remains in the atmosphere, and is calculated over a specified time period, which EPA has determined should be 100 years. The GWP of individual GHGs are set forth at 40 C.F.R. part 98, subpart A, Table A-1.

greenhouse gases (GHGs). These gases primarily include CO_2, methane (CH_4), nitrous oxide (N_2O), hydrofluorocarbons (HFCs), perfluorocarbons (PFCs), and sulfur hexafluoride (SF_6). EPA's mandatory greenhouse gas reporting rule codified at 40 C.F.R. part 98 defines greenhouse gas emissions as the six primary GHGs and other "fluorinated greenhouse gases." Each greenhouse gas differs in its ability to absorb heat in the atmosphere. For example, methane traps 21 times as much heat as CO_2, and nitrous oxide traps 310 times as much heat as CO_2.

hazardous air pollutants (HAPs). Chemicals that may cause serious health and environmental effects. HAPs are released by certain industrial operations and motor vehicles.

hydrocarbons (HC). Formed from the incomplete combustion of fossil fuels. HC was rescinded from the list of criteria pollutants by EPA in 1982.

inspection and maintenance (I/M). Auto inspection programs required for certain nonattainment areas. I/M programs require periodic inspection, usually done annually or biannually, to determine whether a motor vehicle is meeting emission standards and whether emission control systems in the vehicle are working properly.

lead (Pb). A metal emitted by motor vehicles burning leaded fuel and from certain types of manufacturing processes involving combustion, such as incinerators, refineries, and lead smelters. Lead is regulated as a criteria pollutant.

low-emission vehicle (LEV) program. California program for motor vehicles designed to achieve low emission exhaust standards according to vehicle weight classifications.

lowest achievable emission rate (LAER). Source-specific control technology for new and modified sources of air pollution in nonattainment areas. LAER is the most stringent emission limitation contained in a SIP or the most stringent emission limitation achieved by the same source or similar source category in practice. *See* chapter 5.

maximum achievable control technology (MACT). Applies to source categories and subcategories as a specific control technology for existing and new sources of listed HAPs. MACT is the maximum degree of emissions reduction achievable after taking into account certain factors prescribed by the CAA.

mobile sources. Motor vehicles and nonroad vehicles that release pollution, such as cars, SUVs, trucks, buses planes, trains, construction equipment, farm equipment, and lawn mowers.

Montreal Protocol. An international environmental agreement to control chemicals that deplete the stratospheric ozone layer. *See* chapter 13.

National Ambient Air Quality Standards (NAAQS). Standards that establish an acceptable level of a pollutant in the ambient air. *See* chapter 3.

National Emission Standards for Hazardous Air Pollutants (NESHAP). Emission standards promulgated by EPA for HAPs. *See* chapter 7.

New Source Performance Standards (NSPS). Technology-based standards for new, modified, and reconstructed sources of air pollution. NSPS reflect the degree of emission limitation achievable through application of the best system of emission reduction that has been adequately demonstrated, taking into account the cost and any non-air-quality health and environmental impact and energy requirements. *See* chapter 6.

New Source Review (NSR). Program requiring stationary sources in both attainment and nonattainment areas to obtain permits for construction and operation activities. Permitting review of new major sources or major modifications to existing major sources in nonattainment areas is also generally referred to as New Source Review. *See* chapter 5.

nitrogen dioxide (NO_2). A compound formed when nitric oxide (NO) is oxidized in the atmosphere. NO and NO_2 are generally referred to as nitrogen oxides or NO_x. NO_2 is regulated as a criteria pollutant.

nitrogen oxides (NO_x). Nitric oxide (or NO) and NO_2 are referred to as NO_x. NO_x usually occurs during high-temperature combustion processes of boilers, furnaces, utilities, and other combustion sources, as well as from motor vehicles.

nitrous oxide (N_2O). A greenhouse gas released from agricultural fertilizers, land clearing, biomass combustion, and natural biologic processes that occur in soil.

nonattainment area. Geographic areas in which levels of a criteria pollutant exceed the level allowed by the applicable NAAQS.

NO_x allowance. Authorization to emit one ton of NO_x during a particular period. The Clean Air Interstate Rule (CAIR), adopted in 2005, requires power plants in 28 states and the District of Columbia to implement a cap-and-trade program to achieve substantial reductions in NO_x emissions. CAIR requires power plants to possess NO_x allowances covering their annual NO_x emissions and NO_x emissions during the summer ozone season (from May 1 to September 30). The successor program to CAIR—the Cross-State Air Pollution Rule (CSAPR)—will require power plants in 27 states and the District of Columbia to achieve significant reductions in NO_x through a cap-and-trade program using annual and ozone season NO_x allowances.

offset. Primarily used for compliance with nonattainment area NSR requirements for new major sources or major modifications to existing major sources. A continuous credit that is generally good in perpetuity unless restricted by a state or EPA.

opacity. The relative capacity of matter to obstruct the transmission of light.

operating permit. Federal or state permit authorizing the operation of stationary sources. EPA's Title V operating permit program is currently administered by either by EPA, in certain U.S. territories and federally recognized Indian lands; or by state or tribal agencies with EPA-approved programs. Title V operating permits are intended to include all of an emission source's applicable federal requirements under the Clean Air Act, and are issued for a term of up to five years. *See* chapter 10.

oxygenated fuels. Gasoline that has been blended with alcohols or ethers and contains oxygen in order to reduce CO and other pollutants.

ozone (O_3). Ozone consists of three oxygen atoms. Ozone is a gas that is found at both ground level and in the stratosphere. Ground-level ozone is a product of reactions among VOCs and NO_x produced from the combustion of fuels and the use of chemicals found in products such as solvents, paints, and aerosols. Ozone is regulated as a criteria pollutant.

Ozone Transport Commission (OTC). Created by the Clean Air Act Amendments of 1990; a group that oversees the development of strategies to mitigate interstate ozone pollution and recommends potential emission control measures to EPA that may be necessary to ensure that the northeastern and mid-Atlantic states attain and maintain the ozone NAAQS. The OTC is composed of governmental leaders and environmental officials from the 12 northeastern and mid-Atlantic states, including the District of Columbia.

Ozone Transport Region (OTR). The 12 northeastern and mid-Atlantic states, including the District of Columbia, that were identified as a single transport region for ozone pursuant to CAA section 184. The states are Connecticut, Delaware, Maine, Maryland, Massachusetts, New Hampshire, New Jersey, New York, Pennsylvania, Rhode Island, Vermont, and the northern part of Virginia.

particulate matter (PM). Includes dust, soot, and other tiny particles that are released into the air. PM can cause eye, nose and throat irritation and other health problems. PM is a regulated criteria pollutant.

$PM_{2.5}$. "Fine" particulate matter with an aerodynamic diameter equal to or less than 2.5 microns.

PM_{10}. Particulate matter with an aerodynamic diameter equal to or less than 10 microns.

potential to emit (PTE). The capability, at maximum design capacity, of a unit or source to emit a pollutant after application of control equipment.

Prevention of Significant Deterioration (PSD). Program requiring stationary sources to obtain a PSD permit before they can build a new major stationary source or make major modifications to an existing major source of air pollution in an attainment area. *See* chapter 5.

primary NAAQS. Ambient air criteria pollutant limits based on health effects. *See* chapter 3.

PSD increment. The maximum increases to ambient air pollution levels that may be incurred as a result of increased emissions from new major sources or major modifications to existing major sources in Class I and Class II areas.

reasonable further progress (RFP) plan. CAA section 182(b)(1) require each eight-hour ozone nonattainment area designated moderate and above to submit an RFP plan for EPA review and approval into the SIP that describes how the area will achieve actual emissions reductions of VOC and NO_x from a baseline emissions inventory.

reasonably available control measures (RACM). Technologies and other control measures that can be used to reduce air emissions, including RACT.

reasonably available control technology (RACT). Source-specific control technology that applies to existing stationary sources of pollution in certain nonattainment areas. *RACT* is defined as the lowest emission limitation that a source is capable of meeting by applying reasonably available control technology, considering technological feasibility and economic costs.

reformulated gasoline (RFG). Gasoline with a composition specified by the Clean Air Act that is different from conventional gasoline and that is designed to result in lower levels of air emissions.

regional haze. Visibility impairments across a broad geographic area that is caused by particulate matter emissions (e.g., organic carbon, elemental carbon, and soil dust) as well as sulfates and nitrates, which are formed from SO_2 and NO_x emissions through chemical reactions in the atmosphere.

renewable fuels. Biomass and cellulosic-based fuels, such as ethanol and biodiesel, that are used as transportation fuels.

risk management plan (RMP). A plan required of owners and operators of major stationary sources emitting HAPs above threshold quantities. Such owners or operators must prepare and implement an RMP that includes a hazardous assessment evaluating potential off-site consequences of accidental releases of such substances. An RMP is designed to put in place a program to prevent and/or minimize accidental releases and provide a plan for responding to any accidental releases.

secondary NAAQS. Ambient air criteria pollutant limits based on environmental effects, such as damage to property, plants, and visibility. *See* chapter 3.

Significant New Alternatives Policy (SNAP). A program implementing CAA section 612, which provides for the replacement of listed ozone-depleting substantives with alternative chemicals, products, or manufacturing processes that reduce overall risks to human health or the environment.

SO_2 allowance. An allowance worth one ton of SO_2 emitted from an affected unit under the federal acid rain program. The Clean Air Interstate Rule (CAIR), adopted in 2005, requires power plants in 28 states and the District of Columbia to implement a cap-and-trade program to achieve substantial reductions in SO_2 emissions. CAIR requires power plants to possess two acid rain program SO_2 allowances for every ton of SO_2 emitted. The successor program to CAIR—the Cross-State Air Pollution Rule (CSAPR)—will require power plants in 23 states and the District of Columbia to achieve significant reductions in SO_2 through a cap-and-trade program using SO_2 allowances. Under CSAPR, an allowance equals one ton of SO_2 emitted from an affected source. *See* chapters 4 and 9.

state implementation plan (SIP). Collection of EPA-approved state control strategies and regulations that a state implements to carry out its responsibilities under the Clean Air Act.

state implementation plan call (SIP call). An EPA rule requesting revisions to existing SIP rules and/or imposing new SIP requirements. SIP calls may be issued when new statutory requirements trigger the need for SIP revisions, or when EPA makes a finding that an existing state's SIP rules are inadequate to maintain or attain compliance with the applicable NAAQS.

stationary source. Any building, structure, facility, or installation that emits air pollutants. Stationary sources include power plants, industrial plants, and gas stations.

stratospheric ozone. The stratospheric ozone layer that is part of the atmosphere approximately 6 to 30 miles above the Earth. Ozone in the stratosphere protects Earth against harmful ultraviolet radiation from the sun.

sulfur dioxide (SO_2). Heavy, pungent, gaseous air pollutant produced by burning certain fossil fuels, notably coal and oil. Sulfur in the fuel is released during the combustion process. Power plants and motor vehicles are the primary sources of SO_2 emissions.

Title I. Title of 1990 CAA amendments regarding NAAQS, nonattainment/attainment areas, and SIPs.

Title II. Title of 1990 CAA amendments regarding mobile sources.

Title III. Title of 1990 CAA amendments regarding air toxics.

Title IV. Title of 1990 CAA amendments regarding acid rain control.

Title V. Title of 1990 CAA amendments regarding operating permits.

Title VI. Title of 1990 CAA amendments regarding stratospheric ozone.

Title VII. Title of 1990 CAA amendments regarding enforcement.

Title VIII. Title of 1990 CAA amendments regarding miscellaneous provisions.

transportation control measures (TCM). Various measures required to reduce air emissions from motor vehicles, including adjustment of traffic patterns and reduction of motor vehicle use.

tribal implementation plan (TIP). Collection of EPA-approved tribal control strategies and regulations that a native American tribe implements within fee and non-fee land within a reservation (or "Indian Country") to carry out the provisions of the Clean Air Act.

tropospheric ozone. Ground-level ozone. Tropospheric ozone is the primary component of smog.

volatile organic compounds (VOCs). Chemicals that contain carbon and participate in atmospheric photochemical reactions. Certain carbon-containing compounds are excluded from the regulatory definition of *VOCs*, including carbon monoxide and carbon dioxide. *See* 40 C.F.R. § 51.100(s). VOCs are smog-forming chemicals, and include gasoline and solvents such as tetrachloroethylene and perchloroethylene.

Resources

Books and Treatises

F. WILLIAM BROWNELL, CLEAN AIR HANDBOOK (Gov't Insts. 3d ed. 1998).

THE CLEAN AIR ACT HANDBOOK (Julie R. Domike & Alec C. Zacaroli eds., ABA 3d ed. 2011).

CLEAN AIR DESKBOOK (Envtl. L. Inst. 1992).

EPA OFFICE OF AIR QUALITY PLANNING & STANDARDS, NEW SOURCE REVIEW WORKSHOP MANUAL (DRAFT) (Oct. 1990).

EPA OFFICE OF AIR QUALITY PLANNING & STANDARDS, EPA-0400-K-93-001, PLAIN ENGLISH GUIDE TO THE CLEAN AIR ACT (Apr. 1993).

GLOBAL CLIMATE CHANGE AND U.S. LAW (Michael B. Gerrard ed., ABA 2007).

CHARLES H. KNAUSS, SHANNON S. BROOME & MICHAEL E. WARD, THE CLEAN AIR ACT OPERATING PERMIT PROGRAM (ABA 1993).

JAMES P. LIPTON, CLEAN AIR ACT: INTERPRETATION AND ANALYSIS (Nova Science Pub. 2005).

ELIZABETH MORSS & DAVID R. WOOLEY, CLEAN AIR ACT HANDBOOK, 20TH (West 9th ed. 2010).

TOM MOUNTEER, CLIMATE CHANGE DESKBOOK (Envtl. L. Inst. 2009).

ARNOLD W. REITZE JR., AIR POLLUTION CONTROL AND CLIMATE CHANGE MITIGATION LAW (Envtl. L. Inst. 2010).

ARNOLD W. REITZE JR., AIR POLLUTION CONTROL LAW: COMPLIANCE AND ENFORCEMENT (Envtl. L. Inst. 2001).

ARNOLD W. REITZE JR., STATIONARY SOURCE AIR POLLUTION CONTROL (Envtl. L. Inst. 2005).

WILLIAM ROGERS JR., 1 ENVIRONMENTAL LAW—AIR AND WATER (West 1986 & 2010 pocket part).

Law Review Articles

John Cabell Acree III, *Operation Flexibility Under the Clean Air Act Title V Operating Permits*, 3 ENVTL. LAW. 37 (Sept. 1996).

Michael S. Alushin, *Enforcement of the Clean Air Act Amendments of 1990*, 21 ENVTL. L. 2217 (Summer 1991).

Richard E. Ayres, *The 1990 Clean Air Act Amendments: Performance and Prospects*, 13 NAT. RES. & ENV'T 379 (Fall 1998).

Roy S. Belden, *Preparing for the Onslaught of Clean Air Act Citizen Suits: A Review of Strategies and Defenses*, 1 ENVTL. LAW. 377 (Feb. 1995).

Shannon S. Broome, *Implementing the Clean Air Act Amendments of 1990: Major Rules 1995–2000*, 14 PACE ENVTL. L. REV. 79 (Fall 1996).

F. William Brownell & Ross S. Antonson, *Implementing the New Eight-Hour NAAQS for Ozone—What Happened to the 1990 Clean Air Act?*, 11 TUL. ENVTL. L.J. 355 (Summer 1998).

Dale S. Byrk, *The Montreal Protocol and Recent Developments to Protect the Ozone Layer*, 15 HARV. ENVTL. L. REV. 275 (1991).

Margaret L. Claibourne, *The New Air Toxics Program*, 7 NAT. RES. & ENV'T 21 (Fall 1992).

Amy Coy & Eric Groten, *New Growth in the PSD Forest: A Trail Map*, 4 NAT. RES. & ENV'T 453 (Spring 1989).

F. James Cumberland Jr., *EPA's August 1997 Final Rule Regarding Transportation Conformity*, 4 ENVTL. LAW. 611 (Feb. 1998).

Anne D. Curley, *Requirements for Constructed or Reconstructed Major Sources of Hazardous Air Pollutants: Regulations for MACT Determinations Under Section 112(g) of the Clean Air Act*, 4 ENVTL. LAW. 225 (Sept. 1997).

Scott M. Duboff, *The 1990 Amendments and Section 304: The Specter of Increased Citizen Suit Enforcement*, 7 NAT. RES. & ENV'T (FALL 1992).

David M. Driesen, *Capping Carbon*, 40 ENVTL. L. 1 (2010).

Joseph M. Feller, *Non-threshold Pollutants and Air Quality Standards*, 24 ENVTL. L. 821 (July 1994).

Mary A. Gade, *When the States Come Marching In*, 10 NAT. RES. & ENV'T 3 (Winter 1996).

Richard Gaskins Jr. & Shawn F. Sullivan, *New Clean Air Act Enforcement Provisions and the Defense of Enforcement Actions*, 10 J. ENV'T L. & LITIG. 39 (Spring 1995).

Lisa Heinzerling, *Climate Change and the Clean Air Act*, 42 U.S.F. L. REV. 111 (Dec. 2007).

Carol S. Holmes & Arnold W. Reitze Jr., *Inspections Under the Clean Air Act*, 1 ENVTL. LAW. 29 (1994).

William H. Lewis & Hunter L. Prillaman, *Reasonably Available Control Technology Under the Clean Air Act: Is EPA Following Its Statutory Mandate?*, 16 HARV. ENVTL. L. REV. 343 (Summer 1992).

William H. Lewis, *Expanded Enforcement Exposure Under Credible Evidence and CAM Rules (EPA Compliance Assurance Monitoring Rules)*, 13 NAT. RES. & ENV'T 388 (Fall 1998).

Ivan Lieben, *Catch Me if You Can—The Misapplication of the Statute of Limitations to Clean Air Act PSD Permit Program Violations*, 38 ENVTL. L. 667 (2008).

Alan P. Loeb & Tiffany J. Elliott, *PSD Constraints on Utility Planning: A Review of Recent Visibility Litigation*, 34 NAT. RES. J. 231 (Spring 1994).

Bradford C. Mank, *What Comes After Technology: Using an "Exceptions Process" to Improve Residual Risk Regulation of Hazardous Air Pollutants*, 13 STAN. ENVTL. L.J. 263 (May 1994).

Jonathan S. Martel, *The Explosion of Clean Air Act Regulation of Fuels*, 25 ENV'T L. REP. 10,538 (Oct. 1995).

Lesley K. McAllister, *The Enforcement Challenge of Cap-and-Trade Regulation*, 40 ENVTL. L. 1195 (2011).

Paul J. Miller, *Cutting Through the Smog: The 1990 Clean Air Act Amendments and a New Direction Towards Reducing Ozone Pollution*, 12 STAN. ENVTL. L.J. 124, (1993).

James Miskiewicz & John S. Rudd, *Civil and Criminal Enforcement of the Clean Air Act After the 1990 Amendments*, 9 PACE ENVTL. L. REV. 281 (1992).

David P. Novello & Robert J. Martineau Jr., *The New Accidental Release Prevention Program Under the Clean Air Act*, 13 NAT. RES. & ENV'T 464 (Fall 1998).

Craig N. Oren, *Is the Clean Air Act at a Crossroads?*, 40 ENVTL. L. 1231 (2011).

Craig N. Oren, *The Protection of Parklands from Air Pollution: A Look at Current Policy*, 13 HARV. ENVTL. L. REV. 313 (1989).

Alexa B. Pappas, *The Clean Air Act Amendments of 1990: Enhanced Criminal Liability*, 3 VILL. ENVTL. L.J. 181 (Winter 1992).

Vickie L. Patton, *The New Air Quality Standards, Regional Haze, and Interstate Air Pollution Transport*, 28 ENV'T L. REP. 10,155 (Apr. 1998).

Brian H. Potts, *Trading Grandfathered Air—A New, Simpler Approach*, 31 HARV. ENVTL. L. REV. 115 (Spring 2007).

D. Michael Rappoport & John F. Cooney, *Visibility at the Grand Canyon: Regulatory Negotiations Under the Clean Air Act*, 24 Ariz. St. L.J. 627 (1992).

Arnold W. Reitze Jr., *A Century of Air Pollution Control Law: What's Worked, What's Failed, What Might Work*, 21 Envtl. L. 1549 (Summer 1991).

Arnold W. Reitze Jr., *Federal Control of Greenhouse Gas Emissions*, 40 Envtl. L. 1261 (2011).

Arnold W. Reitze Jr., *The Regulation of Fuels and Fuel Additives Under Section 211 of the Clean Air Act*, 29 Tulsa L.J. 485 (Spring–Summer 1994).

Arnold W. Reitze Jr., *Mobile Source Air Pollution Control*, 6 Envtl. Law. 309 (Feb. 2000).

Arnold W. Reitze Jr., *Transportation-Related Pollution and the Clean Air Act's Conformity Requirements*, 13 Nat. Res. & Env't 406 (Fall 1998).

Daniel Riesel, *Forecasting Significant Air Act Implementation Issues: Permitting and Enforcement*, 14 Pace Envtl. L. Rev. 129 (Fall 1996).

Ernest S. Rosenberg, *Clean Air Act Reform: A Necessity of the Act's Survival*, 14 Pace Envtl. L. Rev. 115 (Fall 1996).

Edward B. Sears, *The "Any Credible Evidence" Rule: Is EPA Really Holding All the Cards?*, 4 Envtl. Law. 157 (Sept. 1997).

C. Russell Shearer, *Practical Considerations in the Domestic Sale of CFCs and HCFCs*, 11 Nat. Res. & Env't 58 (Spring 1997).

Robert N. Stavins, *A Meaningful U.S. Cap-and-Trade System to Address Climate Change*, 32 Harv. Envtl. L. Rev. 293 (Fall 2008).

Cass R. Sunstein, *Is the Clean Air Act Unconstitutional?*, 98 Mich. L. Rev. 303 (Nov. 1999).

Cass R. Sunstein, *Of Montreal and Kyoto: A Tale of Two Protocols*, 31 Harv. Envtl. L. Rev. 1 (Spring 2007).

Murray Tabb, *Twenty-Five Years of the Clean Air Act in Perspective*, 10 Nat. Res. & Env't 13 (Fall 1995).

George Van Cleve & Keith W Holman, *Promise and Reality in the Enforcement of the Amended Clean Air Act, Part I: EPA's "Any Credible Evidence" and "Compliance Assurance Monitoring" Rules*, 27 Env't L. Rep. 10,097 (Mar. 1997).

George Van Cleve & Keith W. Holman, *Promise and Reality in the Enforcement of the Amended Clean Air Act Part II: Federal Enforceability and Environmental Auditing*, 27 Env't L. Rep. 10,151 (Apr. 1997).

Henry A. Waxman, *The Clean Air Act Amendments of 1990: A Sympo-sium and Overview of the Clean Air Act Amendments of 1990*, 21 ENVTL. L. 1721 (1991).

Web Pages

For a listing of the websites of more than 150 key federal, state, and local air regulatory agencies and other air-related web pages, visit the ABA Section of Environment, Energy, and Resources Air Quality Com-mittee's web page at http://apps.americanbar.org/environ/committees/airquality/.

EPA Guidance, Technology Transfer Network (TNN), http://www.epa.gov/ttn/.

EPA Region 7 Air Program Database, http://www.epa.gov/region07/pro-grams/artd/air/policy/policy.htm.

Columbia Law School, Center for Climate Change Law, http://www.law.columbia.edu/centers/climatechange.

Other Legal Resources

United Stated Code Annotated version of the Clean Air Act, 42 U.S.C.A. §§ 7401 to 7671q.

Code of Federal Regulations, 40 C.F.R. parts 49–98.

State statutes, regulations, and guidance implementing Clean Air Act provisions.

Legislative history of the Clean Air Act Amendments of 1970, 1977, and 1990.

Case law available on Lexis, Westlaw, and Pacer.

Environmental Law Forum (Envtl. L. Inst.).

Natural Resources and Environment (ABA).

Trade press articles (e.g., Argus Air Daily, BNA, Inside EPA, Environment & Energy Daily, ClimateWire).

Table of Cases

Index